P9-AOZ-397

THE PSYCHOLOGICAL
PROBLEMS
OF RELIGION

RITUAL:
PSYCHOANALYTIC STUDIES

THE PSYCHOLOGICAL PROBLEMS OF RELIGION

—I—

RITUAL
PSYCHO-ANALYTIC STUDIES

BY
THEODOR REIK

WITH A PREFACE
BY
SIGM. FREUD

TRANSLATED FROM THE SECOND GERMAN EDITION
BY
DOUGLAS BRYAN, M.R.C.S., L.R.C.P.

FARRAR, STRAUS AND COMPANY, INC.
NEW YORK
1946

First Published in Great Britain by the Hogarth
Press in 1931 as No. 19 of the International Psychoanalytical Library

TRANSLATOR'S NOTE

APPRECIATING the importance of Dr. Reik's work, I
made a translation from the first German edition
some years ago, and Mr. L. C. Martin was good
enough to revise it at the time. As I was unable to
publish it then it was laid aside, but the delay thus incurred has the advantage of allowing me to make use of
the second, revised and enlarged German edition which
in the meantime appeared. This final draft has been
revised by Mrs. James Strachey and Mr. Roger Money-
Kyrle. I count myself fortunate in obtaining such competent assistance, and I wish to express my gratitude to
those who have so generously rendered it.

DOUGLAS BRYAN

Manufactured in the United States of America

INTRODUCTION TO THE
AMERICAN EDITION

To the average cultured American, psychoanalysis has only one meaning. It is a special treatment of nervous and mental disturbances. As such, it was first of interest only to psychiatrists and, of course, the patients. Certain terms like "Oedipus-complex", "repression", "Freudian mechanisms" and "wishful thinking" became widely known. This treatment has been used as dramatic material in novels, and on the stage and screen, with considerable variation in the degree of understanding. However, Freud and his circle of students had a different concept of psychoanalysis. It was best formulated by Freud himself [1] for whom the term psychoanalysis had three meanings: (1) a method of investigation of psychical processes which are hardly approachable otherwise; (2) a therapeutic treatment founded upon this method; (3) a number of psychological insights won by such a method. It becomes increasingly clear that the first of these meanings will be the most important one in the future.

This method of psychological observation and investigation concerns the realm of unconscious processes and tries to find facts in the field of subterranean emotions and thoughts. The material used by this method are small details, insignificant traits of behaviour, speech and gestures, the remnants of observation. Such trifles are inter-

[1] Freud, Gesammelte Schriften. Vol. XI: p. 201.

1

preted and evaluated as important manifestations of repressed tendencies and thoughts; they reveal their hidden
meaning to the psychologist who has learned to read
them.

When I once compared this method with the art of
interpretation which Sherlock Holmes applied, Freud
said he preferred to compare it with the technique used
by another investigator. He asked me if I knew the studies of Giovanni Morelli and spoke with great respect of
the method of this original and daring art-critic. Morelli
(1816–1891) who wrote under the name of Iwan Ler-
molieff [2] realized that many pictures in Italian galleries
are attributed to painters who did not make them. He
thought that the traditional knowledge of art was unin-
spired and full of prejudices of the scholars. The histor-
ians of art took their point of departure from the general
impression of the paintings, from the choice of their subject and the application of colors. Morelli thought that
these are often fallacious criteria and he found a most
ingenious method to determine the authorship of old
paintings. The superficial views of the traditional scholars, he maintained, should be replaced by a searching
analysis of the individual parts of the paintings. Morelli
studied the personal manner which the individual painters used to draw the fingernails, the lobes of ears, the
nostrils, the disposition of drapery and other peculiarities. In his method of precise observation and compari-
sion such inconspicuous traits as the treatment of the
hair, the drawing of the eye-lid, the indication of the
sinews were evaluated like the signature of the master.

[2] The books of the Italian critic were first published in German (Kunst-
kritische Studien ueber italienische Malerei. 3 vol. Leipzig, 1890–1893;
Die Werke italienische Meister in den Galerien von Muenchen, Dresden u.
Berlin, Leipzig, 1880). Most of his studies are now translated into English.

As in psychoanalytic research, the significance of the apparently unimportant results from the fact that inconspicuous traits are used as evidence, as clues revealing unknown and otherwise unavailable things. The genius of Freud applied a similar method in penetrating into the recesses of the human soul.

During the same conversation in which Freud turned my attention to the studies of Morelli (it was in the spring, 33 years ago), I told him of certain ideas which had occurred to me in regard to the psychology of primitive religions. The two first studies in this volume present this research; they were lectures given to the Vienna and Berlin Psychoanalytic Society in 1914 and 1915. The third paper was a lecture given to Freud alone, who listened attentively, smoking a long cigar, at his home in the Berggasse in Vienna.

The young and ambitious analyst who wrote this book is a stranger to me now; a stranger who reminds me of myself. I look at him with a mixture of sympathy and irony. He would never have believed, had anyone told him, that he would have to flee from his native Vienna, that Germans would kill members of his family and that he would be a United States citizen thirty years later. At that time this prediction would have sounded fantastic.

From the first, Freud took a strong interest in the research of his student. The great man never ceased to encourage him, to admonish him to continue the work, and to promise him that sooner or later many people would be interested. Freud visited the young man in 1915 and told him smilingly that he was awarded the prize for the best work in applied psychoanalysis for the study, "Puberty Rites of Savages", which can be found in this volume. Memories of conversations, and letters which are at this moment on the desk before me, prove that Freud expressed again and again the hope that his student would continue this line of research. In the thirty years of close association and common work with Freud, he was frequently reminded of it, as if of a promise not kept.

The four studies here presented have stood the test of time rather well. When John Farrar and Roger W. Straus, Jr. suggested an American edition (the German and British editions are no longer available),[3] I reread the book and realized that no essential changes were necessary. The line of research here initiated was continued by other analysts in whose books and papers these studies are frequently quoted. Many instances show that they aroused the attention of scholars in the field of comparative religion and of the history of civilization. There are even signs that they found attention beyond the circle of psychological research. A well known writer, my friend William Maxwell, used the material presented in "Puberty Rites of Savages" in his beautiful novel "The Folded Leaf".

The scientific daydreams of the young psychoanalyst who wrote this book were very ambitious. He wanted to penetrate into the psychologic secrets of religion, to discover what are the concealed undercurrents which determine the religious evolution of mankind, and to find the hidden emotional facts behind the historical ones. In his thoughts he compared these studies with the first movement of a symphony. The other movements should concern the psychology of dogma, the unconscious tendencies in the myths, the hidden nucleus of truth in the

[3] The first German edition was published in 1919, second and revised edition 1928, British edition 1931 as No. 19 by the Hogarth Press of the "International Psychoanalytic Library".

Sinai-story, and the origin of guilt-feelings. (A returning theme, a leitmotif, should be the psychology of the
Israelites: "How odd of God to choose the Jews", dealt
with seriously and in the spirit of scientific research.)
Very little of these daydreams was fulfilled; the symphony threatened to remain unfinished. Other books demanded to be written; the problem, of psychoanalytic
practice led to different trains of thought. I imagined I
would return to the planned work in the meantime between writing about other subjects. There are, however,
only three tenses: past, present and future. There is no
such thing as the meantime.

A few books about dogma and obsession-ideas, about
one's own and the foreign gods and quite a few papers
and essays about psychological problems of religion were
published in Vienna. They represent rather the blue-
print than the finished work. The plan to continue the
interrupted research was, however, not given up.

Without saying so, John Farrar and Roger W. Straus,
Jr. give me the impression that they are not disinclined
to publish these books, if and when readers of this volume
show sufficient interest in further volumes of psychological research.

Theodor Reik

New York, May, 1946.

CONTENTS

PREFACE

By Professor Sigm. Freud

PSYCHO-ANALYSIS was born of medical necessity. It originated in the need of helping the victims of nervous disease to whom rest, hydropathy or electrical treatment could bring no relief. A striking case recorded by Joseph Breuer had aroused the hope that the amount of help that could be given to such patients might vary directly with the extent to which it might be possible to understand the genesis, hitherto unfathomed, of their symptoms. Psycho-analysis, therefore, though originally a matter of purely medical technique, was directed, from the first, towards new research, towards the discovery of mechanisms whose nature was concealed but whose effects were far-reaching.

Its further progress led away from the study of the physical conditions of nervous illnesses in a degree surprising to the physician, and gradually the whole mental content of human life came within its sphere, including the healthy—the normal as well as the super-normal. It had to concern itself with affects and passions, and above all, with those constant subjects of the poet's art and enthusiasm, the emotions of love: it learnt to recognise the potency of memories, the unsuspected significance of the early years of childhood in shaping the conduct of later life, and finally the strength of those wishes which lead men's judgements astray and prescribe the paths of human endeavour.

For a time it appeared to be the fate of psycho-analysis to be incorporated into the field of psychology

without being able to indicate in what way the mind of
the sick patient differed from that of the normal person.
But in the course of its development it came upon the
problem of the dream, which is an abnormal mental
product created by normal people under regularly recurring physiological conditions. And in solving the
enigma of dreams it found in unconscious mentality
the common ground in which the highest as well as the
lowest mental impulses are rooted, and from which arise
the most normal mental activities as well as the strange
products of a diseased mind. The picture of the mental
mechanisms of the individual now became clearer and
more complete: it was seen that obscure impulses arising
in his organic life were striving to fulfil their own aims,
and that controlling them was a series of more highly
organised mental formations, acquired and handed on
by man under the pressure of his cultural development,
which had taken possession of parts of these impulses,
developed them ·or employed them in the service of
higher aims—had bound them fast, at all events, and
utilised their energy for its own purposes. This higher
organisation, which we know as the ego, had rejected
another portion of the same elementary impulses as
useless, because these impulses could not accommodate
themselves to the organic unity of the individual, or
because they conflicted with its cultural aims. The ego
was not powerful enough to exterminate those mental
forces it could not control. Instead, it turned away from
them, leaving them on the most primitive psychological
level, and protected itself against their demands by
means of energetic defensive or reactive mechanisms, or
sought to compromise with them by means of substitute-
gratifications. Unsubdued and indestructible, yet in-

hibited in every direction, these repressed impulses, together with their primitive mental content, form the underworld, the kernel of the true unconscious, ever on the alert to urge their claims and to find any means for gratification. Hence the insecurity of our proud psychical superstructure, the nightly emergence of proscribed and repressed things in dreams, and our proneness to fall ill with neuroses and psychoses as soon as the distribution of power between the ego and the repressed is altered to the disadvantage of the former.

It requires but little consideration to realise that such a view of the life of the human mind cannot possibly be limited to the sphere of dreams and nervous diseases. If it be a justifiable view, it must apply also to normal mental phenomena, and even the highest achievements of the human mind must have some relation to the factors recognised in pathology—to repression, to the strivings for mastery of the unconscious and to the possibilities of gratification which are open to the primitive impulses. And now it became an irresistibly tempting task, indeed, a scientific duty, to extend the psycho-analytical methods of investigation from their original field to more distant and diverse spheres of mental interest. The psycho-analytical treatment of patients also pointed insistently in this direction, since it became evident that individual forms of the neuroses showed a marked correspondence with the most highly valued products of our civilisation. The hysteric is undoubtedly a poet, though he represents his phantasies essentially by mimicry, without considering whether other people understand them or not. The ceremonials and prohibitions of obsessional patients force us to conclude that they have created a private religion for themselves; and even the delusions of the paranoiac show an unwelcome external similarity and inner relationship to the systems of our philosophers. We cannot get away from the impression that patients are making, in an asocial manner, the same attempts at a solution of their conflicts and an appeasement of their urgent desires which, when carried out in a manner acceptable to a large number of persons, are called poetry, religion and philosophy.

In an extremely brilliant and suggestive monograph,[1] O. Rank and H. Sachs have collected the results which have so far been accomplished by the application of psycho-analysis to the fields of mental interest. Mythology and the history of literature and religion appear to furnish the most easily accessible material. The final formula which shall assign to the myth its particular province has not yet been found. But in a large work on the incest complex, O. Rank[2] reaches the remarkable conclusion that the selection of subject matter, particularly in dramatic poetry, is limited chiefly by the range of the Oedipus complex, as it is called in psychoanalysis. Through the elaboration of this complex into the most manifold variants, distortions and disguises, the poet seeks to elucidate his most personal attitude to this effective theme. It is in the mastery of his Oedipus complex, *i.e.* his affective attitude towards his family, and in its narrower sense his father and mother, that the individual comes to grief, and therefore it is this complex which regularly forms the kernel of his neurosis. It owes its significance not to any unintelligible concatenation of events. The importance of the parental relationship springs naturally from the biological fact of the

---

[1] *Die Bedeutung der Psychoanalyse für die Geisteswissenschaften*, 1913.
[2] O. Rank, *Das Inzestmotiv in Dichtung und Sage*, Leipzig und Wien, 1912.

long helplessness and slow maturing of the young human being, and the complicated development of his capacity for love; and furthermore guarantees that the lines on which the Oedipus complex is overcome shall run parallel with those on which the archaic and animal inheritance of mankind is most successfully brought under subjection. In this inheritance are contained all the energies necessary for the later cultural development of the individual, but they have first to be sorted out and elaborated. In the form in which the individual brings it with him into the world it is useless for the purposes of social life.

One step more is necessary before we reach the starting point for a psycho-analytical consideration of religious life. What is now the heritage of the individual was once, long ago, a newly acquired possession, handed on from one generation to another. The Oedipus complex itself must therefore have its own process of development, and the study of prehistory can help us to find out something about it. Such a study leads us to assume that the human family as we know it to-day was organised differently in remote primitive times, and this surmise is supported by data obtained from primitive races of the present day. If we submit the prehistoric and ethnological material relating to this archaic heritage to psycho-analytical elaboration, we come to an unexpectedly definite conclusion—namely, that god the father at one time walked incarnate on the earth and exercised his sovereignty as leader of the hordes of primitive men until his sons combined together and slew him; and further, that the first social ties, the basic moral restrictions, and the oldest form of religion—totemism—originated as a result of, and a reaction against, this liberating misdeed. Later religions are filled with the same content and with the endeavour to obliterate the traces of that crime, or to expiate it by substituting other solutions for the conflict between father and sons; while, on the other hand, they cannot refrain from repeating anew the removal of the father. As a result we can recognise in myths the echo of that occurrence which throws its gigantic shadow over the whole development of mankind.

This hypothesis, founded on the views of Robertson Smith, and developed by me in my *Totem und Tabu* in 1912, has been taken by Th. Reik as the basis for his studies on the problems of the psychology of religion, of which this is the first volume. In accordance with psycho-analytical technique he begins by considering details of religious life that have not been previously understood, and in elucidating them throws light upon the fundamental presuppositions and ultimate aims of religion. He keeps steadily in view the relationship between prehistoric man and primitive man of to-day, as well as the connection between cultural activities and neurotic substitutive formations. For the rest, the reader may be referred to the author's own introduction. It is to be hoped that his work will commend itself to the attention of those who are most competent to appreciate it.

INTRODUCTION

Boast not against the branches. But if thou boast, thou bearest not the root, but the root thee.—*Romans* ii. 18.

I

THE four studies in this volume are amplified from lectures delivered before the Berlin and Vienna branches of the International Psycho-Analytical Association in the years 1914 to 1919. The characteristic, therefore, that distinguishes them from other works on the psychology of religion is that the method employed is the psycho-analytical one, and this fact will determine the nature and contents of the book in more than one direction. My presentation of the material must conform to the methods peculiar to psycho-analysis, and I shall have to assume the reader's knowledge of an important part of the results already obtained by those methods of investigation. Reference to the works of the founder of psycho-analysis, Professor Sigm. Freud, and his followers, as well as to the different expositions of psycho-analytical doctrines, must here take the place of a comprehensive introduction.

The systematic adoption of the psycho-analytical point of view will influence the content of this work more especially in the choice of the problems, the manner of their investigation, and the fact that a complete and universal solution of the problem will not be attempted. We shall only deal with questions upon which psycho-analysis is at present able to throw some new light, and shall, furthermore, confine ourselves to the treatment of a few of these very numerous questions only. It is not intended to build up a system of religious psychology founded on psychoanalysis, but to show by a few examples of representative value and significance what psycho-analysis with the means at present at its disposal may accomplish towards the explanation of difficult religious problems.

Psycho-analytical research does not pretend to render the works of the special sciences superfluous, but to make them in certain respects more complete. It should, therefore, aim at bringing out those aspects of the problems concerned which seem most fitted to be understood by the help of its methods. We should not for one moment forget, even where it is not expressly stated, that there are other aspects, that religious phenomena are of a complicated nature, and that only the investigation of them from different points of view can lead to the full appreciation of them. This conscious limitation, whereby we renounce the claim to solve questions from all points of view, seems to us both necessary and desirable; the methods and purpose of psycho-analysis refer particularly to the sphere of unconscious processes, and it can only deal with psychological phenomena of this nature and their connection with consciousness.

We maintain that the psycho-analytical method of investigation in scientific work has an equal claim to recognition with other already accepted explanatory methods. Though conscious of the necessary limitations of psycho-analysis, we maintain further that its application is all the more urgent inasmuch as the scientific study of religion comprises a large number of problems which cannot be solved without its help; and this is true not only for the less important but, perhaps, for precisely the most momentous questions in the psychology of religion. Of course, only the synthesis of the results of all methods can prove what final place will be assigned to psycho-analytical research in relation to the structure of the completed whole. Such a synthesis will be occupied with a task which psycho-analysis is unable to accomplish, namely, with the examination and study of the problems involved from all points of view. It will be concerned to show in what way those unconscious impulses, to which analysis points as determining the genesis and essence of religion, influence the products of conscious and higher activities of mental life, and how to define the sphere of the work of other parts of the psychical apparatus besides the primitive ones of the unconscious. No particular prophetic insight is required to predict that the importance of the material discovered by psycho-analysis will stand out prominently in the light of a synthetic review. When once psycho-analysis has interpreted to us the deeper strata of the structure of the mind and has explained their significance in the history of its development, it will not be so difficult to recognise the character of such a structure itself and the formal and material conditions which govern it. We shall find again and again in the course of our investigation how great is the influence of those deepest strata upon the disposition and development of the whole. In investigating the problems of religion, we are obliged constantly to keep in mind the unconscious processes; otherwise we are in great danger of building an edifice that will be blown down at the first breath of wind.

II

In the following four essays I have put religious ritual in the foreground of interests. There is a good precedent for this, as ritual has already proved a sound starting-point for the scientific analysis of religion. The first analytical comprehension of religious phenomena started from the ceremonies of believers, which Freud has compared with the obsessive acts and religious ceremonials of neurotics. His short paper 'Obsessive Acts and Religious Practices'[1] showed what new, surprising and profound discoveries could result from a comparison of religious and neurotic ceremonials. His *Totem und Tabu*, hitherto the most important work of the kind, and one that will always remain the standard illustration of what psycho-analysis can perform in the sphere of mental science, enables the reader (by its masterly analytical penetration of the affective foundation on which the belief in taboo rests, as well as by its analysis of the

[1] Freud, *Collected Papers*, vol. ii. p. 25.

sacrificial ritual) to recognise the trains of feelings to which religion owes its origin.

It thus seems to be advisable, both on psychological and historical grounds, to start our analytic treatment of religious problems with consideration of ritual. In the light of analysis it is possible to lay bare the motives which have led to the origin of ceremonial and the psychic paths which were taken in its development, by indicating the nature of the repressing forces, and also of the repressed material, as this latter manifests itself in the process of the ' return of the repressed '. It is, like the ceremonial of the obsessional neurosis, the first and most tangible object upon which analytic work can fix, and the disclosure of its meaning admits of the most conclusive inferences regarding the mental foundation upon which it rests. The character of *action* which is such a marked feature of ritual may be more profitably investigated psycho-analytically than the ideas, commands, prohibition, dogmas and complicated sentiments, which have later become the chief content of religion. To the psycho-analyst the compulsive symptoms of a patient, as represented in the carrying out of apparently silly or unnecessary acts, are at first richer in information than are the widely ramified and deep reflections and train of thought of obsessional cases which often can only be understood in retrospect from the meaning of his neurotic ceremonials. This comparison goes beyond a formal and purely external comparison, and is based upon the essential identity of the psychological processes involved in religion and the neuroses. The neuroses represent an individual attempt to solve the identical problems which it is the object of the great institutions of human society to overcome; but we must bear in mind that it is precisely the weakening of the social factor and the corresponding accentuation of the sexual one that is the distinctive sign of neurosis. It is this fact that makes a solution impossible for the neurotic. It is thus that the neuroses come to be caricatures of the great achievements of mankind. Obsessions are in especial a caricature

of religion, and accordingly obsessional neurotic ceremonial is an involuntary caricature of religious ceremonial.[1] In the failure to achieve their psychological task
and in the caricature-like nature of the symptoms which
result from it, the obsessional neuroses show the essential
characteristics of religion in an exaggerated and patho-
logically crude form; and these characteristics stand out
more clearly in them than in group-productions by
reason of the absence of their social aspects.

But though we put ritual at the centre of an analytical
investigation of religious questions, we are perfectly well
aware that this order can only be justified on heuristic
grounds, that ritual is by no means the earliest religious
phenomenon from a psychological point of view, and
that it presupposes very complicated mental processes
behind it. Nor do we wish to assert that it has a unique
significance in a consideration of the nature of religion;
it must simply be looked upon as an avenue of expression
for deep-lying psychological impulses that are only with
difficulty discoverable by other means. There is a
further advantage in that religious customs show a remarkable resistance to external influences; it is true they
undergo certain alterations of a very extensive nature,
but the advance of civilisation and the transformations
of human society have less effect upon them than they
have upon the beliefs, dogmas and other mental products
of religion.

Robertson Smith[2] has set forth with both vigour and
clearness the state of our historical knowledge concerning the origin of rites and religious customs. He says
that 'In all the antique religions, mythology takes the
place of dogma'; and 'these stories afford the only explanation that is offered of the precepts of religion and
the prescribed rules of ritual. But strictly speaking, this
mythology was no essential part of ancient religion, for
it had no sacred sanction and no binding force on the
worshippers. . . . Provided the worshipper fulfilled the

---

[1] See Freud, *The Future of an Illusion*, 1927.
[2] *Lectures on the Religion of the Semites*, p. 17.

B

ritual with accuracy, no one cared what he believed about its origin. Belief in a certain series of myths was neither obligatory as a part of true religion, nor was it supposed that, by believing, a man acquired religious merit and conciliated the favour of the gods.' 'So far as myths consist of explanation of ritual, their value is altogether secondary, and it may be affirmed with confidence that in almost every case the myth is derived from the ritual, and not the ritual from the myth.' Smith seems to be certain that the myth is only the interpretation of a religious custom. This scholar is opposed to the prominent position frequently given to mythology in the scientific treatment of the old religions.

But Smith's statement must certainly not be allowed to pass without some corrections and qualifications. Myth is older than religion; it is one of the oldest wish-compensations of mankind in its eternal struggle with external and internal forces. The origin of myth can perhaps be traced back into the animistic period, and it is of the highest importance for our understanding of the first psychological conflicts of primitive people. Therefore, although the primitive myth originates in the pre-religious period (and traces of this are clearly detectable in the myths and tales of a later period), it allies itself quite with religious cults and shares their history. The same affects, wishes and tendencies are operative in myth and in religion and can be recognised as the unconscious roots of both those products of the mass-psyche. It must indeed be recognised that myth, in its original state, preserves in a far less disguised form the memory of those events which led to the institution of religion than do the other forms of phantasy formation in which the share of unconscious powers and forces of repression can be demonstrated. It is true that Robertson Smith was right so far as the knowledge of his time went, because at that period science had no means of recognising all the later distortions and alterations of the myth and of laying bare its hidden and original meaning. Since psycho-analysis has succeeded in interpreting myths, their significance in folk-psychology has been more and more recognised. The difficult problem of the relations of myth and religion, which still awaits solution, will not be discussed here, but it is evident that Smith's remarks are correct as far as the late forms of the myth are concerned: the value to be attached to the 'aetiological' myth for the understanding of religious questions is indeed only secondary although its closer relationship to ritual, a relationship of which the essential nature is not yet clear, deserves more consideration. From a heuristic point of view, we shall, in accordance with Smith, ascribe for the present the chief importance to the study of ritual. This seems to be quite permissible as long as it is remembered that this attitude is only provisional and that no final judgement is pronounced as to the value and significance of ritual in religion.

In the following essays I have taken four examples of religious ceremonial and have sought by means of analysis to throw light upon the operation of unconscious factors, the mechanisms of affects and the significance of conscious influences, in the origin and development of the ritual concerned. I have selected for this purpose religious customs that are still practised, for my object is to show that in the latest forms of reaction-formation the same mental forces develop their activities in accordance with the same laws as in the earlier stages of development. I shall further show that the psychoanalytical methods make it possible to reconstruct the nature of the original impulses from which the ritual is derived by working back from the forms of expression and the hidden tendencies which the ritual still presents. Thus the analysis of the religious rite paves the way for the myth, dogma and cult, just as an intensive study of the ceremonials of obsessional patients invariably leads us to the larger structures of their dreams, obsessional ideas, conscientious scruples and compulsive acts.[1]

---

[1] The author has since endeavoured to continue his investigations of the psychology of religion along the lines indicated (*Der eigene und der fremde Gott,* 1923, and *Dogma und Zwangsidee,* 1927).

III

It is not of paramount importance what material taken from the history of religion is studied in order to obtain a knowledge of the influence of unconscious forces, since the psychological tendencies are everywhere the same and the difference between races plays no great part in the earliest development of mankind. On this account it is not surprising that problems of religious life of the savages of to-day and those belonging to the civilisation of the time of the Old Testament can be viewed from an identical standpoint. It must not be overlooked that the cultural level of the people to whom Europe owes its ethics and religion was once no higher than that of the Australian natives ; the Jews were not always the evangelists of a morality and system of religious thought whose essence is still accepted by civilised peoples to this day. Like other races, they have risen slowly and gradually from the lowest and most modest beginnings. In spite of the height to which they subsequently reached, many traces remain in their traditions witnessing to the paucity and brutality of their internal and external life in that period when, plundering and conquering with other Semitic tribes, they invaded the Land of Jordan. On the other hand, we must not forget that the primitive peoples of to-day have passed through a long development during which there have been numerous and important advances in civilisation. It is, of course, not permissible to make a direct analogy between the two lines of development, on account of the different conditions that internal and external factors have brought about in the course of thousands of years ; but taking into consideration all distinguishing and separating factors, much illumination can be obtained by the side-lights thrown from the one to the other. The continuity of human mental life, which is established by psycho-analysis, seems at least to point to an agreement in fundamentals. There is no reason why the psychologist should distinguish between so-called positive or revealed religions and others, particularly as his task is to understand the revelation itself as a psychological process.

The history of Judaism, so far as our knowledge of it now goes, presents numerous problems which are not only of interest to the historian, but of even greater interest to the psychologist. The remarkable vitality which has enabled the Jews to weather all storms and to maintain their existence as a distinct people constitutes a problem that cannot simply be explained on biological or historical grounds alone; mental factors must have co-operated in producing such a result. The mystery of why those ideas which came from the small country of Judea exerted such a special influence, and what led to their spiritualisation and transformation, cannot be solved without the aid of mental science.

Two factors determine the fate of the individual and that of races: disposition and experience, δαίμων and τύχη. The mental constitution which the individual brings with him into life is, perhaps, nothing more than a precipitate of the experiences of his ancestors. It is the task of science to trace back as far as possible these experiences in the history of peoples as well as in that of individuals. If, therefore, we desire to recognise and understand the distinctive qualities of a people—the how and the why of their being—we must study their history. History shows us that in the long development of a people, not only external events, but also mental processes are strictly determined by the law of cause and effect.

The beginnings of the people of Israel are shrouded in obscurity. About one and a half thousand years before Christ, warlike tribes from the Arabian peninsula penetrated into the more fruitful land of Canaan where Egyptian and Babylonian civilisations met. We obtain the first accounts of their appearance from tablets found in 1887 in the region of the Bedouin tribes at El Amarna, south of Cairo. We may assume that the Chabiri and the Sa. Gaz tribes (which, probably impelled by hunger, penetrated into the east and west Land of Jordan) belonged to the greater group of Hebrews among which are to be reckoned the later people of Israel. The conquerors came from the desert in the east ; perhaps that trace of patriarchal love which brings Israel into relation with Haran and the land of the 'Sons of the East' is significant in so far that the eastern land of Aramea, between Damascus and Haran, was once the home of these nomadic tribes. In the sagas and tales of their ancestors they seem to be almost entirely unwarlike; the coarse and savage life of earlier generations is almost forgotten; only Jacob and Abraham appear occasionally as warriors and fighters. The Book of Genesis faithfully portrays the life of half-nomads, peasants and shepherds.

These tribes, the state of whose civilisation at that time is unknown, penetrated into the land of Kena 'an (Canaan), which then became the scene of a development of peoples that was to influence profoundly the course of human culture for thousands of years. The small region from the foot of Lebanon to the desert between Arabia and Asia, from the Mediterranean to Syria, saw the birth of great thoughts which were to dominate the world. For the Jews also once conquered the world more permanently than did the Romans.

The fate of the Jewish people was inseparable from that of their religion. In ancient times religion was not, as it is to-day, a private and individual affair, but part of organised social life, an element in citizenship. A man who forsook his land forsook also his gods. However far we go back in history, we always find communities with fixed religious customs which the individual had to carry out if he did not want to place himself outside the tribe. It may be said that this community of religious and social life nowhere shows itself to us Europeans so closely and obviously as in the Jews. Religion itself, however, as we know, is a creation of mental functions born under the pressure of mental forces. And thus every student of the development of Judaism is irresistibly impelled to face the weighty question: What harmonious or discordant psychological forces, acting now as heretofore in their religion as in their national history, invisibly dominate the development of the Jewish people? Their history of suffering, their existence under abnormal conditions of life, and the mystery of their persistence must be of the greatest interest to the psycho-analyst, since it becomes more and more evident that the psychology of consciousness is not able to give us a sufficient explanation. He will feel, as he becomes absorbed in the history and the unique culture of Judaism, that dynamic processes of an unconscious nature, processes which have not hitherto been considered, have taken, and are still taking, a great and important share in its development.

A more comprehensive investigation, beyond the limits of Judaism, might be very fruitful—especially in two directions. Science recognises to an ever-increasing degree that the founders of the Christian religion base their feelings and thoughts on Judaism. Christ came not to destroy the law, but to fulfil it. The religions of the Church represent both the continuation and the transformation of the Jewish religion. An analytical understanding of the religious questions of Judaism should, therefore, throw light on the unconscious factors which have determined the nature and origin of Christianity. Thus, one of the fundamental principles of the civilised world of to-day comes within the sphere of the analysis of the psychology of religion, and it may be possible thus to recognise more easily the dynamics of its unconscious processes.

The analysis of the fundamental stages in the development of Judaism may have a special value and significance for the psychology of religion in a second direction also, in that it may explain the psychogenesis of the claim of the Jews to be the chosen people and to stand in a peculiarly intimate relationship to the Deity. This belief is perhaps demonstrable in the religion of every primitive people, though in different ways and degrees— possibly it arises from mental impulses which are not specifically of a religious nature—and it can be shown in the civilised religions in a form which transcends national frontiers. But the peculiarly clear expression which this claim finds in Judaism makes the latter the best field in which to prosecute our analytical investigation.

The primitive unity of religion and people, which is only beginning to be loosened in the Judaism of the present day, makes it probable that an analytical investigation of the Jewish religion may throw a great deal of light upon the unconscious influences which have played their part in determining the special fate of the Jews—light which anthropology, archæology, history, political economy and other sciences are unable to furnish. A reading of the scientific literature bearing on the group of problems brought together under the misleading designation of the 'Jewish question' is reminiscent of an amusing dialogue in one of Molière's plays between a miserly father and his son's servant.[1] The servant, Scapin, relates with every sign of fear that his young master, Léandre, has met with a great misfortune. The owner of a Turkish galley lying in the harbour had invited him to his ship and overwhelmed him with courtesies. Suddenly the ship had weighed anchor and sailed away. He, Scapin, had been ordered by the Turk to fetch from the father five hundred *écus* as ransom for his imprisoned son. The father, Géronte, asks: '*Mais que diable allait-il faire dans cette galère?*' But the servant answers evasively, '*Il ne songeait pas à ce qui est arrivé.*' The harassed Géronte repeats the question again and again, but the clever Scapin quickly speaks of something else, urges haste, emphasises the danger in which young Léandre is placed, etc. This play of question and answer is often recalled when one reads scientific works, highly illuminating as far as they go, on the problems of Judaism. '*Mais que diable allait-il faire dans cette galère?*' this is indeed the momentous question to be answered. We have to investigate not only the external conditions that help to mould the peculiar destiny of the Jews, but also the mental forces and tendencies which have urged them on their long and painful road. It may be claimed to-day that unconscious

[1] *Les Fourberies de Scapin*, Act ii.

psychological processes in the group-mind of the people are factors of outstanding importance in the formation of the religion and history of the Jews. Only through the co-operation of these factors with other factors such as economic conditions, the nature and climate of their land, etc., could the fate of the Jews develop in one direction or the other.

It may, of course, be asked whether it is necessary to go so far back into the developmental history of the mind of a people in order to understand their racial characteristics, whether the psychical experience of remote ancestors, as it appears to us reflected in religion, is essential for the understanding of the present problems of Judaism. We may answer this question simply by pointing to the fact that regressive investigation has been found to be necessary in the analysis of the individual. The conflicts of the individual, as well as many very significant characterological traits, cannot be fully understood unless we carry back the analysis into the earliest years of his childhood, the occurrences and impressions of which require just as much attention as the later experiences of puberty and manhood. We even believe that it is in the events of his ' pre-historic' childhood that the basis is laid for his later experiences, and that the mental processes of these years (processes which have later become unconscious) possess a peculiar significance and a tendency to produce after-effects in the later years of his life.

If we accept the fact of the continuity of psychological processes beyond the limits of a single generation, we are obliged to consider the effects of such events in pre-history, since they persist and are renewed by the unconscious mental life. The experience of our ancestors is as potent in its influence on us as our experience will be on the mental life of our descendants. Much of what we believe long since dead and buried in us still lives on in the depths of the mind and determines our course in life. As the French say, '*Ce sont les morts qu'il faut qu'on tue*' ('It is the dead whom we must kill').

COUVADE AND THE PSYCHOGENESIS OF THE
FEAR OF RETALIATION[1]

Hier dacht' ich lauter Unbekannte
und finde leider nah Verwandte;
es ist ein altes Buch zu blättern:
vom Harz bis Hellas immer Vettern.
GOETHE.

I. MATERIAL

THE old saying that, when ideas fail, a word will present itself to fill the gap at the right moment, has been repeated in the naming of the phenomena termed 'couvade'. The word is derived from the Basque *couver* (to sit, *i.e.* on eggs).[2] All competent scholars of the present day are agreed that the terms 'couvade' and 'male childbed' correspond neither in extent nor in essence to the observed facts. Couvade, according to the view of Sidney Hartland, is 'a name too deeply rooted now to be changed, albeit one founded on a mistake as to the use of the word and a limitation, untenable on scientific grounds, though inevitable in the then state of our knowledge, to certain remarkable developments of the usage'.[3] The use of this word, though scientifically inaccurate, has become so fixed that we must continue to employ it.

If we ask what is the ethnological significance of the

---

[1] From a paper read before the Berlin Psycho-Analytical Society on April 25, 1914. First published in *Imago*, 1914.

[2] Cordier, 'De la covada en Espane', *Anthropos*, 1910, p. 775. Others prefer to see its origin in a Lyonnais expression *encovar* (*cueva, encerrarse, occultarso* = to hide oneself). The word does not exist in the French vocabulary of to-day. *Dictionnaire de l'ancien language françois* by La Courne de Saint Palaye, 1877, gives the following definition: *Lieu de sûreté, demeure dans l'enceinte et couvert de son parc. D'où vient l'expression faire couvade pour se tenir à couvert dans son parc, dans une assurée retraite.* Monet et Rob. Estienne, *Dictionnaire. Se cacher, se tenir aux aguets.* Cotgrave, Dictionary, vol. iv. p. 358. *S'accroupir comme une poule, qui couve afin de voir ce qui se passe, sans se hasarder.* In Frédéric Mistral, *Lou trésor doù felibrige ou dictionnaire provençal français*, tom. I. p. 662, we find the term *couvado* or *cougado*, the meaning of which coincides with that of couvade.

[3] *The Legend of Perseus: A Study of Tradition in Story, Custom, and Belief,* London, 1895, vol. ii. p. 400.

27

word we must temporarily be content with the following
definition: Couvade is the custom observed among many
races that the father of a new-born child lies in bed for a
certain period, eating only prescribed foods, abstaining
from severe work and from the chase, etc., while his wife
who has just given birth to a child carries on her usual
occupation. (We shall see presently in how many points
this definition needs correction.) The impression which
these phenomena have made on outside observers shows
that in applying the name they were trying to convey
the idea of a lying-in on the part of the man.

Our knowledge of couvade is old although by no
means always based upon trustworthy report. Diodorus
writes of the Corsicans:[1] 'The most singular thing
amongst them is the usual custom at the birth of a
child. When a woman is delivered no one troubles about
her, but her husband lies in childbed for a definite
number of days as though he had pains in his body.'
'Strabo mentions the story that among the Iberians of
the north of Spain, the women, "after the birth of a child,
tend their husbands, putting them to bed instead of
going themselves".'[2]

'Apollonius Rhodius did indeed affirm that among the
Tibareni of Pontus, when a woman had been delivered
of a child, her husband lay groaning in bed with his head
bandaged, while his wife prepared food and baths for
him as if he had been the mother.'[3] Reports of later
travellers from North Spain, South Africa, Sardinia and
Corsica show that the descendants of those old peoples
knew of couvade. Francisque Michel wrote of the inhabitants of Biscay in 1857:[4] 'The women rise immediately
after childbirth and attend to the duties of the household, while the husband goes to bed, taking the baby
with him, and thus receives the neighbours' compli-

[1] Diodorus Siculus, *Bibliotheca historica*, i. 80.
[2] Tylor, *Researches into the Early History of Mankind*, London, 1870, p. 302.
[3] Frazer, *Totemism and Exogamy*, London, 1910, vol. iv. p. 245.
[4] *Le Pays basque*, Paris, 1857, p. 201, quoted by Tylor, *ibid.* p. 301. De
Laborde, *Itinéraire descriptif de l'Espagne*, Paris, 1809, ii. p. 123, also testifies
that the Basques of the Province of Navarre knew of the custom.

ments'. It is strange to find that Marco Polo, the celebrated explorer of the fourteenth century, mentions
similar customs in a province of China.[1] 'When one of
their wives has been delivered of a child, the infant is
washed and swathed, and then the woman gets up and
goes about her household affairs, whilst the husband
takes to bed with the child by his side, and so keeps his
bed for forty days; and all the kith and kin come to visit
him and keep up a great festivity. They do this, because,
say they, the woman has had a hard bout of it, and 'tis
but fair the man should have his share of the suffering.'
Further accounts concerning the inhabitants of the
province show that Marco Polo's description refers to
the Miâo-Tsze, the primitive folk of China, who, living
as they do in isolated woods, possess no written records.
Lockhart has testified to the occurrence of couvade
among the remnants of the Miâo-Tsze.[2] Kunnicke[3] quotes
the text of a picture,[4] 'The father is seen through the
window of the cottage lying on the couch, nursing the
new-born babe, and the mother outside coming with his
food—he must be treated as an invalid in this way, we
are told, for a month, or disaster will result'. A. Crain
(quoted by Kunnicke) reports that a primitive people of
India, the Dravidians, lay the new-born child in its
father's bed, and the man is taboo in the period following. As a reason for the same custom among the Koranas,
Thurston says that 'the life of the man is more valuable
than that of the woman, and the husband being the
more important factor in the birth of the child, it is
fitting that more care should be taken of him'.[5] E.
Tylor[6] states that there exists in South India a custom
that 'a man, at the birth of his first son or daughter by
the chief wife, or for any son afterwards, will retire to
bed for a lunar month, living principally on a rice diet,

[1] *The Book of Ser Marco Polo*, London, 1871, vol. ii. p. 52.
[2] 'The Miâo-Tsze or Aborigines of China', *Transactions of the Ethnological Society*, London, vol. i. p. 187 (New Series).
[3] 'Das sogenannte Männerkindbett', *Zeitschrift für Ethnologie*, 43. Jahrgang, 1911.
[4] Bushell, *Chinese Art*, vol. ii. p. 144.
[5] *Ethnographic Madras*, 1906, pp. 547-51.   [6] *Ibid.* p. 301.

abstaining from exciting food and from smoking; at the end of the month he bathes, puts on a fresh dress, and gives his friends a feast'. Here a detail is brought out which we have not met with previously, *i.e.* the man carrying out couvade has to submit to restrictions in diet. In many islands of the Malay Archipelago we find these restrictions not only applied to food. The customs of the Land Dyaks of Borneo will serve as an example.[1] 'The husband, before the birth of his child, may do no work with a sharp instrument except what is necessary for the farm; nor may he fire guns, nor strike animals, nor do any violent work, lest bad influences should affect the child; and after it is born the father is kept in seclusion indoors for several days, and dieted on rice and salt, to prevent not his own but the child's stomach from swelling.' Already we can recognise that a number of new details threaten to upset our previous idea of couvade. Besides the 'observance of the lying-in bed', the husband among the Dyaks and many other peoples imposes upon himself severe denials at the birth of a child—an event which to us is a 'joyful' one. Among the Caribs, for example, 'when a child is born, the mother goes presently to her work, but the father begins to complain, and takes to his hammock, and there he is visited as though he were sick, and undergoes a course of dieting. . . . They sometimes pass the five first days without eating or drinking anything; then up to the tenth they drink *oüycou*. . . . These ten days passed, they begin to eat cassava only, drinking *oüycou*, and abstaining from everything else for the space of a whole month.'[2] Later he gets a little more than this prison fare, but sometimes abstains ten months or a whole year from many kinds of flesh, such as turtles, pigs, fowls, fish, etc. It is believed that by the eating of these animals the child might be injured. De Rochefort,[3] who also reports these customs, adds that this fasting is only strictly observed at the birth of the first child; after the birth of

[1] Tylor, *ibid.* p. 298.   [2] Tylor, *ibid.* p. 294.
[3] *Histoire naturelle et morale des Isles Antilles de l'Amérique*, Rotterdam, 1665.

others the diet of the Carib father is less rigorous and carried out for a much shorter period. If this strange diet surprises us, how are we to explain this further account given by the same author? 'Some of the Caribs have yet another custom which is even more unpleasant for the father to whom a child has been born. At the end of the fast he is duly bled on the shoulders with a tooth of an agouti. The unfortunate man must not only submit to this, but he must not give expression to the slightest feeling of pain. They believe that the greater the endurance of the father during this trial, the greater will be the bravery of the child.' Our opinion that the commencement of fatherhood is no sinecure for a Carib is confirmed when we notice what another investigator, Du Tertre, relates.[1] 'When the forty days are up they invite their relations and best friends, who being arrived, before they set to eating, hack the skin of this poor wretch with agouti teeth, and draw blood from all parts of his body, in such sort that from being sick by pure imagination they often make a real patient of him. This is, however, so to speak, only the fish, for now comes the sauce they prepare for him; they take sixty or eighty large grains of pimento or Indian pepper, the strongest they can get, and after well mashing it in water, they wash with this peppery infusion the wounds and scars of the poor fellow, who, I believe, suffers no less than if he were burnt alive; however, he must not utter a single word if he will not pass for a coward and a wretch. This ceremony finished, they bring him back to his bed, where he remains some days more, and the rest go and make good cheer in the house at his expense. Nor is this all, for through the space of six whole months he eats neither birds nor fish, firmly believing that this would injure the child's stomach, and that it would participate in the natural faults of the animals on which its father had fed; for example, if the father ate turtle, the child would be deaf and have no brains like this animal, if he ate manati, the child would have little round eyes like this

---

[1] Tylor, *ibid.* p. 294.

creature, and so on with the rest.' 'Among the Arawaks of Surinam, for some time after the birth of his child, the father must fell no tree, fire no gun, hunt no large game, lest his child should become ill and die. The agouti is tabooed among some tribes, lest like that little animal, the child should be meagre; the haimara also, lest it should be blind—the outer coating of the eye of that fish suggesting film or cataract—the marudi is also forbidden, lest the infant be still-born, the screeching of that bird being considered ominous of death.' La Borde tells of a peculiarly ludicrous precautionary measure: a Carib after the birth of a child goes to bathe so that the baby shall not become cold.[1] This author also gives a detailed description of the abstinences to which the father has to submit among the tribes of South America. He fasts for a long period, only goes out at night, visits no one, and fears to see anybody who has eaten fish lest the smell should tempt him to eat some himself, in which case the mother would become ill and the child die. After having had his skin cut and mutilated in different parts, and a mixture of Jamaica peppercorns and tobacco juice rubbed into the wounds, the rich blood which is shed is rubbed on the child's face so that it will be brave. The more unflinching the father the more courageous will be the child.

We must not forget that in most of the tribes who observe the custom of abstemiousness during couvade, a great feast is spread after the period of fasting at which the forbidden animals are placed upon the table. Couvade is observed almost everywhere in Brazil. The same customs exist even among the Indian tribes living at the source of the river Shingo, who exhibit no culture of any sort, and were only discovered in 1887 by the cousins von den Steinen.

Although 'genuine' couvade, *i.e.* the apparent lying-in of the man, exhibits in essential features the same forms in all these widely dispersed peoples, the abstin-

[1] *Voyage qui contient une relation exacte de l'origine des Caraïbes*, Leide, 1704, chap. vii. p. 585.

ence customs of the father vary extraordinarily as regards number, form and content. M. Dobritzhoffer gives
a clear description of the father-rites of the Abipones
from which I will quote an example.[1] 'Francisco Barreda, Deputy of the Royal Governor of Tucuman, came
to visit the new colony of Conceiçam in the territory of
Santiago. To him, as he was walking with me in the
courtyard, the cacique Malakin came up to pay his
respects, having just left his bed, to which he had been
confined in consequence of his wife's recent delivery. As
I stood by, Barreda offered the cacique a pinch of
Spanish snuff, but seeing the savage refuse it, contrary to
custom, he thought he must be out of his mind, for he
knew him at other times to be greedy of this nasal
delicacy; so he asked me aside to inquire the cause of his
abstinence. . . . "Don't you know?" he answered, "that
my wife has just been confined? Must not I therefore
abstain from stimulating my nostrils? What a danger my
sneezing would bring upon my child!" They believe that
the father's carelessness influences the new-born offspring, from a natural bond and sympathy of both.
Hence if the child comes to a premature end, its death
is attributed by the women to the father's intemperance,
this or that cause being assigned; he did not abstain from
mead; he had loaded his stomach with water-hog; he had
devoured underground honey, stamping on the bees with
his feet; he had ridden till he was tired and sweated.
With raving like this, the crowd of women accuse the
father with impunity of causing the child's death, and
are accustomed to pour curses on the unoffending husband.' Among most of the people who observe couvade,
the father should neither perform heavy work nor handle
weapons. Hartland says that 'the Niasese father-
expectant must avoid talking with Malays or Chinese,
lest the child be unable to speak his own tongue, splitting a piece of wood or the *atap*-leaves wherewith the
houses are roofed, lest the infant be born with harelip;
eating of a pig found dead, lest the fœtus be born with-

[1] Tylor, *ibid*. p. 294.

C

out attaining proper development; killing or cutting up
chickens or pigs, lest the babe feel the wounds; eating of
the great beetles of which the natives are very fond, lest
the little one catch a cough'.[1] 'On the Melanesian island
of Saa, both before and after the birth, the father "will
not eat pig's flesh, and he abstains from movements
which are believed to do harm, upon the principle that
the father's movements affect those of the child. A man
will not do hard work; he keeps quiet lest the child
should start, should overstrain itself, or should throw
itself about as he paddles."'[2] An idea of the length of
time these customs have to be observed may be obtained from the following accounts. In Japan a husband
may not eat bananas, fallen cocoanuts, or turtle, from
the fourth month of his wife's pregnancy.[3] Among the
Zambales of Luzon (Philippines) the bridegroom may
not eat sour fruits as early as the last week before
marriage, lest his future children suffer from pains in the
stomach.[4] In other places the wife as well as the husband has to submit to strict prohibitions. For example,
among the Niasese, 'Both parents must abstain, before
the birth, from passing over a spot where a man has been
murdered, or a buffalo slain, or where a dog has been
burnt for the purpose of giving effect to certain impreca-
tions, else the child will be affected by the contortions
of the dying man or beast'. 'The consequence of expressing or boiling-out oil is headache to the child.' The
married people of the Dyaks in south-east Borneo ought
not to cork up anything, lest the child suffer from con-
stipation.

Brett, who observed couvade in Guiana in 1868, says
that the dietetic rules 'are probably observed by very
few in their full rigour, for the forbidden animals form
a large portion of the Indian's bill of fare as found in the
forests, and a Carib or other polygamist with three or

---

[1] Hartland, *ibid*. p. 403.
[2] Hartland, *ibid*. p. 404.
[3] A. Senfft, 'Gefühlsleben bei Südsee-Insulanern', *Völkerschau*, III. München, 1904.
[4] According to Blumentritt in *Globus*, XLVIII. and XLIV.

four wives might be debarred from tasting them during
the whole, or the best period of his manhood'.[1]

If we survey the present sphere of the father-rites
comprised in couvade, we find that they occur only in
South America and south-east Asia, although traces of
them are still found in many lands and even in south-
west Europe. The reports which have been preserved
show that it and similar customs were formerly widely
spread, and all observers agree that their practice has
steadily decreased with the advance of civilisation.
Hartland[2] states, 'America inhabited by a homogeneous
race, displays it everywhere, even among the Eskimos
of Greenland, save apparently in Tierra del Fuego. On
the eastern continent Mr. Ling Roth puts the matter
somewhat strongly when he says that it "is only met
with in isolated and widely separated localities". In
Australia it is unknown; nor is there any record of it
among the extinct Tasmanians. Summing up the facts,
the same writer says: "The custom does not appear to
exist or to have existed among those people to whom the
term 'most *degraded*' is erroneously applied, people which
were better described as savages living in the lowest
known forms of culture, such as the Australians, Tasmanians, Bushmen, Hottentots, Veddahs, Sakeys, Aetas,
and Fuegians. Neither does the custom exist among the
so-called civilised portion of mankind. In other words,
couvade appears at first sight to be limited to people
who hold an intermediate position between those in the
highest and those in [the] lowest states of culture. As
such it may be said to represent an intermediate or
transition state of mental development."' E. B. Tylor
ascribes the same importance to the custom in the cultural history of mankind.[3] 'The isolated occurrences of a
custom among particular races surrounded by other
races who ignore it, may be sometimes to the ethnologist
like those outlying patches of strata from which the
geologist infers that the formation they belong to once

---

[1] *The Indian Tribes of Guiana*, London, 1816, p. 356.
[2] *Ibid.* p. 409.   [3] *Ibid.* p. 303.

spread over intervening districts, from which it has been
removed by denudation.' The same idea is expressed in
the *Encyclopædia Britannica*:[1] 'It is far more likely that
so universal a practice has no trivial beginnings, but it is
to be considered as a mile-stone marking a great transitional epoch of human progress'.

We shall, therefore, be interested to learn what ethnologists and students of cultural progress have to say of
this important subject.

II. THEORIES

We will now consider the attempts that have been
made to solve the riddle of couvade. It will be necessary to examine numerous and mutually contradictory
opinions and hypotheses, and we shall endeavour to
disentangle the most important of them.

The missionary, Josef François Lafitau, 1723, offered
an explanation of couvade from the religious point of
view. According to him it is a remembrance of original
sin, and the isolation and rules of abstinence are signs of
deep repentance.[2] Bachofen seeks a scientific basis for
the explanation of these customs.[3] In his view couvade
is a symptom of the transition from matriarchy to
paternity, and lays emphasis on the father's share in
procreation in contrast to the mother-right which originally existed. The father pretends to go through confinement in order to obtain the right over his child which
earlier belonged only to the mother. Bachofen comes to
the following conclusion: 'Gynæcocracy itself is associated once more with the religious supremacy of the
mother, and this peculiar metamorphosis of the father
signifies his admission into that state of religious sanctity

---

[1] *Encyclopædia Britannica*, Eleventh Edition, 1910, vol. vii. p. 338.
[2] I do not know if this clergyman derived his idea from the Old Testament.
It may be surmised that he had in mind 2 Samuel xii. 16-22. David had taken
the wife of Uriah the Hittite to be his wife: 'And the Lord struck the child that
Uriah's wife bare unto David, and it was very sick. David therefore besought
God for the child; and David fasted, and went in, and lay all night upon the
earth. And the elders of his house arose, and went to him, to raise him up from
the earth; but he would not, neither did he eat bread with them.'
[3] *Das Mutterrecht*, Stuttgart, 1861, S. 256-59.

and inviolability belonging to her. Gynæcocracy could not have celebrated a greater triumph; the father could have found no more speaking expression of his subordination to motherhood.' The phantastic hypothesis of a 'male protest' which found both its expression and its overcoming in couvade customs has been almost completely dropped after a period of great popularity. It was opposed first and foremost by the facts themselves, for couvade exists among peoples in whom the child at the present time belongs to the mother clan.[1] We are reminded by v. Dargun that among the very people who most practise couvade a lying-in of the woman is little recognised or even unknown, so that the idea of imitation seems to be out of the question.[2] He is of opinion, however, that couvade is a sign of incipient paternal authority: the man has become the chief person of the family and carries the greatest responsibility, and on this account has to observe the couvade. It is quite certain that this explanation is opposed to just as many facts as that of Bachofen; on the other hand, it is not possible to make all customs intelligible. Bachofen's view, which was opposed by those relentless and clear-sighted critics, Hartland and Frazer, was adopted by many German, English and French scholars, for example, Bastian,[3] Bernhoft,[4] Giraud Teulon,[5] Letourneau,[6] Tylor,[7] etc. Bastian gives two explanations. The first one assumes that the custom originated in the endeavour to elude the devil of puerperal fever and to protect the new-born child against lurking demons. We shall acknowledge the relative correctness of this hypothesis in our psychological analysis. The second explanation is closely related to that of

[1] E. Westermarck has alluded to this. Cf. *The Origin and Development of the Moral Ideas*, London, 1908.
[2] Lothar v. Dargun, *Mutterrecht und Vaterrecht*, Leipzig, 1892, I. S. 20.
[3] 'Matriarchat und Patriarchat', *Verhandlungen der Gesellschaft für Ethnologie und Urgeschichte*, Berlin, 1886, S. 337. (*Zeitschrift für Ethnologie*.)
[4] *Zeitschrift für vergleichende Rechtswissenschaft*, 1891, IX. Bd.
[5] *Les origines du mariage et de la famille*, Paris, 1884, p. 137, and *La mère chez certains peuples de l'antiquité*, Paris, 1867.
[6] *La Sociologie d'après l'ethnographie*, Paris, 1884, pp. 384-95, and *L'Évolution du mariage et de la famille*, Paris, 1888, pp. 394.
[7] *Ibid.* See below for the opinions of Frazer and Hartland as to Bachofen's views.

Bachofen; the man cannot be recognised as the legiti-
mate father without the male childbed. Max Müller lays
stress on the following hypothesis.[1] The people held the
primitive idea that the child could easily come to harm
through noise, agitation, or violence on the father's part
at the time of the confinement. This was the starting-
point of the strange custom which gradually developed
from this view. Every act that was thought good and
finally became a fixed rule of conduct was in agreement
with it. 'It is clear that the poor husband was at first
tyrannised over by his female relations, and afterwards
frightened into superstition. He then began to make a
martyr of himself till he made himself really ill and took
to his bed in self-defence.' Many objections can be raised
against this idea, of which I shall mention only two. The
idea that the life of the child would be imperilled
through noise and violence on the father's part cannot
possibly be a 'primitive one'. It is quite immaterial
whether we take 'primitive' here to mean inborn (in-
nate) or primary. Moreover, the assumption that couvade was invented and carried out by the women does
not appear to be proved. It is inconceivable that the
savages imposed upon themselves abstinences and endured pains just because their women wished it. The
chivalry attributed by many investigators to primitive
peoples—and these are the only proper subjects of study
where the origin of couvade is concerned—reaches its
acme in Karl Friedrich Oppen's[2] explanation. He considers that couvade is the women's invention, 'to prevent the men troubling them at this time with too much
work, which otherwise they would have in abundance if
the man went out hunting daily and brought home
venison or a quantity of fish'. Quandt has expressed
similar views.[3] Surely such an object as these authorities
assume would have been more easily and more thoroughly

[1] *Chips from a German Workshop*, London, 1867, ii. p. 274; and Oppen, *Das
Ausland*, 1871, Nr. 6, S. 124.
[2] *Das Ausland*, 1871, Nr. 6, p. 174.
[3] *Nachricht von Surinam und seinen Einwohnern, sonderlich den Arawaken,
Waraiien und Karaiben*, Görlitz, 1807, S. 252.

attained by the woman herself staying in bed; the husband lounging in bed or in a hammock only imposed more work upon her. There is as little value in tracing male childbed to the 'effeminacy' of the men—the very men who observe the severest abstinences and uncomplainingly endure the sharpest pains. In the face of such explanations one feels tempted to agree with J. G. Frazer's opinion that 'the astonishment which customs like the couvade have excited in the mind of civilised man is merely a measure of his profound ignorance of primitive modes of thought'.[1] The ease with which the psychological questions raised by couvade may be studied is due in particular to the insight of three English scholars, E. B. Tylor, E. S. Hartland and J. G. Frazer. Tylor was the first to express the opinion that Bachofen's theory was untenable.[2] He points out that among primitive peoples 'the connection between father and child is not only, as we think, a mere relation of parentage, affection, duty, but that their very bodies are joined by a physical bond, so that what is done to the one acts directly upon the other'. He speaks of couvade as an institution which owes its origin to 'sympathetic magic'. Hartland[3] also rejects Bachofen's hypothesis: 'Moreover, the lying-in of the husband, so far as it can be so termed, is only part of a large number of observances, by which he is bound, in the more fully developed forms of the custom, from the moment his wife conceives, or occasionally before, until the child is able to speak, or to digest the usual food of the tribe'. He endeavours to explain this from the 'belief that the child is a part of the parent; and, just as even after apparent severance of hair or nails from the remainder of the body, the bulk is affected by anything which happens to the severed portion, so as well after as before the infant has been severed from the parent's body, and in

[1] *Ibid.* p. 248.
[2] *Ibid.* p. 295. But he afterwards changed his mind and accepted Bachofen's view. See E. B. Tylor, 'On a Method of Investigating the Development of Institutions', *Journal of the Anthropological Institute*, xviii., 1889, p. 254.
[3] *Ibid.* p. 402.

our eyes has acquired a distinct existence, he will be
affected by whatever operates on the parent; and, conversely, the parent will feel whatever happens to him,
as in some parts of England, a mother absent for a while
from her child is believed to feel her breasts painful when
he cries. . . . Gradually, however, as the infant grows and
strengthens he becomes able to digest the same food as
his parents, and to take part in the ordinary avocations
of their lives. Precaution then may be relaxed, and ultimately remitted altogether. . . . The custom, therefore,
is liable to gradual diminution. . . . With the tardy and
half-unconscious recognition of natural laws, it loses bit
by bit its importance, until it fades away into little more
than a ceremony. In spite of decay, however, and, indeed, in consequence of it, it may acquire another significance; and among a few tribes, as, for example, the
Mundurucus, it becomes "the legal form by which the
father recognises the child as his". Accordingly, I venture with all respect to think it is a mistake to see in this
legal form the origin of the couvade, as Dr. Tylor has
done, plausible though the explanation seems.'

Frazer holds the same view.[1] He says that the hypothesis that couvade involves a simulation of childbirth
'is to all appearance an unwarranted assumption made
by civilised persons who misunderstood what they saw
or read about'. He quotes Bancroft's description of
couvade among the Californian Indians[2] as an example.
'When childbirth overtakes the wife, the husband puts
himself to bed, and there, grunting and groaning, he
affects to suffer all the agonies of a woman in labour.'
From the similarity of behaviour, observers interpreted
the custom 'as an imitation of childbirth enacted by
the husband'. 'The assumption and the misunderstanding are embodied in the German name for the custom,
das Männerkindbett.' 'If the couvade, so far as is known,
does not imply any pretence of maternity on the part of
the father, it can hardly be explained as an attempt to
secure for the father under a system of father-kin those

[1] *Ibid.* p. 246.   [2] *Ibid.* p. 245.

rights over the children which had previously been enjoyed by the mother under a system of mother-kin. . . . On the whole, Bachofen's theory may be safely set aside not only as unproved but as inconsistent with the facts. . . . In fact the custom is merely one of the innumerable cases of sympathetic magic. The father believes that there exists between him and his child a relation of such intimate physical sympathy that whatever he does must simultaneously affect his offspring; for example, if he eats food that disagrees with him, the child will be sick or have a pain in its stomach. . . . We have no right, therefore, to reject their testimony and to substitute for their explanation another which, far from explaining the facts, is actually contradicted by them. The fact is that what in this custom seems extravagantly absurd to us seems perfectly simple and natural to the savage. The idea that persons and things act on each other at a distance is as firmly believed by him as the multiplication table or the law of gravitation is by us.'

The customs which refer to childbirth have more than one purpose. Couvade serves, in the first place, to mitigate the mother's pains in that it transfers them by magic to the man. Frazer[1] mentions the following cases in proof of this: 'Among some of the Dyaks of Sarawak "should any difficulty occur in child delivery the *manangs* or medicine men are called in. One takes charge of the proceedings in the lying-in chamber, the remainder set themselves on the *ruai* or common verandah. The *manang* inside the room wraps a long loop of cloth around the woman, above the womb. A *manang* outside wraps his body around in the same manner, but first places within its fold a large stone corresponding to the position of the child in the mother's womb. A long incantation is then sung by the *manangs* outside, while the one within the room strives with all his power to force the child downwards and so compel delivery. As soon as he has done so, he draws down upon it the loop of cloth and twists it tightly around the mother's body,

[1] *Ibid.* p. 248.

so as to prevent the upward return of the child. A shout from him proclaims to his companions on the *ruai* his success, and the *manang* who is for the occasion personating the mother, moves the loop of cloth containing the stone which encircles his own body a stage downwards. And so the matter proceeds until the child is born." '

'Again, in some parts of New Ireland, when a woman is in hard labour and a compassionate man desires to aid her delivery, he betakes himself to the men's clubhouse, lies down, feigns to be ill, and writhes in fictitious agony, whenever he hears the shrieks of the woman in childbed. The other men gather round him and make as if they would alleviate his pangs. This kindly meant farce lasts till the child is born. In both these cases there is a deliberate simulation of childbirth for the purpose of facilitating a real birth. In both cases the mode of operation is sympathetic or imitative magic. . . . But there seems to be this distinction between them that in the first case the immediate object is to hasten the appearance of the child, in the second it is to relieve the woman's pangs by transferring them to the pretended mother. . . . In Borneo an attempt is sometimes made to shift the travail-pains to an image.' 'In other cases the same notion of vicarious suffering appears to be applied for the relief of women at the expense of their husbands. In Gujarat "among a very low-caste set of basket-makers (called Pomlā) it is the usual practice of a wife to go about her work immediately after delivery, as if nothing had happened. The presiding Mātā of the tribe is supposed to transfer her weakness to her husband, who takes to his bed and has to be supported with good nourishing food."' Among the Erukalavandlu, a tribe in Southern India, 'directly the woman feels the birth-pangs, she informs her husband, who immediately takes some of her clothes, puts them on, retires into a dark room, and lies down on the bed, covering himself with a long cloth. . . . During the days of ceremonial uncleanness the man is treated as the other Hindus treat their women on such occasions.'

Frazer differentiates between the South American and South Indian couvades; he considers they represent two quite different phenomena which are incorrectly included under the name couvade. 'The South American couvade consists in a certain diet and regimen observed by a father for the sake of his child, the South Indian couvade, if we may call it so, consists apparently in a simulation of childbirth enacted by the husband for the sake of his wife.' Frazer quotes numerous customs existing in Europe which testify to a widely spread belief in a 'transference of pains'. 'In Ireland, "there is also a way by which the pains of maternity can be transferred from the woman to her husband. This secret is so jealously guarded that a correspondent in the west of Ireland, who had been able to investigate the matter, was at last obliged to report: 'In regard to putting the sickness on the father of a child, that is a well-known thing in this country, but after making every inquiry I could not make out how it is done. It is strictly private.' . . . It is asserted by some that the husband's consent must first be obtained, but the general opinion is that he feels all the pain, and even cries out with agony, without being aware of the cause."' 'The local doctor of Kilkeiran and Carna, in south Connemara, reported in 1892 that a woman occasionally wears the coat of the father of the expected child, "with the idea that he should share in the pains of childbirth"; and similarly, Dr. C. R. Browne writes that in the counties of Tipperary and Limerick "women in childbirth often wear the trousers of the father of [the] child round the neck, the effect of which is supposed to be the lightening of the pains of labour".' An Esthonian woman on the marriage evening gives her husband 'plenty of beer to drink seasoned with wild rosemary (*Ledum palustre*), that he may fall into a deep sleep. While he lies in this narcotic slumber, the woman must creep between his legs without his perceiving it (for if he wakes up, all the good of it is lost), and in that way the poor man gets his share of the future travail-pains.' 'At Langholm in Dumfriesshire in

the year 1772 the English traveller, Pennant, was shewn
the place where several witches had suffered in the last
century, and he adds: . . . "I saw the reputed offspring of
such a labour; who kindly came into the world without
giving her mother the least uneasiness, while the poor
husband was roaring with agony in his uncouth and
unnatural pains".'

Although Frazer includes all these cases in his elucidation of the couvade, bringing them under the head of
sympathetic magic and the belief in the 'transference of
evil ', he considers 'in regard to some of the cases it may
perhaps be doubted whether the dread of demons and
the wish to deceive them has not its share in the transference. Certainly women in childbed are supposed to be
peculiarly obnoxious to the machinations of evil spirits,'
which have to be scared away. The demons are cheated
by means of the 'mock-birth'; 'the real patient steals a
march on them by giving birth to the child before they
can discover the deceit that has been practised on them
and hasten back, with ruffled temper, to the real scene of
operations. For example, the Tagals of the Philippines
believe that women at childbirth are the prey of two
malignant spirits called Patianac and Osuang. . . . To
protect women in their hour of need against these dreaded
foes, the people resort sometimes to craft, sometimes to
intimidation, and sometimes to sheer physical force.
Thus they bung up the doors and windows to prevent
the ingress of the devils, till the poor patient is nearly
stifled with heat and stench. They light fires all round
the hut; they stuff mortar-pieces with powder to the
muzzle and let them off again and again in the immediate
neighbourhood of the sufferer; and the husband, stark
naked and armed to the teeth, mounts the roof and
there hews and slashes in the air like a man demented,
while his sympathising friends, similarly equipped with
swords, spears, and shields, and taking their time from
him, attack the demons with such murderous fury, that
it is a chance if the poor devils escape with a whole skin
from the cataract of cuts and thrusts. These are strong

measures. Yet they do not exhaust the resources of the
Tagals in their dealings with the unseen. . . . They will
sometimes carry the sufferer softly into another house,
where the devils, they hope, will not be able to find her.
For the same purpose the nomadic Turks of Central Asia
beat with sticks on the outside of a tent where a woman
lies in childbed, and they shriek, howl, and fire off their
guns continually to drive away the demon who is tor-
menting her. . . . Sometimes they pepper the woman
with gooseberries, in the hope that the devil will stick to
them and so drop off from her. . . .[1] And for a like reason
they bury a sword in the ground, edge upwards, under
the place where the poor suffering head is lying.' Particularly remarkable is the fact that sometimes 'a bard
rushes into the tent and beats the woman lightly with a
stick under the impression that the blows fall not on her,
but on the devil'.

Frazer gives the following résumé: 'I. Under the
general name of couvade two quite distinct customs,
both connected with childbirth, have been commonly
confounded. One of these customs consists of a strict
diet and regimen observed by a father for the benefit of
his new-born child, because the father is believed to be
united to the child by such an intimate bond of physical
sympathy that all his acts affect and may hurt or kill
the tender infant. The other custom consists of a simulation of childbirth by a man, generally perhaps by the
husband, practised for the benefit of the real mother, in
order to relieve her of her pains by transferring them to
the pretended mother. The difference between these
customs in kind is obvious, and in accordance with their
different intentions they are commonly observed at
different times. The simulation of travail-pangs takes
place simultaneously with the real pangs before the child
is born. The strict diet and regimen of the father begin
only after the child is born.' Frazer considers it quite
evident that the two procedures are totally different,

[1] Similar examples are quoted by S. Seligmann, *Der böse Blick*, and E.
Samter, *Geburt, Hochzeit und Tod*.

and proposes that the difference should be indicated in the name. 'One, for example, might be called the prenatal and the other the post-natal couvade, on the ground of the different times at which they are observed; or the one might be called the dietetic couvade and the other the pseudo-maternal couvade, on the ground of the different modes in which they are performed. 2. Both customs are founded on the principle of sympathetic magic, though in different branches of it. The post-natal or dietetic couvade is founded on that branch of sympathetic magic which may be called contagious, because in it the effect is supposed to be produced by contact, real or imaginary. In this case the imaginary contact exists between father and child. The prenatal or pseudo-maternal couvade is founded on that branch of sympathetic magic which may be called homœopathic or imitative, because in it the effect is supposed to be produced by imitation. . . . 3. Neither the one custom nor the other, neither prenatal or dietetic couvade, nor post-natal or pseudo-maternal couvade, appears to have anything to do with an attempt to shift the custom of descent from the maternal to the paternal line, in other words, to initiate the change from the mother-kin to father-kin.'[1]

III. Psycho-analytical Interpretation

We can only accept Frazer's proposal to differentiate, even in name, between the two forms of couvade with

---

[1] I cannot go into the explanation of couvade customs that have been published since the first edition of this book, because their description would take us too far afield. My interpretation has, as far as is known to me, only been appreciated by analysts (Róheim, Jones, Flügel, etc.). I shall, on the other hand, only mention Ferd. v. Reitsenstein's explanation. He considers that the purpose of couvade is fourfold: '1. To stress that importance of the father which followed the recognition of the connection of cohabitation and conception. 2. Where polyandric marriage is recognised by law, to establish paternity. 3. During transition from matrilineal to patrilineal society, to adopt the child into the father's family. 4. To secure the health and growth of the child and to prevent it from being changed, in short, to protect it from any injury from its maternal ancestors.' (Max Marcuse, *Handwörterbuch der Sexualwissenschaft*, Bonn, 1823, S. 56.) Without wishing to discuss these theories with the author one has to admit that who brings much will bring something to many (*wer vieles bringt, manchem etwas bringen wird*).

certain reservations. For we observe that practically nowhere is a pure form of the one or the other kind of couvade to be met, that their boundaries fluctuate and that the distinction is only a provisional one and employed for descriptive purposes. We shall be prepared to give up that distinction as soon as the results of our investigations show that the object of our study is in fact a psychical unity, only expressed under two different forms. We believe that we have considerable reasons for giving preference to the second of Frazer's two divisions. It is quite clear from various reliable reports that the time at which couvade is carried out varies greatly among different peoples, and therefore a classification in regard to time cannot be a very exact one. On the other hand, we suggest that a psychological consideration of couvade customs promises better results if we start with the analysis of their external manifestations.

A. *The Pseudo-Maternal Couvade*

We have been told that this form of couvade consists of a conscious representation of childbirth carried out by the man in order to ease the mother's pains. This representation rests on imitative magic; it is based on the belief that relations between things correspond to those between ideas, or that, through imitation of a process, the process itself is actually brought about. We know that magic signifies the technique of the animistic system of thought.

If we adopt Frazer's explanation we shall have to suppose that half-civilised people have developed sympathy for their suffering women in a high degree. It might be pertinently asked whether many of us Europeans would not be most unwilling to take upon ourselves our wives' labour pains. Nevertheless, we may rely provisionally upon Frazer and assume that such strong feelings of sympathy do actually exist in these people. It is clear that the practice of couvade rests upon a psychical identification. We see to-day cases of marked identifications of this kind in the mental life of hysterics and other psycho-neurotics. Neurotic men sometimes show a tendency to imitate conditions specifically proper to women. I am indebted to Dr. Karl Abraham for the report of a case in which a neurotic man imitated menstruation, *i.e.* he suffered from severe headaches every four weeks, could not bear the light, and was completely incapacitated from work. During these attacks he remained in bed most of the time, getting up on the fourth day. He was imitating his mother's menstrual periods during which the children had not been allowed to disturb her. A male hebephrenic, treated by Dr. Abraham, had passed through a fictitious pregnancy when fifteen years old, which very closely resembled a real one. The imitation and identification were unconscious in these patients, whereas our half-civilised people consciously identify themselves with the woman in childbed in the service of magic tendencies. Although we are prepared to admit that love and tenderness in the man play their part, yet we shall have to assume that other motives underlie the magic measures which have as their conscious purpose the easing of the woman's pains. At present we are unable to see what those motives are, and must be content for the time being with the knowledge that that act of imitative magic which we have recognised as pseudo-maternal couvade rests upon the 'omnipotence of thought', the real meaning of which has been indicated by Freud.[1] Frazer suggests the outwitting the demons as a second possible explanation of couvade, but he believes that only a secondary significance should be ascribed to this. Nor do we know what this idea really means. We ought not to place it in the category of magic, but of sorcery, since the human being outwits the demons, struggles with them and overawes them, as though they were of the same nature as himself.[2] The magic act, as Freud explains, is the earlier and the more significant of the two. Since both acts refer to the same

---

[1] Freud, *Totem und Tabu*, Hugo Heller, Wien, 1913.
[2] Freud, *ibid.* p. 72.

situation and serve the same conscious purpose, namely, to ease and nullify the pains of the lying-in woman, we may assume that the procedures of magic and sorcery represent two successive stages of one practice. Although ethnologists have shown that the procedures of couvade pertain to magic or to sorcery, they have given us no satisfactory information concerning the motive which underlies them. It seems as though we can only raise a corner of the veil which conceals the secret of couvade.

In this unsatisfactory state of affairs the psycho-analytic method of interpretation comes to our aid. It tells us that the unconscious motives of the custom— and it is concerned only with these—can be discovered on account of the indestructibility of unconscious processes and the impossibility of altering them even in their later more disguised stages; and in virtue of this knowledge the way is opened to a psychological understanding of the habits of an earlier period. Psycho-analysis helps, too, by showing how human beings manage to create demons like those which beset the bed of the poor woman in childbed. Psycho-analytic investigations have shown that the belief in demons is the product of the psychic mechanism of projection.[1] In a person whose state of mind is governed by contradictory feelings of hostility and tenderness towards the same object, the situation is deprived of its gravity and tension if he can transplant the unconscious part of his impulses, usually the hostile tendencies, from his inner perception into the external world—can detach them, as it were, from himself and apply them to others. Henceforth it is not he who has hostile feelings towards his father, but wicked demons who are malevolently inclined towards his father, while he, in contrast, feels only love and tenderness towards him. If, therefore, we look upon demons as the projection of a person's own latent hostility, we must conclude that in this heightened fear of demons among many people lie reactive feelings of punishment and remorse, which conceal and over-compensate wicked

[1] As regards the following explanation, see Freud, *ibid.* p. 69.

D

wishes directed against the lying-in woman. We shall then have to assume that in the very measures of protection which the Tagals, let us say, employ against the demons in order to save the woman from pain during her labour, there is also active the hidden unconscious wish to increase her pains. This would seem absurd if we were to confine ourselves to the sphere of the psychology of consciousness, but it is quite intelligible if we take into consideration the great and important part played by unconscious processes. If this is the case, then different couvade customs, like those of the Tagals and the Turks in Central Asia, represent the expression of a compromise between two strong currents of feeling struggling with each other. The one, conscious, is evident in the trouble taken to ease the woman's pains—it is tenderness and love; the other, unconscious, is proved to exist from the analysis of the fear of demons—it is a concealed hostility against the woman. What are the reasons for this strange constellation of feeling? What is the explanation of these hostile undercurrents? We know that every intimate emotional relation between human beings is characterised by ambivalence. The relations between man and wife regularly contain both tender and hostile emotions, the latter being betrayed by various signs to the experienced observer. The analysis of neurotics has enabled us to recognise this attitude in an extreme form, but there are also indications that it is usually to be found in normal people as well. The death of the wife affords an opportunity for studying the husband's emotional reaction to his latent hostility. The same situation can be observed at the time when the wife incurs the risk of death in her hours of labour. The conflict between the contrary currents, which remains hidden from the man's consciousness, is acute in such hours.[1] His unconscious hostility tempts him to obtain pleasure out of the sight of the woman's pains, and this temptation is severely repulsed by the conscious part of his mental life. As a result the repressed hostility is pro-

---

[1] Concerning a further co-operating cause, see later.

jected on to the demons. They alone are the ones to experience satisfaction in the suffering of the lying-in woman; and the tenderness of the man, increased by reaction, now struggles against them as the representatives of his own unconscious hostility. The severity and difficulty of this struggle cannot fail to be recognised when we discover who are the real opponents. Those acquainted with psycho-analysis who have observed a neurotic man when his wife has lain in the throes of childbirth, are easily able to see in his abnormal agitation and anxiety how well the situation is suited to awaken his slumbering hostility; and they will no longer doubt that this extreme sympathy is of the nature of a reaction, built up upon repressed sadistic pleasure. If the assumption is correct that the outwitting and overcoming of demons oppressing the woman in labour represents a reaction to evil impulses projected into the external world, then we should expect to find traces of this causal connection. Among the Tagals confined women become seriously alarmed when their husbands lay fire round the huts and discharge firearms in their immediate vicinity. The unconscious hostile motivation of the protective measures against the demons comes out more clearly in that custom of the Turks where a sword is laid under the woman's bed. It seems like a re-emergence of the repressed in the repressive forces themselves when the same people beat the poor woman with a stick, ostensibly to ward off the demons, but really to gratify their own hostile impulses. The proverb 'The sack is beaten but the ass is meant', if one may apply it so ungallantly, is here much to the point.

Assuming, then, that the magic customs of couvade belong to a stage preceding sorcery and based on the same psychic motives, we can now proceed to their investigation. Nevertheless, we ought not to overlook the differences of period and cultural development involved. The acts of sorcery, of which we have just attempted an analysis, are found mostly among half-civilised peoples, whereas the magic practices, of which we are about to speak, belong to less cultured if not to actually savage tribes. (The customs reported by Frazer from Europe are residual vestiges of magic distorted and degraded into acts of superstition.) We will assume with Freud that in these primitive tribes there is a still higher degree of ambivalence than in the more advanced people in whom we have recognised an ambivalent attitude as the chief motive underlying acts of sorcery. There exists among the Dyaks of Sarawak and the Pomlā of Gujarat a still stronger latent hostility towards their women. The couvade of these and other people rests upon imitative or homœopathic magic. The magic act, like that of sorcery, is to ease and nullify the woman's labour pains. While, however, sorcery attains this object by outwitting the demons, the ostensible purpose of the magic cere- monial is to transfer the labour pains from the woman to the man. We know already what the principle of the magic is—'the omnipotence of thought'. The savages believe that by imitation of a process they can bring about its real appearance. Their wish is not only father to the thought, but also to the reality. Let us recall a few cases of this form of couvade. The man sometimes puts on the woman's clothes, betakes himself to bed, and writhes in pain. There is no doubt that sympathy with the woman is the motive which leads to such a marked identification; but we consider that pity and sympathy appearing in such intensity is a very complicated phenomenon, founded upon the repression of the sadistic instinctual components and the sublimation of the masochistic ones. It seems probable that we shall get nearer the explanation if we assume that the pains were at one time not simulated but real. The pains were imagined by the men (moreover, in a pleasurable way), and were at the same time actually felt by them. We must admit that the existence of such genuine and un- divided sympathy is very unlikely in primitive human beings, since it is lacking in us—in so far as we consider ourselves mentally healthy. We must remember, how- ever, that we meet with the same identifications in the symptomatology of the neuroses. I quote the following case as an example. A woman, suffering from an obsessional neurosis, felt hurt by a friend's tactless remark. She overcame her strong feeling of annoyance and entirely hid all expression of it from her friend. Next day she felt quite exhausted and miserable, and described her condition as follows: 'I am as bruised as though someone had severely thrashed me'. The patient, in virtue of her unusual intellectual talents, could see that repressed wishes for revenge on her friend had led to this reaction. She had suppressed an intense wish to give the tactless person a good beating, and her own sensations were the expression of a self-punishment for the unfulfilled intention. It is now clear why the men who carry out couvade allow themselves to be treated as though they were ill and miserable: it is as though they had actually suffered the pains which they had wished for their wives, making no distinction between wish and reality. The 'neurotic standard' (Freud) which stands so near to the primitive one predominated. We know that in the old codes of law the precept of punishment was an eye for an eye, a tooth for a tooth, and that the *lex talionis* obtained everywhere, and it will therefore not surprise us to find that exactly the same pains were felt by the men which they had wished for the women in labour. Although we have assumed that couvade originated in the ambivalence of emotional feelings, we must not forget that the origin of the custom lies very far back, and that to a great extent the custom now exists as a ceremonial without intelligible meaning or with a new meaning ascribed to it.

Having assumed that malevolent wishes of a sadistic nature are awakened in the husband, it follows that the suppression of these wishes will bring about a relatively increased intensity of the masochistic instinctual components. In the play of forces between sadistic and masochistic tendencies, and in the struggle between hostile and tender impulses, the latter, which alone could become conscious, have obtained the victory.

Having explained the pseudo-maternal couvade in this way, we find ourselves for the most part in agreement with Frazer, who lays stress on the time of occurrence of this form of couvade as being just before or at the confinement. Nevertheless, we have gained an advantage over him in having explained certain phenomena which he has failed to account for. If his hypothesis had been right we should still be in the dark as to why the man remains in bed and behaves like an invalid, while his wife goes calmly on with her daily work. Logically his magic action should stop when her confinement is over. Here, again, psycho-analytic investigation helps us by pointing to the mechanism of displacement. The prohibition of the realisation of hostile wishes towards his wife, which the primitive man has imposed upon himself, exceeds the period of her confinement because his unconscious wishes continue to press towards active expression through the motor system. The temptation to realise these wishes is not overcome; it is merely displaced, and the protective measures against it have also to move with it. This keeping the man in bed has also the object of protecting his wife from his sexual and hostile wishes. Although up to now we have especially emphasised the preponderating share of aggressive tendencies in the building up of couvade, it must not be forgotten that by means of them an inhibition of sexual wishes may also arise. The participation of sexual wishes is certainly accessory to the high psychic tension of this period. We must also, of course, take into consideration the primitive stage of the people in question: a man has no sexual intercourse with his wife when she is far advanced in pregnancy, and her increased helplessness through her condition is a constant temptation to him.[1] On the other hand, superstitious fear prohibits him from

[1] Attention must be drawn to the fact that the woman in this condition is especially prone to awaken the unconscious comparison with the first love object of the man—his mother—and that perhaps the prohibition observed among many peoples against sexual intercourse with the woman during the latter period of her pregnancy corresponds to an unconscious re-establishment of the incest barrier.

having sexual intercourse. His inhibited libido joins itself to those inborn sadistic instinctual components which the woman's condition brings to the fore and is turned into latent hate against her. Wicked desires now awaken towards the pregnant woman for whose body the man longs and which is forbidden to him.

It must be admitted that if we ask the people who practise couvade the reason for this custom we shall receive quite unexpected answers, the meaning of which at first sight seems to be forced and artificial. The Miâo-Tsze, for example, say that it is quite right that the wife who has suffered long should now rest. Among the Koranas, Thurston was told as a reason for couvade, 'that the life of the man is of more value than that of the woman and, therefore, more care should be taken of him'. Other explanations are of the same nature. We should regard such feeble attempts at explanation as rationalisations if we met them in the analysis of a neurotic. We have to admit that it is of little use to question the people themselves regarding the purpose of couvade, since it is probable that the ancient custom, which manifestly had a meaning, has now become a ceremony which is carried out traditionally, but without a clear idea of its purpose. If we keep, however, to our results, we can confidently affirm that the originators of the custom, *i.e.* the ancestors of those people who practise couvade at the present time, could have given us no satisfactory information as to its purpose, because the very strong impulses that were necessary for its institution were unconscious. It is for this reason that we assume that a distortion of the actual motives has taken place in the explanations. As the people could not conceive the actual situation they have constructed another, which by rearrangement of the material has given rise to a new, fictitious aim, namely, that the man is lying-in. Freud has demonstrated the great significance of the same process in the system-formation of the neuroses and of delusions, and has given as an explanation that the intellectual inconsistency and unintelligibility that

characterise a series of symptoms originating in unconscious processes have been done away with, and those
symptoms endowed with new meaning by the process
of 'secondary elaboration'. The best way of characteris-
ing this 'system-formation' is, according to Freud,[1] that
'each product shows that at least two motivations, one
arising out of the premises of the system—that is, ultimately a delusory one, and the other, a hidden one which
we must recognise as the actually effective, real one'. In
our case couvade is to be looked upon as a male childbed only as a result of 'secondary elaboration'. The
secondary motivation regards the man's remaining in
bed after the confinement as a consequence of the
fictitious male childbed. But the unconscious motive
shows that it is a protective measure against the pressing forward of hostile and sexual wishes. The social purpose of couvade is therefore twofold: primarily, to protect the woman against the latent hostility and sexual
aggression of the man; secondarily, and fictitiously, to
ease the woman's labour pains.

We have still to consider two phenomena which help
to confirm this hypothesis. The first is the general taboo
of a pregnant woman among the most primitive peoples.
This also affords evidence of protective measures against
the desires of the man. For instance, Frazer mentions
that 'among the Saragacos Indians of eastern Ecuador,
as soon as a woman feels the travail-pangs beginning,
she retires into the forest to a distance of three or four
leagues from her home, where she takes up her abode in
a hut of leaves which has been already prepared for her.
"This banishment", we are told, "is the fruit of the
superstition of these Indians, who are persuaded that
the spirit of evil would attach himself to their house if
the women were brought to bed in it." '[2]

The second piece of evidence is those cases of superstition which Frazer quotes from European peoples. If
they put on some of their husband's clothes, the women,

[1] *Ibid.* p. 88.
[2] Frazer, *The Golden Bough: Taboo and the Perils of the Soul*, Third Edition,
London, p. 152.

on the one hand, ease their labour pains, and on the other, transfer those pains to the man who knows nothing of the birth and writhes in mysterious travail. In this superstition, which undoubtedly owes its origin to imitative magic, it is quite clear that the ambivalent attitude of feelings which we have supposed in the man is also met with in the woman; it has here found its expression in the 'transference of pain'. For when the woman lessens her pains by putting on some of the man's clothes, what else could be the purport of her primitive therapy, but that she finds her pains less severe if she constantly keeps before her the fact that she suffers them for the sake of the beloved man who is indirectly their cause? In the memory of his love lies the mitigation of her pain, but nevertheless the hostile attitude towards him asserts itself; the pains are transferred to the man; the impatience of the parturient woman accuses him of her sufferings. A primitive human being, when suffering pain, always believes that another is the cause of it, and so the lying-in woman projects her hostile feelings on to the man.

It is obvious that this explanation involves no claim to have considered and investigated all the factors which lead to the origin and development of the pseudo-maternal couvade. There are certainly other mental impulses which participate in its psychogenesis, and religious and social conditions have certainly had a very great influence on its development. One of the difficulties in the investigation of this form of couvade arises from the fact that measures relating to the carrying out of the post-natal couvade have become intermixed with it and have helped to modify its later forms, so that now both kinds often merge into each other. As this point seems to me to be important I will quote some interesting examples of such mixed forms taken from a recent work by Isidor Scheftelowitz.[1] 'Among the Moorish Jews

---

[1] 'Das stellvertretende Huhnopfer', *Religionsgeschichtliche Versuche und Vorarbeiten*, Bd. xiv. Heft iii, Giessen, 1914. See also Seligmann, *Der böse Blick*, ii., S. 39.

during the first eight days after the birth of a boy the
father carefully closes the doors every evening and reads
aloud from the Bible for several hours in the presence of
the nearest relatives who have gathered in the room of
the woman in childbed; then he draws a circle with the
point of a sword round the bed in which is the mother
and child. . . . A similar custom existed formerly among
the Jews. A sword was laid at the head of the woman in
childbed and was flourished round about the bed, on
the walls, and on the ground each night for thirty days.'[1]
At one time in Karlsruhe a knife was flourished about in
a circle around the head of a woman in childbed and the
child, after the child had been laid in her bed in the
evening, and these words were spoken: 'I encircle you,
woman in childbed and your child. As many angels
shall watch over you as there are stars over this roof.'
This custom is called 'encircling'.[2] Among the Slavonian
Jews it is the custom to make circles on the walls of the
bedroom with a coal or saltpetre in order to protect a
woman in childbed against wicked spirits. The words
'Adam and Eve without the demon Lilith' are written in
the circle.[3] These are again so many various protective
measures against demons, similar to those we have mentioned above. The wielding of the knife or sword also
reminds us of the procedures among the Turks in
Central Asia. These forms of sorcery are to protect the
child as well as the mother from demons. Are we to
suppose that hostile impulses towards the new-born
child are active in the young father? We must turn now
to the far more significant and widely spread dietetic
couvade.

B. *The Dietetic Couvade*

We know already of what this form of couvade consists; of abstaining from definite foods, and of a number
of other rules of behaviour. The precautions and con-

---

[1] E. Samter, *Geburt, Hochzeit und Tod*, 1911, S. 48.
[2] Reported by Frau Abr. Dünner, Köln, *née* Wormser of Karlsruhe.
[3] Abraham Löwysohn, *Sefer Mequore Minhagim*, Berlin, 1846, S. 91.

siderations which the unfortunate father of a new-born child has to observe seem almost incredible to us. If we came across them in the analysis of a neurotic we should regard such extraordinary consideration as a mental reaction to repressed hostile impulses towards the child. The foundation of all these customs is regularly stated to be care about the child. We are used to regarding the painful conscientiousness, the excessive tenderness, and exaggerated apprehension that dominate the obsessional neurotic as a reaction against the temptation lurking in his unconscious to realise his own evil wishes. We do not hesitate to affirm that all these rules of conduct are of a protective nature and are intended to set up an effective barrier against the impulse to do harm to or kill the child. Nevertheless, we do not yet understand how it can harm the unborn child if the father chops wood or eats the flesh of turtles. Neither are we satisfied with Frazer's explanation that it is a question of sympathetic magic.

It seems as though the analogy to the symptoms of the obsessional neurotic might afford us some explanation of these apparently absurd father-rites. One of Freud's patients who suffered from an obsessional neurosis was constantly troubled with this idea:[1] 'If I marry Fräulein X. something will happen to my father (in the next world)'. The similarity of the thought to that of the people we are considering is quite evident. For example, 'If I make a violent movement this will harm my child (yet unborn)'. But does this formal similarity correspond in content and spirit? We know that in obsessional neurotics we can re-establish the actual train of ideas by a reconstruction of the missing links. Freud's obsessional patient had made a false connection (substitution) of ideas which made the actual meaning of his obsessive thoughts unrecognisable to himself and others. These thoughts arose from a memory of childhood scenes in which vindictive wishes were awakened in him against his father. What then is the

[1] 'Bemerkungen über einen Fall vom Zwangsneurose', *Sammlung kleiner Schriften zur Neurosenlehre*, 3. Folge, Leipzig und Wien, 1913, S. 123.

meaning of forbidding an Indian father, for example, to
perform hard work, to tread on the place where an
animal has been killed, or to kill or eat certain animals
before the birth of his child? Here substitutions have
also taken place in the association of ideas of peoples. It
is not difficult to restore the lost meanings to some of
these procedures by means of the psycho-analytic method
of interpretation; while others will be less easy to
explain in proportion to the degree of distortion, omission and displacement that the original true association
has undergone. Nevertheless, in all of them we recognise
prohibitions of substitutive actions which originate in
the conflict between the urge to gratify the impulse and
the contrary current produced by social considerations.
'The pleasure in the impulse is constantly displaced in
order to avoid the state of exclusion in which it finds
itself, and it seeks surrogates for the prohibited things,
in the form of substitutive objects, and substitutive
actions. Every new advance of the repressed libido
brings with it an aggravation of prohibition.'[1] The
majority of the ceremonials which the father has to
observe in couvade come into being by way of displacement. The feared consequence of doing the forbidden
things—the child would become sick and die—was once
the desired consequence of the breaking out of hostile
impulses. When the Dyaks forbid the prospective father
to do anything of a noxious character the primary basis
of the prohibition is evident. The measure is allied to the
taboo regulations among uncivilised peoples which pro-
hibit the keeping of sharp weapons and cutting instruments in the house.[2] It is fully justified in its provision
that the father should touch no weapons, perform no
severe work, kill and eat no animal, since these actions
are substitutive actions for the forbidden realisation of
his death wish towards the child.

Let us attempt to represent the mental attitude of the
primitive human being who has just become a father.
One cannot conceive him having much fatherly tender-

<hr>

[1] Freud, *Totem und Tabu*, S. 28.   [2] Freud, *ibid*. S. 91.

ness. A strange being has come into his home and he feels
no pleasure in supporting the little creature. On the
contrary, he feels impelled to kill and devour the child.
The deeper motive of this wish will become clearer later.
For the present we need only refer to the fact that to-day
the killing and eating of children is not unknown among
certain peoples. These original wishes are not destroyed
with the development of fatherly feelings, about which
we have yet to speak, but are pushed back and finally
repressed: they become unconscious, though none the
less effective. The prohibition is constantly endangered
by the urging of unconscious impulses and is forced to
alter and extend its limits, because it is unwilling to
grant instinctual gratification even through substitutive
actions. Psycho-analysis can demonstrate the mental
paths which lead from the wish to the building up of
protective measures of this kind.

In order to confirm our statement that the protective
measures have been instituted against these aggressive
tendencies of the man, we must allude to the taboos
regarding new-born children (and the mother) which are
found among the most primitive peoples.[1] Among some
Bantu tribes a man 'dare not take his child in his arms
for the three first months after the birth'. 'In the island
of Tumleo, off German New Guinea, after the birth of her
child, a woman is shut up with her infant for five or eight
days, during which no man, not even her husband, may
see her.' 'When a Herero woman has given birth to a
child, her female companions hastily construct a special
hut for her to which she is transferred. Both the hut and
the woman are sacred and "for this reason, the men are
not allowed to see the lying-in woman until the navel
string has separated from the child, otherwise they
would become weaklings, and when later they *yumbana*,
that is, go to war with spear and bow, they would be
shot".'

Some of the usages of dietetic couvade claim our

---

[1] Frazer, *ibid.* p. 151. See also Heinrich Ploss, *Das Kind in Brauch and Sitte
der Völker*, 3. Auflage, Bd. i. S. 30.

special attention. What is the meaning of the cruel blood-ordeals which we have found among Caribs and other peoples? Du Tertre tells us that among the Caribs deep wounds are made in the fathers by their friends at the end of the fasting period, and the tortures to which the victims are subjected by their wounds being washed in spices are willingly endured with astonishing patience and fortitude for the sake of the child. Hartland[1] refers to a similar, if less severe, custom among the primitive inhabitants of the Celebes. 'If the first-born be a son, the mother bathes the child in the nearest water-course, while the father, fully armed and dressed in his finest garb, awaits her return. In his turn he then goes to bathe, and when he steps out of the water, his neighbours are waiting for him to beat him with reeds all the way back to his dwelling. On arriving there, he seizes his bow and shoots three reed arrows over the hut, saying: "I wish much happiness to my son, may he grow up to be a valiant man".' This ceremony consists, therefore, in a chastisement of the father and an incantation. We know that magic formulas correspond to the protective formulas of neurotics who use them to ward off their own evil impulses. Every Minahassee man who wishes his son much luck, and that he may grow up into power-ful manhood, has to struggle against an impulse within him to murder that son. The detail that he shoots arrows over the hut gives us a suggestive clue as to whom the arrow should really strike. The shooting is a compromise action in which hostile and tender impulses are found together in a common expression. It is, moreover, not difficult to arrive at the psychogenesis of that terrible chastisement. It is suffered for the sake of the child. Hartland says that 'in his person his son undergoes the first tests of his endurance, valour, and skill'. But the basis of that identification is only this, that in the blood-ordeal which has taken place on behalf of the child, there is at the same time a punishment which is be-stowed upon the father by the members of the tribe.

[1] Hartland, *ibid.* p. 407.

They punish him as though he had really committed the crime which he unconsciously desires to do, as though he had overstepped the taboo prohibition. This punishment also rests on the 'omnipotence of thought'. It is as though the overstepping of the taboo had not spontaneously revenged itself on the offender, and the tribe which is threatened through the wished outrage now carries out the punishment.[1] Freud has shown us that the strict expiation for overstepping the taboo is based on the fear of the infectious quality attributed to the taboo, that is to say, fear of temptation.[2]

Certain characteristics make it seem probable that the cruel ceremony of scarifying and beating signifies a religious expiation for unconscious impulses. Among many peoples the father has to undergo expiation and atonement ceremonies after the birth of his son. On the other hand, if the child dies prematurely, he is accused of causing its death and punished by the women.[3] 'Signor Modigliani, sojourning with a native of Nias whose wife was in "an interesting condition", was the innocent cause of an amusing domestic squabble. For his host, in leaving his room one day, stepped across the traveller's outspread legs. This was a serious matter, because it was apt to cause misfortune to the unborn child. The wife did not fail to remind her imprudent husband of his folly and carried her anger to such a height that he was glad to flee from the blows administered by means of the firewood intended for the domestic hearth.'[4] In this very unceremonious scene we see a private analogy to that ceremony in the Celebes, at least as regards its unconscious motivation. Finally, we can support our interpretation further by a description borrowed from La Borde. In the Caribbean ceremony of drawing blood, the father's precious blood is rubbed into the

---

[1] At the same time the neighbours gratify their hostile desires against their own father, who is unconsciously represented by the one who has just become a father.
[2] Freud, *ibid*. S. 66.
[3] See Dobritzhoffer's earlier quoted statements.
[4] Hartland, *ibid*. p. 402.

child's face in the belief that this will serve to make the child generous. We cannot doubt that in this act there survives the memory that the blood originally belonged to the child, and that the child itself was once the victim of that cruel pleasurable impulse which now finds in the father a suitable object as the instrument for the strengthening of the baby. If further proof be needed we may refer to the fact that among all peoples blood serves as an extremely effective apotropaic measure. The meaning of the blood-ordeal is especially clear in the following ceremony.[1] Among some of the wandering gipsies of northern Hungary, the child, immediately after its birth, is wrapped in rags on which there are some drops of the father's blood. It is believed that the child up to baptism is thereby protected against the snares of witches and demons of illness. For the same reason a father of a new-born child among a Transylvanian tribe of gipsies allows some of his blood to run into a fire which is flaring before the tent, saying: 'If you want blood I here give it to you, but the blood of my child belongs to the great Master in Heaven, to Christ, who will chain you with Jewish chains'. It is sufficient to refer to the analysis given above of the fear of demons in order to recognise what mental impulses give rise to this ceremonial.[2]

It will not be surprising, if we remember the retaliative nature of the taboo, that the father should suffer the same torture which he wished to inflict on his child. In the analysis of neurotics it is clear that their self-injuries and suicidal impulses are self-punishments for the emergence of wicked wishes. The symptomatology of neurotics who are not treated analytically also shows the same tendencies.

Having noted how fear of the infectious power of the taboo is operative in the punishment of the father, we can also attribute to the same cause the prohibition against leaving the house, although it seems that there

---

[1] H. v. Wlislocki, *Aus dem inneren Leben der Zigeuner*, 1892, S. 95. Quoted by Scheftelowitz, *Das stellvertretende Huhnopfer*, S. 48.

[2] It may be briefly pointed out here that in all these rites a blood brotherhood is founded at the same time between father and child.

must also be other motives for this prohibition. In itself
it appears to be an extension of the restrictions to which
the father has to submit among the people practising
couvade customs. Kings among primitive peoples, as
Frazer has shown, also have to submit to the prohibition
against leaving their house by day. As regards the father
it might be due to the fact that the temptation to do
forbidden things, namely, to kill animals, fell trees, etc.,
is more likely to be yielded to outside the house than in
it. Nevertheless its motive is made clear through the
anxiety lest something may befall the child during his
absence, which, if he wished for it, could be fulfilled in
virtue of the omnipotence of thought. What is therefore
represented as excessive tenderness is really a reaction
to malevolent impulses against the child: the increased
tenderness is to be attributed to the intense repression
of these impulses. Again the psychology of the neuroses
can bring parallels for this behaviour. A hysterical
patient treated by Freud, expressed her over-tender care
for her mother by having to hasten home at all times in
a state of anxiety to convince herself that nothing had
happened to her. The analysis showed that this excessive
care was only apparently unfounded, since there existed
in her the fear that malevolent wishes which she had
once cherished against her mother might be fulfilled
during her absence. The mechanism of displacement
common to taboo and the neuroses enables us to understand how among certain people the whole family is
affected by such a prohibition, for example, among the
Abipones. Hartland[1] reports of the Galician Jews that
they 'permit no member of a household where there is a
young child to stay out after sunset, else the little one
will be deprived of its rest'. When, in our civilised
countries, young married people, full of the zest for life,
declare that they are constantly prevented from going
out by having to look after their child, although considered objectively, sufficient protection for it may be
found, for instance, by a trustworthy person remaining

[1] *Ibid.* p. 411.

E

at home, we may see in their attitude traces of this primitive prohibition against going out, in which it appears excessive tenderness associated with unconscious hostility play a leading role.

It seems to me that this is the place to pursue the analogy, to which we have frequently alluded, with the mental life of the neurotic person. A man of my acquaintance, about fifty years of age, interested me on account of his constant and extremely intense anxiety regarding his children, and his peculiar treatment of them, which is best described by the expression 'torturing tenderness'. As grounds for his anxiety he stated that his children had no talent, would achieve nothing in life, and would suffer harm through their stupidity. There were no indications that these prophecies would be fulfilled. His supervision of his three sons was so detailed that he carped at all their movements, feared harm would come to them in their most trifling and unimportant actions, and was constantly warning and admonishing them.[1] All these things he did with a strange mixture of hostility and most touching tenderness. He suffered quite as much from this eccentricity as his children did; for not only did his unreasonable anxiety disturb him in his business, it also determined the whole course of his life and destroyed all his happiness. When his second son —certainly under the pressure of this paternal influence— developed an obsessional neurosis the father's anxiety and hatred for him increased to such a serious degree that only a removal from home obtained a respite, though a short one, for the father. He often spoke to me of his son's condition in a manner which at the best could only be characterised as pity infused with hatred. He once said that he suffered so much from sympathy with the young man that he (the father) would receive with

---

[1] His conduct reminds me of the undoubtedly conscious tactics of Petruchio in Shakespeare's *The Taming of the Shrew*. The defiant little Kate complains of it as follows (iv. 3):
    'And that which spites me more than all these wants,
    He does it under name of perfect love:
    As who would say—if I should sleep or eat,
    'Twere deadly sickness, or else present death.'

equanimity the news that the patient—who, during this period of psycho-analytic treatment, felt well in himself —had committed suicide by shooting himself with a revolver. In this remark and in many conversations with the patient the latent hostility of the father was quite evident, but his conduct towards his son was essentially characterised by the excessive tenderness described. No sacrifice seemed too dear, no trouble too great, no self-denial too hard for him to take upon himself for the welfare of his sons. Here, as well as in numerous similar examples of neurotic fathers, the symptom of exaggerated tenderness and conscientiousness may be regarded as a reaction to opposite impulses of an earlier period. There was a time when the little child could not claim the father's love in the same degree as to-day, and in which the child was sometimes felt to be an inhibiting factor in the relations between the man and the woman.[1] Similarly Freud was able to show, in the analysis of a symptomatic act in a young man who tenderly loved his child, how these unconscious impulses of a previous period remain effective, and may be recognised as repressed death wishes.[2]

If we now call to mind Hartland's and Frazer's explanations we must admit that the hypothesis of sympathetic magic is fully justified as a motivation of couvade customs; but, on the other hand, the investigation of the unconscious processes renders possible a fuller and more satisfactory explanation. Kinship is the only band which unites human beings of the primitive period to one another. What happens to the father must affect the child. 'Omnipotence of thought' as a principle of explanation enables us to recognise the father-rites as compromises, the result of the psychic play of forces between conscious tenderness and unconscious hostility. The atonement and expiation ceremonial of couvade shows that here the guilty conscience, built up on wicked

---

[1] Compare Ibsen's *Little Eyolf*. Similar psychic situations are analysed in my book *Arthur Schnitzler als Psychologe* (J. C. Bruns, Minden, 1914).
[2] *Psychopathologie des Alltagslebens*, S. Karger, Berlin, 2. Auflage, S. 89.

wishes, plays the part of a central psychic force in the origin of a social institution.

A comparison of the consequence feared from an over-stepping of the taboo among primitive people and among obsessional neurotics brings out the following difference: among savages every breaking of a taboo results in expectations of misfortune which will harm the evil-doer himself, whereas the obsessional neurotic mostly fears the disastrous effects of his infringement as they concern others—that these latter would then become ill and die. Freud has noted this difference: 'The neurotic behaves altruistically, the savage egoistically'. We find that the behaviour of the people who keep the dietetic couvade is similar to that of neurotics. An explanation of this may be found in the fact previously mentioned that the custom is not met with among primitive and savage peoples, but seems limited to tribes who take a mid-position between the highest and lowest forms of civilisation. If we bring this fact into relationship with the displacement of expectations of misfortune from oneself on to others, the following reconstruction of the course of events may be put forward as having a good deal of probability. In a period of remoter civilisation, taboo regulations making for the protection of the new-born child persisted among these peoples. Every breach of the taboo was prevented by expectations of mis-fortune which the father anticipated for himself. As an effect of age-long repression it happened that the more the mental origin of the father-rites was lost to con-sciousness, the more the fears associated with the breach of the prohibitions were directed on to the beloved child. A return of the repressed wishes also shows itself in dis-torted form, because the consequence of a breach of the prohibition is feared on behalf of that very object—the child—whose existence originally gave rise to the pro-hibition. This may be supported by two arguments. We have already quoted taboo laws among really primitive peoples which separated the father from his child for a certain period. If the father broke one of the taboo laws misfortune would befall him, *e.g.* he would be killed in battle, or the like. Here we can see the preliminary stage of the father-rites designated as couvade. Furthermore, reference to the psycho-neurotic shows that the fears of misfortune harboured by obsessional neurotics at first concerned their own persons, and are only transferred to other beloved persons during the course of their disease.[1]

We feel tempted in this place to trace the story of couvade customs still further back. If we do so we arrive at a stage in which a pregnant woman and new-born child were exposed defenceless to the sexual and hostile impulses of the savage man. But we should also be interested to know whether traces are still to be found of these peculiar couvade usages in our present-day customs. This will probably not be very difficult since we may assume that the ambivalent emotional disposition of the primitive mind has yielded gradually to a regulated and balanced state, and to a better adaptation to the real claims of life. We may therefore suppose that all the arrangements that make for the well-being both of the wife, who has just become a mother, and the newly born infant, have had their origin where reality and the repression of malevolent wishes have been victorious. It sounds paradoxical, admittedly, but it is not the less correct, that institutions of an eminently social character, namely, protection of the mother and care of the infant, have developed from couvade and similar customs.

C. *The Psychogenesis of the Fear of Retaliation*

This paper might have been concluded with the preceding attempts at explanation if the universal and most prominent mark of the dietetic couvade were not worthy of a special investigation. We have recognised in the prohibition against the killing and eating of certain animals an actual aggravation of totemistic restrictions. The question arises as to the motives whence this prohibition received its severity and practical significance.

[1] Freud, *Totem und Tabu*, S. 66.

If we are to believe superstitious peoples we have to suppose that the killing of an animal would harm the child. The animals would then, according to our interpretation, be substitute-objects for the child, and the pleasure in killing them transferred to them only secondarily. Still some weighty considerations compel us to avoid this relatively simple idea. The prohibition in most instances refers to large animals; at least it is certain that these fall primarily under the ban. It is hard to see why the emu, bear, kangaroo and other large animals should be spared for the sake of the child. It would be more to the point if the little being, often still unborn, were represented and spared in the form of a small animal. Another observation gives food for thought. Among the Urabunna tribes in Australia the husband, in the early stages of his wife's pregnancy, 'does not kill any large game necessitating the use of spear or boomerang. . . . It is supposed that the spirit of the unborn child follows him about and gives warning of his approach to large game. Should the man attempt to throw his spear or boomerang at any animal, then the spirit child will cause the weapon to take a crooked course, and the man will know that he has lost his skill in the chase and that the child is angry with him.'[1] In this more primitive tribe, as well as in the Unmatjera tribe in Australia, the father fears on his own behalf the result of a breach of the hunting prohibition, and a new factor is added, the spirit of the child accompanies him. Frazer reports the following beliefs among tribes where couvade is still in vogue.[2] 'The Indians of Cayenne refuse to eat certain large fish, because they say that the soul of some one of their relations might be in the fish and that hence in eating the fish they might swallow the soul.' 'The Indians of California formerly refused to eat the flesh of large game, because they held that the bodies of all large animals contained the souls of past generations of men

---

[1] Spencer and Gillen, *Native Tribes of Central Australia*, London, 1899, p. 471.
[2] Frazer, *The Golden Bough: Spirits of the Corn and of the Wild*, vol. ii. p. 285.

and women.' 'Californian Indians have been known to plead for the life of an old grizzly she-bear, because they thought it housed the soul of a dead grandam, whose withered features had borne some likeness to the wrinkled face of the bear.' Freud, on the basis of much data, and by convincing deduction, has shown that the totem animals originally formed a substitute for the father. It therefore seems to be extremely probable that the primitive folk perceive their ancestors and not the child in those prohibited animals. What, then, is the meaning of the fact that the prohibition to kill and eat the father was made stricter on the birth of the child? It seems to me that the sacrificial customs after childbirth may give some explanation of it. Immediately after the birth of a child a Dyak of Borneo sacrifices a fowl to the children's demon, Indu Rarawi. In Assam the father sacrifices two fowls to the spirits of his ancestors on the birth of a child ; also among the Miâo-Tsze in Canton and among the Limbu (Bengal) the priest sacrifices a fowl to the ancestors.[1] The Pampas Indians in Argentina, and also the Patagonians, sacrifice a horse which is eaten in company with the relatives. There seems to be a palpable contradiction here. On the one hand, certain animals are to be preserved on account of the child; on the other hand, just the same animals are sacrificed on the child's account. Frazer once more enlightens us.[2] He shows by many examples that the custom of killing the first-born was widely spread in many parts of the world. 'In some tribes of New South Wales the first-born child of every woman was eaten by the tribe as part of a religious ceremony.' 'The natives of Rook, an island off the east coast of New Guinea, used to kill all their first-born children.' 'In India, down to the beginning of the nineteenth century, the custom of sacrificing a first-born child to the Ganges was common.' 'In Uganda if the first-born child of a chief or any important person is a son, the midwife strangles it and reports that the

---

[1] J. Scheftelowitz, *Das stellvertretende Huhnopfer*, S. 8.
[2] Frazer, *The Golden Bough: The Dying God*, p. 179.

infant was still-born.' 'The Kutonaqa Indians of British
Columbia worship the sun and sacrifice their first-born
children to him. When a woman is with child she prays
to the sun, saying, "I am with child. When it is born I
shall offer it to you. Have pity upon us."' When the
king of Moab was besieged and hard pressed by the
Israelites, he took his son, who was to reign in his stead,
and sacrificed him on the rampart as a burnt offering.
Phoenician history, says an old author, is full of such
child-sacrifices. The prophet Micah said:[1] 'Shall I give
my first-born for my transgression, the fruit of my body
for the sin of my soul?' Jahve Himself demands that all
first-born human beings as well as animals should be
sacrificed to him.[2] 'The first-born of thy sons shalt thou
give unto me.'[3] Later a distinction is made between
sheep, oxen, rams, and human beings, asses, etc. The
first-born of the former had always to be sacrificed, the
latter were redeemable. A similar alteration and modification is met with among Sabine tribes. '"But since", says
Festus, "it seemed cruel to slay innocent boys and girls,
they were kept till they had grown up, then veiled and
driven beyond the boundaries."' 'In later times the Italian
peoples appear to have resorted to measures of this sort
only in special emergencies; there was a tradition that
in former times the consecration of the first-born to the
gods had been an annual custom.'[4]

We see, then, that the killing of animals really formed
a substitute for child murder. Nevertheless a deeper
insight into this complicated question can only be
obtained by investigating the motive that underlies this
horrible religious practice of infanticide. It could not
have had any such rationalistic basis as regard for
threatened famine in the future, since savages give no
thought to the following day. If such had been their idea,
'they would be more likely to kill the later children than
the first-born.'[5] Frazer believes that the evidence he has
collected indicates that the custom has different motives

---

[1] Micah, v: 6-8.   [2] Exodus, xiii. 1, 2.   [3] Exodus, xxiii. 29.
[4] Frazer, ibid. p. 186.   [5] Frazer, ibid. p. 188.

among different peoples. 'With the Semites, the Italians, and their near kinsmen, the Irish, the sacrifice, or at least the consecration of the first-born, seems to have been viewed as a tribute paid to the gods, who were thus content to receive a part though they might justly have claimed the whole. In some cases the death of the child appears to be definitely regarded as a substitute for the death of the father, who obtains a new lease of life by the sacrifice of his offspring.' Neither explanation, however, claims to have revealed the fundamental psychic motives which lie behind the religious sacrifice of children. A deeper penetration is required.

We know that among primitive people their god, who desires the sacrifice of the child, is regarded as their father. Psycho-analysis has proved that the idea of God in the life of the individual and of the people has its origin in the veneration and exaltation of the father. The command to sacrifice the first-born child to God as an atonement is therefore really a command to give the grandfather his grandchild. Moreover, the idea is always present that the father is being appeased and satisfied by the sacrifice as though his dignity had before been infringed by a misdeed on the part of his son. The religious sacrifice of the child is always in the nature of an atonement. What offence of primitive man is to be made good thereby, and why by such a horrible and inhuman custom as this one?

Perhaps we shall gain light on this point if we turn to the second motive given by Frazer in regard to child-sacrifice, *i.e.* that the death of the son will lengthen the life of the father. In Peru, for example, 'the son died that the father might live. But in some cases it would seem that the child has been killed, not so much as a substitute for the father, as because it is supposed to endanger his life by absorbing his spiritual essence or vital energy.'[1] Frazer assumes that this belief originates in ideas of the migration of souls. The belief in the migration of souls is actually given as the determining factor

[1] Frazer, *ibid.* p. 188.

in this fear. For example, a Bantu negro of the Lower Congo would be much offended if it were remarked that his son resembled him. He would then firmly believe that he would soon die himself. 'The Galelareese fancy that if a child resembles his father, they will not both live long; for the child has taken away his father's likeness or shadow, and consequently the father must soon die.'[1] Nevertheless we have more unequivocal evidence. The Hindoos are of the opinion that a man is literally reborn in the person of his son. 'Thus in the *Laws of Manu*, we read that "the husband, after conception by his wife, becomes an embryo, and is born again of her; for that is the wifehood of a wife, that he is born again by her". Hence, after the birth of a son, the father is clearly in a very delicate position. Since he is his own son, can he himself, apart from his son, be said to exist? Does he not rather die in his own person as soon as he comes to life in the person of his son? . . . In some sections of the Khatris, a mercantile caste of the Punjab, funeral rites are actually performed for the father in the fifth month of his wife's pregnancy. But apparently he is allowed, by a sort of legal fiction, to come to life again in his own person; for, after the birth of his first son, he is formally remarried to his wife, which may be regarded as a tacit admission that in the eye of the law at least he is alive. . . . It is plain that fatherhood must appear a very dubious privilege ; for if you die in begetting a son, can you be quite sure of coming to life again? His existence is at the best a menace to yours, and at the worst it may involve your extinction. The danger seems to lie especially in the birth of your first son; if only you can tide that over, you are, humanly speaking, safe. In fact, it comes to this, Are you to live? or is he? It is a painful dilemma. Parental affection urges you to die that he may live. Self-love whispers, "Live and let him die. You are in the flower of your age. You adorn the circle in which you move. You are useful, nay, indispensable, to society. He is a mere babe. He never will be missed." Such a train

[1] Frazer, *The Golden Bough: Taboo and the Perils of the Soul*, p. 88.

of thought, preposterous as it seems to us, might easily lead to a custom of killing the first-born.'[1] It is still not clear whether we have any prospect of assigning to this absurd fear of the first-born its true place in the mechanism of the human mind. What mental processes could have given the first impulse to such a belief? The idea of the rebirth of the father in his eldest son may have produced the remarkable law of succession in Polynesia. As soon as the king had a son born to him he was obliged to abdicate the throne in favour of the infant, who was at once proclaimed the sovereign of the people. His father was the first to do him homage, by saluting his feet and declaring him king. This custom of succession was not confined to the family of the sovereign, it extended also to the nobles and the landed gentry; they, too, had to resign their rank, honours and possessions on the birth of a son. A man who but yesterday was a baron, not to be approached by his inferiors till they had ceremoniously bared the whole of the upper part of their bodies, was to-day reduced to the rank of a mere commoner with none to do him reverence, if in the night time his wife had given birth to a son, and the child had been suffered to live. All marks of respect were at once transferred to the child, for the spirit of the father was supposed to quit him at the birth of his first son and to reappear in the infant.

The psychogenesis of the belief in the migration of souls is still not sufficiently explained. Again psychoanalytic investigation throws a ray of light into the darkness. It shows that the situation of the man who has become a father signifies the fulfilment of an old desire originated in the infantile Oedipus complex. The son, who in childhood had wished the death of the father in order to take his place with the mother, has now himself become a man and father. A fundamental change in the mental life of the man now sets in. We know that the welling-up of the so-called fear of retaliation starts from this point.[2] The new-made father fears that his son's

---

[1] Frazer, *The Golden Bough: The Dying God*, p. 188.
[2] See Rank, *Das Inzestmotiv in Dichtung und Sage*, 1912, S. 99.

attitude towards him will be the same as his own once
was towards his father. Many emotions now unconsciously awaken in him. The situation is well suited to
arouse a feeling of triumph; he is now a father himself
and can bring to partial fulfilment his old infantile impulses—those impulses which impelled him to do the
same things as his father did. In this feeling of triumph
there is a kind of deferred defiance come to expression in
the reality, since the previous paternal sexual prohibitions have been so completely overstepped that he has
become a father himself. On the other hand, feelings of
remorse and tenderness are so strong in him and so
strongly does his deferred obedience operate, that it
seems expedient to conciliate the father's wrath. We
have pointed out earlier that Frazer mentions that a
second motive for infanticide is the sacrificial offering of
the child to the Deity as an atonement. We understand
now—since psycho-analysis has proved the Deity to be
the deified father—why such an expiation is necessary.
It appears now as a reaction to the reanimation of old
infantile impulses. We should say that memory traces
of the infantile situation are aroused in the man who
has become a father.

We may now return to the belief of primitive people
in the migration of souls. It was the fear of retaliation,
besides other factors, which gave rise to the belief in the
reappearance of the father in the son, and led to infanticide in order to safeguard the father's life. The individual identified himself with his own father in order to
activate paternal feelings towards his child. Consciously
these feelings are only tender ones; nevertheless, the
harsh treatment he has experienced from his own father
causes cruel and hostile influences to mingle in his
identificatory tendencies. He is afraid that his child
might feel and carry out the wishes which were once the
object of incest prohibitions. We have already seen,
however, that he also fears his own father. A two-sided
fear of retaliation therefore actually prevails in the new-
made father. He is afraid of being punished by his own

father on account of his partial fulfilment of forbidden impulses, and he is afraid that his child will entertain the same wishes against him.[1] The mental origin and mechanisms of these complicated feelings will become clearer if, having regard to facts soon to be mentioned, we assume that the two-sided fear of retaliation on the part of the new father was originally unified and singly directed. The savages are firmly convinced that an ancestor—his grandfather, we should say—comes to life again in the child. Frazer quotes a great number of examples which show that the name of a dead person is carefully avoided.[2] On the other hand, he proves by just as many examples that after some generations have passed, the primitive peoples witness the resurrection of their ancestors in the names they bestow. This belief appears in both positive and negative forms. If the giving of the dead person's name was intended to keep his memory fresh and was evidence of the longing for him, then the forbidding of the names would be an expression of that superstitious fear regarding the dead which we have recognised as the fear of retaliation. Thus we find here again the typical ambivalent attitude. How can this belief, that the grandfather lives again in the child, be compatible with the earlier one, that the child will kill the father? It seems to me only through the fear of retaliation. At the sight of the child the savage must unconsciously remember the breach of prohibition to which the child owes its existence. It is as though he said, 'I also was a child and wished wicked things against my father, and my child will likewise wish to do wicked things to me'. The two thoughts merge into each other— the fear of punishment proceeding from his father, and fear of retaliation threatening from his child. And the two trends of feelings find their expression in the belief

---

[1] This double fear of reprisal and its significance in connection with the Hamlet problem is treated by Rank, *Das Inzestmotiv in Dichtung und Sage*, S. 221. I am aware that I have here laid stress upon only one of the mental motives which have led to infanticide; discussion of the other motives will be left to a later part of this work.

[2] See Freud, *ibid*. S. 51.

that the child is none other than the father whose revenge is feared. This is really the primary superstition, the child is his own resurrected grandfather. Karl von den Steinen reports of the South American Indian tribes that they call the man and his new-born son the 'big father' and the 'little father' respectively. It is only necessary to take literally the phrase, 'the child is father of the man', to arrive at the root of the primitive belief in the migration of souls. The fear of retaliation is the real motive in the teaching of the migration of souls. Memory-traces of old infantile malevolent and incestuous impulses would be actually reanimated by the child's arrival. We now fully understand what the father has to fear from the newly arrived baby; he fears the revenge of his own father. We see also more precisely why he kills the child; he carries out once more the impulse of hate towards the deceased father; he kills once more his own father in the child.

It may be objected that we have ascribed a too complicated mental life to primitive man, for which there is not sufficient evidence. To meet this objection we will only quote one example—out of many—from Frazer's work:[1] 'At Whydah, on the Slave coast of West Africa, where the doctrine of reincarnation is firmly held, it has happened that a child has been put to death because the fetish doctors declared it to be the king's father come to life again. The king naturally could not submit to be pushed from the throne by his predecessor in this fashion; so he compelled his supposed parent to return to the world of the dead from which he had very inopportunely effected his escape.'

We may now survey the result of our work. We started from the analysis of couvade customs and have arrived —as I believe—at a new and surprising explanation of the teaching of the migration of souls. We suspect that the importance of this latter teaching has not yet been fully appreciated, and that it may yet throw light on many strange and peculiar processes in the life of

[1] Frazer, *The Golden Bough: The Dying God*, p. 188.

individuals and of people. We may now consider it as
the intellectually disguised outcome of the unconscious
fear of retaliation, as well as of the longing after the
father. We have learned that its psychogenesis rests on
the fact that the father of the child's father appears to
be born again in the child. If the primitive people assume
that the child will kill them, then their fear is justified in
so far as it relates to this resurrected father. But the
interpretation given by ethnologists needs correction. In
the belief of the savage people the child represents not
the rebirth of its father, but the rebirth of its father's
father. Naturally this statement refers to a very early
stage, because later the child was effectually identified
with its own father. We have seen, however, that unconscious processes point strongly to the conclusion that,
to begin with, it was the first and third generations which
were associated in the belief of primitive people.

The theory of the migration of souls as we have found
it among primitive people has, as Ernest Jones shows, a
significant analogy in the phantasies of many children.[1]
For instance, some children believe that as they grow up
their parents become proportionally smaller, so that in
time the position of both would be reversed. 'This strange
phantasy, which is probably one of the sources of the
belief in reincarnation, is, of course, intimately connected with incestuous wishes, since it is an exaggeration
of the more frequent wish to be one's own father. Nevertheless, it also serves the hostile attitude towards the
parents and fulfils the wish so to change the actual
situation that the child can command the person who
now commands him.' In this 'Reversal of Generations
Phantasy', as it is called, the past and future generations are blended into a unity.

We will now return to Frazer's second hypothesis, that
infanticide is a tribute rendered to God. We have
previously shown that this religious ceremony has the
quality of a psychological reaction-performance, that it
is a wish to conciliate the angry father by the sacrifice of

[1] *Papers on Psycho-Analysis*, Third Edition, 1923, p. 668.

the child. From what has been said we can conclude that
such a ceremony was not originally united absolutely
with the practice of infanticide—probably this happened
at the beginning before any religion had originated.
Infanticide was originally nothing else than the realisation and carrying into action of the son's hostile wishes
towards the father who he believed was born again in his
son. The unconscious motivation of the wishes which
tended to infanticide is chiefly to be found in the fear
of retaliation (from the man's own father). Later, this
murder awakened remorse, and the longing to atone for
the crime took possession of the primitive people. In this
sacrificial scene, as in the totem sacrifice,[1] the father
appears twice. The murder of the father (in the child)
has gratified the hostile feelings, the offering of the
victim signifies the victory of the tender feelings. The
propitiation sacrifice of the child is therefore shown to
be the expression of a compromise from the fact that 'it
offers to the father compensation for the outrage committed on him in the very act which perpetuates the
memory of this monstrous crime'.[2] The religious sacrifice
of the child is certainly later than the entirely non-
religious murder, which, we may assume, was once
common. As in the totem sacrifice so also here the double
presence of the father has two successive meanings; the
father is at first the victim himself, then he to whom the
victim is brought.

We will now venture to amplify Freud's important
hypothesis of what took place in the primitive horde.
After the murder of the father, which was the most important event of primitive development, perhaps of
human development, the brother clan was formed. After
successful detachment from incestuous objects—in what
way this happened need not be discussed here—each of
the brothers took one or more wives. The child who resulted from this new union awakened its father's
memory of that outrage, since the child was the result
of a breach of the paternal prohibition and made the

[1] Freud, *ibid*. S. 138.   [2] Freud, *ibid*. S. 131.

son himself a father. His guilty conscience was changed into the fear of retaliation. The memory of the father found its primitive expression in the belief that the newly arrived child was the father himself who had come to take revenge on his murderer. For how came this strange, peculiar little creature into his home? (The ideas of primitive peoples concerning the connection between sexual intercourse and birth are the same as the infantile sexual theories of the children of to-day.) Who else could this sinister being be than the demoniac father whose memory was perpetually present in the son's guilty conscience? The son now fought for his life and defended his possession, the woman, whom the father, risen again in the form of a child, wished to take; impelled by fear of retaliation, he once more killed and devoured the immortal father. Feelings of remorse and tenderness strengthened by reaction soon set in, but the ambivalent tension remained, and the crime of parricide was repeated in the religious sacrifice of the child. The longing after the father again made itself felt and in the case of the later children—or in the children of a later generation—there occurred severe mental conflicts within the man between hostile and tender impulses towards his father born again in his child. In this ambivalent struggle the tender feeling gained the victory and the hostile impulse was forced into the unconscious. The later children were spared. As civilisation proceeded, a sacrificial animal was substituted for the child. Still the unconscious impulses ever and again tempted primitive man to commit the old act of parricide, and to become reconciled with the father through the killing and devouring of the child, for whom the totem animal had been substituted. The taboo was made stricter, and finally extended so far that the killing of the animals at the period when the man became a father was also included in it. Here we perceive the origin of the rules of the dietetic couvade. Proceeding, therefore, from other premises, we have arrived at the conclusion expressed in the Freudian totem theory, which recognises a father-

F

surrogate in the totem animal. Now we need not hesitate to suppose with Lafitau that in the dietetic couvade
there is a memory of original sin—parricide—and that
its rules are really of an expiatory character, since they
can be recognised in their entirety as a reaction to the
impulse to kill the father.[1] There is no reason at all for
assuming that the sacrifice of the child was originally an
attempt to become reconciled with the Deity. We believe that we have shown that infanticide preceded
child-sacrifice, both temporally and psychologically,
and that it was not an act of propitiation, but an act,
dictated by fear of retaliation and by yearning for the
father, which, through the devouring of the father, represented at the same time a sign and seal of tribal unity.
We can still further trace how the sacrifice of the child
gradually yielded to the sacrifice of the totem animal.
The Russians under Svatoslav, for instance, carried out
nocturnal death sacrifices at Dorostolum on the Ister, by
strangling cocks and infants and sinking them in the
waves of the great river.[2] In South Togo as soon as a
woman can get up again from her childbed she takes a
hen, wipes the body of the new-born child with it, and
then offers it as a sacrifice.[3] Abraham, at the command
of God, sacrificed a ram, representing his son, Isaac.[4]
Scheftelowitz[5] quotes the prohibition which Rabbi Salomon Ben-Aderet, who lived in Barcelona in the thirteenth
century, issued against the vicarious fowl-sacrifice in his
parish.[6] 'This custom was carried out in our city in addition to other similar customs, as for example, the
following: An old cock was killed as propitiation for a
new-born boy; its head was cut off and the head with
the feathers hung up with garlic at the entrance into the

---

[1] The explanations given here enable us to see clearly enough that the idea of
sacrifice put forward by C. G. Jung in his 'Wandlungen und Symbolen der
Libido', *Jahrbuch für psychoanalytische Forschungen*, Bd. iv. 1912, is untenable.
[2] Hehn, *Kulturpflanzen und Haustiere*, 1914, S. 326.
[3] J. Spieth, *Religion der Eweer*, 1912, S. 229.
[4] I. Moses, 22, 13. Regarding the significance of the ram compare the section
on the Shofar.
[5] Scheftelowitz, *Das stellvertretende Huhnopfer*, S. 32.
[6] In his work *Šeelot utešubōt*, Wien, 5572, Bl. 47a, § 395.

house; this I held to be heathenish and hence have forbidden it.'[1]

We see, therefore, how the totem animal appears in the place of the father and of the new-born child. The prohibition in the dietetic couvade against killing and eating animals is the repetition of the totem prohibition against eating and killing the father—we have recognised the child as his *revenant*—just as infanticide was a repetition of the original parricide. The renewal of this is due to the prohibition against the state of fatherhood, a state which has been realised and in which memories of the primitive wishes of one's own childhood are called forth, and occasion a strong fear of retaliation. The people, therefore, are only apparently making an absurd statement when they say that the killing of an animal by the father will bring injuries and even death to the child, since this animal represents the child itself.[2] We can now understand the fasting prohibition which originally only referred to the devouring of the child. We can also recognise the remains of an old totem meal in the repast which is taken by the tribe or family after the birth of a child.

We have stated that primitive people see in the animal a surrogate not only for the child but also for the father —and this at one and the same time, as appears from the analysis of the dietetic couvade and the belief in the migration of souls. Neurotics sometimes have the same idea; and dreams, which stand so near to primitive mental life, show the same identifications. I am indebted to Dr. Karl Abraham of Berlin for the report of two dreams, the analysis of which gave the following result. The cats about which a female patient dreamed were substitute objects for her parents. A month later, the same patient had a dream in which she represented herself as a cat which had a little kitten with it. A dog

---

[1] I cannot here go into the question of ritual murder among the Jews, but I shall return to it in another place. (*Der eigene und der fremde Gott,* 1923.)

[2] In this idea may be seen one of those compressions comparable to obsessional neurotic forms of expression, which, translated into the language of consciousness, would run as follows: 'If I kill and devour the animal which is really my father, then my father will revenge himself through the death of my child'.

in the dream of another female patient signified at the same time her father, the dreamer, and her child. Recently E. Weiss has been able to trace a similar identification in a dream analysis.[1]

I regret having no case at my disposal which demonstrates precise analogies in the mental life of the neurotic to the psychological material of the dietetic couvade customs. I have no doubt, however, that other psychoanalysts could produce cases of this kind. It seems to me, nevertheless, not out of place to adduce here, as a sort of confirmatory evidence, a poem which has already once been the subject of psycho-analytic study.[2] Count Ulrich in G. Hauptmann's *Griselda* has many traits which seem to show his close resemblance to the primitive father. He is supposed to have shown no spark of natural paternal feeling, and to have taken steps to make away with the new-born child without its mother's knowledge. It reminds us of the ideas which we have attributed to the people of the primitive horde, when we find him calling out, 'What does this mean? Why does she give birth? I want no son! I hate the child in her womb. She is mine. I poisoned the cats because she stroked them. Have I begotten some strange toad that sucks the blood from her breasts?' The Countess Eberhard avows that Ulrich becomes as angry about the poor little unborn child, 'as if he had had an irreconcilable blood feud with him in another world'. We cannot help thinking of the primitive theory of the migration of souls when we see the hostility of the Count thus referred back to a conflict with the child 'in another world'. The foe in the 'other world' is certainly the Count's father and the old hate is now turned upon his ghost, the child. The Count confirms this in his reply to the doctor's question as to what were the principles and who the teachers of his

---

[1] 'Totemmaterial in einem Traume', *Internationale Zeitschrift für ärztliche Psychoanalyse*, Märzheft, 1914. Compare *Talmud Gittin*, 57a; *Berakot*, 57a: 'He who sees a cock in a dream will soon have a boy, he who sees many cocks will soon have many boys'. A similar belief prevails among the Sudanese. If a woman dreams of a hen, then she will soon have a child (Globus, 44, 349).

[2] Otto Rank, 'Der Sinn der Griseldafabel', *Imago*, 1912, Heft. 1.

youth. 'A wild boar, if you like, that eats its young.' It seems like a return of totemism and impulses to commit infanticide in the neurotic when Ulrich cries out in the stress of the hours of birth: 'I would rather any wild animal broke out of some menagerie in the neighbourhood'. Count Heinz says, 'I assure you he does not know where he is. He is positively unloosening his dagger.' With the Count, just as among primitive people, the killing of an animal is a substitute for the murder of the hated child.[1]

It seems likely that our investigation of the father-rites of primitive peoples may yield some more particular information regarding couvade customs. We are now better able to understand why the restrictions of couvade were observed with special strictness as regards the first son, while a lessening and mitigation of the prohibition was allowed as regards later children. The fear felt by primitive people which, as Frazer says, led to infanticide, is especially strong as regards the first son. The reason for this will be clear if we are right in regarding this feeling as the fear of retaliation. The first-born son grows up soonest and can earliest become dangerous to the father through his hostility and through the incest impulse towards his mother. Again the son is a ghost of the grandfather; on the birth of the first son, the primitive man is for the most part still young; hate impulses and the memory of wicked wishes towards his father are more active than at a later age, as the identification with the father is always increasing in intensity.

When the psychogenesis of the fear of retaliation is taken into account, another detail of couvade becomes

---

[1] I will here allude to a detail which seems of interest. Griselda will only return to the castle when commanded to wash the stairs as a servant. It is as though the house had become unclean (taboo) through the anger and covetousness of the man towards her. Also Count Ulrich's separation from his wife during and after the birth of the child offers an analogy in the life of an individual to the customs of uncivilised peoples; it is a kind of couvade. The feeling which prevails in the Griselda poem of the father's jealousy of his son's love for his mother (that jealousy whose repression has contributed to the building up of the couvade) becomes more prominent still when the son has reached the age of puberty, as he can become dangerous to the father. See the following section on the Puberty Rites of Savages.

more intelligible and takes on a more intimate connection with the unconscious mental life of savages: I refer to the blood-ordeal among the Caribs and other peoples.

The wounds which are inflicted on the new father by his friends and relatives prove to be a substitute for castration. We know that castration originally represented punishment for incest. It is as if the man had consummated incest by becoming a father. We can understand this if we recognise that the circumstances of childbirth have brought back the infantile incest complex to unconscious memory. Rank has collected many examples which show that mutilations and woundings form a substitute for castration.[1] We need only allude to the two forms of the Kronos saga in order to find again the psychological motive which dictates this partial castration. Kronos cut off his father's generative organs when the latter made overtures to his wife. Having become a father himself he feared from his children the same fate which he had meted out to Uranus, and devoured them immediately after their birth. According to the Orphic theogony, however, Kronos is supposed actually to have been emasculated by Zeus, as Uranus was by Kronos. The progress of repression, however, has resulted in the same situation being represented in the third generation by a wounding. Zeus is weakened in the feet by Typhon, having the tendons cut out with a sickle. The blood-ordeal among the Caribs represents a modified form of emasculation of this kind, since the father suffers punishment for his breach of the paternal sexual prohibition. We have no need to retract any part of our earlier interpretation according to which the tortures of a Carib father are regarded as punishment for his wicked wishes; the new explanation is only a deeper view of the earlier one. In reality the man wishes to cut off the organ of the child—the ghost of the father—because he is dominated by the fear that the new being (his child and at the same time, his father) might take back his

---

[1] Otto Rank, *Das Inzestmotiv in Dichtung und Sage*, Kap. ix. 2. Wien und Leipzig, 1912.

wife. He had also wished when he was little to cut off his father's penis (compare the tales of Uranus and Kronos). The man is, as it were, robbed of his own penis as a punishment for the castration-wish once directed against the father, and he must now permit wounds to be inflicted on him. The breach of the paternal sexual prohibition is, so to speak, subsequently atoned for by the fact that means are used which, if they had been adopted earlier, would have made the breach impossible. A custom which prevails among the Borans in southern Abyssinia seems to support our contention.[1] The children are sacrificed to a sky-spirit called Wak. 'When a man of any standing marries, he becomes a Raba, as it is called, and for a certain period after marriage, probably four to eight years, he must leave any children that are born to him to die in the bush. . . . After he ceases to be a Raba, a man is circumcised and becomes a Gudda. The sky-spirit has no claim on the children born after their father's circumcision, but they are sent away at a very early age to be reared by the Wata, a low caste of hunters. They remain with these people till they are grown up, and then return to their families.'[2] Frazer rightly supposes 'that the circumcision', in this custom, 'is regarded as an atoning sacrifice which redeems the rest of his children from the spirit to whom they would otherwise belong'.

If we remember that the child seems to the savage the reincarnation of his father, then we can understand how it is that, being governed at the time of the birth by unconscious fear of retaliation and unconscious feelings of revenge, he allows emasculation, or its substitute, mutilation, to be carried out on himself as a deferred sign of obedience towards the resurrected father, and as a self-punishment to which his guilty conscience impels him on account of the wishes he once held.

As already pointed out, only a small number of the

---

[1] Frazer, *The Golden Bough: The Dying God*, p. 181.
[2] The Jewish traditions also necessitate the conclusion that circumcision is a castration symbol.

mental determining factors of couvade customs are
analysed in this work. Only a careful analysis of the
puberty rites of primitive peoples[1] will throw further
important light on the male childbed.[2] The view will
there be reached that the displacement of the birth from
the mother to the father has actually a real meaning
besides the meaning we have already discussed ; this
real meaning has, of course, nothing to do with father-
and mother-right. It corresponds to the phantasy of
the father having given birth to the child, and is equivalent to a nullification of the child's birth from the
mother. The affective basis of this phantasy lies in the
unconscious incestuous fixation of the child on the
mother which was created by the birth; and on this
basis also rests the father's striving to detach this libido
fixation from its object, and to transfer to himself the
child's love. This nullification of incestuous attitude can
have no more radical enforcement than by the denial of
its first and most essential cause; it is not the mother
who has given birth to the child, but the father; to him,
therefore, the child's love must go. Here again we find it
best to believe in what the rites represent, however
senseless and stupid their external appearance may
seem at first sight. If we consider that in the puberty
rites a kind of rebirth of the boys from their father takes
place, we have couvade represented as a temporarily
displaced form of this phantasy charged with strong
affects. We may compare this to the great rôle played
by the father's unconscious fear of retaliation in couvade
customs, and the particularly strict observance of the

---

[1] See the following section.

[2] The connection between the rites of couvade and of puberty become still
closer when one thinks of the dieting, the ordeals and the symbolic castration
of the novices. To the unconscious of the young father, the birth of his child is a
disproof of the castration threats of his own father; it is before everything a
triumph over his father, for he has reached the same state. Thus his reaction of
anxiety (demon avoidance), and his homosexual and feminine identification
with the woman who bears children becomes clear. Géza Róheim in a letter to
me has reduced the rites of couvade to the theory of the anal child, in which the
conception is orally (diet) represented. As a punishment for the unconscious
tendency to kill the father (=the child) the man is himself impregnated and
compelled to bear a child.

ritual at the birth of the first-born. Couvade and the puberty rites would, therefore, be the effects of the same unconscious attitude of feeling expressed in different forms, in which the ambivalency towards the son stands out with special prominence.

The scholars who affirm that couvade signifies a landmark in the development of mankind now seem to be justified. For it is, as it were, the boundary stone of a definite stage of civilisation, which marks the victory of the tender impulses for his wife and child on the part of the man. It shows us that the unconscious identification with his own father now begins to be a lasting one, and that his affection for him has so successfully suppressed the fear of retaliation that his concern about the new generation now becomes the central point in his emotional life as a parent. This signifies, however, a partial renunciation of the gratification of his impulses—a necessary condition in the advance to each higher stage of civilisation. At the same time it means that the father, in thus renouncing his own claims, regains the gratification he has lost in his new unity of feeling with his son.

If I may be permitted to conclude this study on a lighter note I may venture to sum it up by saying that among the half-civilised peoples who practise couvade lives a glimmer of that wisdom which, quoting freely from Wilhelm Busch, we may express thus: '*Vater sein ist nicht schwer, Vater werden dagegen sehr*'. (It is not difficult to be a father; it is not easy to become one.)

THE PUBERTY RITES OF SAVAGES

SOME PARALLELS BETWEEN THE MENTAL LIFE OF SAVAGES AND OF NEUROTICS[1]

Und hat mit diesem kindisch-tollen Ding
Der Klugerfahr'ne sich beschäftigt,
So ist fürwahr die Torheit nicht gering,
Die seiner sich am Schluss bemächtigt.
GOETHE.

I

THE significance of initiation and puberty rites with their elaborate and impressive ceremonial can hardly be overestimated in the religious life and social organisation of primitive peoples. H. Schurtz says that they are for the most part more imposing and of longer duration than the marriage celebrations.[2] Their importance is intelligible if we bear in mind that the puberty rites not only mark an epoch of life, but also indicate that the age has arrived when sexual intercourse and the procreation of children is legally permitted; that they initiate the young man into the religious ceremonies of the tribe; and that they confer upon him all the rights and impose the obligations which are valid for the adult members of the tribe.

In spite of the numerous scientific investigations that have been devoted to the initiations of youths the meaning of the very complicated ceremonials that accompany these rites has not been elucidated up to the present. That penetrating scholar, J. G. Frazer,[3] has recently stated that it can be easily shown from a great number of facts that in the mind of savages sexual relations at the time of puberty are associated with serious risks, but the real

[1] Read before the Vienna Psycho-Analytical Society in January, 1915. First published in *Imago*, Bd. iv. 1915-16.
[2] *Altersklassen und Männerbünde*, Berlin, 1902, S. 96.
[3] *The Golden Bough: Balder the Beautiful*, vol. ii., Third Edition, London, 1913, p. 278.

nature of the feared danger is obscure. Frazer expresses
the hope 'that a more exact acquaintance with savage
modes of thought will in time disclose *this central mystery
of primitive society*,[1] and will thereby furnish the clue,
not only to totemism, but to the origin of the marriage
system'.

Without claiming to be able to satisfy such lofty expectations, the following exposition is an attempt to
solve the problem of the primitive puberty rites. My
justification for making this attempt is that I propose
to attack material which has already been much discussed, with a new instrument, namely, psycho-analysis,
the value of which in its application to folk-psychology
has already been brilliantly demonstrated.[2]

If we seek for a theme which, under various forms, is
common to the initiation rites of primitive peoples and
which will present a convenient starting-point for our
psychological analysis, we shall find it in the ceremonials which ostensibly have in view the killing and
resurrection of the youths about to be initiated. This
theme, which Frazer includes under 'the drama of death
and resurrection', can be observed especially well in the
puberty rites of the Australian natives; but it has also
been found and described in primitive tribes of Africa
and America.

In order to form a general picture of the puberty rites
of primitive peoples we will first of all consider some
typical examples from Australian tribes. In the Wonghi
tribe of New South Wales a part of the puberty rites
consists in knocking out a tooth. 'When the tooth is
knocked out, a loud humming noise is heard, which is
made with an instrument of the following description:
a flat piece of wood is made with serrated edges, and
having a hole at one end, to which a string is attached,
and this swung round, produces a humming noise. The
uninitiated are not even allowed to see this instrument'
(called a 'bull-roarer'). 'Women are forbidden to be
present at these ceremonies, and should one, by accident

---

[1] Author's italics.   [2] Freud, *Totem und Tabu*, Wien, 1914.

or otherwise, witness them, the penalty is death. . . . It is said that the youths are sent away a short distance one by one, and that they are each met in turn by a Being, who, so far as I can understand, is believed to be something between a black-fellow and a spirit. This Being, called Thuremlin, it is said, takes the youth to a distance, kills him, and in some instances cuts him up, after which he restores him to life and knocks out a tooth.'[1] Frazer[2] gives the following account of the initiation ceremony in the Jabim tribe of German New Guinea.[3] 'The initiation of young men takes place at intervals of several years, when there are a number of youths ready to be initiated, and enough pigs can be procured to furnish forth the feasts which form an indispensable part of the ceremony. The principal initiatory rite consists of circumcision, which is performed on all youths before they are admitted to the rank of full-grown men. The age of the candidates varies considerably, from four years up to twenty. Many are married before they are initiated. The operation is performed in the forest, and the procession of the youths to the place is attended by a number of men swinging bull-roarers. As the procession sets out, the women look on from a distance, weeping and howling, for they are taught to believe that the lads, their sons and brothers, are about to be swallowed up by a monster called a *balum*, or ghost, who will only release them from his belly on condition of receiving a sufficient number of roast pigs. How, then, can the poor women be sure that they will ever see their dear ones again? . . . The place where the operation is performed on the lads is a long hut, about a hundred feet in length, which diminishes in height towards the rear. This represents the belly of the monster who is to swallow up the candidates. To keep up the delusion a pair of great eyes are painted over the entrance, and above them the projecting roots of a betel-palm represent the monster's hair,

---

[1] J. G. Frazer, *ibid.* p. 227.
[2] *The Belief in Immortality*, vol. i., 1913, p. 250.
[3] [Now Papua—Trans.]

while the trunk of the tree passes for his backbone. As the awe-struck lads approach this imposing creature, he is heard from time to time to utter a growl. The growl is, in fact, no other than the humming note of bull-roarers swung by men, who are concealed within the edifice. When the procession has come to a halt . . . they raise a shrill song like a scream and sacrifice pigs to the monster in order to induce him to spare the lives of the candidates. When the operation has been performed on the lads, they must remain in strict seclusion for three or four months, avoiding all contact with women and even the sight of them. They live in the long hut, which represents the monster's belly, and their food is brought to them by elder men. . . . Sometimes, though perhaps rarely, one of the lads dies under the operation; in that case the men explain his disappearance to the women by saying that the monster has a pig's stomach as well as a human stomach, and that, unfortunately, the deceased young man slipped by mistake into the wrong stomach and so perished miserably. But as a rule the candidates pass into the right stomach, and, after a sufficient period has been allowed for digestion, they come forth safe and sound, the monster having kindly consented to let them go free in consideration of the roast pigs which have been offered to him by the men. Indeed, he is not very exacting, for he contents himself with devouring the souls of the pigs, while he leaves their bodies to be consumed by his worshippers. . . . When the time of seclusion is up . . . the young men are brought back to the village with much solemnity. An eye-witness has described the ceremony. . . In marching back to the village, they had to keep their eyes tightly shut, and each of them was led by a man who acted as a kind of god-father. . . . The women were much moved at the return of the lads; they sobbed and tears of joy ran down their cheeks. Arrived in the village, the newly initiated lads . . . stood with closed eyes, motionless as statues. Then a man passed behind them . . . saying, "O circumcised one, sit down". But still the lads remained standing, stiff and motion-

less. Not till another man had knocked repeatedly on
the ground with the stalk of a palm-leaf, crying, "O circumcised ones, open your eyes!" did the youths, one after
another, open their eyes as if awaking from a profound
stupor.' Frazer points out that 'the candidate is supposed to die or to be killed and to come to life again or
be born again; and the pretence of a new birth is not un-
commonly kept up by the novices feigning to have forgotten all the most common actions of life, and having
accordingly to learn them all over again like new-born
babes. We may conjecture that this is why the young
circumcised Papuans march back to their village with
closed eyes; this is why, when bidden to sit down, they
remain standing stiffly, as if they understood neither the
command nor the action.' The rites among the Bukaua
and the Tami are of a similar kind. In these rites 'it is
given out that the lads are swallowed by a ferocious
monster called a *balum*, who, however, is induced by the
sacrifice of many pigs to vomit them up again. In spew-
ing them out of his maw he bites or scratches them, and
the wound so inflicted is circumcision. . . . The youths
are shut up for several months in a house specially built
for the purpose in the village' (called *balumslum*).[1] The
same procedure is carried out very realistically in the
Kai tribe.[2] 'A long hut, entered through a high door at
one end and tapering away at the other, is built in a
lonely part of the forest. It represents the monster which
is to swallow the novices in its capacious jaws. The process of deglutition is represented as follows: In front of
the entrance to the hut a scaffold is erected and a man
mounts it. The novices are then led up one by one and
passed under the scaffold. As each comes up, the man
overhead makes a gesture of swallowing, while at the
same time he takes a great gulp of water from a coco-nut
flask. The trembling novice is now supposed to be in the
maw of the monster; but a pig is offered for his redemption, the man on the scaffold, as representative of the
beast, accepts the offering, a gurgling sound is heard,

[1] J. G. Frazer, *ibid*. p. 260.   [2] J. G. Frazer, *ibid*. p. 290.

and the water which he had just gulped descends in a jet on the novice, who now goes free. The actual circumcision follows immediately on this impressive pantomime. . . . Women are strictly excluded from the neighbourhood of the circumcision ground; any who intrude on it are put to death.[1] The mythical monster who is supposed to haunt the ground is said to be very dangerous to the female sex. Among the Tami[2] the women are even banished from the village at the time of the puberty rites, and are accommodated in quarters specially erected for them. 'To impress women and children with an idea of the superhuman strength of the dragon [whose bite is the circumcision], deep grooves are cut in the trunks of trees and afterwards exhibited to the uninitiated as the marks made by the monster in tugging at the ropes which bound him to the trees.'

'In the west of Ceram boys at puberty are admitted to the Kakian association. . . . The Kakian house is an oblong wooden shed, situated under the darkest trees in the depth of the forest, and is built to admit so little light that it is impossible to see what goes on in it. . . . Thither the boys who are to be initiated are conducted blindfold, followed by their parents and relations. Each boy is led by the hand by two men, who act as his sponsors or guardians, looking after him during the period of initiation. When all are assembled before the shed, the high priest calls aloud upon the devils. Immediately a hideous uproar is heard to proceed from the shed. It is made by men with bamboo trumpets. . . . Then the priests enter the shed, followed by the boys one at a time. As soon as each boy has disappeared within the precincts, a dull chopping sound is heard, a frightful cry rings out, and a sword or spear, dripping with blood, is thrust through the roof of the shed. This is a token that the boy's head has been cut off, and that the

---

[1] During one of these festivals among the Kai, a woman, impelled by curiosity, ventured too near to the forbidden dwelling in the forest; she was discovered, seized, and immediately thrown into a pig's hole where the men trampled her to death without pity. Cf. Richard Neuhauss, *Deutsch-Neu-Guinea*, Berlin, 1911, Bd. iii. S. 36.　　　　　[2] Frazer, *ibid.* p. 301.

devil has carried him away to the other world, there to regenerate and transform him. So at sight of the bloody sword the mothers weep and wail, crying that the devil has murdered their children. In some places, it would seem, the boys are pushed through an opening made in the shape of a crocodile's jaws or a cassowary's beak, and it is then said that the devil has swallowed them. The boys remain in the shed for five or nine days. Sitting in the dark, they hear the blast of the bamboo trumpets, and from time to time the sound of musket shots and the crash of swords. . . . When they are not sleeping, the lads must sit in a crouching posture without moving a muscle. As they sit in a row cross-legged, with their hands stretched out, the chief takes his trumpet, and placing the mouth of it on the hands of each lad, speaks through it strange tones, imitating the voice of the spirits. He warns the lads, under the pain of death, to observe the rules of the Kakian society, and never to reveal what has passed in the Kakian house. . . . Meantime, the mothers and sisters of the lads have gone home to weep and mourn. But in a day or two the men who acted as guardians or sponsors to the novices return to the village with the glad tidings that the devil, at the intercession of the priests, has restored the lads to life. The men who bring this news come in a fainting state and daubed with mud, like messengers freshly arrived from the nether world. . . . When they [the lads] return to their homes they totter in their walk, and enter the house backward, as if they had forgotten how to walk properly; or they enter the house by the back door. If a plate of food is given to them they hold it upside down. They remain dumb, indicating their wants by signs only. . . . Their sponsors have to teach them all the common acts of life, as if they were new-born children.'[1]

L. Frobenius reports similar initiation customs in the secret societies of Africa.[2] The youths who enter into a certain society in the Congo are subjected to a number

---

[1] Frazer, *The Golden Bough: Balder the Beautiful*, vol. ii. p. 249.
[2] *Die Masken und Geheimbünde Afrikas*, Halle, 1898.

G

of tests, and are then put into a trance and immured in
the fetish house. On being brought to life again they
have lost the memory of all things that have gone before,
even of their father and mother, and they cannot remember their own name. When a youth is initiated into
the Ndembo society the priest instructs him to act as
though he were suddenly dead at a given signal. The
novice then falls down in any public place, shrouds are
laid over him, and he is borne out of the town. The other
young men follow suit in simulating death. It is believed that the youths who have thus died decompose
until only a single bone is left. After a certain time,
which fluctuates from three months to three years in
different places, the priest takes these bones and resur-
rects each young man.[1]

In central and north Australia the spirits which drag
away, kill and reanimate children often replace the
human organs by spirit ones; sometimes they place
stones which have magic power, or a serpent, for example,
in the body of the new-born person. After the youth has
been called back to life with a new heart, a new pair of
lungs, etc., he returns to his native village in a more or
less stupefied condition.

We may be satisfied with these few typical examples
which show again and again in different forms what a
great part the motives of death, resurrection, and sudden
amnesia play in puberty and initiation rites.

Before passing to the analysis of these strange rites
we must remember the difficulties of finding a precise
interpretation. We may assume that we see before us in
the ritual of puberty celebrations institutions among the
primitive people of to-day which have a long developmental history, in the course of which their original
meaning has been lost, new forms have replaced old
ones and a new meaning has been imposed upon the unintelligible elements; this process resembles the dreams

---

[1] Similar examples are found in abundance in the three works quoted, by
Frazer, Frobenius and Schurtz respectively, and also in the ethnographical
literature mentioned by these authors.

of adults to which consciousness has given a secondary elaboration. The psycho-analyst's task is to break up these distortions, condensations, displacements, etc., which the dream-work has produced, and thus expose the latent meaning of the dream freed from its superimposed layers.

II

If we ask the Australians who carry out the puberty rites what these signify, we are given the surprising information which was once put by a native in the following way: 'We eat the pigs and lie to the women'.

We need not be discouraged by so superficial an answer; it is clear that this lofty ambition could be achieved by shorter and less circuitous methods, and in reality we have a fairly patent rationalisation which refers to an advantage obtained only supplementarily from old rites which are anything but meaningless. There must have been a time when the natives attributed an important significance to the puberty ceremony which has now degenerated into a farce.

The youths are killed by a monster or spirit whose voice, represented by the noise of bull-roarers, inspires fear. Who is this spirit or monster that claims the young people for itself? Perhaps we can learn something of the nature of this mysterious being from its name. Among the Tami the monster is called *kani*; the same name is also given to the bull-roarer and to the spirits of the dead. Frazer concludes from this circumstance that in the mind of the Tami the initiatory rites are closely associated with their conception of the state of the human soul after death.[1] Among the Kai people both the bull-roarer and the monster are named *ngosa*, which means 'grandfather'. Most of the tribes, however, call the being *balum*. Among the Bukaua *balum* denotes (1) the secret cult of the male Papuans which centres round an uncanny being to whom is ascribed all unfortunate events,

[1] Frazer, *ibid*. p. 301.

such as spring-tides, earthquakes, etc. (*Balum* is often personified as the chief ancestor of a village clan whose name he bears. He is also represented as a gluttonous monster who demands young people); (2) the bull-roarer or the voice of the spirit; (3) the soul of each deceased person.[1] This last feature agrees with the fact that bull-roarers bear the name of prominent and deceased men, and also have the same defects that were peculiar to those men, such as a nasal twang, a striking construction of the body, prominent hip bones, etc. An old Papuan told the missionary, Stefan Lehner, that 'the *balum* is the spirits of people long since dead that have reappeared'.[2]

We may now venture to assume that the preying monster who ostensibly devours the youths represents the totem animal which, as is well known, the primitive people worship as their chief ancestor. The significance of the word *ngosa* leads us to suppose that in reality behind that chief ancestor there is concealed a special figure, namely, the grandfather of the youths who are to be initiated. The intimate connection of the grandfather with his grandson has been constantly noted in the ideational life of primitive peoples. A typical example from Frazer's book[3] enables us to recognise the nature of this relationship. In Vanua-levu, one of the largest of the Fijian islands, 'a child was considered to be more closely related to his grandfather than to his father. Hence, when a grandfather died, his ghost naturally desired to carry off the soul of his grandchild with him to the spirit land. . . . If the survivors preferred to keep the child with them a little longer in this vale of tears, they took steps to baffle grandfather's ghost. For this purpose, when the old man's body was stretched on the bier and raised on the shoulders of half-a-dozen stout young fellows, the mother's brother would take the grandchild in his arms and begin running round and round the corpse. Round and round he ran, and grand-

---

[1] R. Neuhauss, *Deutsch-Neu-Guinea*, S. 402.
[2] R. Neuhauss, *ibid.* S. 418.   [3] *Ibid.* p. 416.

father's ghost looked after him, craning his neck from side to side and twisting it round and round in the vain attempt to follow the rapid movements of the runner. When the ghost was supposed to be quite giddy with this unwonted exercise, the mother's brother made a sudden dart away with the child in his arms, the bearers fairly bolted with the corpse to the grave, and before he could collect his scattered wits grandfather was safely landed in his long home.' Frazer sees in this peculiar custom an expression of that belief so widely spread in the whole of the primitive world that 'the soul of the grandfather is actually reborn in his grandchild.'[1] A dead grandfather reclaims his own soul before he sets out for the spirit land.

We feel that we have here a clue to the enigma of the puberty rites. Why does the grandfather devour his grandson in the initiation rites? What does the resurrection of the youths and their subsequent amnesia signify? What part do the boys' fathers play in the drama?

Perhaps we obtain a clearer insight into the origin of these rites if we consider more carefully the share of the father-generation in them. It is the adult men of the tribe who drag the youths to the monster, terrify them, and perform circumcision upon them; yet these same men ostensibly protect the boys from the monster and even fight for them. The men's behaviour towards the boys has given many observers the impression that the intimidation and terrifying of the novices was the chief object of the initiations. For example, Schellong in his report of the *balum* festival in Kaiser Wilhelms Land[2] says that the men make the preparations for the circumcision with refined deliberation, while the novices await the operation in the stomach of *balum*. The men make the most hideous noise, striking their shields, shrieking, whooping, whistling through their hands, and appear as noisy and unrestrained as possible, 'with the unmistak-

[1] As to this belief and its psychic motivation compare the preceding section on Couvade, p. 76.
[2] 'Das Balumfest der Gegend Fischhafen', *Internationalen Archiv für Ethnographie*, 1889 (Supplement), S. 145.

able intention of thoroughly intimidating the trembling youths'. P. W. Schmidt,[1] who reports in detail the secret initiation of youths among the Karesau islanders in Papua, says that while the youths are waiting to be devoured one of the men addresses the spirit thus: 'We have not got as many children this year, and so you cannot have any now; perhaps another time'. Thereupon loud and mysterious sounds of a flute are heard which are interpreted as the urgent demands of the spirit. Then the man says: 'No, you must wait, not now, but perhaps later; you must go home'. The men now go to the two houses in which the youths are and shake and beat them so that the youths are afraid and begin to cry. On the next day different spirits appear in the masks of animals, and on their approach the men say to the boys, 'They will eat you'; whereupon the boys begin to cry. Among these islanders a fight often takes place between the men and their sons. During the period of the novices' seclusion the men come from the forest with arrows and spears in their hands as in war. A man places himself before each boy and throws a spear or shoots an arrow over the boy's right shoulder close to his body and into the ground. Thereupon the boys spring up, run behind the men and throw spears at them which they pick up from the ground, sometimes hitting one of the men.

The women seem to have the idea that the men have hostile feelings towards their sons, since it is reported of the Bukaua[2] that the mothers do not sleep on the night preceding the day of departure. They cry continuously, and caress and fondle the youths whom a monster is to devour in the morning. In the morning when the fathers come to take the boys away they often meet with a rough reception from the sorrowing mothers. Although we may now assume that the fathers show malicious and hostile feelings towards the youths, we must not forget that they are also represented as their protectors and friends. We have already heard that the youths

---

[1] *Anthropos*, 1907, Heft 6.   [2] R. Neuhauss, *ibid*. S. 402.

receive men as godfathers when on their way to the circumcision. Among the Bukaua feigned attacks coupled with a frightful noise are made on the boys, and their protectors have to guard them from the blows.[1] The men's human kindness appears, moreover, in the fact that they so fasten the hut which represents the monster that it cannot run away and harm the women and children.[2]

It seems as though the attitude of the fathers towards the boys were a complex one composed of two opposite feelings, namely, hostility and affection. This mental attitude, containing two opposed emotions directed towards the same object, psycho-analysis characterises as an ambivalent attitude. In these primitive fathers the two strong emotions of hate and tenderness towards the boys struggle for predominance, but without a final victory being attained by either feeling.

The presence of unconscious hostile impulses in the mental life of the men is best shown in the refined tortures which they impose on the youths. Among the Kai, for example, after the circumcision the men stand in two rows facing one another, and the youths have to pass down between the men who rain violent blows upon them. The boys are beaten with birches, thorny branches, nettles, etc., ostensibly to awaken their warlike spirit. Also among the Tami the youths have to run the gauntlet twice; and it is said that formerly some were left dead on the ground.[3] Among the Karesau islanders the novices are led into the forest to a tree, kakar, on which black ants run up and down, and the boy is placed against it with his head bent forward. A man strikes the tree and an ant falls down and bites into the boy's neck. At each blow the men give the candidates

---

[1] R. Neuhauss, *ibid*. S. 407.

[2] In Kaiser Wilhelms Land. Compare Ploss, *Das Kind in Sitte und Brauch der Völker*, 3. Aufl., II. Bd., S. 210 und 196, Leipzig, 1911.

[3] This running the gauntlet is called by the natives 'settling the account'. Compare later details for the justification of this description. For the present we may refer to the report of missionaries, to the effect that on this occasion many a deserted husband takes revenge on the seducer of his wife. (R. Neuhauss, *Deutsch-Neu-Guinea*, S. 499.)

for circumcision they say, 'If anyone does you any harm,
then spear him'. There is a parallel to this procedure
among civilised people: the ceremonial of knighting in
the Middle Ages was associated with the admonition to
avenge every future blow. Among many Indian tribes
the growing youths have to endure unspeakable tortures.
Formerly among the Maskoki the candidate at puberty
was whipped by the chief until the latter's hands became
powerless.[1] Among the Mandan Indians the youth, who
has not been allowed to eat or sleep for four days, has a
knife with a saw edge thrust through his arm, forearm,
thigh, knee, calves, chest, and shoulder, and then has
pointed pieces of wood pushed into the wounds. Then a
rope is let down from the roof of the medicine hut and
fastened to the pieces of wood in the chest or shoulder,
and the youth raised off the ground by it. The sufferer,
swinging thus in the air, is turned round and round at an
increasing rate until he loses consciousness and hangs
motionless.

What do these cruel rites signify? The explanation
given by comparative ethnology, that they represent
tests of courage and endurance, does not satisfy us. This
certainly may be a secondary motive, but we prefer to
take these refined acts of cruelty at their face value,
i.e. as cruel and hostile acts of the men against the
youths.[2] We have seen that the men among the Australian natives drag the youths to the monster, circumcise and torture them, but at the same time hypo-
critically assist the novices in the fight against the
monster. The rôle of these fathers now becomes clearer
to us. The fathers identify themselves with the *balum*
monster. It is they who harbour those wicked impulses
against the neophytes which are ascribed to the monster.[3]

[1] Compare the whippings of the *Ephebi* in Sparta. Ploss gives a detailed
account of similar cruelties to the novices in the second volume of his above-
mentioned work.
[2] Of course the particular form each of these cruelties takes is mentally determined and over-determined. (Compare the detailed work of Dr. Moritz Zeller,
Die Knabenweihen, Bern, 1923.)
[3] We are reminded of the ceremonies among the Kai, where the man on the
scaffolding—instead of the monster—makes the gesture of devouring.

We do not yet know whence arise the hostile impulses of the fathers, nor why, in realising them, they make use of the *balum*, which represents the novice's grandfather. The psycho-analytic investigation of the institution of circumcision comes to our aid here.

We know that the monster is supposed to bite the young men, and that this constitutes the circumcision. This idea seems very puzzling; we can find no analogy for it in our conscious minds. The explanation will be clearer if we take into account the results obtained from the psycho-analysis of unconscious mental processes. For instance, little Hans's constant anxiety about being bitten by a horse has been explained by Freud as the infantile expression of an unconscious fear of castration.[1] Similarly, Ferenczi's little patient, Árpád, said that he had been bitten by a hen.[2] We have previously mentioned the idea among certain Australian tribes that the youth was robbed of his intestines by one spirit, and received new ones in their place from a benevolent spirit. This idea is very similar to a wish-phantasy produced by little Hans:[3] 'The plumber came, and first he took away my behind with a pair of pincers, and then gave me another, and then the same with my widdler'. As in these infantile phantasies, so in the ideas of the savages an over-compensating assuagement of castration anxiety is to be discerned.

We know that circumcision represents a castration-equivalent and supports in the most effective way the prohibition against incest.[4] The fear of castration would be stimulated by the unconscious fear of retaliation which is felt by the man who has now become a father himself. The unconscious memory of incestuous and hostile impulses of childhood which were turned upon his parents still lives in him. He fears the realisation of these wishes, in which he might be the object injured at the hands of his own child.

---

[1] Freud, *Collected Papers: Analysis of a Phobia in a Five-Year-Old Boy*, vol. iii. p. 149.
[2] Ferenczi, *Contributions to Psycho-Analysis: A Little Chanticleer*, p. 204.
[3] Freud, *ibid.* p. 240.　　　　[4] Freud, *Totem und Tabu*, S. 141.

The reason for the primitive man's identification of the monster with the grandfather now becomes clear; and the youth's fear of the monster is comparable to little Hans's fear of horses. Thus one motive of the savages' *father-identification* is the fear of retaliation.[1]

If we understand circumcision as a punishment for incestuous wishes, then the different tests of courage and fortitude which we have denoted as tortures will be punishments for wicked wishes against the father. The rite of being devoured by the monster is a threat of death and a psychic reaction to the youth's unconscious intention to murder his father.

This interpretation is forced upon us by certain facts. By the Talion law of the unconscious, a killing, as we see it here represented in regard to the novices, corresponds to death wishes which are expiated by that punishment. In support of this interpretation we may adduce other facts from varieties of the puberty rites, in which the death of persons other than the youths plays the chief part. The festival of youths among the tribes of the south coast of New South Wales described by A. W. Howitt,[2] and the initiation ceremonies of the Nanga society, carefully reported by Lorimer Fison,[3] are other varieties of the initiation of youths. 'In New South Wales the drama of death and resurrection was presented to the novices in plastic form. After the boys have been raised to the dignity of manhood by having a tooth knocked out, the men dig a grave in their presence. There was some discussion as to the shape of the grave, but the man who was to be buried in it decided the question by declaring that he would be laid in it on his back at full length. . . . Six performers were clothed from head to foot so that not even a glimpse could be obtained of their faces. Four of them were tied together by a cord which was fastened to the back of their heads, and each of them carried two pieces of bark in his hands. The

---

[1] As to another motive, see below.
[2] See Frazer, *The Golden Bough: Balder the Beautiful*, vol. ii. p. 235.
[3] 'The Nanga or Sacred Stone Enclosure of Wainimala-Fiji', *Journal of the Anthropological Institute*, xiv. (1885) pp. 15-26.

other two walked free, but hobbled along bent double, and supporting their tottery steps on staves to mark the weight of years; for they played the part of two medicine-men of venerable age and great magical power. By this time the grave was ready, and the eagle-hawk man stretched himself in it at full length on a bed of leaves, his head resting on a rolled-up blanket, just as if he were a corpse. In his two hands, crossed on his chest, he held the stem of a young tree, which had been pulled up by the roots and now stood planted on his chest, so that the top of it rose several feet above the level of the ground. A light covering of dried sticks filled the grave, and dead leaves, tufts of grass, and small plants were artistically arranged over them so as to complete the illusion. All being now ready, the novices were led by their sisters' husbands to the grave and placed in a row beside it, while a singer, perched on the trunk of a fallen tree at the head of the grave, crooned a melancholy ditty, the song of Yibai. . . . Then to the slow, plaintive but well-marked air of the song the actors began to move forward, winding among the trees, logs, and rocks. On came the four disguised men, stepping in time to the music, swaying from side to side, and clashing their bark clappers together at every step, while beside them hobbled the two old men keeping a little aloof to mark their superior dignity. They represented a party of medicine-men, guided by two reverend seniors, who had come on pilgrimage to the grave of a brother medicine-man, him of the eagle-hawk totem, who lay buried here in the lonely valley. . . . When the little procession, chanting an invocation to Daramulun,[1] had defiled from among the rocks and trees into the open, it drew up on the side of the grave opposite to the novices, the two old men taking up a position in the rear of the dancers. For some time the dance and song went on till the tree that seemed to grow from the grave began to quiver. "Look there!" cried the sisters' husbands to the novices, pointing to the trembling leaves. As they looked, the tree

[1] A spirit similar to the *balum* of other tribes.

quivered more and more, then was violently agitated
and fell to the ground, while amid the excited dancing
of the dancers and the chanting of the tuneful choir the
supposed dead man spurned from him the superincum-
bent mass of sticks and leaves, and springing to his feet,
danced his magic dance in the grave itself, and exhibited
in his mouth the magic substances which he was supposed
to have received from Daramulun in person.'[1]

We see here that he who ostensibly dies and comes to
life again is a representative of the men and the father-
generation. The novices are, so to speak, passive spectators of the whole drama. But since the representation
takes place in the middle of the puberty celebrations it
must have some significance for the novices. It is obvious
that the drama is enacted in their presence in order to
stamp an impressive scene on their imagination in after
life. But what can be its meaning? Perhaps we shall
discover this if we consider the initiation of youths in
the Nanga society,[2] which in some respects is similar to
the above. Here also we find the motive of death and
resurrection as the central point of the rites. 'But on the
fifth and great day of the festival, when they again
entered the sacred ground [Nanga tambu-tambu], they
beheld a sight which froze their souls with horror.
Stretched on the ground was a row of dead, or seemingly
dead, and murdered men, their bodies cut open and
covered with blood, their entrails protruding. At the
further end sat the High Priest, regarding them with a
stony glare, and to reach him the trembling novices had
to crawl on hands and knees over the ghastly blood-
bedabbled corpses that lay between. Having done so
they drew up in a line before him. Suddenly he blurted
out a piercing yell, at which the counterfeit dead men
started to their feet and ran down to the river to cleanse
themselves from the blood and guts of pigs with which
they were beslobbered.'[3] These are initiated men who,
according to Fison, represent the deceased ancestors on

---

[1] Frazer, ibid. p. 235.   [2] Frazer, ibid. p. 245.
[3] It may be surmised that originally the men were actually dead.

this occasion. According to Fison the general purport of these initiation rites seems to be to present the young people to the ancestral spirits in their holy place, and to introduce them into the large community which comprises all adult men of the tribe whether alive or dead. We cannot, however, be contented with this explanation. It does not explain the ceremony whose purpose is to frighten the boys, nor does it explain the resurrection of the ostensibly dead men. The connection between this initiation rite and those in Papua, described above, is clear despite their differences. The conception of death and resurrection is the central point in the two rites. In the Nanga society the men whose simulated death fills the youths with terror represent their ancestors: in the first rites we described it is the novices themselves who are to be killed and devoured. We are perhaps correct in assuming that the differences between the two initiation ceremonies are only external ones, and that their latent, unconscious meaning is the same in both cases. In the latter the cruel picture of the realisation of the novices' hostile impulses against the fathers is represented to them in a plastic manner, so as to fill them with fear and feelings of remorse; in the former the novitiates are imbued with fear by the threat of the punishment of death for their unconscious wicked wishes against the fathers. Both rites, however, owe their origin to the fear of retaliation which dominates the father-generation in its relations to its growing sons.

Schurtz's[1] account tends to confirm this idea by expressly stating that one of the old men in the initiation celebrations of the Nanga society reproaches the novices with being guilty of the death of the men lying in the holy place.

Perhaps we can now comprehend the peculiar conduct of the primitive fathers: they project their own hostile feelings towards their sons on to the monster which devours the youths, and in so doing make it evident that an essential part of those feelings is derived from an

[1] *Altersklassen und Männerbünde*, S. 389.

unconscious fear of retaliation. Their apparently affectionate and protective actions merely serve to conceal their hostility towards their sons.

The men who have so long protected themselves from their growing sons by means of intimidation now have no objection to those sons having a glance behind the scenes, so to speak, since they have received them into their society. In central Australia the women and children are always thrown into a state of terror by the humming of the bull-roarer, which is ostensibly the voice of the mythical being called *Twanyirika*. In many tribes, after the circumcision, the men give the youths a bull-roarer and explain its secrets to them. This takes place, for instance, among the Arunta, as the missionary, Carl Strehlow,[1] reports in the following terms: 'We have always told you that it was *Twanyirika* who caused your pains. You must give up the belief in *Twanyirika* and believe that this, *i.e.* the bull-roarer, is *Twanyirika*. We have only told you, as children, and the women, about this bull-roarer (*nankara*), and have compared *Twanyirika* to it. As we have told you, so you must always tell the children about *Twanyirika*, so that it shall not be known that there is no *Twanyirika*; for if you did, we should all disappear from the earth, and it would be known everywhere that we were extinct. O circumcised one, like ourselves, you are never to spread the news so that it is told to the children. Keep the *Churinga* (bull-roarer) secret and tell the children of *Twanyirika*. Retain it for yourself; you are now a man like our ancestors. If the children learnt about it from you, you would become sick unto death. As we have lied so must you, and say there is undoubtedly a *Twanyirika*.' The men frankly confess that it was fear of the growing generation that compelled them to allow the demon to play their part. The admonition to follow their example, as well as the warning that the youths who had become men would be sick unto death and that the tribe would

[1] *Das soziale Leben der Aranda- und Loritjastämme*, Frankfort am Main, 1913, S. 25.

become extinct, is justified if its unconscious significance is recognised, *i.e.* if these protective measures were omitted the young men would abandon themselves to their rebellious feelings and kill the fathers; the tribe would really perish in the struggle between the two generations.

It might also be pointed out that in the sagas of the ancient Semitic peoples the same displacement on to gods who demand circumcision takes place, just as in primitive peoples. Among the Jews this command comes from Jahve; the patriarchs (Abraham and Joshua) carry it out as representatives of the father-generation. The Arunta of central Australia derive the institution of circumcision (and subincision) from god-like beings, just as in the Jewish myths. The operation was introduced by the Mangarkunjerkunja who formed human beings in the primeval period; when it fell into disuse, or was carried out badly, two hawk-men came from the north and performed the circumcision with a stone knife on the men dwelling in the south.[1]

Only two points need here be mentioned in order to strengthen the connection that we have assumed. The first refers to the right to carry weapons, which in certain tribes is only conferred after the celebration of puberty. Among the Kikuyu, Oigob, Wakwafi, etc., in east Africa the youths are not allowed iron weapons before their initiation, which takes place when they are sixteen or seventeen years of age; and so they make weapons of wood as playthings. They must not even possess an iron knife.[2] We see in this prohibition a measure instituted by the fathers to prevent the possibility of their sons carrying out, in the vigour and passion of adolescence, their unconscious wishes of hatred against their procreators.

The second factor, however, appears to contradict what has just been said. In many tribes one of the usual conditions for acceptance into the society of fighting-

---

[1] C. Strehlow, *ibid.* S. 10.
[2] Ploss, *Das Kind in Sitte und Brauch der Völker*, Bd. II., S. 173.

men is the fulfilment of the order to kill a human being.
Most of the tribes who carry out head-hunting on a
large scale demand that the youths bring home a hostile
skull before they are looked upon as mature—perhaps
like many German student societies that only look upon
their members as fully qualified after their first duel.[1]
For instance, among the Waniki in east Africa the
marriageable young men go into the forest and remain
there until they have succeeded in killing a human
being. If we recognise in the prohibition to carry weapons
a means of protection against the realisation of death
wishes in the youths, it is easy to deduce the latent
meaning of this last condition from the same hypotheses.
The cruel impulses of the young people are turned away
from their real object, the father, and are directed upon
a substitute object outside the tribal organisation. That
this measure is in the nature of a compromise is clear.
The cruel unconscious impulses that persist and are
active in the youths obtain a partial gratification, but
another object is substituted for the father.[2]

III

We have learnt that the cruel monster of the Australian
tribes ostensibly devours the youths. The cannibalistic
aspect of this act must also be fitted into our theory and
shown to substantiate it if our interpretation of the
unconscious processes is correct. Why does the father-
monster eat his sons at the time of puberty? If we trust
to our belief in the validity of the Law of Talion, then
the answer should be because the sons have killed and
eaten their father.

We shall get nearer to an explanation of this process
if we consider some strange details in the puberty rites

---

[1] Schurtz, *ibid.* S. 99. Compare with this the deeds of valour claimed by the
heroes of the sagas.

[2] The above psycho-analytical assumption naturally does not exclude the
idea that the fulfilment of the command, as Schurtz notes, is at the same time a
test of the courage and a manifest proof of the fact that the boys deserve acceptance as warriors. This purpose is, however, certainly a secondary one.

of the Australian tribes. The candidates for circumcision are subjected to great restrictions; these are not confined to the avoidance of definite animals that are forbidden the rest of the tribe.[1] 'For example, in some tribes of New South Wales youths at initiation were forbidden to eat eggs, fish, or any of the finer sorts of opossum or kangaroo. . . . "Indulgence in forbidden foods is supposed to be punished with sickness and cancerous sores." ' The novices' bill of fare is a very meagre one, but the older they become the more lax becomes the prohibition; there is a certain tragic irony in the fact that only the old men are free to eat anything. 'In the Encounter Bay tribe old men appropriated to themselves the roes of fishes, and it was said and believed that if women, young men, or children ate of that dainty they would grow prematurely old.' 'The Kulin of the Goulburn River in south-eastern Australia "believed that if the novice ate the spiny ant-eater or the black duck, he would be killed by the thunder".' An Arunta youth who tastes certain forbidden foods will bleed to death at his circumcision. In the Warramunga tribe the novices may not eat eagle-hawks; it is believed that these birds feed on the bodies of dead natives.

These prohibitions would seem to represent certain intensified totemistic restrictions that come into force at the period of puberty, but the reasons for this are unknown to us. A hygienic factor is certainly present in these prohibitions; we shall learn that during the period of initiation the youths must have no intercourse with women, and that above all heterosexual practices are made completely impossible to them. The instinctual renunciation contained in the abstention from many kinds of flesh is motivated in part by primitive hygienic ideas: a sexually stimulating effect is ascribed to the flesh of many animals and particularly to the roe of fish; the taking of these foods might lead the novices into sexual temptation. During this period they are placed

[1] J. G. Frazer, *Totemism and Exogamy*, London, 1910, vol. iv. p. 217.

H

on scanty and 'non-stimulating' fare in order to ensure
their sexual continence.

Certain religious and social reasons, besides this
practical therapy, have been a decisive factor in the
severity of the prohibitions. Their precise nature becomes clear if we consider the descriptions of certain
mystic meals of the novices. It is to be noted that in
many tribes certain kinds of flesh are proscribed before
initiation, but permitted after completion of the puberty
rites. For instance, the Anin Bush people forbid their
sons to partake of venison before they are grown up. In
the maturity ceremonies, however, they imitate the cry
of the rutting deer and from that time the prohibition
is removed.[1] It is evident here that a close relationship
exists between the prohibition and the worship of
certain animals.

This connection will become more obvious if we re-
count the sacramental meal of the Nanga society,[2]
which immediately followed the resurrection of the dead
men. 'Four old men of the highest order of initiates now
entered the Holy of Holies. The first bore a cooked yam
carefully wrapt up in leaves so that no part of it should
touch the hands of the bearer; the second carried a piece
of baked pork similarly enveloped; the third held a
drinking-cup full of water and wrapt round with native
cloth; and the fourth bore a napkin of the same stuff. The
first elder passed along the row of novices putting the
end of the yam into each of their mouths, and as he did
so each of them nibbled a morsel of the sacred food; the
second elder did the same with the hallowed pork; the
third elder followed with the holy water, with which
each novice merely wetted his lips; and the fourth elder
wiped all their mouths with his napkin.' Here the
religious factor is obviously the central point. We see in
this ceremonial a kind of communion of believers with
their god, 'an act of social fellowship between the deity
and his worshippers'.[3] We know to-day through the

---

[1] Ploss, *ibid*. S. 726.
[2] Frazer, *The Golden Bough: Balder the Beautiful*, vol. ii. p. 245.
[3] Robertson Smith, *The Religion of the Semites*, Second Edition, London, 1907.

investigations of Robertson Smith, Frazer and Freud,[1] the origin and development of these sacrificial meals. The act of sacrifice is derived from the totem meal of the primitive people, and this act is a memorial of that significant event in the history of mankind which led to the institution of religion, art and social organisation, namely, the killing and devouring of the father of the primitive horde.

In this solemn meal of which the youths of the Nanga society partake, we recognise an act of communion which unites the younger members of the tribe to the older ones, and all of them to their god. We find here a stage of development in which the sacrifice has not yet lost its relation to the totem meal. The holiness of the food[2] and the solemn partaking of it point to the fact that this food was originally taboo, prohibited. Thus is explained the apparent contradiction that exists between the prohibition of flesh food in the period of puberty, and the solemn breaking of the prohibition in the totem meal. The totem meal is not only an act of identification of the youth with the father, but also a repetition of that criminal deed, in that the flesh of the father is symbolically devoured. We have come to understand the temporary sharpening of the totemistic prohibitions in the period of puberty by analysing the breach of those prohibitions in the totem meal: it is to prevent the sons who have become marriageable from killing and devouring their fathers. On a closer consideration of these prohibitions, we also recognise that the savages in their rationalisations unconsciously give the reason for the prohibitions which they impose upon the youths. For instance, the belief that by partaking of the roe of fish the youths become prematurely old, can be translated from the unconscious into the language of consciousness as follows : the novices are not to devour the father in order to take his place and to assume the rights that are alone his.

---

[1] Freud, *ibid*.
[2] The food is so holy that it must not touch the hands of the oldest man.

The psycho-analytic recognition of the psychological mechanism of displacement enables us to recognise also why the food restrictions become less severe as the men grow older, until they finally cease. The temptation to kill and devour the father which originates unconsciously from the Oedipus complex is natural to the young and passionate man; the older he becomes, the stronger is his tendency to identify himself with his own father, and the weaker becomes the temptation.

IV

We have recognised the relationship that exists between the ostensible killing and the circumcision of the youths. The circumcision is carried out for the purpose of punishing and preventing incest; the killing for the punishment and prevention of parricide. We may be surprised to find that in the puberty rites the gates are once more closed to the two primitive wishes of childhood. Since both the renewed prohibitions happened at puberty we may conclude that the realisation of the wishes giving rise to them must be specially feared in this period of life; and with good reason. For such a fear is borne out by the alterations that take place in the instinctual life of the individual during puberty. His sexual development enters upon a new stage after it has passed through the latency period; the impulse which hitherto obtained its gratification auto-erotically now finds a sexual object. In this period 'the infantile tendencies existent in all persons and now increased by somatic pressure reappear, and among them, appears, naturally and chiefly, the sexual feeling of the child for its parents, already for the most part influenced by sexual attraction, the son towards the mother and the daughter towards the father'.[1] Feelings of jealousy, and consequently hatred, towards the parent of the same sex arise in conjunction with this new urge of the libido which is unconsciously directed towards the infantile object.

[1] Freud, *Drei Abhandlungen zur Sexualtheorie.*

Both unconscious urgings, the sexual and the aggressive, strive for motor discharge. This is opposed by inhibitions. Unconsciously circumcision and the various cruelties practised on the youths signify the suppression of their sexual and aggressive impulses; consciously primitive peoples regard these procedures as institutions for the actual promotion of those impulses. This phenomenon does not mystify the psycho-analyst, for he meets with an analogous process in the structure of the mental systems in delusional diseases and in the psycho-neuroses. In patients suffering from these disturbances, the conscious factor of their mental life demands coherence and intelligibility. When for any reason such a proper coherence cannot be supplied, their consciousness does not hesitate to establish an incorrect one. 'In every case we can show that a rearrangement of psychic material takes place towards the new aim, and this rearrangement is often fundamentally a very forcible one, provided it fits into the point of view of the system. The distinctive sign of system-formation lies in the fact that each of its results can be shown to have at least two motivations, one of which springs from the hypotheses of the system itself, and is, therefore, eventually delusional, and a hidden one which we have to recognise as the true and effective motivation.'[1] The character of a 'system' can now hardly be denied to the ostensible motivations of circumcision and ordeal among savages. Circumcision is supposed to increase the young men's capacity for procreation, and the cruelties they undergo to strengthen and test their warlike spirit. The rearrangement of the psychic material was so violent as to cause a complete reversal of the real motivation.[2]

---

[1] Freud, *Totem und Tabu*, S. 88.

[2] It is astonishing that none of the numerous anthropologists, ethno-psychologists, and students of religion, who have taken up the problem of circumcision, have recognised the hostile character of this operation. (Compare a review of the various ideas by James Hastings in the *Encyclopædia of Religion and Ethics*, Edinburgh, 1910.) Most students are satisfied with the hypotheses given by the savages. This kind of intellectual blindness can be understood if it is remembered that psychical prohibitions similar to those which keep the real motivation of circumcision from the consciousness of the primitive may operate in that of the modern professor. Compare, on the other hand, the older literature

We may easily recognise the motive underlying this rearrangement; it is the ambivalency of feelings and the relegation into the unconscious, caused by age-long repression, of cruel impulses. In the same way the systematic motivation of circumcision and tortures at puberty was concerned to stress the friendly and tender purpose of the two rites towards the young man. In the separating out of the ambivalent feelings, these latter impulses only could become conscious, while the hostile impulses gradually became more and more withdrawn from consciousness.

In this part of the puberty rites, therefore, we see a compromise expression of two intense impulses struggling with each other in the primitive fathers. This conflict leads to a diagonal effect like the resultant of the play of two component forces, namely, to a partial suppression and a partial fulfilment of the two wishes which dominate mental life in childhood. We may add that to some extent a free path is left to the impulses, but towards an object other than the original one.[1]

V

Up to the present the puberty rites have been relatively easy to understand, but we shall meet with much greater difficulties when we turn to the second act of the great drama of the initiation ceremonies. The whole rite defies comprehension if we follow the folk-psychologists, whose methods are very different from those of psycho-

---

regarding the meaning of the operation. Philo, 'De circumcisione', *Opera*, ed. Mangey, ii. 210, and Maimonides, *More Nebuchim*, xlix. 391, hold that the purpose of circumcision was to check sexual pleasure. H. J. F. Autenrieth, *Abhandlung über den Ursprung der Beschneidung*, Tübingen, 1829, Frederic Baumann, *Origine, signification et l'histoire de la castration, de l'eunuchisme et de la circoncision*, Palermo, 1883, Bruno Bauer and others among the old authors come near to the real state of affairs.

Baumann, for example, says, *la castration, l'eunuchisme et la circoncision ne sont que des modifications amoindries l'une de l'autre*. A deeper knowledge of the latent meaning of circumcision can certainly only be reached if the results of psycho-analytic research are taken into consideration.

1 Compare the obligation to kill a man (described in the second section of this essay) and the sexual licence after circumcision, which will be dealt with later.

analysis, in regarding the resurrection rite as a direct continuation of the death drama.

To this very complicated product of primitive mental life we will therefore apply the same heuristic method which has afforded us such valuable information in the analysis of the apparently foolish and senseless acts of neurotics.

We have seen that the ostensible killing of the youths is a punishment for their unconscious desire to murder. This punishment proceeded from the father-generation, and was the expression of hostile and revengeful wishes on the part of the grown men towards the youths. A certain connection does, indeed, exist between the death and resurrection rites, but we cannot possibly assume in the latter the operation of the same train of feelings which gave rise to the former cruel ceremonies. On the contrary, we shall find in the resurrection rites the expression of two contrary tendencies, namely, affectionate and hostile ones. We know that such apparently incompatible contrasts of feelings are found in the mind. But what is the significance of the fact that the primitive fathers first of all allow free play to their cruel feelings towards their sons, and then afterwards express their tender feelings towards them?

The psychology of the neuroses is instructive on this point in virtue of its theory of the 'two-period compulsive actions of neurotic patients'. In symptoms of this kind two strong contrary feelings are gratified singly, the one after the other. It frequently happens that hate is expressed in one compulsive action, though this is difficult to recognise, and love and tenderness in the other. The neurotic, like the fathers among the primitive people, attempts to establish a kind of logical connection between these two incompatible tendencies.

Let us now give a brief résumé of the death and resurrection rites. The primitive fathers signify to their sons by means of these rites that they are ready to receive them into the company of men, but only on one condition, namely, the youths must renounce their incestuous and hostile impulses. This is a *conditio sine qua non*, and the threat of death very clearly indicates what awaits the youths if they do not carry out this condition. It must not be overlooked that these rites represent an advanced stage in the development of 'savage' peoples. Originally the punishment of death was actually carried out by the infuriated fathers. A long path is traversed in the development of the peoples from the actual killing of the youths and the consequent strong remorse of the fathers up to the two-period rite-sequences which say in effect, 'We love you, but we must rid you of your infantilisms'.

One of the most essential characteristics in the resurrection rites as an expression of affectionate feelings is the tendency towards the identification of fathers and sons. In the festivals of the masks among savages, which, according to H. Schurtz,[1] are traceable to the initiation of boys, we often find that the ministrants of these initiations, priests, teachers and old men, wear wooden masks, and that the boys also are disguised by masks and in other ways. The fact that the totemistic cult appears so prominently in the initiation of boys is also due to this unconscious tendency to identification. The totem is nothing but a primitive symbol of the father.

As in the generation of fathers so in that of the sons, we find the same contrast of feelings is represented in the two-period rite of death and resurrection. The child Árpád, whom Ferenczi[2] analysed, recounted that he cut off the head of the hen who had bitten him. Later on the bloodthirsty little boy made attempts at an identification which he expressed by constantly crowing and cackling. This example is eminently suited to throw light upon our subject. In little Árpád tenderness as a reaction to hostile impulses was over-emphasised, and was manifested in his complete identification with the previously hated object. A similar over-compensation is shown in the death and resurrection rites of the primitive youths.

---

[1] *Ibid.* S. 105, 115.
[2] Compare the work quoted above.

In the ostensible killing of the novices we see a kind of retaliation punishment for their wicked and incestuous wishes, and in their reanimation their identification with the father-generation.

Some further examples from the initiation rites will help to make the mental processes that we have assumed appear more probable. John R. Jewitt[1] reports the following initiation rites among the Indians of Sondka Sound. The chief discharges his pistol close to his son's ear, and the son immediately falls down as though he were dead. The women utter terrible cries, tear out their hair and wail, thinking the youth is dead. Two men covered in a wolf's skin, and having a wolf's mask on their heads, approach on their hands and feet and carry the youth away. Jewitt saw the boy later wearing the wolf's mask. This tribe of Indians belong to the totem clan of the wolf. Frazer suspects there is some connection between the totem animal and the youth's transformation, though he does not know how to explain it; but it seems like a confirmation of our view as to the latent meaning of the death and resurrection rite. Frazer,[2] however, points out how characteristic of the primitive is the belief that mind and body can be transformed. A parallel may be drawn between the death and resurrection rites and the story of the Basque hunter, 'who affirmed that he had been killed by a bear, but that the bear had, after killing him, breathed its own soul into him, so that the bear's body was now dead, but he himself was a bear, being animated by the bear's soul'. The identification of the man with the totem plays the chief part in the totemistic system of belief; but we must not forget that the totem animal affords protection and assistance to its worshippers and believers by means of this identification.

'Among the Thompson Indians of British Columbia, warriors who had a knife, and arrow, or any other weapon for their personal totem or guardian spirit, enjoyed this

---

[1] *Narratives of the Adventures and Sufferings of John R. Jewitt*, Middleton, 1820, p. 119. [2] *Ibid.* p. 272.

signal advantage over their fellows: that they were for
all practical purposes invulnerable. If an arrow did hit
them, which seldom happened, they vomited the blood
up, and the hurt soon healed. Hence these arrow-proof
warriors rarely wore armour. . . . So convinced were the
Thompson Indians of the power of their personal totem
or guardian spirit to bring them back to life, that some
of them killed themselves in the sure hope that the
spirit would immediately raise them up from the dead.
Others, more prudently, experimented on their friends,
shooting them dead and then awaiting, more or less
cheerfully, their joyful resurrection.' [1] We find a transitional totemistic stage in the initiation rites of the
Carrier Indians. The youth to be initiated puts on a
bear's skin, goes into the forest and remains there three
or four nights. Each night some of his neighbours go in
search of the missing 'bear'. He answers with angry
growling their loud call of 'Come on, Bear!' Reference
may also be made to the sleeping on the graves of
ancestors, and to the dreams of the totem which the
young people are supposed to have at the time of
puberty. For example, a young man in Australia who
was a fisherman said that 'he was compelled to live for
two nights on the grave of one of his ancestors, who had
also been a fisherman of some note; by this means he
was supposed to inherit all the good qualities of his
predecessor'.[2] Among the Niska Indians of north-west
America the novice resorted to a grave, took out a
corpse, and lay with it all night wrapt in a blanket.[3] The
youths after their 'death' rise again, no longer as themselves, but as their ancestors with whom they have
become identified; they are now adult men and on an
equality with their ancestors. We see that an ambivalent feeling operates in this apparently complete
identification, since not only tender, but hostile impulses
find adequate expression by means of it. The youths, by

[1] Frazer, *ibid.* p. 275.
[2] Frazer, *Totemism and Exogamy*, vol. iv. p. 227.
[3] Frazer, *ibid.* p. 228.

their resurrection, now actually take the place of their father, as they wished to do through the unconsciously planned parricide. We may now regard the killing and reanimation of the novices as a primitive way of representing the play of forces which causes the young men to fluctuate between tender and hostile impulses towards the totem animal or father. We are reminded of little Hans's fear of being bitten by horses, which represented his unconscious wish that the horse might fall down and die, and of his imitation of the animal, *i.e.* his identification with the horse. We might point out further that a repetition of the primitive situation in which the totem system originated[1] takes place in the puberty rites; in both cases a reactive tenderness succeeds to the forcible acting out of hostility and hate, and finds expression in almost all religions in the process of identification with the totem.

Ethnologists who have made the puberty rites the subject of their investigations have failed to explain them up to the present, not only on account of their lack of psycho-analytic knowledge, but because they have allowed themselves to be deceived by the manifest content of the rites, and therefore only see a direct continuation of the death rites in the ceremony of resurrection.[2] By analysing the latent trains of thought we have found that that ceremony is not a continuation of the earlier psychic current which created the rite of killing, but a reaction to such an impulse. The killing of the youths is a rite representing the hostile desires of the young men which are rooted in the incest complex, whereas in the identificatory character of the resurrection rites we see the affectionate and homosexual reaction to those desires becoming manifest.

[1] Freud, *ibid.*

[2] It has to be constantly remembered that these rites, taken in their entirety, originate from different periods and different psychological situations, *i.e.* they are only to be conceived historically. The rites of killing are certainly more primitive than the others. In their genesis is clearly recognisable the share taken by the repression of hostile feelings, by psychic reaction-formation, and by the operation of mental displacement due to the growth of repression.

VI

We have already noted the connection between the pretended killing of the boys and their circumcision. Circumcision does not take the place of the human sacrifice; the killing and the circumcision are two separate acts that are only associated unconsciously. The first represents a punishment for the unconscious desire to murder the father, the second, a punishment for the incestuous wishes of the young men now at 'the most dangerous age'. Taking into consideration the intimate connection between these two fundamental factors, we shall not be surprised to find in the resurrection rites a reaction to the threat of castration which circumcision represents both genetically and symbolically. Such a reaction actually exists. We must recall those varieties of the initiation ceremonies in which it is believed that the spirits take away from the youths in the forest certain parts of their body and replace them by new ones, for example, better intestines, lungs, etc. Let us assume further that the boys, in virtue of their identification with the totem animal or spirits of the ancestors, are endowed with the power, capabilities and bodily characteristics of the totem. We shall then easily discover in this identification the factor which represents a refuge from the threat of castration—namely, the boy's wish-phantasy to exchange his own small penis for his father's big one. It is even possible that in the conscious minds of the people this wish-phantasy in a more or less distorted form is the sole meaning of circumcision. The primitive people give the same reason for it as anthropologists and ethnologists[1] do—that it is an operation for

[1] C. Strehlow may be mentioned as one of the few praiseworthy exceptions who did not share the idea prevalent among ethnologists as to the purpose of circumcision. (See *Die Arranda- und Loritjastämme*, S. 11.) This missionary states that by means of this painful operation 'the young people who were not accustomed to obedience were subjected to the authority of the older ones; they are to obey the old ones. . . . Viewed from this aspect the circumcision, so cruel in itself, has a salutary influence on the unrestrained children of nature who are unaccustomed to any order, since it checks the wildness and insubordination of the youth who is entering into years of discretion and makes him conscious of the authority of the old people whose will must now be obeyed. This reason

facilitating sexual intercourse and increasing its pleasures. The wish-phantasy of the primitive people to obtain by means of identification with the father his (or the totem's) bigger penis in the place of that which has been cut off, offers a precise ethno-psychological parallel to certain infantile reactions to the threat of castration. The operation and the substitution of an organ by spirits in the primitive initiation rites are closely analogous to the phantasy of little Hans from whom the plumber was supposed to have taken the 'buttocks' and the 'widdler' in order to give him two bigger replicas of those valuable parts of the body 'like his father's'. An unconscious connection between the two rites appears in the fact that the states of being dead and rising again represent symbolically the flaccidity and erection of the penis.[1]

Having thus recognised the mental forces which made the resurrection an expression of the tender reactions to unconscious death wishes, we can conclude that a part of ancestor worship has found its manifestation here. The analysis of the fear of retaliation clearly shows that the fathers of the youths had identified themselves with their own fathers, *i.e.* with the grandfathers of the novices. The resurrection, which represents this identification in

---

is given in the sagas of the two hawk men, Lakabara and Linjalenga, who instil into the men the strict observance of this custom, and in case of its non-observance pronounce the threat that a youth on whom they omitted to perform this ceremony would become an *erintja* who would kill and eat his own companions in the tribe.' This belief of the natives points very clearly in the direction of the definite intentions of murder on the part of the young people towards their fathers, as the result of incestuous impulses. The second reason given by Strehlow is somewhat similar: 'By means of circumcision a check has been put upon the sexual excesses of the adult youths. This operation is performed at a period during which the sexual impulse awakens in these youths, impulses which naturally appear in an unusually strong degree in the children of nature.'

Among these culturally very low tribes of Australian blacks the original motive of the cruel treatment of the youths stands out crudely in the behaviour of the father-generation. Strehlow reports of their initiation rites (S. 24): 'The chosen operator now appears; after running about wildly he comes to a standstill near to the men who are collected together, he grasps his beard with one of his hands, sticks it into his mouth and bites it as though he were very angry....' Then the men call out loudly, 'Furious, look! circumcise [the boy raised up] on high.' 'With rolling eyes as though 'furious' the man grasps a stone knife and performs the operation.

[1] More details on this point are given by Otto Rank, 'Die Matrone von Ephesus', *Der Kunstler*, 4. Aufl. For parallel phenomena in myths, see the same author's *Das Inzestmotiv in Dichtung und Sage*, Wien, 1912, S. 283.

plastic form, signifies not only the entrance of the youths into the present tribal community of men, but it makes them a link in the great chain which leads from the primitive ancestors to the youngest generation. All the customs of ancestor worship which Trilles cites in his book on the totemism of the Fan[1] and which Frobenius[2] characterises as 'manistic' come under this explanation. We shall return later to this very important aspect of the initiation of youths.

Another part of the puberty rites requires explanation, namely, the peculiar conduct of the youths after their return into their village and their amnesia. It will be necessary to call attention to a few characteristics of this part of the initiation of youths in order to explain this very strange custom. The youths behave as though they had forgotten their previous life. On the return of the initiated youths of the *ndembo* society, their parents, brothers and sisters call them by their names, but they give no expression of joy and not a muscle of their face moves. Whatever they may feel at this reunion, it has to be suppressed; it is supposed that they come from the land of spirits and can no longer recognise their relatives. The old men lead the boys to their parents, brothers and sisters, and to their dwellings. The novices pretend to be unable to speak their mother tongue, and to have forgotten how to eat. Everything has to be shown and explained to them, for example, the usual household utensils; their guides even place food in their mouths. Among the Indians of Virginia there exists an initiatory ceremony in the course of which the youths dwell in the forest for several months, and receive very little food except an infusion of intoxicating roots. It is supposed that these poor creatures have so much of this drink called 'wysoccan' that they lose their memory of all earlier events, impressions and knowledge. As soon as the medicine-man finds that they have had enough of this drink he brings them back to consciousness by re-

---

[1] P. H. Trilles, *Le Totemisme chez les Fans*, Münster i. W., 1912, p. 372.
[2] *Masken und Geheimbünde Afrikas*, S. 214.

ducing the quantity; and shortly afterwards takes them home. They are unable to speak, they understand nothing, and do not recognise their relatives, etc. They anxiously avoid showing any recollection of their earlier existence, for if they did they would have to go through' the whole cure again. The second course is so strict that a youth seldom escapes with his life. We have already quoted Schellong's report of the return of the youths in Kaiser Wilhelms Land. The youths come home with closed eyes and only open them after repeated commands from the chief.

Frazer believes that the temporary amnesia of the boys can be explained from the hypotheses of the rites;[1] it is 'a natural effect of the shock to the nervous system produced by resuscitation from the dead'. We also consider that the peculiar phenomena of the return have a definite connection with the rest of the characteristics of the puberty celebrations; but we have seen that numerous customs on these occasions have a meaning other than their outward appearance signifies, and that they contain a latent significance which is revealed by psycho-analysis besides the manifest content that is unintelligible and often absurd. Any explanation, therefore, would fail which regarded these phenomena as a single whole, and which sought to explain them, like the symptom structures of the obsessional neurosis, from a definite peculiarity of the illness. Illumination may come from two directions; by a comparison of these customs with other details of the initiation rites, i.e. through an extension of our knowledge in this sphere; and by the application of the psycho-analytic method and the information gained by it from similar symptoms in the neuroses.

VII

If we wish to understand the conduct of the youths in this situation our first question will be: What do the

[1] Frazer, ibid. p. 238.

candidates do during the time between their being
'killed' and their return home? We know already that
they are for the most part housed in their own huts in
the depth of the forest and watched over by old men,
and in all sorts of ways subjected to limitations and
privations. Perhaps the most important prohibition they
have to observe during this period is that which forbids
association with women. The circumcised youths among
the Amaxosa remain in their huts in isolation. If they
leave the huts for a short time they have to cover their
faces in case they should see girls and women, and in
particular, they must not see their own mothers.[1] Among
the Unmatjera tribe in central Australia the prohibition
goes so far that the circumcised youth 'must hide himself away in the bush, and if by any chance he should
see a lubra's (woman's) track he must be very careful to
jump over it. If his foot should touch it then the spirit of
the louse which lives in the lubra's hair would go on to
him, and his head would get full of lice. Not only this,
but if he were to touch the track he would be sure, sooner
or later, to follow up the lubra, who would ask him, "Why
do you come and try to catch me?" and she would go
back to the camp and tell her brother, who would come
and kill him.'[2] Among the tribes of the Meranke river,
the puberty candidates on their journeys by boat have
to lie down when a boat with women in it passes, so as

[1] Albert Schweiger, 'Der Ritus der Beschneidung unter den Amaxosa und
Ama-Fingo in der Kaffraria (Südafrika)', *Anthropos*, 1914, Hefte 1 und 2.
[2] Spencer and Gillen, *The Northern Tribes of Central Australia*, London,
1904, p. 342. I will give the explanation of another rite in this place. In the same
tribe each circumcised youth receives a fire stick from his mother, which he is
told he must on no account lose or let go out, else he and his mother will be
killed. This fire stick is a penis symbol, and the meaning of the threat associated
with it is quite clear. Spencer and Gillen in another work (*The Native of Central
Australia*, London, 1899, p. 322) state that the future mother-in-law presents
to the Arunta youth a fire stick, and tells him that he must always keep it for
his own fire, 'in other words, he should have no intercourse with women who
belong to other men'. At the circumcision in Lukuledi the blood of a cock is
smeared on a tree; the Hova in Madagascar cut a branch in the house of the
circumcised youth; the Karesau islanders in the puberty celebrations decorate
a tree which the old men first admire and then tear up, appropriating the
decorations. (Ploss-Renz, *Das Kind in Sitte und Brauch der Völker*, S. 180, 191,
200.) As in dreams, myths and jokes, trees, sticks, etc., here signify the male
genital. Concerning the archaic and primitive nature, as well as the psychogenesis of the symbols, compare Freud, *Die Traumdeutung*, 4. Aufl.

not to be seen.[1] Among the Arunta the youths, after
their circumcision, are given a number of moral precepts
and prohibitions regarding food, the non-observance of
which means death.[2] One of the most significant precepts
is as follows: 'You are not to go in the way of women'.
Among the Luritcha the chief utters the following exhortation to the young people after the subincision:[3]
'You are always to go about with young men; you are
not to go in the neighbourhood of women; you are not to
go after girls or married women; you are not to have any
intercourse at all with the "beautiful sex", *ngalumba*. If
we hear that you go after women and girls we shall cast
you into the fire.' It must be admitted that these ex-
hortations leave nothing to be desired as to stringency
and clearness. Among the Wa-yaos in Africa, according
to a report of Professor K. Weule,[4] no boy after his
initiation must sit on the same mat or the same bed as
his mother. Also among the Makua a circumcised youth
must never enter his mother's house without loudly
announcing his arrival. Among the Yaos the mentor
pronounces the following exhortation to his pupils;[5]
'You, my apprentice, are now circumcised. Your father
and your mother—honour them. Do not go into the
house unannounced, you might find them in tender em-
brace. You must have no fear before girls; sleep together;
bathe together; when you are ready she is to massage
you; when you are ready she is to greet you, *masakam;*
then you reply, *marhaba*. At the new moon take care,
you might easily become sick. Avoid cohabitation
during menstruation (you might die); menstruation is
dangerous (it brings many illnesses).' Let us consider
this exhortation for a moment. It contains a mixture of
prohibitions and commands, moral admonitions and
hygienic counsels. We may take two factors from them

---

[1] Ploss-Renz, *Das Kind in Sitte und Brauch der Völker*, Bd. ii. S. 764.
[2] Strehlow, *ibid*. S. 27.
[3] Strehlow, *ibid*. S. 58.
[4] Prof. Dr. Karl Weule, 'Mitteilungen aus den deutschen Schutzgebieten',
Ergänzungsheft, Nr. i., Berlin, 1908, S. 28.
[5] Prof. Dr. Karl Weule, *Negerleben in Ostáfrika*, Leipzig, 1908, S. 304.

to form as it were two nuclei. 1. The prohibition to witness parental coitus. 2. The formal permission, even the order to have sexual intercourse with girls. There is no doubt that these factors not only follow each other in time, but also stand in an intimate connection. The prohibition to disturb parental coitus, or to sit on the bed or mat with the mother is to prevent the realisation of incestuous wishes, while the allusion to coitus with girls suggests other channels for the libido which is so active at the time of puberty. In so far as object-choice always forms an unconscious partial realisation of infantile desires for incest, it can be said that this hint paralyses the effect of the first prohibition. This connection between the two again represents, therefore, one of those compromises which we have to conceive as a historical product. The primary one is certainly the incest prohibition, whose object is to guard against the threatening outbreak of incestuous desires at the time of puberty.

We can now understand the prohibition to go with women as a generalisation emanating from this more special incestuous avoidance. The prohibition originally had in view the young man's earliest object, his mother, and was extended from her to all women.[1] We have seen that after their period of seclusion the youths have access to women who are not relatives. Another characteristic of the puberty rites which has hitherto been obscure is now clear, namely, the sexual licence that takes place in many tribes after the period of the rites. It seems to run counter to the avoidance of women that in many tribes the puberty celebrations are accompanied by wild orgies. For instance, in the Amaxosa tribe it is customary for the circumcised youths to commit un-

---

[1] The missionary, S. Bamler, relates of the Tami, Papua, that the youths are told, 'Do not put yourselves under other people's roofs (*i.e.* do not seduce strange women)'. Immediately after this, however, the youths are instructed by their fathers how to win the favour of women belonging to other people when they are on their journeys, and the old men boast of their conquests. This contradiction is explicable if one remembers that the prohibition imposed upon the youths refers to the women of their own tribe, and above all to their mothers, while the women of other tribes are looked upon as fair game. (Richard Neuhauss, *Deutsch-Neu-Guinea*, Bd. iii. S. 504.)

restrained excesses with girls. Each youth may possess any mature girl. The final celebration of the circumcision among the Zulu Basutos and other people is also characterised by sexual excesses.[1] Some central Australian tribes believe that the youths must have sexual intercourse after their initiation or they will die. Immediately after the circumcision the young man in Serang, one of the Molucca Islands, must have intercourse with girls, no matter whom, 'in order that the wound may heal'.[2] This has to be continued until the wound has ceased to bleed. Chazac reports of the Kikuyu of West Africa that they believe that the first coitus which the newly circumcised youths perform leads to their death or that of their partner. They endeavour to avoid this gloomy fate by the following procedure. After the puberty rites have been carried out, fifteen to twenty men collect together, seize some old women in a lonely spot, misuse them sexually, and then kill them. The death of these old women frees the youths from all danger.[3] This and similar sexual freedoms Crawley[4] has explained as a kind of 'test' of the one sex on the other, 'as if the preparations necessitated putting it to the test; and thereby each sex is practically inoculated against the other by being "inoculated" with each other in view of the more permanent alliance of wedlock'.

We see here that the strictest sexual abstinence is followed by complete sexual freedom, the unchaining of instinctual life. This contradiction we can easily understand from our hypotheses. The prohibition against seeing women and having intercourse with them is intended to prevent the incestuous union of the maturing youth with his mother, and in the sexual freedom of those festivals we see a breaking through of this prohibition. Here (as in the previously mentioned case of the mentors' address to the initiated youths) sexual gratification is a substitute, as it were, a compensation

[1] Ploss-Renz, *ibid.* S. 181, 718.
[2] Crawley, *The Mystic Rose*, London, 1902.
[3] 'La Religion des Kikuyu', *Anthropos*, Bd. ii., 1910, p. 317.
[4] *Ibid.* p. 309.

for that unattainable incestuous act. The intimate connection, both in time and thought, of these events with
circumcision leads us to suppose that that operation in
some way receives its vindication from them; as though
to show that what on this one occasion breaks through
with elemental force would always have prevailed, but
for the introduction of castration (or its milder form,
circumcision), and would have endangered the social
organisation of the tribe or even destroyed it. The idea
that the young men in some tribes must have sexual
intercourse so that the wound of the penis can heal, if
translated from the language of the unconscious into
that of consciousness, with all the distortions of the
original meaning rectified, signifies that he has received
this wound because he desired sexual gratification too
impetuously and without considering any restrictions.
This gratification is now accorded him, but with inhibited enjoyment, and no longer with the original
object of his desires. We easily see how the shadow of
the incest prohibitions hovers over the removal of the
sexual barriers set up by the moral code of the tribe,
from the fact that the Kikuyu believe that either the
youth who performs his first coitus after initiation or
his partner must die.

Our insight into the genesis of neurotic symptoms enables us to understand why the youths have recourse to
old women. These old women are unconscious substitutes
for that forbidden love-object, the mother; and thus a
way has been found for the realisation of the unconscious tendency to incest in the very celebration which
has as its purpose the annulling of incestuous desires.
The choice of old women as love-objects after the circumcision is a 'return of the repressed from repression',
and the fact that these first loves die such an unnatural
death indicates that the union took place under the
gloomy auspices of a substitutive incestuous gratification.[1] The behaviour of the father-generation towards

[1] A. Le Roy, *La Religion des Primitives*, Paris, 1909, p. 236, is quite right in
referring to circumcision and *interdit levé*, and we believe with him that the

the sons is best explained by analogy with the 'two-period' actions. In the castration (circumcision) and in the sexual licence following it, their hostile and tender impulses are gratified in succession. But we must not overlook the fact that the after-effect of the hate-tendencies is still recognisable in the permission to have sexual intercourse after the operation. Is it not a brutal mockery that this licence should be granted the young men who have just been castrated (circumcised)? The woman is but a Greek gift after the deprivation or lowering of their potency. If we judge by the standard of the low-cultured Australians, it seems most likely that it was a long time after circumcision that permission to have sexual intercourse came to remit the general prohibition against it, and that this permission is proper to an advanced stage of development. Originally the prohibition was enforced in spite of the operation. For instance, in the 'good old times' among the Arunta and other tribes of central Australia, the young men had to wait for the women who had been promised them until the first grey hairs showed in their beards.

We have seen that the celebrations of puberty in the life of the primitive man signifies an alteration of his attitude towards women; he has now the right to sexual intercourse and marriage, and the half-childish free intercourse of the boy with his mother comes to an end. The permission for sexual intercourse is bought with the renunciation of the most beloved sexual object, the mother.

We also now understood why a kind of confession is insisted upon before or after circumcision in some tribes. For instance, among the Amaxosa, if a youth's wound has not healed in a definite time after circumcision, the men gather together and decide that he is to confess his sins before a great number of people, so that he can be healed. If he says that he is not prepared to do this, then

---

permis d'user is bought with the blood sacrifice of penis mutilation. However, we consider that the prohibition, the partial removal of which is associated with the puberty festivals, was at first strictly limited to the family, and the limit only later extended.

he is violently beaten until he yields and accuses himself
of his sins, whether he has really committed them or not.
The Amaxosa generally assume that a youth who had
carried out sexual intercourse with his blood relatives
could not be healed after circumcision within the fixed
time. *Bula*, meaning 'confess your incest', is said to the
circumcised youth.[1] The relationship of the unhealed
circumcision wound to incest is here clearly established
through this association.[2]

The period of segregation of the sexually mature
youths receives its importance from the circumstance
that during it instruction is given to the young people
concerning tribal traditions and rites. Livingstone saw
an old man among the Bechuanas who instructed the
youths during this period in dancing, politics and the
administration of their country.[3]

Among the Basutos the circumcised youths are instructed during the last month in the religious mysteries
of the tribe. In most of the Australian tribes the youths
are initiated into the totemistic cult. The most important result of the instruction received in the bush is the
changed attitude of the youths towards the men of the
tribe. A young Karesau islander is told that he must no
longer quarrel with men; and if his father reproves him,
he is not to make opposition.[4]

The circumcised youth of the Binbinga tribe was told
'that he must no longer speak to or even look at the
Tjuanaku men who are his tribal fathers-in-law'. He
was also told 'that he must not quarrel with older men'.[5]
In the Luritcha tribe the *tatata* (circumcised youth) is

---

[1] Albert Schweiger, *ibid*. S. 60. For similar confessions among the Basutos,
see Ploss-Renz, *ibid*. S. 760.

[2] As an illustration of the working of the psychic mechanism of displacement,
which tends to shift a fact out of its special situation, it may be mentioned that
the *ukubula* (the confessions of the Amaxosa youths) was in earlier times confined to the admission of having committed incest; to-day, however, it includes
the confession of any kind of immorality, and is even extended to 'impure'
dreams (A. Schweiger).

[3] Ploss-Renz, *ibid*. S. 759.

[4] See W. Schmidt's article, quoted earlier, as to the secret initiations of the
Karesau Islanders.

[5] Spencer and Gillen, *The Northern Tribes of Central Australia*, London,
1904, p. 367.

told impressively:[1] 'You are to be obedient as we are obedient. You are to conduct yourself as we do. We are very prone to anger; when a circumcised youth does not obey, then we kill him. If you wish to live, conduct yourself well, lest you be cast into the fire.'

We have seen that following on the observance of sexual abstinence, complete sexual licence is allowed in the puberty celebrations. A similar antinomy is also found in the present connection. The young people on whom are impressed the laws and moral code of the tribe which they have henceforth to observe, are given the opportunity to 'have their fling' once more.[2] In Australia the boys throw mud at everyone they meet. Among the Janude in the Cameroons the youths who are to be initiated destroy everything that falls into their hands; and in Darfur they steal fowls. The boys, who are often conducted by their teachers, make attacks by night on the villagers of their tribe and plunder them. The circumcised youths ravenously attack the paternal kraals, steal cattle, and misuse anyone who opposes them. The youths during this period have the right to steal and to carry out other acts of violence.[3]

We have called particular attention to the commands and prohibitions of this period which refer to the relationship of the young people to their fathers and all men of the tribe, that the boys are not to quarrel with the men, not to oppose their fathers or quarrel with them, not to look at their fathers-in-law, etc. We have to assume that strong impulses exist in the initiated youths with regard to these forbidden acts. We imagine that these prohibitions were originally intended for much more potent excesses of the young people, against which the men wished to protect themselves. The threats of the Australian fathers issued to their sons point clearly in this direction. Their teachings prove to be prohibitions, the aim of which is to check the hostile impulses of the

---

[1] Strehlow, *ibid*. S. 51.
[2] Schurtz, *ibid*. S. 107. See also Frobenius, *ibid*. S. 216.
[3] Murder is said to have been frequently committed during these excesses.

novices towards their fathers and the older generation.
At the same time, however, they aim at a kind of reconciliation between the older generation and those who
have just attained manhood. The latter, for example, by
learning the secrets of the totem receive the privileges of
manhood from the men's standpoint, *i.e.* the identification is completed. The unconscious desires that urge the
novices to deeds of violence and murder against their
fathers find outlet in their unrestrained conduct during
the period of seclusion: robbery, plundering and mal-
treating of others are substitutes for actions originally
intended against their own fathers.

In conclusion we might say that the most important
counsel given to the circumcised youths is of two kinds,
namely, to have no incestuous intercourse and to renounce hostile impulses towards the father. We have
now arrived at the chief principles of the totemistic
system of primitive people, namely, exogamy and the
preservation of the totem;[1] and we recognise how necessary it is to erect these barriers just at the period of
puberty, with its reanimation of incestuous and aggressive tendencies.

We have recognised that there is one indispensable
condition for reception into the community of the men
of the tribe; the putting away, or rather, the psychological mastering of the anti-social current of feelings
arising from the incest complex.[2] Freud has formulated
the social significance of the erection of the incest
barriers at the time of puberty as 'a cultural demand of
society, which has to guard against the absorption by
the family of interests needed for the establishment of
higher social units. Society, therefore, uses every means
to loosen in every individual, especially in the boy, the
family ties, which apply only in childhood.'

We seem now to have found a meaning in the peculiar
and apparently senseless puberty rites of savages. They
are for the purpose of erecting barriers against incest, to

---

[1] Freud, *Totem und Tabu.*
[2] Freud, *Drei Abhandlungen zur Sexualtheorie*, 3. Aufl., S. 86.

release the youth from the family tie and introduce him into the society of men, and at the same time, of transforming his unconscious impulses of hostility against his father into friendly ones. Schurtz has stated the social significance of the puberty rites in almost the same words as Freud has used to characterise the erection of the incest barriers in puberty.[1]

VIII

We may now, equipped with new knowledge, turn back to our task of explaining the peculiar conduct of the novices. What relationship exists between the instruction given to the youth during the period of seclusion, sexually matured and capable of bearing weapons as he is, and his amnesia on his return? There appears to be a very intimate one. The prohibitions that are impressed upon the novices respecting their future life, concern desires that belong to that part of their life which has now been forgotten. The amnesia on their return is, as it were, the test of the effectiveness of their instruction. In other words, the youths are to forget, or better, 'repress' what constituted hitherto their chief desire, namely, to put the father out of the way and take his place with the mother. One objection merits our attention here. The youths have apparently forgotten everything about their earlier life, not only their family relationships, for they have to be taught how to eat and drink, and through which door to enter the hut. This

---

[1] *Altersklassen und Männerbünde*, S. 99. 'The initiation of boys involves not only the acceptance into the society of the youths and warriors, but at the same time, a turning away from the conditions obtaining before. The young man is no longer subordinate to his mother, he no longer dwells in the hut of the women or helps in their domestic affairs; "he has become a new man". The words with which Wallenstein's sergeant addresses the recruits might, with some alterations, be used in the initiation of boys; he belongs henceforward to a group which is separated spatially from the family, and which, through its views and customs, is in more or less obvious opposition to it.' See S. 108 of Schurtz's work. If the prohibitions and commands in the puberty rites of the Australian blacks in particular are compared with the Jewish story of the Exodus, the Decalogue and the Book of the Covenant, a striking and hitherto unconsidered similarity becomes apparent. I hope to throw some light on the reasons for this in another work.

difficulty, however, is solved if we keep in view the
theories and observations of psycho-analysis. The unconscious, faced with denial, seeks substitutive objects
and gratifications; it knows how to find hidden relationships to desired objects and practices in the most everyday and most insignificant things. The fathers of the
circumcised youths in their obscure way are well aware
of the right method to adopt. In order that these two
primitive wishes may be banished from the mental life
of the young people, they have to forget all their previous
existence, their everyday life with which these wishes
are so intimately associated. Otherwise the mental
mechanism of displacement would still allow an emergency exit for the impulses barred by the censorship.

We certainly do not wish to assert that the result
answers to the intention of the older generation—that
the boys have really forgotten everything that has gone
before. Yet such an intention certainly exists, although
unconsciously, and it would not be very unlikely that
under the combined impressions of very great privations,
tortures and the mystical meeting with spirits, a repression of those tendencies should take place in the youths.
Their behaviour on returning would then be similar to
that of the neurotic patients out of whose memory a
whole year or even longer periods of their life may have
gone. Analysis shows that in these patients the repression originally concerned relatively few and typical
feelings and occurrences which to the patients were
incompatible with their ego feelings, and that the
amnesia of these painfully characterised things only
gradually extended to greater periods of time by way of
displacement.

We are now in a position to understand the rites concerning the return of the youths more especially. The
Australian men, in saying to the returned novices, 'This
is your father, this your mother', mean, 'This is the
father and the mother to whom you stand in an altered
relationship'. Among the Indian youths of Virginia the
intoxication that causes forgetfulness recalls the lethal

drink of the ancients and the expiatory customs of other primitive tribes.[1]

When the youths (according to Schellong's report) approach with their eyes closed, and only open them after repeated commands, we may see in this closing and 'opening of the lids two actions which resemble in character the sexual abstinence and licence of the initiations. An important rôle is assigned to the eye, among the bodily organs, in the finding and wooing of an object, because it is stimulated by beauty. Besides this erotogenic significance of the eyes, there are certainly other critical factors in this behaviour of the novices. It might be said that they are to awaken, as it were, from their blindness in order to look upon the world with other eyes. With what eyes? The answer is simple: With eyes like the eyes of those who bid them see; like the chief's, like their fathers' and adult brothers'. Here we again come upon the identification tendency. To our surprise, however, we note that what happens in reality is a repetition of the same processes; for the killing and resurrection in the rites signify the same thing as the simulated amnesia, blindness and changed 'attitude'— this word is here used dynamically—towards the world and towards the self, namely, repression and punishment of the infantile primitive wishes, and identification with the father or totem. Among the Arunta and Luritcha the circumcised youth speaks of various men who played a part during his circumcision, for example, the one who held the prepuce during the operation, or the one who had previously painted it, as 'those towards whom one has to observe silence'. He must not speak to them before the wound is healed, and has to pay them

[1] We must remember that when there is no effect the youths receive a stronger drink which leads them finally into the land of the Lethal River. What it is that they have to forget is easily recognisable if this rite is compared with the confession of the circumcised youths among the Basutos. Ch. Stech, *Daheim*, 1879, Heft 24, S. 384 reports that offences which come to light through the confessions of the novices are severely punished. A big pot full of magic medicine is handed round and each youth has to drink of it. The medicine will not harm anyone who has spoken the truth, but the liar is seized with terrible pains and finally dies.

tribute in the form of venison. This ceremonial silence signifies unconsciously being dead, just as in dreams, and is a self-punishment for the youth's murderous desires.

As psycho-analysts we ought not really to be astonished at this, because our experience teaches us that the unconscious delights in such repetitions in varied forms. We have recognised in the interpretation of dreams [1] how frequently—sometimes in a single night —the same wish will rebuild the dream façade in another form. In bringing the same wishes again and again to the scene of dreams, the unconscious behaves like the ancient languages (cf. the 'Song of Songs'). Both express the importance and significance of a process by means of repetition.

Comparison between this rite-sequence and dream life is not only justified by the dream-like and mysterious character of the initiations of puberty, but also by their dramatic and plastic form.[2] It follows from this quality that logical relationships, as in dreams, cannot be represented in the rites except plastically. It might be said that the amnesia of the youths is nothing but the plastic representation of the process of repression.

It may be pointed out that the parallel between amnesia, circumcision and blindness, which we previously supposed to exist, is verified by the forms through which unconscious mental life finds expression. The unconscious cannot get rid of something that is painful to the ego more radically than by forgetting. ('It is not to be thought of.') Blinding (to which the closed eyes refer) as an unconscious equivalent to castration is not only known from the Oedipus myth, but also from many analyses of dreams.[3]

It almost seems as though the primitive fathers are acting with refined hypocrisy in instructing their 're-

---

[1] See Freud, *Die Traumdeutung*, 4. Aufl., Wien und Leipzig, 1914, S. 248.
[2] Compare the suggestions on the origin of tragedy detailed below.
[3] Compare the contributions of O. Rank, M. Eder, R. Reitler and S. Ferenczi, 'Über Augenträume und Augensymbolik', *Internationaler Zeitschrift für ärztliche Psychoanalyse*, März 1913.

born' sons in daily affairs; for it is they themselves who
compel the youths to forget all these things.

A hitherto unconsidered part of the puberty rites receives new light from the knowledge we have now gained.
We have received the impression that acceptance into
the community of men has to be purchased by under-
going two things, castration (of which circumcision is
the equivalent) and tortures and cruelties of another
kind. We have found one relationship between these two
processes in their expiation of incestuous and hostile
impulses. A second one is shown by the following facts.
A firm comradeship exists between the youths who go
through the initiations of puberty together; and between
these boys and older men who have already been initiated, a ceremony of blood brotherhood takes place on
the occasion of the puberty rites.

IX

Among most of the Australian natives, youths who
are circumcised at the same time are considered to be
very closely united; the Narrinyeri give a special name
(*wirake*) to this relationship. Among the Herero these
young people are regarded as friends, and the festival of
circumcision is not held until there is a great number of
youths, and these then form a kind of age class. Among
the negroes youths who have been circumcised together
form a band under the leadership of the chief's son. The
Kaffirs often put off the circumcision of the youths for
several years until a chief's son has grown up, and then
those youths become subject to the young prince.[1] The
bond of friendship which unites such a group of youths
lasts for the whole of their life.

More important even than the formation of these
alliances are the ceremonies by which the older men of
the tribe—*i.e.* the father-generation—are bound to the
youths. Spencer and Gillen report the Kuntamara cere-

1 I take these accounts from Schurtz, *ibid*. S. 126.

mony in central Australia as follows:[1] 'On this particular occasion, after the performance of a sacred ceremony on the corroboree ground, all of the men gathered together in the bed of the creek, where the youths were camped, and performed the *kuntamara*. Each man took a sharp flake of stone or glass, and cut himself until the blood flowed freely, the newly initiated youths following their example. . . . When it was all over the Thakomara [circumcised] youth first of all touched the head of his actual father with a little of the blood from himself, and then, taking a green twig, stroked the head of a very old Thakomara man, who was his *Kankwia* or grandfather.' This ceremony is to unite the men initiated a long time ago with the youths who have just been subincised. It is said that this ceremony is to aid the healing of the youth, and to strengthen the bond among the men of the tribe. Among the Mara and Anula tribes, after circumcision some blood from the wound is allowed to drop on the man upon whom the youth lies during the operation; this is done in order to produce an especially intimate friendship. In the Urabunna tribe the foreskin and circumcision knife are handed to the elder brother of the youth, and he touches the stomach of each *nuthi* (the man who stands to the circumcised youth in the relationship of elder brother) with the foreskin.[2] Among the Karesau islanders, the youths and men collect together for the following ceremony which is described by W. Schmidt.[3] The men make a shallow hole of stones and pour fresh water into it. Then they pierce the penis and allow the blood to flow into the hole and mix with the water. The blood that collects on the edge of the hole and coagulates there is scraped off and thrown into the water, so that there are thick bits swimming about in it. Finally one of the men tastes it and all the boys have to drink of this precious fluid.

We see forms of blood brotherhood in all these rites.

[1] *The Northern Tribes of Central Australia*, p. 360.
[2] Compare with this ceremony the Exodus story where Jahve attacks Moses.
[3] Compare W. Schmidt's article in *Anthropos* above cited.

Blood bonds of this kind are very old and are disseminated over the whole world.[1] But what do they signify in this connection? Why do the older and already circumcised men draw blood from the penis?

We have to remember that it was these older men who, dominated by the unconscious fear of retaliation, instituted castration, *i.e.* circumcision and subincision, as an expiation for the unconscious incest impulse of the youths. In carrying out upon themselves a kind of castration by means of the incision they perform an act of community which can only spring from similar psychical processes. This act implies a confession of the wishes which they themselves once had, the same which have now forced them to take such cruel precautionary measures against the youths. It also implies an expiation of these infantile impulses, and a mental approximation to the young people. We now understand how this blood bond came about. As so often in life, judge and accused, executioner and criminal, are impelled by the same hidden tendencies. If castration is a hostile measure directed against the sexually mature youth, this blood ceremonial represents the expression of a homosexual feeling, an act of community in which is clearly shown the tender side of the father's ambivalency.

One detail of these rites is so interesting that I cannot refrain from quoting it. Little Boniface, a Karesau islander, who had been through the puberty celebrations, both actively and passively, and who gave the ethnologist, W. Schmidt, a detailed report of them, said that the men told the boys after the ceremony of incision of the penis and drinking the mixture of blood and water, that if they wished they could draw blood from the penis incision each day. It was not obligatory on the boys to do this, but if one of the boys fell ill it was believed to be due to his not having drawn blood. By carrying out this well-meant advice, the boys often became so weak that they could not work. One youth who did it daily could

[1] See Robertson Smith, *Lectures on the Religion of the Semites*, Second Edition, London, 1907.

go no farther in the forest because of weakness and could not be found by the men who sought him. A woman by chance met him crawling on the ground 'like a pig', as Boniface realistically expressed it, and she carried him home on her shoulders. The men, in whom obviously remorse and the tender part of the ambivalent complex of feelings now had the upper hand, told him not to do it any more. The little Karesau islander concluded his tale with the indignant remark, 'The men are fools; first they say, do it, and then, don't do it'. The little savage need not be ashamed of this dictum; well-known professors, who teach psychology in the German Universities, cannot relinquish the idea of expecting the logic of conscious thought from unconscious mental life, and of looking for purely intellectual processes where latent effects play the chief part.

We have seen that the father-generation identifies itself with the father totem, and we have found a basis of explanation in the feelings associated with the fear of retaliation. On the side of the father-generation, the puberty rites represent a number of hostile and homosexual acts, which in this form correspond to the paternal ambivalence towards the youths. Special attention must be called to the fact that both these characteristics are intimately bound up with each other, so that both sadistic and homosexual tendencies are evident in the frightful cruelties meted out to the youths, just as so often happens in neurotic symptoms, especially among obsessional cases.[1] The homosexual tendencies stand out more clearly in the ceremonies of acceptance into the community of men. In the Urabunna tribe 'at the camp the women sit a little distance behind the men, and the boy, approaching, walks past the men and sits down close to the women. Then two old men who are *kadnini* (grandfather) to the boy come up, take the string from his

---

[1] The tender motivation which is effective in this rite besides the unconscious and hostile one, is specially emphasised by the savages themselves, by their giving as the object of the tortures that the boys should become strong, brave and steadfast.

head and lead him by a roundabout way to the men's camp.'[1]

We recognise in all these rites the strong tendency to detach the youths from their mothers, to chain them more firmly to the community of men, and to seal more closely the union between father and son which has been loosened by the youth's unconscious striving towards incest. We have described the numerous rites in which the youth is devoured by the spirits or totem and born again. What does this absurd pretence signify—that the novice is born again from a totem that is certainly male? We might consider this feature as senseless and disregard it, but psycho-analysis warns us to pay attention and attach significance to ideas that are apparently quite nonsensical.

Let us put aside all logical considerations for the moment and place ourselves on a level with the primitive mind. If the youth was not born of his mother, but of the totem (or his father), what is the consequence of this unnatural birth? We remember that in the puberty rites rebirth is related to the detachment of the novices from their mothers, *i.e.* to the prevention of incest. Thus such a rebirth has therefore a negative character. Is not the peculiar practice of being born from the totem explicable from this? The men of the primitive people behave as though the birth of the boy out of his mother was because of the erotic attraction between him and her. A kernel of truth can indeed be found in this naïve idea; if another being had given birth to the boy then his first strong inclination would not be towards his mother. If it is desired to detach the sexually mature youth from the unconscious fixation of his libido then it is necessary to remove the basic cause of his desire for incest—he must be born again. This radical attempt to nullify a fact arises from the men's fear that the unconscious desire of their wives and sons for incest might be realised. That the youths have to be born again from the spirit or totem points to the wish of the men to transfer their sons' inclinations from the mother on to themselves; the homosexual current of feeling is manifested in these rites as also in other ways. This ceremony, therefore, like the resurrection rites, has a negative character; it serves to detach the youths from the women, and is designed to loosen their relation to the mother, a relation which derives its quality from an unconscious incestuous tendency. It nullifies the birth of the boy from the woman, and is thereby supposed to have removed the incestuous libido.[1]

We get quite another view of the meaning of these rites, if, like C. G. Jung,[2] we approach investigation of them with modern ideas which are quite foreign to the realistic and plastic thinking of primitive peoples, and imagine that there is a highly developed and sublimated symbolism in the ceremonies. We have noted that one of the most essential and unconscious motives of the puberty rites—the checking of incestuous tendencies—is dictated by the fear of retaliation. Jung, who has successfully suppressed his previous convictions, has recently stated that 'the fundamental basis of the desire of incest is concerned not with cohabitation, but with the peculiar idea of becoming a child again, of returning to the protection of the parents, of returning into the mother in order to be born again from her'. Jung [3] not only finds this self-rejuvenating idea in the mysteries of the ancients, but also in primitive peoples, in connection with whom he expressly refers to Frazer's investigations in *The Golden Bough*. According to him psycho-analysis has overcome the misunderstanding that this rebirth signifies a giving up of the usual sexual wishes, or their cessation, and in reality the problem

---

[1] Compare the last section of the preceding essay (on Couvade), regarding the motivation of the imitation of birth. Couvade, on the one hand, represents an anticipatory form of puberty rites (the fiction of being born from the man is a nullification of birth from the woman), on the other hand, a renewal of those rites as regards the man who has become a father, as though fatherhood called for expiation on account of having overstepped the prohibition. In Couvade, therefore, the double-headed fear of retaliation comes to expression.

[2] 'Wandlungen und Symbole der Libido', *Jahrbuch für psychoanalytische und psychopathologische Forschungen*, Bd. iv. 2 Hälfte, Wien und Leipzig, 1912.

[3] *Ibid.* S. 267.

concerns the sublimation of the infantile personality, that is, expressed mythologically, 'a sacrifice and a rebirth of the infantile hero'.

I cannot here attempt to show the incorrectness of Jung's ideas so far as they refer to the psychology of the neuroses, dreams, character formation, etc.,[1] but it must be expressly pointed out that there is nothing in the great number of facts of the puberty rites to indicate such a theological conception on the part of savages. Jung is unjust in calling Frazer as a witness, for this scholar, in discussing the meaning of the initiations, argues that the aim of the puberty rites is reincarnation and rebirth in a physical (not a moral) sense.

It does not accord very well with the 'sublimation of the infantile personality', the sacrifice and rebirth of the infantile hero, that sexual orgies, thieving, and deeds of violence regularly take place at the end of the initiations. In reality nothing is farther removed from the primitive world of thought than an 'anagogic' significance in the rites.[2] Moreover, it would be very difficult for Jung to explain how the being devoured and born again from the spirit or totem, *i.e.* from a male being, is intended to signify that the novice again gets into the body of the mother and is born again from her. Such a process as to rebirth from the mother would certainly have been represented much more realistically by a people at a primitive stage, as, for instance, is shown in the customs connected with adoption.[3] In Jung's inter-

[1] Compare the criticism of Jung's doctrines by Freud, Abraham, and Ferenczi.

[2] The expression 'anagogic' originates from Herbert Silberer, *Probleme der Mystik und ihrer Symbolik*, Wien und Leipzig, 1914, S. 138, and is meant to signify an occult religious idea in contrast to the psycho-analytical one, 'that which as it were leads us upwards to high ideals'. This author, like Jung, treats the rebirth theme one-sidedly as a womb-phantasy, and, as it seems to me, he unjustifiably gives too great significance to the interpretation called by him anagogic, S. 149.

[3] In ancient Greece if one who was said to be dead returned contrary to expectation, he was considered unclean until he had gone through a rebirth, *i.e.* he had to pass through the lap of a woman, be washed, wrapped in swaddling-clothes and suckled. Adoption in ancient Rome was concluded by imitation of the birth act, and without this ceremony adoption was invalid. The Graeco-Roman myth states that Hera when she adopted Heracles pressed the hero to her bosom and dropped him on the ground through her robes. Among the Circassians the woman offered her breast to the person she was adopting.

pretation the idea of rebirth, applied to the myth of the
hero, reads: 'One is a hero if she who bare him had
already once before been his mother, *i.e.* he is a hero
who is able to beget himself anew with his mother'. The
opposite to this is actually the case. The condition of
heroship seems rather to be that the birth of the hero
from the mother is nullified. One might mention, in
support of this, Mithra, who was cut out of a stone;
Dionysus-Zagreus, whom Semele previously bore and
whom Zeus sewed into his thigh and then rebore him;
the story of Macduff in Shakespeare's *Macbeth*; the
customs of the Anabaptists, etc. We have seen that in
the puberty rites the accounts of the savages have to be
taken seriously in spite of all apparent contradictions,
and that their latent meaning can be recognised through
psycho-analytical investigation. The rebirth is a detachment from the women, and is for the purpose of attract-
ing the young men more closely to male society. Its
most serious motive is to prevent the now unconscious
incest tendency. The idea of initiation and sublimation
found an entrance into the rites and mysteries at a very
late period, and forms only the upper layers of the
mental determining processes, as its secondary nature
would lead us to expect. Every psychological investigation that is not merely superficial is able to prove that
such an idea represents neither the essential nor the
effective thing. We have seen, for example, that it plays
no rôle at all in the puberty rites of the savages, which
illustrate these ceremonies at an early stage of their
development.

Having put this difficulty out of the way, we shall
attempt in the next section to sketch the significance of
the puberty rites in the social life of the primitive people.[1]

Among the Dyaks of Sarawak in Borneo, the adopting mother is seated on a
high seat in the presence of many guests, and makes the one to be adopted
crawl through her legs from behind. These examples are quoted from Ploss-
Renz, *ibid.* S. 675. A comparison of these rites with those of the 'rebirth' in the
puberty rites shows the differences between them.

[1] On the significance of the puberty rites compare Zeller, *Die Knabenweihen,*
Bern, 1923, and Géza Róheim, *Australian Totemism,* London, 1925, p. 42.

X

We have seen that in the puberty rites there are two generations, each hostile and tender at the same time in their feelings towards one another, and therefore each exhibiting an ambivalent attitude. The rites themselves form a most significant term to a period of life among primitive peoples; they denote the passing from one age-class to another. We have noted a certain contrast between the two age-classes, and also a contrast between the older men, *i.e.* the father-generation and the women of the tribe.

We now enter a sphere in which the ethnologist, Heinrich Schurtz, has made a detailed investigation in his valuable book.[1] I refer to the subject of the development and classification of social organisation in primitive society.[2]

In the first section, that on age-classes, he states[3] that 'the age-classes, which represent an attempt at division consciously carried out, though resting on a natural basis, stand in opposition to the most simple and natural unions which arise from blood relationship. A discussion as to whether grouping in accordance with blood relationship or with the period of life is the older and the more original would serve no real purpose. Both kinds of separation already exist in the fundamental and ever recurrent contrast between parents and children, and both develop side by side, not one after the other.' Schurtz has investigated the institutions of age-classes and men's societies in all primitive peoples and has shown how relics of these institutions exist among civilised peoples. At the same time he has made researches into the initiation of boys, club-like associations, and those secret societies which are spread among the

---

[1] *Altersklassen und Männerbünde.*

[2] I may remark here that I am acquainted with the arguments brought forward by Jonghe, Trilles, and other authors against Schurtz's book, but that in my opinion they do not affect the essential conclusions of his work.

[3] Schurtz, *ibid.* S. 82.

whole of the primitive peoples of the world. He shows very clearly that the men's societies are 'the real bearers of almost all higher development'.[1]

It is not my intention to give a résumé of the whole of Schurtz's work. I shall only quote some of his principal views, which have importance for our subject, without reproducing his detailed line of argument, fascinating as it often is.

Schurtz assumes, as the primary basis upon which the men's societies are founded, that a definite contrast exists between relationships among men, which depend on natural sympathy, and those of the man to his wife and children, a contrast which has far-reaching cultural consequences. He also shows how the men's societies have developed from the age-classes, and that they have their natural centre of gravity in the puberty rites. When we compare and connect the results of Schurtz's studies, which have been carried out in accordance with sociological and ethnological methods, with the results obtained by psycho-analysis, we arrive at the following conclusion. The important and widespread institution of age-classes is conditioned by the ambivalent attitude of feelings of the older generation towards the younger generation, *i.e.* of the fathers towards their sons, and *vice versa*. Clans, age-classes, and men's societies have not developed concurrently, as Schurtz believes, but successively as a result of a development of primitive society which has yet to be investigated. The original purpose of these institutions can be determined from the fact that they are recognisable as attempts to bridge

---

[1] Cf. S. 5 of the introduction to Schurtz's work. I would like to quote one sentence from another work of his, *Urgeschichte der Kultur*, Leipzig und Wien, 1900, S. 99, because it provides effective support of Freud's theory of the brother clan in the primitive horde, and still more, because the knowledge formulated in it has been arrived at by other paths and independently by psycho-analysis. 'In effect we have already seen that the relations of the sexes to each other are the indispensable pre-conditions of social life, but hardly the causes of its development; but that as in communities of animals and also of peoples of higher civilisation the mutual sympathy of the men, above all those of the same age, renders possible the closer social union of larger groups.' Richard Thurnwald declared the seat of the men's society, the men's club-house, to be the 'first tangible forms of state organisation' (*Zeitschrift für vergleichende Rechtswissenschaft*, Bd. xxv. Heft 2-3, 1911, S. 424).

over the gulf between fathers and sons produced by the Oedipus complex. The latent meaning of the men's societies is to prevent incest, to afford protection against the hostile impulses of the sons that arise from incestuous desires, and to establish a reconciliation between fathers and sons, deriving its support from unconscious homosexual tendencies. This view Schurtz, to some extent, corroborates when he says [1] that the age-classes 'are a primitive attempt, in its nature highly remarkable and in a certain degree successful, to reduce the dangers of sexual life to the uttermost, since each individual is assigned to the particular age-class to which he belongs'. We are mistaken if, like Schurtz, we expect to find such dangers in excessive sexual enjoyment, and we incline to the view that these dangers consist in the opposition between fathers and sons which originates in incestuous desires. Schurtz points out that germs of the secret societies that are spread throughout almost all primitive peoples can already be found in the details of the puberty rites. We have mentioned some of these factors in the first section, the orders, for example, that no woman is to witness these rites under pain of death, that no woman is to see the bull-roarer, for if she did, she would become sick and die, and that women and the uninitiated are to be kept in the belief that the novices are devoured by a wicked spirit or monster. If we add that the women are careful to avoid meeting their sons and brothers during the puberty rites, then we can say that a good part of the rites also concerns the intimidation of women and youths not yet initiated; an intimidation which is equivalent to the erection of an incest barrier.

Another significant part of the rites that we have already discovered is the gradual attraction of the young men to their own sex which is dictated by unconscious homosexual feelings. These two factors, suppression of the maternal tenderness for the son on the grounds of the unconscious fear of retaliation, and the growing attraction of the son to the side of the father, are mutually

[1] *Ibid.* S. 85.

complementary. It will not escape the psycho-analyst how much there is that is typical in this mental constellation. In every normal marriage we can observe these two unconscious tendencies operating in the father: the husband endeavours to lessen a part of his wife's affection towards her son on account of his unconscious recognition of its incestuous origin, and simultaneously he seeks unconsciously to attract to himself the affection of the growing youth in order to detach him, as it were, from his mother. It seems that in every satisfactory marriage, besides the man's libido for his wife, there exists also distrustful and hostile impulses towards her, as well as a homosexual tendency towards his son.[1]

If Schurtz's idea is correct that the age-classes, men's societies and secret societies arose from the initiation of boys, we have in the puberty rites institutions which give us an insight into the primitive forms of human society. We have to assume the existence of the same strong feelings in these forms of society. In the primitive horde, the first form of human society, a definite opposition between father and son must have prevailed, the same opposition which in the course of development found its expression in the age-classes and the initiation of boys. Have we now got a basis upon which we can reconstruct the course of events in the primal horde with some degree of probability?

XI

The typical psychical constellation we have described, and which stands out clearly in the puberty rites, reminds us of the processes in the primitive horde as Freud has pictured them.[2] The jealous and violent father of the

---

[1] In an article, 'Narzissmus und Vaterschaft', *Internationale Zeitschraft für Psychoanalyse*, Bd. iii., 1915, I have endeavoured to show that a part of this homosexual tendency referred originally to the man's own father and is only later transferred to his son.

[2] Freud, *Totem und Tabu*, S. 131.

primal horde who drives away the adolescent sons became himself the victim of his sons, who together accomplish what would have been beyond the power of
one individual, *i.e.* they kill and devour the hated and
admired man who was their superior rival in life and
love. But the plurality of brothers made it necessary to renounce the realisation of incestuous wishes,
and thus appeared a re-establishment of the incest
prohibition and the foundation of the brother clan.
Freud assumes[1] that in this way the brothers saved the
organisation 'which had made them strong and which,
possibly based on homosexual feelings and practices,
may have formed in them during the period of banishment'.

We can, perhaps, now supplement this latter remark.
The homosexual tendencies which formed the motive
for the foundation and preservation of the primitive
organisation are actually considerably strengthened by
the parricide. Each of the brothers seemed to the others
a kind of father, as each wished to be, and each one's
claim for the possession of the mother indicated this.
Tenderness towards the slain father was increased by
reaction, and showed itself after the deed in the form of
feelings of remorse and guilty conscience, later transferred from the original object to the companions in that
deed as substitutes (*imagines*, one might say) of the
murdered father.

A second source of the strengthening of the homosexual libido may also be suggested. We are accustomed
to represent the relation of the sexual impulse with the
sexual object as a very intimate one; but observations
of children and nervous patients show that originally
object-choice is independent of the sex of the object, and
that only by a process of limitation do distinct types of
object-choice develop. The psycho-analytical investigations of Freud, Sadger, etc., seem to show that every
human being unconsciously oscillates between heterosexual and homosexual object-choice. Among the 'acci-

[1] *Ibid.* S. 133.

dental' conditions influencing object-choice, privation
plays a very important part.[1]

If we take into consideration these results of psycho-
analytical investigation in examining the libidinal processes dominating the brother clan, we arrive at the following situation. There was an actual privation in the
realisation of the heterosexual libido, arising essentially
from the number of the brothers and their consequent
sexual rivalry. The emotions excited by the mother, who
was a common libido-object denied to all, had to find a
new object. It was transferred to a male object, and thus
the tender (homosexual) feelings of the brothers towards
each other found reinforcement from a second source.
I must now call attention to a second factor that originated in the ambivalence of feelings of the brothers, and
in the psychical after-effects of the parricide. Freud has
already alluded to it when he says that failure to carry
out the murder was far more favourable to a moral reaction than gratification of this wish.[2]

The erection of the incest barrier within the brother
clan is not only a prohibition that has proceeded from
the rivalry of the brothers; it belongs also to the mental
reaction from the parricide. The brothers had already
accomplished a partial turning away from their libido
object, the woman, through their strengthened homosexual tendencies. On the other hand—and this seems
to me important—impulses of hate based on ambivalency of feelings must have manifested themselves against
the woman on whose account the dreadful and fruitless
deed was carried out. The brothers' abnormal and intense libido that was turned upon the mother burst out
in full force in the crime of parricide, and thus attained
its maximum psychical effect. The hostile part of their
ambivalent attitude, powerfully increased by remorse
and guilty conscience, now made a way for itself. We have
seen how an unconscious hostile attitude towards the

[1] Compare Freud, *Drei Abhandlungen zur Sexualtheorie*, 3. Auflage, S. 11,
where he shows that these psychic processes play a regular part in the genesis
of inversion.
[2] Freud, *Totem und Tabu*, S. 173.

women is clearly expressed in the puberty rites of primitive peoples.

It seems credible that all these phenomena—exclusion of women, secret societies, etc.—showed unconscious reactions of hostility persisting towards the women, and at the same time a warning to the men amongst whom heterosexual craving causes discord.[1]

Freud says in his work that 'a process such as the removal of the primordial father by the union of the brothers must have left behind indelible traces in the history of mankind'. We now recognise as such traces the most important institutions of the primitive races— the men's societies, secret associations, and age-classes —as well as the whole system of puberty rites, and we may attempt an extension of the Freudian hypothesis concerning the events in the primitive horde, and suggest that what happened was this.

After all prohibitions of incest instituted by the brother clan had been overcome, *i.e.* new families were formed, fathers reappeared, and in a certain measure a re-establishment of the once primitive horde took place. The social changes the brother clan had achieved were not given up, however; rather were they strengthened in that the men now combined to secure themselves against a repetition of their deed on the part of their growing-up sons. This arrangement was bound to consolidate the close association of the men. The primitive fathers were compelled to re-erect the same prohibitions which they had once torn down—a process constantly recurring in the history of mankind.

We have to consider the puberty rites as the expression of these prohibitions, and at the same time as the plastic representation, for educative purposes, of the two fundamental taboos of totemism. We have shown that in these rites homosexual tendencies play a part

[1] Max Moskowski thinks that the origin of the male clubhouse is to be sought 'in certain strivings of the men to emancipate themselves from the tyranny of the women' (*Die Völkerstämme am Mamberamo, u.s.w.*, S. 339). Schurtz, who prefaces his book with a misogynistic theory, has expressed similar views.

that has hitherto been little considered. The effectiveness of these tendencies is permanently shown in
men's societies and secret societies, the object of which
was the preservation of the social organisation, as well
as the handing down of the laws of the race to the
ensuing generation. The mental factor which we have
recognised as the turning away of the brothers from the
female libido-object in the primitive horde is still manifested in the intimidation and exclusion of women. Not
only is the organisation of the tribe intimately connected with the institution of the initiation of men;
acceptance into the society of men is the kernel of the
formation of the State, and is of fundamental significance
for the beginnings of the primitive morals. The principles
that were impressed on the youths on their initiation
are, according to Howitt and Strehlow, essentially the
same as those which the ancients have left behind as the
foundation of ethics. When the Australian natives affirm
that the *mura-muras* (mythical beings) taught their
fathers how to make weapons and tools, and initiated
them in the ceremonies, we have no hesitation in recognising the primordial fathers in these god-like beings.[1]
The foundation of morality without the active co-
operation of the father-generation is unthinkable.

XII

Before concluding this study, which has led from an
analysis of puberty rites among savages to a hypothesis
as to the beginnings of human society, we must touch
upon the general historical significance of those rites as
they are revealed to us by psycho-analytical investigation. I refer to the growth of religion. The bond which
the primordial fathers of the Jews concluded with their
god is represented in a later part of this work as a
glorified and emended account of an initiation ceremony.
The connection of the *B'rith* with circumcision is just as

[1] Among the Kurnai the name of this mythical being is the same as that of
the father (Howitt, *The Native Tribes of South-East Africa*, p. 475).

little an accident as the covenant meal in which the worshippers of Jahve identified themselves with him; and the giving of the law—*B'rith* can also signify law— which stands in such an intimate relationship to the concluding of the covenant (Sinai) should be set side by side with the procedures of the puberty rites. The promise of numerous descendants corresponds to the primitive permission for sexual intercourse, just as the Promised Land symbolises sexual possession of the beloved mother. The threats which Jahve issues in the case of a breach of the covenant are essentially the same as those which the Australian natives make to the youths on attaining manhood. Psychological analysis of the puberty rites enables us to recognise in the Sinai passage a historical counterpart to the important present-day rites of initiation that take place in the bush. Repression victorious, but ever exposed to constant temptations from impulses that have been rejected by the moral idea of the tribe, has continued from the old dispensation into the new. The strengthening of the moral urge through the ages has not been able to prevent reactions and the temporary breaking through of forbidden tendencies. Other factors must have come in to strengthen the son in his ever-persisting defiance; for the father-gods become replaced by son-gods. Christianity is culturally the most significant instance of such a radical replacement. Freud has indicated the transformations in the mental life of mankind which brought about the replacement of father-religions by son-religions. The part played by an oppressive sense of guilt as well as by defiance in the son is clearly recognisable in these later forms of religion.

The son-gods among the ancients have certain typical traits in common respecting their nature and the fate they suffer. They are, like Tammuz, Adonis, Attis and Osiris, lovers of the great mother-deities of the west; they die an unnatural death and thus do penance for the incest they have committed. Adonis, the beloved of Aphrodite, is killed by a wild boar; Attis, the lover of the

mother of the gods, Cybele, castrates himself; Osiris, the
favourite of Isis, is slain by Typhon; and Dionysus-
Zagreus is dismembered by the Titans. The violent
deaths of these youthful gods is by no means the end of
their vicissitudes; they are bemoaned and mourned for
by their lovers and mothers—for instance, Osiris is
bewailed by Isis, etc., and their resurrection is hailed
and celebrated with loud jubilation.[1]

Death, mourning by the mother and other women,
and resurrection of the killed god have been taken over
into the ritual of the world religion of Christianity. Freud
has shown us that the self-sacrifice of Christ was the
expiation for an attempted murder—a parricide, since
original sin was a sin against God the Father.

The sacrificial death of the Son of God is an attempt
at expiation; it has the character of a compromise, for it
ensures the attainment of the son's most urgent wish,
namely, his own enthronement at the side of his father.

Death, mourning by the mother and resurrection, as
well the ascension of Christ, offer us, as do the corresponding myths of the Attis, Adonis and Osiris cults, the
best analogies to the devouring of the candidates at
puberty by the *balum* monster, the lament of the mothers
from whom their sons are torn, the resurrection of those
sons, and their acceptance at the side of the fathers.[2]

The myth of the killing of Adonis by a boar presents a
significant parallel to the killing by the totem animal,
the father, in the puberty rites. Other features can
similarly be recognised as common to the myth of the

---

[1] Respecting these gods who die and come to life again, compare J. G. Frazer,
The Golden Bough: Adonis, Attis, Osiris, Third Edition, London, 1914. Compare
also W. Wundt, *Völkerpsychologie*, Leipzig, 1909, Bd. ii. S. 713.

[2] How realistically the myth of Christ was originally conceived by the community is shown in the report of C. Wachsmuth, *Das alte Griechenland im
neuen*, S. 26, on the Easter celebrations in the Greek Church. According to the
report the community solemnly buries its Christ as if he had really just died.
Finally the wax image is deposited again in the Church and the same comfort-
less bewailing hymns are again heard. This mourning is continued with strict
fasting until Saturday midnight. At the stroke of twelve the bishop appears
and announces the glad tidings that 'Christ is risen', to which the multitude
answers, 'Yes, he is risen indeed', and immediately the whole town resounds
with jubilation expressed by a yelling noise and the letting off of fireworks of
all kinds. (Quoted from Hugo Hepding, *Attis: seine Mythen und sein Kult*,
Giessen, 1903, S. 167.)

son-religions and the ceremonies of puberty. The self-castration of Attis, the dismemberment of Dionysus-Zagreus[1] by the Titans, Osiris slain by Typhon, as well as Christ's wound[2] approximate to the mutilation of the penis in the initiation of boys among the primitive peoples. The complete turning away from women, as found in the puberty rites, is expressed in the words, 'Woman, what have I to do with thee?'[3]

Looked at in this way the myth of the suffering, death and resurrection of the Saviour, *i.e.* the account of the passion (*Passio domini*), can be denoted as a complex of the puberty rites.

A characteristic common to all the son-gods is worth notice; they are redeemers and bringers of culture. For instance, Dionysus is called ἐλευθερεύς or λυαῖος and Christ of Nazareth, the Saviour. The justification of this title is quite clear since they are deities who took upon themselves the primordial guilt, the hereditary sin, and thereby freed humanity from the burden of its guilty conscience. Dionysus, like Jesus Christ, shed his blood for the salvation of the world.

It can therefore happen that the death and resurrection of these deities appear to believers as the glad tidings (*Evangelium*), and as the symbol of liberation from their old guilt.[4] The rites of religious initiations

[1] Concerning the motive of dismemberment as a modification of emasculation, compare Otto Rank, *Das Inzestmotiv in Dichtung und Sage*, Wien und Leipzig, 1912, S. 309.

[2] The representation of wounds as castration equivalents in neurotics has repeatedly been demonstrated in Freud's analyses.

[3] It is characteristic that the lower estimation of the woman is brought into connection with original sin, so that the love for the woman (the mother) becomes clear as the strongest motive of the 'fall' in this distorted form. 'And Adam was not deceived, but the woman being deceived was in the transgression' (1 Tim. ii. 14; compare *Jesus Sirach*, 25, 32; 2 Cor. xi.). Tertullian (*De cultu feminarum* i. 18) designates the woman as 'the devil's door', and accuses her of having so easily deceived God's image, man, 'because your guilt brought death into the world, God's son had to die' (*De virginibus velandis*, v. 7-8). On the other hand the incestuous tendency is reanimated in the tale of Mary and shows the return of the repressed, just as the reception of Christ at the right hand of the Father-God signifies the realisation of the ambitious wishes of the son. Concerning the development of these tendencies see my books, *Der eigene und der fremde Gott*, 1915, and *Dogma und Zwangsidee*, 1927.

[4] In the Adonis celebration in Antioch, the capital of Syria, the death and resurrection of Adonis was portrayed in dramatic form. His corpse, represented by an image, was buried amid wild wailing songs of the women, and on the next

observed by the worshippers of Mithra, Attis, Adonis and Christ, by means of which the mystics are identified with their god, present the same death and resurrection forms as the puberty rites. We may trace this persistent element of identification from the ceremonies of the savages to the analogous legends of the son-deities and the religious initiations of Christianity.

The solemn identification of the novices in Viti Levu by means of a sacramental meal finds its parallel in the holy totem meal of religious initiation. The old totem meal could now be renewed, only the flesh and blood of the father was replaced by that of the son. In the orgiastic celebration of Dionysus-Sabazius, the mad Bacchantes fell upon the bull destined for sacrifice, which represented the god himself, tore it, and devoured the raw flesh. The formula of the novices in the Attis mysteries runs: 'I have eaten from the tympanon, I have drunk from the bowl, I have become a mystic of Attis'. The Christian Fathers regarded the meal of bread and wine at which the worshippers of Mithras, like the Christians at the Communion, eat the body of the god,

---

day the resurrected god was greeted. 'The master lives, Adonis has come to life again', was shouted in the streets of the town. The priest anointed with oil those who had previously been lamenting, saying the following words:

'Courage, pious ones! As God is saved
So shall we receive salvation from our troubles.'

In the Eleusinian mysteries, too, the initiated person carried away with him the certainty of his own immortality. The prohibition against informing any-one of the real content of the initiation of the boys recalls the command of silence imposed on novices in the ancient mysteries, the *fides silentii*, which persisted as an occult discipline in keeping secret the baptismal and last-supper celebrations of the Church. As in the puberty feasts so here it is the women who appear to have most cause for grief—here as well as in them the death of the son guilty of incestuous love is represented. ('Un trait commun du culte de ces héros, c'est que les femmes célèbrent l'anniversaire de leur mort par des lamentations.' Salomon Reinach, *Cultes, mythes et religions*, Paris, 1905, Bd. ii. p. 88.)

The identification with the god in the Attis cult, etc., is reflected in the many self-mutilations of the priests and novices which were carried out at the great Attis feast on the twenty-fourth of March as a sign of grief, (Compare the penis-mutilations of the initiated boys amongst the savages.) The boundless joy, the transgression of all usually respected barriers during the celebration of the resurrection of the god (for instance, in the Hilaria in Rome), recalls the sexual excesses of the feasts of circumcision. The psychogenesis of feasts, as brought out by Freud, shows that such excess is necessarily bound up with them. In this case the rejoicings were at first at the demise of the father, or god, in the unconscious, and were only later displaced on to the resurrection of his murderer, the son-god.

as a devilish imitation of the Holy Eucharist. As the
Bacchantes became ἔνθεοι with Diónysus by their totem
meal, so the partakers of the Christian Supper were
originally in a physical sense full of God (ἐν Χριστῷ).
The science of comparative religion teaches us that in
the Communion the ancient idea of union by means of
eating and drinking still exists.[1] Students of religion
long ago revealed the connection of the ritual of baptism
with the primitive initiation ceremonies.

Freud has shown that the sacramental meal expresses
not only the son's affection for his father, through identification, but also his feelings of defiance. The Christian
Communion, itself fundamentally a new and later setting
aside of the father, is therefore a repetition of that
primordial crime, the killing and devouring of the father.[2]

The puberty rites, with their intensely dramatic character, also remind us of another situation which is apparently far removed from them. It is the situation in
the older Greek tragedy.[3] We know that the content of
the Greek tragedy in the first period was the sufferings
of the divine ram, Dionysus, and the bemoanings of the
rams which formed his following. We know already in
what the tragic guilt of Dionysus, like that of all the
heroes of the Greek tragedies, consists—in rebellion
against a divine authority, *i.e.* in 'hybris'. The heroes of
the great dramas atone for this crime by the most excessive pains and suffering. The fate of the divine ram,
Dionysus, has already reminded us of the multiform

---

[1] See W. Heitmüller, *Taufe und Abendmahle bei Paulus*, Göttingen, 1903.
The process of the deification, *i.e.* of the identification of the believers with
Jesus Christ, was recognised as a product of the Christian religion. 'When it
speaks of *adoptio* by God, of *participatio dei*, etc., it also always means a spiritual
union; this, however, derives its basis and effectiveness from a sacramental,
physical re-creation: *non ab initio dii facti sumus, sed primo quidem homines
tunc demum dii'* (Adolf Harnack, *Die Mission und Ausbreitung des Christentums*,
2. Aufl., Leipzig, 1906, Bd. i. S. 205). The fasting prior to Communion also
recalls the renunciation of certain foods during the time of seclusion of the
circumcised youths in the bush.

[2] Freud, *Totem und Tabu*, S. 143.

[3] I here follow Freud's suggestions (*Totem und Tabu*, S. 143). A short and
clear account of the beginnings of the Greek drama with mention of its relation
to the initiation ot youths among savage peoples is given by Jane Harrison,
Ancient Art and Ritual, London and New York, 1914. See also Alfred Winter-
stein, 'Der Ursprung der Tragödie', *Imago-Bücher*, viii.

cruelties suffered by the puberty candidates. The crime of this son of god coincides with that for which the novices had to atone so strictly in the initiation of boys, *i.e.* with the attempt to put the father out of the way.[1] But the form of the Dionysian ceremonies as well can be derived from the puberty ceremonies of savages. The masks in the initiation of boys served the same purpose as the disguises of the actors in the Greek dramas, namely, a magic identification with the father (primitive god) whose removal was originally desired and accomplished.[2]

Students of folk-psychology tell us that the masks of the savages serve magic purposes; they are to transform the brethren of the tribe into demonic beings or totem animals. They are the primitive means of identification with the father.[3]

What rôle devolves upon the chorus of the original tragedy? Freud has shown that it represents the brothers of that great primordial tragedy, who bemoan, as it were, with refined hypocrisy, the hero who has taken upon himself the guilt common to all of them. The first hero of the tragedy was the murdered primordial father, who, in the drama, as in religion, was replaced by the son. The state of affairs was distorted, the brothers, *i.e.* the chorus, were no longer guilty of the murder of the hero, he himself had to bear the burden of a tragic guilt. In the late substitution of the father-hero by the son, the members of the chorus, who gradually took over the rôle of the warning and admonishing generation of fathers, behave in a peculiarly hypocritical manner; they are like the members of an Australian tribe who

---

[1] As stated by Nomus, Dionysus ascends the throne of Zeus when a child and imitates the god-father. The cruel death of Dionysus-Zagreus points to the fact that in the original version he killed his father Zeus and assumed his place.

[2] 'Nous savons en effet que Dionysus était appelé fils de taureau' (Reinach, *ibid.* p. 94).

[3] 'The masks mostly represent the spirits of those who have died or also totem animals' (H. Schurtz, *Urgeschichte der Kultur*, Leipzig und Wien, 1900). Compare the manistic theory of the masks by L. Frobenius, *ibid.* S. 214. The religious or magic genesis of the drama is treated by Frazer, *The Golden Bough*: *The Scapegoat*, London, 1913, p. 384, with reference to the mask-dances of the savages.

treat their initiation candidates so cruelly, and yet pretend that they want to protect them against the attacks of the *balum* monster.

We have recognised that the content of the oldest tragedy was the son's rebellion against his father's authority, and his painful atonement for this deed. This rebellion, however, had its essential and unconscious motive in the incestuous desires of the representatives of the son-type. It is, therefore, not to be wondered at that in the Middle Ages, the theatre adopted this tradition, which held its ground on account of the strong feelings which all mankind has experienced. The dramatised passion of the Saviour became the successor to the story of the suffering of Dionysus (Διονύσου πάθη). The crime that weighed down humanity and that underlay this as well as the other myths ensured the success of the Passion-play.[1]

The powerful motive which struggles for expression in the Dionysian celebrations and in the earliest Greek tragedy, namely, the rebellion, based on incestuous impulses, of the son against the father and its tragic expiation, has remained the real theme of all dramatists from the *Oedipus* of Sophocles up to the present day.[2]

---

[1] In a deeper sense than shown by Karl Kautsy, *Der Ursprung des Christentums*, Stuttgart, 1908, we may denote Christ as a 'rebel', since he rebelled against the father-god. See my book, *Dogma und Zwangsidee*, Wien, 1927.

[2] Compare Otto Rank, *Das Inzestmotiv in Dichtung und Sage*, Wien und Leipzig, 1912.

It may be pertinent to observe in connection with the original and afterwards unconsciously retained content of the drama, that actors and counteractors are indispensable for it; for the essence of tragedy is to be found in an originally external combat, the rebellion of the son against the father. Only later did this combat give way to internal conflicts.

In the scenes of boundless joy over the resurrection of Dionysus (originally over the murder of the father) are contained the germs of ancient comedy. ('Le double caractère des fêtes bacchiques, qui contient en germe la tragédie et la comédie, n'a échappé ni aux anciens ni aux modernes.' S. Reinach, *ibid.* p. 90). We may recall that in this later form of jubilation the after-effect of that more original reaction of feeling to the parricide is clearly recognisable: if Dionysus comes to life again his crime, parricide, has not been seriously expiated; the authority is not sufficiently powerful to revenge adequately the crime committed against it. How many subsequent comedies will be devoted to the derision and outwitting of authority? A more particular investigation of the origin of the comedy should take into consideration the masked dances of the savages, in which

This derivation of the drama perhaps enables us to approach the solution of one of the most important æsthetic problems, namely, that of the mental effect of tragedy. In Aristotle's much-discussed view, tragedy is the imitation of an occurrence which stimulates fear and pity and, at the same time, brings about a catharsis of these affects. Might we not try to apply this definition to the Greek tragedy of the early period?

The material upon which this tragedy was originally built was, as we know, a single theme, the suffering and death of Dionysus, *i.e.* of the son-deity, who wished to remove his father, and suffered death in consequence. We now understand why the spectators of this tragedy are seized with fear and pity; it was the same crime which they themselves had once unconsciously wished to commit in their early childhood. The unconscious sense of guilt arising from it continues to operate and causes a dread of stern retribution. The original significance of the catharsis is also evident. Dionysus redeems guilt-laden humanity (*i.e.* the spectators) by the blood he sheds at his death. He takes upon himself the whole guilt; he is the really guilt-laden one; the spectators have no longer to fear punishment. But the feeling of pity also finds its 'abreaction' in the spectators. The spectators have 'empathised' with the suffering hero, *i.e.* have identified themselves with him. In his punishment they complete the self-punishment of their own unconscious, hostile and incestuous tendencies, and condemn those wishes. Besides this effect, which explains the deep 'empathy', in fact, identification of the spectators with the hero, as well as their psychical differentiation from him, the catharsis has to be regarded as a means of objectivisation. In the same way as the patient does in the course of his psycho-analysis, the spectators see what they unconsciously wished and feared, live again through what once impelled and moved them, and still does; and they allow their moral consciousness to speak, where before

they identified themselves with the father, as well as the ancient feasts of the Saturnalia, the carnival, etc., and estimate the psychic factors in both contexts.

only unconscious impulses were urging them.[1] The genesis
of the successive stages of the earliest tragedy, in which
first the father and then the son appeared as hero, becomes clearer if they are compared with the two forms of
initiation of youths as represented in the initiation of the
Nanga society and other rites. In the one case the killed
men (fathers) are shown to the youths or their death
plastically represented; in the other the youths themselves are terrified by their own apparent death. Only
the form and not the essential and hidden content of the
tragedy is changed; and it is on this account that its
effect is the same to-day as it was then. Schiller is quite
right in speaking of the theatre as a moral institution[2]
seeing that tragedy illustrates the expiation of the first
crime which humanity punished, namely, parricide, and
that the traces of this origin had never been entirely lost
in spite of the long history of its development.

Before we leave this suggestive subject, it may be
well in reviewing all that our psychological analysis of
the puberty rites of savages has contributed to our
knowledge of the development of mankind, to repeat
Freud's dictum,[3] that 'the beginnings of religion, morality,
society, and art converge in the Oedipus complex'.

Starting out from other themes we seem to have
arrived at a not unimportant confirmation, and an ex-

[1] It may be recalled that Freud and Breuer denoted as 'cathartic' their
method of psycho-therapy which led to Freud's psycho-analysis (*Studien über
Hysterie*, Wien und Leipzig, 1895).

[2] Another problem of psychological æsthetics may also hope to be explained
along these lines: the fact that the distinction between realities and make-
believe, truth and falsity of what is represented, should have so little effect in
calming the feelings of the onlookers.

The spectators at the Dionysian celebrations, from which ancient tragedy
developed, really believed in the death and resurrection of the god; they lived
through the relevant affects just as fully as the naïve peasants did who wanted
to beat Franz Moor at the theatre. (Compare the regressive attempt of the
romantics like Zacharias Werner, etc., to found the drama on a new mythology.)
The knowledge that the drama did not represent real episodes is the result of a
later recognition brought about by cultural developments. It seems to me as if
this feeling of distance, like the corresponding feeling in the anxiety dream ('it
is only a dream'), may represent an attempt at self-tranquillisation which forces
itself from the conscious factors of the mind into the process of the spectator's
complete identification. By means of it the anxious and moved spectator
assuages the feeling of his own guilt which threatens him with the same
punishment as the rebel Dionysus.

[3] *Totem und Tabu*, S. 145.

tension of the Freudian theories about the origin of totem
and taboo,[1] and we have found parricide in the primitive
horde and its expiation to be the most important events
in the development of primitive man. According to the
individual point of view, it may be described as either a
curse or a blessing that this wicked deed will never cease
producing its reaction in the history of mankind. At the
beginning of human morality and religion we find the
sense of guilt, that creative force which can never afterwards be extinguished.

[1] We may recall Frazer's statement about the puberty rites, quoted in the
first section above, according to which the explanation of this 'central mystery
of primitive society' would furnish at the same time the key to the understanding of exogamy and of the totemism of savage races.

KOL NIDRE

Were my bosom as false as thou deem'st it to be,
I need not have wander'd from far Galilee.
It was but abjuring my creed to efface
The curse which, thou say'st, is the crime of my race.
                                    BYRON, *Hebrew Melodies.*

I. INTRODUCTION

SOME time ago I stayed as a guest in the house of a
music-loving family, and there I heard a composition played by a 'cellist which, although I am by
no means musical, made a peculiarly strong impression
on me. A particularly solemn and impressive minor
passage occurred three times and awakened a feeling of
pre-acquaintance in me that mingled curiously with the
sombre emotions the melody itself had aroused. I was
unable to recall when and where I had heard the melody
before, and conquering a disinclination to exhibit ignorance of a well-known composition in such a circle, I asked
my hostess the name of the piece. She expressed astonishment that I did not know it, and then told me that it was
Op. 47 of Max Bruch, entitled 'Kol Nidre', a modern
free setting of the ancient melody which is sung in all
the synagogues of the world before the service on the
Jewish Day of Atonement. This explained to me my
feeling of pre-acquaintance; but failed to account for the
intense emotion accompanying it and for the subsequent fact that the tune ran persistently in my head
throughout the following day. Gradually, however, a
distinct association grew with the recurrence of the
melody. I saw myself as a child and remembered that
my holidays over a period of years had been spent in a
little Hungarian town with my mother and sister at my
grandfather's home. In this town there was a Jewish
street—a relic of the old Ghetto—and it had seemed to
me as though the inhabitants of the street, in spite of
their recent emancipation, favoured the isolation to

which they had become attached. The Jews held but little intercourse with the Christian population, and appeared absorbed in their families, their religious practices and the routine of business. During my visits to the little town I had often heard the ancient melody of the Kol Nidre, and there grew into my mind a picture of the primitive synagogue; of long-bearded men in white robes, moving their bodies rhythmically in prayer; and of my grandfather at my side. I remembered the mysterious trembling that possessed the congregation when the cantor began the Kol Nidre. I remembered the visible signs of deep contrition exhibited by all these serious men, and their emotional participation in the text, and, how I, child as I was, had been carried away by that irresistible wave of feeling. Yet I was unconscious of any specific wrongdoing that might have called for contrition, and moreover, was certainly incapable of understanding the full meaning of the words. Needless to say, my grandfather, a taciturn and fanatically pious man, had never explained to me the meaning of the Kol Nidre.

Later, there emerged a second reminiscence, closely associated with the first. Years after, when a student, I had joined the Jewish National Association. Holding no positive religious belief, my mind had been occupied in following the conflict of contemporary political opinions —a subject on which I felt strongly. My interest at the time had been aroused by an annually recurring event, as regular to me as the budding of the trees in spring. This event was the appearance of the Vienna *Deutsche Volksblatt* on the eve of the Day of Atonement, when the full text of the Kol Nidre was printed in Hebrew type, with a German translation in juxtaposition. The text was to the effect that all oaths which believers take between one Day of Atonement and the next are declared invalid. The *Deutsche Volksblatt* invariably availed itself of the opportunity to deduce from this edict a moral depravity on the part of the Jewish race. In spite of the logical force of this deduction, it effectually aroused in me a feeling of intense opposition, and, at the same time, I was conscious of a feeling of humiliation at my intellectual limitations and inability to disprove the charge. I do not intend here to repeat the uninteresting process of self-analysis that started from this point, and the political discussions which were involved in the whole question; only those parts will be adduced which are actually necessary for purposes of explanation. The saying, 'A political song—a nasty song', is more true to-day than ever. We desire, however, to approach the question free from bias on either side, and to observe a neutral standpoint between anti-Semitic fervour and over-zealousness in favour of the Jews. These controversies are only to serve as a starting-point. Though at the time I failed to find a solution I might have consoled myself for my lack of insight; no one else had solved the riddle of the song in spite of the many and ingenious attempts to do so which, as we shall see, had been made. We may now find that this first attempt to apply new methods to certain difficult liturgical problems may carry us further than we had anticipated.

II. The Problem

In what does this riddle consist? It appears to me to consist in three principal facts, each of which contradicts the others. The first is that this prayer, if we may so term it, is a mere formula which declares that certain vows, oaths, curses and the like are invalid. The purport of the formula is in complete contrast with the high estimation in which obligations, whether taken on oath or otherwise, are held in biblical and Talmudic Judaism. The second fact is that this bare and almost juridical formula is accompanied by a deeply affecting melody that is quite foreign to the character of the text. What should we say of an advocate pleading a nullity suit in the courts and presenting his legal arguments with the pathos of an Alexander Strakosch? The third fact resembles the second. Whence comes the power of this

prosaic declaration to cause the strong feelings that are
released, the deep emotion that comes to the surface, and
the profound contrition that is manifested in the tears of
those who are praying? These puzzling facts give rise to
a number of subsidiary questions, concerned with the
text and origin, with religious and psychological motives,
with the liturgical significance of the formula, and so
forth. Some may feel sceptical regarding the second fact.
Are the qualities of solemnity and impressiveness really
to be attributed to the melody, or are they only perceptible for some obscure reasons to the adherents of the
Jewish religion? Reliable witnesses have confirmed the
former view. The Kol Nidre, for instance, was a favourite
melody of Field-Marshal von Moltke, who often asked
Joachim to play it to him on his violin. Nikolaus Lenau[1]
compared the melody with Rakoczy's 'March' and with
the 'Marseillaise': 'More than by these two warlike hymns,
however, I am affected by a third song—a song draped
with the veil of grief; a night song dying away in the
innermost recesses of penitent, contrite, repentant human
hearts. Kol Nidre is the name of this prayer of pain. Years
ago I heard it in my home. The Day of Atonement had
come. I squeezed myself into a corner of the synagogue
in order not to disturb the believers. Gigantic wax
candles were alight, and the people, crowded together
in flowing, snow-white robes, were before me with their
bowed heads. Then the cantor began to chant that profoundly solemn and heart-rending song of absolution, so
fraught with terror, and yet so rich in mercy. I struggled
with an inexplicable emotion. I sobbed convulsively
while hot tears poured from my eyes. Then I ran out into
the night; my spirit torn and purified. I believe in that
never-to-be-forgotten hour no single stain remained upon
my soul! Who has created these strains? The good people
who sing the Kol Nidre do not know. They can but tell
you that the song has been handed down from grandfather to grandchild. It seems to me that such a song,
redolent of a people's suffering, can hardly have been

---

[1] According to Karl Beck, *Diaries*, 1843–44.

composed by one brain, however much inspired. I would
rather say that mysterious songs, such as this wonderful
Kol Nidre, have resulted from the composite inspirations
of hundreds. Ah! would that my friends might sing it at
my death-bed!'

Even though we allow for the pathological sensitive-
ness of the poet in his response to emotional impulses,
there still remains abundant proof of the ineffaceable impression wrought by a recital of the Kol Nidre; and this
impression is stamped upon the composition of the celebrated Max Bruch. Nothing is known of the age of the
melody itself; but, admittedly, its age is extreme. The
Karaite Judah Hadassi described it in 1148, nearly eight
hundred years ago. Further details respecting it are to
be found in the *Jewish Encyclopædia*.[1]

Most of us will be curious to know the text of this
melody. It is in the Aramaic language and reads: 'All
vows, obligations, oaths, and anathemas, whether called
'ḳonam', 'ḳonas', or by any other name, which we may
vow, or swear, or pledge, or whereby we may be bound,
from this Day of Atonement unto the next (whose happy
coming we await), we do repent. May they be deemed
absolved, forgiven, annulled, and void, and made of no
effect; they shall not bind us nor have power over us.
The vows shall not be reckoned vows; the obligations
shall not be obligatory; nor the oaths be oaths.' This
ordinance is proclaimed by the cantor. The leader and
the congregation then say together: 'And it shall be forgiven all the congregation of the children of Israel, and
the stranger that sojourneth among them, seeing all the
people were in ignorance'.[2] This is also repeated three
times. The *hazzan* then closes with the benediction:
'Blessed art thou, O Lord our God, King of the Universe,

[1] New York and London, 1904, vol. vii. p. 540. Compare the old setting of
the Kol Nidre melody and the compositions of Bruch, Lewandowski, Sulzer, etc.
Attention has been drawn to the similarity of the melody with the first five bars
of Beethoven's C sharp minor quartet, op. 131, period 6, 'adagio quasi un poco
andante'. In fact, only a slight alteration of the rhythm and the repetition of a
few notes are needed to reproduce the beginning of the Kol Nidre melody note
for note.
[2] Numbers xv. 26.

who hast preserved us and hast brought us to enjoy this
season'. The wording of the formula varies with the language according to the different old manuscripts. The
text of the prayer of Amram, the old *Mahzor Soncino*,
1485, and others is entirely in Hebrew. In the later books
it is always in Aramaic; but in each the reference to the
period is invariably given in Hebrew.

The history of the opposition to this formula by the
people among whom the Jews lived is an old one. It is
probable that the so-called Jew's oath of the Middle
Ages, the origin of which dates back to the tenth century,
is derived from such an opposition. As an example of
such an oath I quote from one of Frankel's books: [1] 'The
Jew had to put a girdle of thorns around his loins, stand
in water, and spit three times on his circumcised penis,
then he took the oath in the following form, "By Barase
Baraa, Adonai, and Eloi, who led Israel dry-shod through
the Red Sea, etc. By the law which Adonai decreed, by
the spitting on the circumcised penis, and by the thorns
with which I have girded my loins I swear not falsely the
name Sabaot. If, however, I swear falsely then cursed be
the descendants of my body; I will tap the wall like a
blind man and fall like one who has no eyes. Besides this,
may the earth open its mouth and devour me like Dathan
and Abiram."' These and more terrible formulas were
prescribed for the legal taking of oaths by Jews right up
to recent times. Already in 1239 Nikolaus Donin accused
the Jews of annulling their oaths by means of the Kol
Nidre.[2] Since that time the sanctity of Jewish oaths, to
which this formula is supposed to be in opposition, has
always been questioned. In 1895 Deputy Ernst Schneider
brought in a motion in the Austrian Parliament in which
it was stated that Jews were permitted to break oaths
and thus to injure their Christian fellow-citizens. We
have already mentioned the perennial article in the
Deutsche Volksblatt. The *Staatsburger-Zeitung*, Berlin,

---

[1] D. F. Frankel, *Die Eidesleistung der Juden*, Dresden und Leipzig, 1840.
[2] Mentioned by Rabbi Jehiel, *Vikuach*, Paris. Compare *Revue des Études
Juives*, vol. ii. p. 267, and vol. iii. p. 56.

September 3, 1910, followed up this brilliant example by concluding an article on the Kol Nidre with this remarkable paragraph: 'The Kol Nidre prayer, like the Talmud, is an insult to civilisation, it is a culpable deception of the Aryans by the Jews. A Jew can commit perjury in court; his religious convictions allow him to do it. He may brand truth as a lie and ruin his fellow-men; his religious convictions stifle any conscience there may be in him. . . . These moral views of Judaism are . . . criminal assaults on humanity and civilisation.' With these sensational statements this section may be concluded.

III. Theories

What have the representatives of Judaism to say to these bold assertions—as far as they are competent to express an opinion on questions bearing on the science of religion? It must be admitted that they have a good deal to say, yet it is remarkable how one argument always cancels the other. I have endeavoured to collect all the variant types of these arguments, and I believe they can be divided into four main groups, examples of which I give.

1. General defence. Those who advance this argument lay the greatest stress on proving the particular sanctity and inviolability of oaths in all Jewish laws. In fact, starting from the Decalogue,[1] 'Thou shalt not bear false witness against thy neighbour', the high esteem in which oaths are held runs like a red thread through the whole legal system of Judaism. This attitude in regard to oaths is brought out in Numbers xxx. 2: 'If a man vow a vow unto the Lord, or swear an oath to bind his soul with a bond; he shall not break his word, he shall do according to all that proceedeth out of his mouth'. The *Nedarim* treatise in the Talmud quotes the opinion of Jehudai Gaon (about 760): 'No one may annul vows or oaths'. Oaths are particularly dealt with in the *Shebu'ot* treatise,[2] and here an extreme conscientiousness is

---

[1] Exodus xx. 16. [2] Section iii.

shown. The following sentence, taken from this treatise, shows an almost ridiculously exaggerated scrupulousness in keeping holy an oath or even only a promise: 'everything that has come from his mouth'. The law-book *Shulḥan 'Aruk*[1] considers it necessary to state that 'if a person has promised another person to dine with him and he or his son falls sick or a river overflows its banks', then his promise is not binding. Maimonides, a philosopher of religion, regarded an oath as an act of veneration;[2] he declares that the obligation of an oath is quite independent of the language in which an oath is taken, and that the obligation remains in force if a Jew has taken an oath to seal a promise to a heathen.[3] A false oath is said to be one of the gravest sins, and is not atoned for by suffering the worldly punishment prescribed for it (castigation), but is also subject to divine punishment. Another professor of religion, Hai Gaon of Tunis, who died in 1038, writes in his work[4] that an oath binds a Jew even when it is taken at the request of a Mohammedan in the name of Allah. In addition to such quotations as these, the apologists make reference to the conduct of Jews at the present time, particularly of those who follow the religion of their fathers with absolute loyalty. Dr. Alfred Stern, President of the Vienna Society of Israelites, mentions in the preface to a recent book by Bloch[5] on the Kol Nidre that in his experience as a solicitor for more than sixty years, he has come across instances in which orthodox Jews, when asked to take an oath, have refused and preferred to give up their case, although they could have sworn with the clearest conscience. According to the laws of the Jewish religion, every *reservatio mentalis* is prohibited, and no artificial interpretation of any word, etc., is permitted in any circumstances. The post-Talmudic literature is increasingly severe on this subject, and declares that every word that is spoken, if it even in the least represents a

---

[1] *Yoreh De'ah*, 232, §. 12.   [2] *Yad Ḥazaḳah*, xi. 1.
[3] *Ibid.* ii. 1.   [4] *Teshubot Ha-Ge'onim*, fol. 14B.
[5] See later reference.

promise or a vow, is a sin. How great a precaution was exercised regarding promises and consents is further shown by current phrases in the everyday language of orthodox Jews, *'im yirze hashen'* ('so God will') and *'bli neder'* ('without my intention involving any kind of vow').

If we examine this argument *sine ira et studio* we become more and more astonished that a religion which attaches an almost exaggerated importance to oaths and promises should by a single special formula cancel all oaths, and, moreover, those which are to be taken during the coming year. Theoretically this possibility exists, and therefore we can only say that the formula stands in striking contrast to the ordinary theory and practice of law-abiding Judaism.

2. This argument is followed by a more important one which may be termed the exegetic argument. It is asserted that the meaning of the formula is quite different from what it appears to be on superficial consideration. This is proved by the manner in which oaths may be broken. Oaths and vows between two people are unbreakable except in one way. The person who wants to be released from a vow can only obtain this release by the consent of the other party. If that consent is obtained, he has to give minute details of the vow to a cleric or to three lay persons, and also the reason why he desires to be released from it; and, further, he has to show signs of repentance.[1] Since the fourteenth century the clerics have renounced this privilege;[2] there is now a general release from future vows by a solemn declaration which is prescribed in the *Nedarim* treatise: 'Whoever wishes all the vows he may make throughout the year to be null and void shall come at the beginning of the year and say: "May all the vows which I shall vow be annulled".'[3] According to some, all he has to do is to think of this declaration at the time of taking a vow;

---

[1] *Bekorot*, 36 sq. *Shulḥan ʿAruk Yoreh Deʿah*, 328, § 1; compare Eisenmenger, ii. S. 429 sq., and Bodenschatz ii. S. 370 sq.

[2] Frankel, *ibid*. S. 63.

[3] *Jewish Encyclopædia*, vol. vii.

according to others, he must not remember it. In the post-Talmudic period this custom has changed, so that the declaration is made: 1. On the eve of the Day of Atonement (according to Strack,[1] 'because then the congregation was particularly large in the synagogue'); 2. By the whole congregation and not by individuals; 3. With reference to the past and not to the future. Here we discover fresh and interesting problems. Why is the declaration to be made on the Eve of Atonement and not on New Year's Eve? Why is it extended to the whole congregation? And why is it made to refer to the past instead of the future? We shall return to these questions later. For the present, we shall concern ourselves with the true exegetic argument according to which it is affirmed that the misunderstanding has arisen because the text is not correctly translated or understood. The whole weight of the argument rests on the subordinate sentence, *di assarna al nafshathna* ('which we have taken upon our souls', or expressed in more modern language, 'which we have taken upon ourselves'). The significance of these words is clear. The Kol Nidre formula does not concern oaths valid at law regarding other persons, but it concerns obligations, oaths, vows, etc., which one imposes upon oneself, therefore a contract with one's own ego. That notorious opponent of the Jews, Professor Eisenmenger, who lived two and a half centuries ago, has to admit this in his work.[2] 'It appears that in accordance with the doctrine referred to, Jews cannot be absolved either by the release from oaths which it is customary to obtain through the Kol Nidre on the Day of Atonement or by a rabbi, or by three lay persons, from an oath which they take in the presence of a Christian or a Christian authority.' The late Jewish code of the *Shulhan 'Aruk*[3] also points expressly in this direction, and states with regard to the Kol Nidre formula: 'All this (that is to say, the annulment of vows, oaths, etc.)

---

[1] *Realenzyklopädie für protestantische Theologie und Kirche.* Published by Albert Haugk, Leipzig, 1901, 3. Aufl. S. 650.
[2] *Entdecktes Judentum*, Part II. S. 501.
[3] *Yoreh De'ah*, 211, § 4.

only applies to an oath or a vow which he himself has sworn and taken upon himself; if, however, another person causes him to take a vow or an oath, then this annulment is of no value to him.' Most of the old Jewish prayer books endeavour, some very clumsily, to explain the meaning of release from an oath by the Kol Nidre in accordance with this ordinance. In the middle of the text of the formula a Russo-Jewish prayer book adds, 'for instance, if somebody has taken a vow to forego bread'. In another Russo-Jewish edition,[1] the Kol Nidre is preceded by the following:

'Declaration of the Rabbis

'In the name of God, on the authority of the *Torah*, we annul oaths and vows by which a man foregoes something, and in general we annul vows and oaths which a man takes and swears of his own accord and only towards himself, but God forbid that anyone should believe that we annul vows and oaths which a person has sworn or vowed before authority or at the law courts, or vows and oaths which concern the interest and well-being of others, irrespective of creed or race. The oaths and vows as regards which the *Torah* says that if they are broken, God will not let the perjurer go unpunished, have to be kept, and held to, and must be carried out to their full extent without any alteration. And the wrath of God will descend upon him who violates them; he is condemned to eternal ignominy and shame.'

So far the Jewish theologians. Their position has received support from an unprejudiced quarter in the work of two well-known Oriental scholars, Professor Friedrich Delitzsch and Professor Hermann Strack. The former states that the Kol Nidre formula is limited to 'those vows which a man has imposed upon himself voluntarily, that is to say, self-obligations taken on oath and recognised as sinful or impracticable: but it does not include legal oaths, and sworn obligations towards another

---

[1] Printed in Vilna by Romm in 1866.

M

person with that person's knowledge.'[1] Professor Strack
in his article, 'Kol Nidre',[2] states as follows; 'Above all
it is to be observed that the formula does not speak of
oaths which are taken regarding others, but of vows and
obligations which one imposes upon oneself'. He adds
emphatically, 'But vows and, of course, also oaths which
have been taken in regard to another person are unbreakable, except when the person concerned is present
and gives his consent'.

The value of the exegetic argument is certainly not to
be underestimated, but we do not wish to suppress our
doubts about it. Regarding the explanation in the
Shulḥan 'Aruk and those in the more recent prayer books,
it is quite possible that they represent reactions against
the accusation that oaths can be cancelled by the Kol
Nidre. If this is so, it is obvious that the Jews, for many
centuries past, have understood the formula only in the
sense indicated by Delitzsch and Strack—but no sensible
person doubts this. Our present purpose is not to refute
anti-Semitic agitators, but to find the real meaning of
the Kol Nidre, to recognise its origin, and to understand
the motives giving rise to it. Does the phrase 'Which
we have imposed on our souls (or upon ourselves)[2] exclude the participation of a second person? Only apparently, we think. Apart from philological doubts, it is
quite possible that oaths as well as vows which we impose upon ourselves concern a second person. I swear to
myself, for instance, I will support a poor relation. Of
course, in such a case it is not a matter of a contract between two persons, but fulfilment or non-fulfilment of this
vow that affects the other person. Or is Jephtha's vow[3]
and its fulfilment without influence on his daughter's
fate? If, however, we adopt the idea of the exegetic
apologist, then from the point of view of a rigorous ethic
holding up an ideal standard of conduct, most serious
doubts could be raised against the breaking even of such
a self-imposed obligation.

[1] Rohlings, *Talmudjude*, 7 Aufl. S. 52.
[2] *Realenzyklopädie für protestantische Theologie und Kirche.*
[3] Judges xi. 30.

3. The third argument is the historical one. This argument asserts that the formula arose from a definite cause or that it refers to vows, oaths, etc., arising from this cause. What do we know about the facts of its history? Strangely enough, the first sign of its existence appears on a vase in the National Museum in Paris. On this vase, which dates from the seventh century, and which Babelon and M. Schwalb have minutely described,[1] are engraved fragments of the Kol Nidre. Amram (869/81, Gaon of Sura) in his order of prayer, which is, however, supplemented from more recent services, recognises the formula as one used by many people. Saadia Gaon (942) concludes from the answer of the congregation[2] that the formula refers only to the congregation as a whole and not to individuals. An important alteration in the wording of the Kol Nidre was made by Rashi's son-in-law, Meïr ben Samuel: hitherto release from vows of the past year had been pronounced, but he had the vows of the coming year declared void. His son, Jacob ben Meïr, usually called Rabbenu Tam, reports[3] this and adds that according to the *Halakah*, it is impossible subsequently to make legally valid the breaking of a vow or promise; the existing interpretation is an erroneous one because no one is able to cancel his own vows. If one recalls the above-quoted expression,[4] this alteration is seen to be really a return to the old setting, *i.e.* a reconstruction of the original text. Many *Maḥzorim* keep to the formula from the last Day of Atonement, and a *Maḥzor* manuscript (oriental rite) quoted by Strack combines both expressions, 'from the last Day of Atonement to the present one, and from this to the coming one'.

We will now discuss the historical arguments. In the first place we may mention L. J. Mandelstamm, who attempts to trace back the formula historically.[5] He refers

---

[1] 'Un vase judéo-chaldéen de la Bibliothèque Nationale,' *Revue des Études juives*, iv. p. 164.
[2] Numbers xv. 26.
[3] *Sefer ha'Yashar*, Vienna, 1810, vol. xvii. column 1, § 144.
[4] *Nedarim*, 23B.
[5] 'Horae talmudicae', *Biblische und Talmudische Schriften*, Part IV., Berlin, 1860, ii. 6-16.

to an old custom which dates back to Meïr of Rothen-
burg (second half of the thirteenth century), according
to which, so-called transgressors, *i.e.* lip-Christians, were
permitted to pray with the congregation before the commencement of the Kol Nidre. These apostates were under
a ban and were not allowed to take part in the public
worship. Mandelstamm thinks that the Day of Atonement would really have been the most suitable to bring
divine pardon to those Spanish apostates who during the
year would have to submit to vows, oaths and penances
extorted under pressure of the Inquisition. The Kol Nidre,
therefore, would be their solemn declaration that everything they would be compelled to vow and to swear to
in the course of the coming year might be looked upon as
extorted and forced from them, and that they, nevertheless, would remain in their hearts always loyal followers
of Jehovah. Mandelstamm's view is wrong, for the
reason that he underestimates the age of the Kol Nidre
—it is much older than the Inquisition, as J. S. Bloch
proves in his recent work on it.[1] According to Bloch, the
Kol Nidre dealt with vows of the past year—not, however, with those which had already been transgressed,
but with those which had been about to be violated by
the intended participation in the service. In this manner,
which we must admit is ingenious, he endeavours to
settle the difference between the two ways of reading the
Kol Nidre. Christians who were Christians by compulsion had to swear before a Christian tribunal not to take
part in any Jewish ceremony. The Kol Nidre, which is
said at the beginning of the service on the Day of Atonement, renders those enforced oaths invalid. This formula
did not contain empty words for those obligatory Christians. It was the 'cry of a torn soul', the 'tragedy of their
life-lie'. Bloch asks why the congregation speaks of having erred as a whole. The origin of the Kol Nidre manifestly dates back to the period of the Western Goths.
Their kings, Recared, Sisebut, Chintilla, vied with each
other in the most cruel persecution of the Jews. Whole

---

[1] *Kol Nidre und seine Entstehungsgeschichte*, Wien, 1917.

communities were compelled to undergo compulsory
baptism at that time. The Jews then gathered in hiding-
places on the *Yom Kippur* and uttered this formula in
order not to be weighed down with the heavy sin of
breaking an oath. The use of the formula during the
period of the Inquisition belongs to a second historical
layer. At the time of the domination of the Western
Goths in Spain there were whole communities who, conscience-stricken, inserted the Kol Nidre in their liturgy;
later, individual *Maranos* were permitted to participate
in the service. 'This is the great mystery, Kol Nidre—a
pathetic document, a thousand years old, of Jewish
mental torment and Jewish martyrdom.' In the introduction to this work of Bloch's, Dr. Alfred Stern says
that it has such a high degree of probability that it will
withstand the criticisms which presumably will be
raised against it.

The first impression of this ingenious and most recent
hypothesis will certainly be astonishing. Nevertheless
the theory is no less incorrect than Mandelstamm's.
Whereas anti-Semitic aggression had been led astray
through a most ludicrous misunderstanding by which
it deduced from the Kol Nidre moral depravity in all
Jews, the views of Bloch go to the opposite extreme.
According to him, the Jews are innocent as lambs
brought to the sacrifice, and the Kol Nidre becomes a
tragic accusation against the barbarism of the rest of
humanity. Turning to more concrete objections—which,
by the way, concern also Mandelstamm's theory—is it
likely that this song should have sprung up suddenly in
consequence of a particular Jewish persecution, without
having a connection with the preceding religious history
of the Jews? The oldest reading of the formula with
which we are acquainted refers to vows of the coming
year. This is a fact; no later new interpretation can in
any way alter it, and no explanation which fails to throw
light on this fact can be regarded as satisfactory. Further,
from whence comes it that this old formula makes such
a strong impression upon modern Jews who are no

longer forced to become Christians by means of rack and thumb-screw? They certainly know nothing of this history of its development, and if they had this knowledge it could not alone produce in them such a powerful emotional state as is actually to be observed. In all probability we should have very few scruples in breaking an oath so cruelly enforced. The old formula lost its meaning through allowing the *Anusim* (Christians by compulsion) to take part in the whole service, and became superfluous. Many more objections might be added to these,[1] but there is one which disposes of this new and startling hypothesis on religious grounds, namely, an enforced oath does not require to be annulled, it is in itself invalid. We quote Frankel's work: 'An oath is not to be based on any injustice, *i.e.* it must be taken voluntarily; if it is taken under compulsion, *i.e.* if a rite is violated and the person in question is compelled to take an oath by which he has to consent to this injury, the oath is not binding, it is assertory or promissory. According to the opinion of the most enlightened legal experts, oaths extorted by unlawful means are not valid. The objection that even such an oath must be kept is refuted in the definition of an oath itself. An oath is a reminder of the truth through God, but God can only be appealed to in the interests of justice; truth never goes with injustice.'

4. The weightiest and most convincing argument is the psychological one, which has been set forth with special clearness in Frankel's book.[2] This book seems to us remarkable in this connection for a double reason: it

---

[1] Dr. Bloch was kind enough to let me see the first proof of a critical article, *Eine neue Hypothese über die Entstehung des Kol Nidre*, by Samuel Poznánski. This author is of the opinion that if the formula had really been framed by Spanish Jews in the seventh century these would certainly not have had sufficient authority to have caused it to be acknowledged in other countries, for instance, Egypt. 'Then there is another question: what reason would there be to recite a formula, which originated for a certain known reason in Spain, in countries where this reason did not exist?' He calls attention to the fact that in Spain the Kol Nidre was not said in the thirteenth and fourteenth centuries. He considers that the formula originated in Palestine, and was originally written in Hebrew, and only later translated into Aramaic. In a *Supplement* Bloch endeavours to refute his opponent's arguments.

[2] *Die Eidesleistung der Juden*, Dresden und Leipzig, 1840.

does not start from the Kol Nidre, but from oaths in general among the Jews, and its psychological method of approach leads us to expect that light will be thrown upon the mental forces on which the formula is based, upon the psychic motives to which it owes its origin, and upon the requirements it fulfils by its present use.

Frankel starts by separating promissory from assertory oaths. The original oath, the oath of the ancients, was a promissory one; the hope for well-being was, therefore, united with the fulfilment of the oath. A not unusual formula ran: 'May I ruin myself and my house if I transgress anything of this oath, but if I keep my oath then may everything desirable and good be my lot'. We recognise a remnant of this in our present-day asseveration: 'So God help me'. The expression of the prohibition in the Decalogue, 'Thou shalt not take the name of the Lord thy God in vain' (in the Septuagint ἐπὶ ματαίῳ, points to the fact that every asseveration in the name of God which was not necessary was forbidden, and was equivalent to blasphemy. Besides the distinction between promissory and assertory oaths, there is a distinction between direct and indirect ones. The direct oath is of the type: 'I swear that . . .'; the indirect: 'May I be cursed if I do not . . .' The more interesting and certainly the older is that of the curse. Remnants of this form are still found. Thus in the *Midrash Wayikra*, chap. 6, it is said that the person taking an oath was shown an inflated skin to signify that just as this skin once contained bones and flesh and is now empty, so will it happen to him who swears falsely. Rabbi Hai (tenth century) recommends that when a person takes an oath he should produce a bier in the same way as at a burial, light candles and put ashes on his head, etc. We also learn to our surprise that in the later law there was a gradation of the oath among the Jews: there was one oath, in the ordinary direct or indirect form, under the sanction of truth, and, in more important cases, another oath in the name of God. We learn of a further limitation. According to a somewhat later ordinance (from the sixteenth century) a Jewish judge is not to demand the judicial taking of an oath during the days of repentance, that is to say, during the eight days between the New Year's Feast and that of the Day of Atonement.[1] Frankel's explanation of this is:[2] 'During the days of repentance many people might be little disposed to take an oath: an oath solemnly taken demands a certain peace of mind, an exact balancing of all the circumstances of which the contrite person is not capable; there constantly arise in him fresh scruples, and he does not attain the certainty which should accompany an oath.'[3] One would have thought that the man who is searching his conscience, and has resolved to avoid all sins, would be in a better position to take an oath than the man who is free from such cares. We shall revert to this point. According to Frankel an oath is based on a positive principle; it is not based upon terror and punishment, but on truth. The Jewish law originally did not have such a thing as the oath of a witness. That is on account of the nature of the promissory oath which referred to the future. Nor can such an oath be used for the purpose of confirming a statement, since the person who vows it is under no suspicion. Oaths and counter-oaths are excluded; if the plaintiff has sworn the defendant has to be silent. We can say that an oath is a promise which the person imposes upon himself. The vow, therefore, would be a promise given to God. There is no definite boundary between the content of oaths which refer to God, and those in which God is appealed to as a witness. Frankel considers it a remarkable psychological fact that the taking of vows has been more and more restricted by law. 'Whoever takes a vow is a sinner and blasphemer, even if he carries it out', says the Talmud. Vows which are intended to combat one's own vices and wicked tendencies are certainly meritorious, they are 'a dividing fence' (by means of such vows, the man separates himself from the sin); vows, however, should not be multiplied, and a man

---

[1] *Orah Hayyim.* Cap. 602.   [2] Frankel, *ibid.* S. 35.
[3] *Nedarim.* 22, 76.

should accustom himself to live free from sin without taking vows. In the Talmud there is a saying which witnesses to a profound knowledge of mental habits: 'Whoever accustoms himself to vows learns at last to play with oaths'.[1] Philo,[2] at a later period, says that there are men who swear to commit thefts, sacrileges, murder and adultery, 'and they carry out such acts at once, using their oath as a pretext'. Again, he says, there are asocial individuals who, from enmity to mankind, or from hatred, swear never to do anything good to anyone, or to accept anything from anybody. Some people keep up this hatred beyond a person's death and will not fulfil the last duties. According to Frankel the Kol Nidre formula is for the purpose of fighting against, or, more correctly, freeing oneself from hasty and impossible vows of this kind, as such vows are bound to give rise to very serious quarrels in civil life: 'In the hand of the excitable Oriental, over whom a momentary impression has an untameable power and who rarely allows reason to act upon his unbridled phantasy, vows were a double-edged sword with which he wounded himself and others. . . . The mania to take vows was irresistible.'

A psychological explanation is also to be found in the *Jewish Encyclopædia*, the tenor of which is contained in the following sentence:[3] 'The religious consciousness, which felt oppressed at the thought of the non-fulfilment of its solemn vows, accordingly devised a general and comprehensive formula of dispensation which was repeated by the *ḥazzan* in the name of the assembled congregation at the beginning of the fast of Atonement'.

We fully admit that Frankel has gone as far as it was possible for a scholar and keen observer of men to do with the means then at hand in accounting for the Kol Nidre formula, and has put most of his successors into.

---

[1] *Nedarim* 20A.
[2] *De Spec. Leg.*, p. 771; quoted by Frankel, *ibid*. S. 59.
[3] New York and London, 1904, vol. vii. p. 539. Ismar Eltbogen, *Der judische Gottesdienst in seiner geschichtlichen Entwicklung*, Leipzig, 1913, S. 153, believes that the Kol Nidre 'has nothing to do with the thoughts and liturgy of the Day of Atonement; only by stretching a point can a connection be established'. We shall see how erroneous this view is.

the shade, even if he has not succeeded in explaining the riddle and solving its numerous contradictions; for he had an idea of the true situation, since he recognised that only a psychological explanation supported by historical facts could give the solution. Each later attempt will have to start from his theory, and supplement it in three directions: first in tracing the oath to a larger complex by means of our advanced knowledge in the science of Old Testament religion and Hebrew archæology, secondly in adducing other peoples' customs for purposes of comparison, and thirdly in deepening the psychological methods of investigation.

IV. The Psycho-analytical Interpretation

What can the students of religion and the ethnologists tell us about oaths? Originally an oath was a matter of divine judgement. Invisible powers threatened perjurers with disease and death. The same invisible powers were invoked to take vengeance on those who swore falsely. Originally the formula of an oath was everywhere a self-curse, an invoking of evil upon oneself if one had committed perjury. Here are a few instructive examples taken from Albert Hermann Post's[1] voluminous work. If a Yakut is accused of having stolen cattle he has to place himself behind magic tokens with his face turned towards the sun, and swear an oath which comprises the curse that if he has sworn falsely he may lose everything that is dear to him. The Kandhs in India swear by their own eyes. Among the heathen Samoyeds the persons concerned stand stark naked and swear: 'May God punish us, the earth devour us, and wild animals tear our body'. Among the old Magyars the person swearing put a handful of earth on his head and cursed himself and all his descendants in the event of his perjuring himself. An essential part of the oath was an action symbolising the misfortune which was to descend upon

---

[1] *Grundriss der ethnologischen Jurisprudenz*, Bd. ii. S. 478.

the one who swore falsely, for instance, to be eaten by
a wild animal. The Khonds of Orissa in India took an
oath while standing on a tiger's skin, and believed that
he who swore falsely would be wounded or killed by a
tiger. The Garos, when taking an oath, put tiger's bones
between their teeth. The heathen Samoyeds on this
occasion gnaw the skin or the snout of a bear and say:
'May the animal gnaw me in the same way as I am
gnawing it'. Among the natives of Nias a pig was killed,
and among the Dyaks a black fowl. Among the Samoyeds a dog was killed before an idol and the curse that
he who swears falsely may die just like this dog was
uttered. But what has all this to do with the Kol Nidre
formula? We may feel some surprise at the similarity of
the ceremonies of oaths of savage peoples to the Jewish
oath of the Middle Ages; but this similarity contributes
just as little to the clearing up of the riddle as the knowledge that the oath originally was a self-curse and was
regularly associated with gloomy and solemn rites.
Possibly we shall obtain more light by comparing these
customs of primitive peoples with the results obtained
by students of the pre-Jahve Judaic religion. Is there
something common to both? Certainly among the ancient
Jews the asseveration was a self-curse as in the savage
peoples of our time.[1] This self-curse had even its own
name: אלה Alah. Is there a difference between the oath
(שבועה) and the self-curse, the אלה? Their relation, perhaps, will best be seen by reference to the ancient B'rith
rite. What is a B'rith? It is not easy to define this as the
word 'bond' only gives a part of the meaning. We will be
satisfied for the time being with the definition Kraetzschmar has given.[2] According to him, a B'rith is the
most extreme form of an asseveration, 'it is the form by
which settlements between two parties are made unconditionally binding'. The fact that the two words are
interchangeable shows that 'oath' and 'B'rith' are cog-

[1] Compare Valeton in *Zeitschrift für alttestamentliche Wissenschaft*, Bd. xii.
S. 226.
[2] Richard Kraetzschmar, *Die Bundesvorstellung im Alten Testament*, Marburg,
1896, S. 15.

nate ideas. Kraetzschmar,[1] however, states that they are
not quite identical, but are related to each other as the
part is to the whole. A *B'rith* consists of three parts:
the asseveration, the curse, and the symbolic action
which represents the asseveration, as fulfilled—'or, if
one associates the two latter, it consists of *Shebu'ot*
and *Alah'*. Kraetzschmar assumes the logical relation
of these parts to one another to be as follows: 'The
asseveration contains the conditions agreed upon, and
is thus the positive part. Then follows, as is so frequent among the Semites, a curse in the form of a self-
curse, in the case that the person transgresses the clauses
of the *B'rith*; this is the negative part. The *Alah*, and
with it the whole bond, was able to inspire more fear, in
that a solemn ceremony was connected with it, which
was carried out with the shedding of blood. The parts of
animals used were probably neither used afterwards for
a meal nor for a sacrifice, because a curse clung to them.'
The meal which was generally associated with the conclusion of the *B'rith*—for example, the feast of the Elders
on the mountain before Jahve, as described in a fragment of the oldest E-account concerning the Sinai bond
—created, according to Robertson Smith[2] and Wellhausen,[3] a communal bond both between Jahve and
guests and between the guests themselves. Kraetzschmar supposes that the real purpose of the meal is to
secure peaceful relations; but he thinks it might possibly
have been simply an act of hospitality. It is perhaps
necessary to separate the concept of the *B'rith* from that
of the bond.[4] Above all, it is not of the essence of the
B'rith that it should be completed by two parties of
equal standing; a single person, by carrying out the
B'rith, can bind himself to a performance without a
counter-performance being expected. A besieged city,
for example, will use this form to declare itself ready to

---

[1] *Ibid.* S. 15.
[2] *Lectures on the Religion of the Semites*, London, 1901, p. 269.
[3] *Prolegomena*, S. 73.
[4] Compare *Die Religion in Geschichte und Gegenwart*, Tübingen, 1918, Bd. i.
S. 1432.

adhere to the conditions of surrender.[1] Through this
solemn promise alone, a superior party can take upon
himself obligations, as Jahve did to Abraham, Genesis
xv. Two typical examples of this ancient rite may
be quoted. Dictus Cretensis states[2] that the Grecian
generals committed themselves to the Trojan war in the
following manner: The seer Calchas obtained a pig,
divided it, and laid the two halves east and west of each
other; then he made the leaders pass between them
singly with drawn sword. The oldest characteristics of
such a rite are to be found in a relatively late story, in
Genesis xv. 1-18:

1. After these things the word of the Lord came to
Abram in a vision, saying, Fear not, Abram: I am thy
shield, and thy exceeding great reward.

2. And Abram said, Lord God, what wilt thou give
me, seeing I go childless . . . ?

4. And, behold, the word of the Lord came unto him,
saying, This shall not be thine heir; but he that shall
come forth out of thy own bowels shall be thine heir. . . .

9. And he said unto him, Take me an heifer of three
years old, and a she goat of three years old, and a ram of
three years old, and a turtledove, and a young pigeon.

10. And he took unto him all these, and divided them
in the midst, and laid each piece one against another:
but the birds divided he not.

11. And when the fowls came down upon the car-
cases, Abram drove them away.

12. And when the sun was going down, a deep sleep
fell upon Abram; and, lo, an horror of great darkness fell
upon him. . . .

18. In the same day the Lord made a covenant with
Abram, saying, Unto thy seed have I given this land. . . .

Ed. Meyer[3] believes that the idea of the rite may be
that the person swearing enters into the animal and

---

[1] 1 Samuel xi. 1.   [2] *Ephemeris belli Trojani*, lib. i. cap. 15.
[3] *Die Israeliten und ihre Nachbarstämme*, S. 560.

identifies himself with it, and in the case of breaking the bond calls down upon himself its fate. Modern biblical exegesis has not gone further than this up to the present. Even Gunkel in his third edition of the commentary on Genesis can only remark, by way of explanation, that such ceremonies originate from time immemorial, and that their meaning is now no longer comprehensible. 'The details of the sacrifice described here are, as often happens in such cases, impossible to interpret.' It is much to be questioned whether this opinion is not hasty, and whether the hidden meaning of this complicated ceremonial could not be found in the association of various features of this tale, hitherto little considered, such as Abram's fear, his deep sleep, the killing of the animals, and the prophecy of an heir, and by means of comparison with religious rites of other ancient peoples as well as those of savages. Kraetzschmar is wrong in regarding the communal meal as an inessential adjunct of the ceremony. For the same reason the asseveration in the ritual is not the most original and significant thing, nor is the separation into asseveration, curse and division of the animal justified for any but descriptive purposes. Probably the difficulties cannot be solved unless more precise explanations be found of the psychological origin of the oath, vow, curse and blessing, and unless their connection with the *B'rith* ritual be investigated. I anticipate the results of later inquiries by stating here that the *B'rith* precedes in development the sacrificial sacrament. It represents an intermediate form which has developed historically from the primitive forms of the totem meal. The self-imprecation is to be regarded as a reaction from an earlier act of violence, the nature of which is suggested by the rite of the division of an animal, especially if we consider it in the light of Freud's view of the beginnings of totemism. This self-imprecation was only later joined with the asseveration. As in mourning rites, tearing of the hair and self-injury, it originally represented a by no means merely symbolic self-punishment for unconscious murderous impulses.

The asseveration is a later institution, and its connection with the earlier one is explicable through the inhibition of unconscious impulsive tendencies towards repeating the murder of the god and the father. The *Alah* re-awakens the memory of the old crime and the fearful threat of punishment in case of its repetition. The character of a bond which adheres to the *B'rith* becomes comprehensible when we think of the situation of the primitive horde after parricide, as broadly sketched by Freud, and of the prolongation of that situation in the sphere of the primitive stages of religion. The son's tender feelings and his feelings of identification, both of which are strengthened by reaction, here play a rôle of primary importance. From the standpoint of the members of that primitive religion, the *B'rith* represents a vow not to repeat the murder; from that of the murdered god a promise of protection and help if no repetition of this deed takes place. This divine promise sounds paradoxical, coming as it does after the deed, but its meaning becomes clearer when we remember the savage's exceedingly tender treatment of the skulls of his slain foes, and when we take into consideration the obsessional thoughts of psychoneurotics, so far as they refer to the influence of dead persons whom they loved, upon their own fate. God's help and benediction are on the side of him who refuses to gratify his subversive and hostile impulses. The *B'rith* shows us the first solemn attempt at reconciliation with the dead father-god. Its most primitive form perhaps lies farther back than the periodic totem meal, and we may still hope to find easily intelligible traces in it of the events which followed upon the parricide. If we call to mind the *B'rith* between God and the Jewish community on Sinai, the law-giving—the word *B'rith* itself is often used to mean law—and the foundation of religion and morality, the essential qualities of which institutions have held their ground for thousands of years, we can see how very true is Freud's statement that morality, religion and guilty conscience are bound up with that great primordial crime. A deeper investigation of the *B'rith* ceremonies would lead us to a confirmation and development of the Freudian totem hypothesis.

But where have we strayed? We started from the numerous attacks upon the Kol Nidre formula and have arrived at the problem of the *B'rith*—the central point of ancient Judaism. We have fared almost like Saul who set out to seek his father's asses and found a king's crown. We have left far behind the pros and cons, the whole dispute about the old wording. We have now quietly to find the way back to our starting-point. Was this digression necessary? In what way is the prosaic formula of the Kol Nidre similar to the vivid and gruesome *B'rith* rite? These are the questions that must now be faced. For the moment we must accept them as justifiable, but at the same time we feel that we have not traversed this long path of our own choice, but that the facts and the theories related to them have impelled us along it. These theories have developed out of the question of the oath. We have now traced the oath back to its origins and have thus come upon the very important problem of the *B'rith*. It may perhaps cause us some surprise to find that the oath actually stands in the central point of all the early mentioned theories. It is quite open to us to regard it as a sign either of inattention or of superficial scientific treatment, that the renunciations, vows and curses expressly mentioned in the formula were not equally the object of a thorough scholarly investigation starting from the Kol Nidre text. The Kol Nidre is originally a formula of consecration, since the Hebrew word נדר signifies to consecrate, like the Arabic *nedara*. One can consecrate a material thing and one can consecrate oneself (for example, by a pilgrimage or war). To consecrate signifies to put a thing or a person under a taboo. We may say that the elements of the Kol Nidre formula already mentioned, if regarded in their ancient meaning as holy and effective actions, and not merely treated as modern customs, can be related to a specific mental phenomenon, namely, the ambivalence

of feelings. The unconscious side of the tendency to hate
and injure that manifests itself in the form of self-
punishments makes itself felt no less in vows, renunciations and asseverations (which are a cursing of oneself
under certain conditions), than in the analogous symptoms of obsessional neurotics; these tendencies are
directed against one's own person. We note that in the
B'rith these three enunciations existed *in nuce*; self-
imprecation, vows and renunciations are not distinguished in this primitive rite. The object of the vow
or the imprecation is partly the inhibition of the tendencies which urge the renewal of the primitive act
of violence and partly its future avoidance; the self-
imprecation is directed against the perpetrators of the
crime; and the renunciation is effected by the refusal to
gratify the impulse. The origin of these three institutions
points to the conscious victory of the honourable and
tender impulses in the ambivalence, the impulses which
form a 'bond' between the father-god and his followers.
Is there anything else in common between the old ritual
of the *B'rith* and the Kol Nidre formula? The most we
can point to is the gruesome impression and the uncanny
and gloomy nature of the situation, and it thus seems
as if our historical inquiry has brought but little profit.

The position is now precarious enough, but possibly
there may still be a way out. Let us keep strictly to what
the formula actually says, to its release from oaths, vows
and renunciations. We know already that after all it
speaks only of release from obligations assumed through
the *B'rith*, against the observance of which unconscious
contrary streams exist in the mind of believers. When
an obsessional patient, whom we know as a thoroughly
estimable and ethical person, says that to his horror he
frequently feels an impulse to murder persons standing
in close relationship to him, we analysts accept the idea
unhesitatingly as though it were unexceptionable and
intelligent. Let us treat moral valuations and purely
reasonable criticism in the same way, and believe that
the formula has as its content actually the annulling of

N

oaths, etc. How then are we to explain this much discussed exception to the high esteem in which obligations
taken on oath are held in Judaism? Must we give up the
attempt, or do we know of similar cases in which ideas
that have been highly respected and carefully guarded
are broken through at some point suddenly and unexpectedly by a diametrically opposite idea? Is it possible
that in the same person impulses emerge which suddenly
call all moral gain and all carefully defended acquire-
ments in question? Yes, we know instances of such surprising human inconsistencies. There is a Jewish joke
which affords an example of it. Two Jews, having become bitter enemies owing to business differences, have
broken off all intercourse with each other.   They meet
on the Day of Atonement, on which day, according to
religious precept, the worst enemies have to be reconciled to one another, and one says to the other, 'Well, I
wish you everything that you wish me'. 'Beginning
again already?' was the answer. This joke expresses in
paradoxical form profound recognition of the indestructibility and everlastingness of all original human impulses
in the face of every moral demand. The old residue of
hostility has come to the fore in spite of all the best
and most peaceful intentions. (Perhaps, as in the Kol
Nidre, the reference here to the Day of Atonement is
not merely accidental.) The fact that it is in a funny
story that such an open acknowledgement of the situation is made is no longer surprising now that Freud has
indicated the full psychological importance of jokes.[1]

Children frequently behave with a similar remarkable
inconsequence. I once witnessed the following pleasing in-
cident. Little Arthur, three years old, was once punished
because he kept taking crockery from the kitchen and
smashing it in spite of his mother's repeated warnings.
His mother asked the weeping child, 'Will you be a good
boy?' He answered, sobbing, 'Bubi wants to be good,
but Bubi can't be good'. Is not this sincere admission

[1] Freud, *Der Witz und seine Beziehung zum Unbewussten,* Second Edition,
Vienna and Leipzig, 1912.

like an infantile counterpart of the Kol Nidre formula with its naïve and unnatural antithesis of two tendencies?

There are, however, a great many human beings whose whole life is characterised by similar mental situations. I refer to obsessional patients. It happens fairly frequently that swearing, oaths and denials are the central point of all complicated compulsive actions, and of the thoughts and reflections which these neurotics feel as obsessive. I quote the following example: 'A lady who dearly loved her husband could not avoid swearing by his life on the most trifling occasions, although she fought against this impulse. She would swear, for example, "May my husband die if I ever again give an order to this dressmaker who has made me so angry".' We should say that even among superstitious persons this form of oath might be a very convenient one since the person who swears it is not endangered; but this lady's great affection for her husband contradicts any such idea. The mental processes which used to follow asseverations of this kind testified to her love. She suffered severely, for instance, from the temptation to carry out the resolutions against which she had sworn, i.e. to give an order to the dressmaker, etc. If the oath referred to past things, she suffered from grave and tenacious doubts whether she had really done this or that thing, and whether she had not sworn falsely. She was also constantly afraid that her asseveration might result in her loved husband's death. Since she could not free herself from her tendency to swear by his life, she procured herself some relief by only swearing, 'If that is not so or so, may my husband die to-day'. Her scruples and anxiety then only lasted one day, but they were no less intense. She admitted to having an anxious curiosity as to whether her swearing would have some effect upon the life of her husband. This patient, like others, was accustomed to destroy the effect of her compulsive swearing and prohibitions by a formula, either thought or uttered, which corresponded in character to the Kol Nidre. The formula annulled the effect of her oath and prohibitions from the outset—but this, it is true, almost always became a source of far-reaching doubt and gave rise to new compulsive actions.

There is here certainly a striking analogy between the two phenomena. But is there a similar mental correspondence; and by what mental paths does one arrive at such declarations of invalidity? Should they perhaps be compared to diplomatic covenants and international agreements which are most strictly weighed and defined, and in which the tacit assumption is that they are to be treated as worthless scraps of paper when circumstances compel? Perhaps our comparison of the ritual with the symptoms of obsessional patients is not merely limited to the similarity of external forms, but can be extended to the essential content. In a paper—unfortunately all too short—written in 1907, Freud has drawn a parallel between religious practices and the symptoms of obsessional neurosis, and has traced the latter back to their psychical roots.[1] Although we are well aware of the essential difference between the two phenomena, we will assume, for the purpose of investigation, that the Kol Nidre is an obsessional symptom. In that case we might say that there exists a type of obsessional patients who state as one of their unintelligible obsessive thoughts that they declare all vows, swearing, denials, etc., invalid for the coming year. Analysis would trace this symptom to its starting-point and its first appearance, and proceed from occurrences at the time of puberty to impressions and events of earliest childhood. Following this same regressive path, we notice the high esteem in which the oath is held in the Jewish legislation, the various doubts concerning the possibility of its annulment, the scruples concerning its extension, and other reflections. Let us consider for a moment the very scrupulous exposition of the *Shulḥan 'Aruk* regarding the person who has undertaken to pay a visit and breaks his leg. We note here that this excessive caution is applied not

[1] See the Introduction.

only to the oath, but to everything 'which comes out of his mouth', as the Bible says. But is not this due merely to great conscientiousness? In some cases of obsessional neurosis, scruples and obsessive ideas appear to be exaggerations of genuine conscientiousness; the fear of bacilli appears to be merely increased caution, and so forth. This semblance, however, is destroyed as soon as we penetrate deeper into it. In the patient whose symptoms Freud has described,[1] an oath played a large part. His oath, 'Now you must really give the money back to A', which it was impossible to fulfil, is the starting-point of many of his conflicts. During a night of torture he argued backwards and forwards as to whether he should or should not fulfil his oath, and endeavoured to postpone that fulfilment without being able to come to a decision. It is clear at once that these obsessive doubts are of the same nature as the arguments about the oath in the *Shebu'ot* and *Nedarim* treatises. Perhaps in these Talmudic discussions only two factors can be seen which distinguish them from obsessional symptoms, namely, their relation to religious matters, and the apparent omission of affective factors. We know what the scruples and doubts of psychoneurotics signify: they indicate failure of the process of repression, resulting from the pressure of strong impulses. 'A special conscientiousness respecting the aims of these impulses is created by their repression; but this psychical reaction is felt to be insecure on account of its being constantly threatened by impulses lurking in the unconscious. The effect of the repressed impulses is perceived as temptation.'[2] We also know from many analyses that the doubt originally proceeded from the oscillation of the individual between love and hate, and we can surmise that this is the case here, though we do not know where such a mental substructure exists in connection with oaths, vows and denials. Obsessional symptoms of this nature are not

---

[1] 'Bemerkungen über einen Fall von Zwangsneurose', *Sammlung kleiner Schriften zur Neurosenlehre*, 3. Folge, 1913, S. 123.
[2] Freud, *ibid.* S. 128.

intelligible at once, but can only be interpreted by means
of historical inquiry. The repeated strict admonitions of
the Old Testament and the instructions of the Decalogue
to hold to oaths and vows unconditionally, as well as the
increasing definition of such obligations by law, lead us to
conclude that a temptation to withdraw from these obligations had to be conquered. The question arises, however, whether this is not one of those generalisations,
so characteristic of obsessional phenomena, by means
of which the obsessive act is unconsciously protected
against causal investigation on the part of the conscious.
Perhaps the obscure wording of the formula points in
this direction. We know that the striving for precision
which obsessional patients aim at in their manner of
expression is only a semblance, and the unreality and
obscurity of their thought processes, as well as their
abstract structure, are often unconscious devices to hide
the essential thing. Do, therefore, the strict prohibition
and the numerous arguments about it, perhaps, originally refer to a quite definite obligation? The answer to
this question is found by going still farther back—to the
earliest stages of the oath and to its original cause. We
know already that the oath was a self-imprecation. This
self-imprecation, however, also represents a self-punishment, especially if we call to mind the strong belief of
the ancients in the effectiveness of the curse. The self-
imprecation and the self-punishment suggest that the
curse was a means of retaliation, and therefore that
hostile impulses had been directed against other persons.
We are brought back to the *B'rith* ceremony which contains *in nuce* oath, vow and renunciation; the *Alah* and
division of animals gave us a hint of the hidden meaning
of the ritual. It represents one of the forms of reaction to
the primordial crime from which proceeded the founding
of religion. In the *B'rith* ritual the love side of the ambivalence is manifested by the grief and self-punishment
of the younger generation. By means of the *B'rith*, the
believers are placed under an obligation never again to
commit that old crime: it forms the remembrance, and—

if the division of the animal's body be considered—
also the repetition of that primordial deed which they
are supposed to forswear. In this primitive picture of
oath, vow and renunciation of an impulse, we find the
unconscious return of the repressed from repression.
This mechanism, by means of which repressed material
breaks through into the upper world from the depths of
the unconscious, just as in the symptomatology of the
neuroses, will frequently be met with in the course of
these inquiries. Freud has occasionally referred to a
picture by Rops as an example of the mode in which this
reversion operates. In this picture, the ascetic, oppressed
with the burden of his sin, falls down contrite before the
Cross, and there appears before him a beautiful and
voluptuous woman instead of the form of the suffering
Saviour. Let us return to the repression of the subversive impulses as it appears in the *B'rith* ritual. Later history has shown that the repression of those old wishes
only partly succeeded, and that those powerful impulses,
the partial overcoming of which reached its temporary
acme in the *B'rith*, did not cease urging a repetition of
the deed. The oath of the *B'rith* no longer sufficed
against this pressure of the impulses, and therefore the
scope of the prohibitions was more and more enlarged
and the range of their effect grew ever wider, the defensive and protective measures against the breaking
through of the forbidden impulses became more and
more numerous and urgent, and the forms of reaction
became more and more pronounced. Not only is this displacement of the limits of the prohibition extremely
well worth notice, but also the displacement of affect.
The whole strength of the affect, which originally was
intended for the wish-fulfilment of the deed, was transferred from the forbidden act to the reaction and displaced on to the defensive measures which it now took
care to preserve most strictly. The Old Testament
teaches[1] that death is the result if the *B'rith* is broken.
The same punishment which was expressd in the ritual

[1] See the asseveration formula of the *Alah*, Ezekiel xvi. 14: Kraetzschmar, S. 48.

in the form of the division of the animal with the sword, was meted out to the oath breaker. The memory of this punishment emerged with the temptation to break the oath; the original form, however, of this association was lost to consciousness when behaviour became more gentle, and when a symbol was substituted for the threat of punishment that was formerly so vividly enacted before the eyes of those taking the oath; there remained only a vague anticipation of harm, an obscure anxious apprehension attached to each fresh temptation. The overpowering sense of guilt, which was associated with the idea of breaking oaths and vows, referred to its earliest source, namely, parricide and god-murder. To break the *B'rith* signifies unconsciously a repetition of this murder. On account of the indestructibility and unchangeableness of unconscious impulses the intensity of the affect of later oaths, vows and renounced impulses is due to the energy which flows perpetually from this primary source. It is as though the *B'rith* has become the unconscious prototype of all solemn obligations for all time.

The gradual separation of the idea from the situation in which it originated can be demonstrated here just as in the case of obsessional ideas; the purpose of this separation is to prevent the conscious recognition of its real meaning. The original form of the oath, *i.e.* the indirect oath, showed a connection with the *B'rith* and the god-murder in virtue of the self-curse contained in it, but this connection was broken when the direct oath took the place of the indirect one as a result of a repression that became more and more exacting as the ages passed by. The *B'rith* had been the most solemn asseveration by the life of God; it is, as it were, an assurance given on oath not to plot against this precious life. Originally one swore by God—'truly Zeus or Jahve lives'—then later the conscious idea of his death became more and more irreconcilable with the sublimated concept of God[1] and it was therefore altered to an oath

---

[1] The painful memory of the god-murder was connected with this.

by the life of the king, and this also was subsequently dispensed with. Thus we see here also how a compulsive act was carried out without its chief significance being recognised by those practising it.

In the symptomatology of obsessions we meet with a similar process to that seen in our comparison between the threat of death in the *B'rith* and the later, more general, warning: for the connection between punishment and the overstepping of prohibitions is quite clear to the patients at the beginning; the obscure anticipation of harm only appeared in its place later. Still later, the relationship between the occasions on which this anxious anticipation appears and the actual nature of the threatened calamity becomes hidden from the patient. That striking mediæval ritual—the asseveration in connection with which a skin is shown or a bier produced—illustrates the intermediate stage between the punishment by cutting asunder 'with the edge of the sword' and the characteristic indefiniteness of the anticipation of harm if an oath is broken. We are now in a position to understand the reflections, scruples and devious discussions of the oath in the Talmud and the Talmudic writings: they are obsessional phenomena of certain composite form; they are practical and reasonable considerations which are opposed to the obsessional thoughts, but which accept certain assumptions of the obsession, and thus, under cover of reason, place themselves on the level of morbid thinking. Freud calls such a psychical activity a *delirium*.

We cannot avoid seeing that displacement is perhaps the most important mechanism in the psychological evolution of the oath. Originally the prohibition imposed by the oath only referred to the overstepping of the *B'rith, i.e.* the repetition of the primordial crime. The more this connection was lost to consciousness in later generations, the more extended its field became. It came to include oaths, vows and renunciations in general, whose observance was demanded with ever greater stringency and conscientiousness. But, on the other hand, the protective measures against the harm which might result from their breach became multiplied and displaced. The apparently grotesque distinction be- tween oaths of higher and lower degree, which we have heard about earlier, is one of these extended protective measures against the lurking temptation to break oaths. We have to regard all those clauses, limiting phrases and customs—for instance, the shyness of orthodox Jews to swear at all—as far-reaching protective measures.

What place does the Kol Nidre take in this process of evolution? The Kol Nidre seems to be a breaking through of all protective measures, a radical rupture with all the conscientiousness that went before. It actually contains the intention of breaking an oath, the intention not to carry out vows and abstinences—this much must not and cannot be denied. This fact only becomes compre- hensible through genetic and psychological investiga- tion and is only explicable if the analogy with obses- sional neurotics is taken into consideration. In the life of these patients who value their oaths and promises so scrupulously and over-conscientiously, there comes a moment when they attempt to get rid of their whole obsession, and they declare their oaths and promises in- valid in advance. It seems to us that such actions directly serve the breaking through of forbidden im- pulses for whose far-reaching protection they were originally instituted (return of the repressed from re- pression). At the same time, however, they are of service in relieving the person from the burden of his extreme conscientiousness. We can, therefore, compare the Kol Nidre with the typical symptoms of the obsessional neurosis, in which unconscious processes succeed in forcing their way into consciousness from some level of unconscious ideation in a relatively undistorted form.

We must not forget, however, to emphasise the fact that we can only fully understand the rite if we equate it with those very pedantic and painfully observed pro- hibitions which are associated with oaths. It is a necessary consequence of that heightened moral sense and, like it, is a defence measure; but with this difference, that its power is no longer directed against the unconscious impulses, but used by them against the moral precept itself. In the same way we have often heard how very devout and repentant monks would think of blasphemies in the midst of their prayers, and how ascetics and holy men were tempted to commit the worst kind of sins in their deepest contrition. The obsessional neurotic patient, described by Freud, was compelled—a converse Balaam—to mingle curses with his prayers.[1] The Kol Nidre formula is therefore to be understood as an antithesis to the very high esteem in which oaths are held among the Jews, and also as a necessary reaction against their caution and conscientiousness. In the Kol Nidre it is only *in appearance* that the extension of protective measures for the defence against temptation has been carried to extreme limits, and the psychical process of displacement accomplished its highest task;[2] *in reality*, this excessively increased conscientiousness has only effected a breaking through of the repressed impulses.

We now recognise that the formula has the character of a wish. The congregation expressed the wish to break oaths, vows and promises, although they are accustomed to attribute the greatest importance to their strict observance—and we know already that this wish, in its deepest sense, refers to a particular observation, the *B'rith*. It is not a matter of trivial vows and everyday oaths, but, deep down, there stirs the unconscious wish to carry out anew the ancient deed of violence. Our assumption that the Kol Nidre is of the nature of a wish need not be disturbed by the fact that the indicative mood is used in the formula instead of the optative. We know from the teaching of the neuroses that the boundaries between reality and phantasy fluctuate, and also

[1] Freud, *ibid.*
[2] See Frankel's psychological explanation in the *Jewish Encyclopædia*, and the commentaries usually contained in modern prayer books respecting the Kol Nidre.

that our unconscious wishes appear as fulfilled in dreams. But in any case the peculiar form of the declaration will require further explanation.

At this point we are threatened with an important objection: How did such a criminal wish get into the religious service, and above all, into that of the Holiest of Days? Is it possible that the congregation acknowledges openly such an unheard-of wish, which goes far beyond blasphemy? The answer to this question lies in its own formulation: there is *no wish at all*, only *the acknowledgement of one, an avowal, a confession of a wish*. If we translate the formula into language which is intelligible to all of us, we must preface it by an invocation to God: 'Lord, Jahve, hear us, we confess to Thee that we feel within us the wish not to keep oaths and vows, etc.'; or, 'See! we confess to Thee we are a congregation of perjurers'. This, however, renders absolutely necessary an addition, an essential complement; the prayer for mercy and forgiveness—for pardon. The acknowledgement of the wicked wish is really an appeal to God, it serves to support the prayer for pardon and mercy: God is to see how much His people are devoted to and enmeshed in sin. The frailty of human nature, its relapse into sin, and the impossibility of completely renouncing the gratification of impulses is demonstrated to Him *ad oculos*; let Him take into consideration these weaknesses, and be thereby the more disposed to grant pardon and impunity. The congregation expects divine absolution precisely in virtue of their unreserved confession. The fact that the cantor actually pronounces this prayer for pardon after the Kol Nidre may be taken as a confirmation of our view. He says: 'O pardon the sins of this people according to the greatness of Thy mercy, and as Thou hast pardoned this people of Mizraim heretofore', whereupon the congregation answers in full confidence and hope: 'And the Eternal One said, I have pardoned according to thy word'. The original meaning of the rite must have been intelligible to the community at one time, but became lost to their consciousness in the course of centuries. Its further development has proceeded from an erroneous conception of the wording, and has been accepted without considering that it required a preceding or additional sentence, and thus finally the religious-juristic formula has been reached. It will be useful to compare the beginning of the confession of sins with the formula in its original shape and liturgical significance. This confession, in its oldest constituent parts, can be traced back to about A.D. 250, and was uttered on the Day of Atonement by the congregation:[1] 'Our God and God of our fathers, our prayers come before Thee; do not hide Thyself from our supplications, for we are not bold of face and stiff-necked as to say to Thee, Jahve, our God and God of our fathers, we are righteous and have not sinned; but, of a truth, we are sinners'.

In spite of the powerful force of psychic displacement, we have recognised that the temptation to break an oath originally concerned the overstepping of the first solemn obligation, the *B'rith*. We can now also show that in our relatively recent formula there still exist traces of the obscure expectation of harm, replacing the definite threat of punishment for the horrible act of murder. It cannot now escape our deeper insight that the phrase, 'Unto the next Day of Atonement (may it come for good)', contains an optative which betrays the original anxious expectation. Is it of no significance that the cantor, at the conclusion of the rite, thanks God that He allows the believers to live? Here again any person with insight can trace a residue of the old expectation of harm. Finally, the deep contrition of the believers during the prayer points in this direction. Even in this indistinct form one can surmise that the ultimate source of the affect is the apprehension of impending evil which always follows the temptation to parricide, and which prevents the breaking of that old obligation.

But why is this peculiar method of expression used, and why does not the Kol Nidre say what it has to say in a direct manner? The real thought has become dis-

---

[1] *Die Religion in Geschichte und Gegenwart*, Tübingen, 1909, Bd. ii. S. 1585.

torted and unrecognisable. We are acquainted with this technique of distortion in dreams, jokes and the symptomatology of the neuroses. As an example, the typical obsessive thought of Freud's patient may be mentioned: 'If I marry a certain lady, misfortune will happen to my father'. If we insert the intermediate, but unconscious, missing words the thought reads: 'If my father were living, he would be averse to my marrying the lady, and would also be very angry, as he was when I was a child, so that I should again wish him every evil, and this wish could be fulfilled in virtue of the omnipotence of my thoughts'. The principal aim of this technique of ellipsis and abbreviation is to guard against recognition of the real obsessing thoughts in the obsessional neurosis. We shall have to assume the existence of the same processes in our analytical interpretation of the Kol Nidre. The abbreviation of the formula, which we have already substantiated, helps to conceal its old connection with the *B'rith* and the crime—the latter was the sole reason for the institution of oaths, vows and renunciations. We have here again an opportunity to admire the marvellous capacity for displacement shown by unconscious tendencies in their detachment from the original situation and in their far-reaching generalisations.

We are now in a position to solve those three contradictions which form the chief enigma of the Kol Nidre. The content of the formula is in no way opposed to the high esteem in which oaths are held among the Jews; rather it proves this, although this does not seem to be the case at first sight. The deeply affecting melody, to which has been set this apparently prosaic formula, is justified, since it is not related to the present wording, but to the secret feelings which have become unconscious. This music brings adequately to expression the revolutionary wish of the congregation and their subsequent anxiety; the soft broken rhythms reflect their deep remorse and contrition. Thus, the song is really full of terror and mercy, as Lenau has observed. The high mental tension, the contrition and bewailing of the congregation during this prosaic ceremony, do not refer to the actual formula they are repeating, but to its latent content. At the deepest level the ancient *B'rith* and its cause are closely related to our unconscious feelings through our own ambivalent attitude to the father. The powerful temptation, which at one time necessitated the institution of the *B'rith*, recurs in the phantasies of every individual, and those same disturbing and continuous struggles which have given the impulse to the formation of great religious and moral and social institutions in the history of peoples, also take place in his individual unconscious mental life.

We can now venture to reply to some questions which we have been unable to answer before. It will be remembered that we felt we could not agree with Bloch's and Mandelstamm's view that the Kol Nidre originated in a definite historical event. Nevertheless, an unconscious discernment of the true situation can be seen in these scholars' views, and it may be that even their errors show an obscure appreciation of the true facts, not certainly in their view that the formula owes its origin to lip-Christians, but that its unconscious source is that first falling away, that first mighty denial of God which we consider to be the origin of the *B'rith*. We have seen, however, that there is also a certain justification for the explanation that the Kol Nidre is only an expression of excessive and refined conscientiousness. We now understand, too, the difference between the readings of the formula: the formula, or rather the affect underlying it, refers equally well to the past as to the future year. The assumption, that not only past obligations but also future ones are subject to obsessive conscientiousness, is justified by the mechanism of displacement, and necessitated by our psychological explanation of the rite as a protective measure against impending evil. The example of the obsessional neurosis with the anticipated annulment of all resolutions enables us to understand the primary form of the Kol Nidre which declared the vows of the future year null and void. The displacement to the past year is quite in accordance with obsessive neurotic symptoms, and results from the extension of the anxious expectation. We have heard of the legal institution of the sixteenth century whereby judges were not to administer oaths on days of repentance, and I may recall Frankel's ingenious attempt to explain it, namely, that on these days, devoted to contrition and remorse, the believer will not have the necessary peace of mind to take the oath. We can now add: This regulation also contains the idea of excluding during those days, which are devoted to repentance, the temptation which, in view of its origin, is found in every oath. For in this case, just as on the Day of Atonement, there is the risk that the aim of all remorse and of all prayers will be frustrated through a sudden return of the repressed.

We have learned that the formula of the oath was originally pronounced at the Feast of the New Year, as we have already surmised, and was only later transferred to the Day of Atonement. Strack suggests[1] that the displacement occurred because the congregation was particularly numerous in the temple on that day. I must confess, however, that this idea hardly seems convincing; it is not correct, so far as the ancient Jews are concerned, that the congregation only visited the temple in unusually large numbers on this day. Strack derives his idea from the modern circumstances. Further, it seems to me, that for such a displacement to occur, there must have been some relation between the content of the Kol Nidre and the Day of Atonement. In my view it can only be explained historically. The Day of Atonement was the last of all feasts of the Jewish religion to be instituted. Ezekiel[2] is the first to prescribe such an observance, and the celebration of absolution of the *Yom ha-Kippurim* is first demanded in the codex of the priests.[3] With the increasing significance of this feast, which Delitzsch with some justification has called the Good Friday of the Old

---

[1] Compare the opinion quoted above from the *Realenzyklopädie für protestantische Theologie.*
[2] Ezekiel xlv. 18-20.   [3] Leviticus xvi.

Testament,[1] the formula was transferred to the great Day of Atonement. This displacement is made possible by two circumstances. The festival of the Day of Atonement probably represents a splitting off from the New Year celebration, and its purpose is to give believers an opportunity for remorse and repentance. It is no mere accident that the high priest on this day renews the congregation's *B'rith* with the Lord at the same time as he gives absolution to the congregation through the sacrifice. The sacrifice of expiatory animals on the Day of Atonement was later replaced by other expiatory rites, in particular by the repeated confession of sins. The repetition of the ancient crime of god-murder and its expiation was embodied in the old sacrificial ritual. It was precisely this expiatory act, the offering of the totem animals, which represented the renewal of the crime. Thus, in the name of religion, an act was performed which in itself was an offence, just as in the Kol Nidre a blasphemy is uttered in the midst of the service. As in the ancient cult, so also in the later form of the confession of the Kol Nidre, the suppressed impulse which suddenly succeeds in breaking into the region of consciousness is for a moment victorious. Absolution and the confession of guilt form the essential content of the Day of Atonement in ancient as in recent times.[2] And we see that this must be so when we consider the strength of that temptation which urges the breaking of the *B'rith*. Only on such a memorable day could the Kol Nidre obtain the place to which it is psychically entitled. Finally, I may mention that a general confession of sins (*'Al Het*) is made repeatedly by the congregation on the Day of Atonement.

Another question arises here. Why was the Kol Nidre put at the beginning of the service? It might be supposed that the reservation of such a special position for it was

[1] Friedrich Delitzsch, *Prolegomena eines neuen hebräisch-aramäischen Wörterbuches*, S. 183.

[2] The Talmud says, concerning the liturgy on the Day of Atonement, 'Judas' prayer consisted in the confession of his sins' (Meg. 25B: compare also Sot. 7 and 10).

due to its latent relation to the *B'rith*. But the position can also be accounted for by the meaning of the feast. All the expiation and repentance that is about to take place is liable to disturbance by the compulsive breaking through of counter-impulses, in the same way as Freud's obsessional patient interspersed his prayers with denials of their meaning. This patient invented the rapid uttering of phrases, abbreviations and other devices as protective measures against such disturbances. It was perhaps for similar reasons that the Kol Nidre formula was taken out of its setting in the liturgy and placed at the commencement of the service. It would thus serve as a protective measure against the harm which unconscious impulses might cause during the feast. Many obsessional neurotics endeavour to isolate every protective act in a similar manner.

We can now understand that sentence in the Kol Nidre which is spoken by the whole congregation in reply to the cantor, namely, 'And it shall be forgiven all the congregation of the children of Israel, and the stranger that sojourneth among them, seeing all the people were in ignorance'. This does not mean, as Bloch would have us believe, that possibly whole communities were made lip-Christians at the time of the domination of the Western Goths, but that the *B'rith* was concluded between God and the whole race, and not between a single individual and God, since all members of the race felt themselves together guilty of the primal crime against God. The expression 'in ignorance' alludes only in a derivative way to 'errors through ignorance', to involuntary faults. According to our view it originally applied to the unconscious root of all temptation to break prohibitions. The fact that the melody of the Kol Nidre[1] showed certain similarities with the Catholic forms of repentance of the Middle Ages accords with this view. The justice of our conception as to the latent meaning of the formula is substantiated by the manner in which it is replaced in the Reform Synagogue. We have

---

[1] According to the *Jewish Encyclopædia*, vol. vii. p. 543.

come to the conclusion that the Kol Nidre is the acknowledgement of forbidden wishes of pious people expressed
in a distorted and unrecognisable form. The unconscious
recognition of this meaning has led, for example, to the
text of Psalm cxxx. being set to the melody in Lewandowski's adaptation:

1. Out of the depths have I cried unto thee, O LORD.
2. Lord, hear my voice: let thine ears be attentive to
the voice of my supplications.
3. *If thou, Lord, shouldest mark iniquities, O Lord, who
shall stand?*
4. But there is forgiveness with thee, that thou mayest
be feared.
5. I wait for the Lord, my soul doth wait, and in his
word do I hope.
6. My soul waiteth for the Lord more than they that
watch for the morning: I say, more than they that watch
for the morning.
7. Let Israel hope in the Lord: for with the Lord there
is mercy, and with him is plenteous redemption.
8. And he shall redeem Israel from all his iniquities.

The text 'God of love and mercy', used in some Reform
congregations,[1] is quite similar.

We are at last in a position to point out in what way
this formula differs from the analogous symptoms of
obsessional neurotics which rest on the same mental
motives. The difference lies principally in the social
character of our formula—a character which is also
expressed in the answer of the congregation to the
cantor. The obsessional neurosis is indeed, as Freud puts
it, 'the religion of an individual'.

V. CONCLUSION

In concluding this inquiry it is desirable to consider
the mental environment in which the Kol Nidre origin-

---

[1] More details are given in Professor Emil Breslaur's short monograph, *Sind
originale Synagogen- und Volksmelodien bei den Juden nachweisbar?* Leipzig,
1898, S. 34.

ated. Just as this rite unites acknowledgement of one's own infirmities and sins with the defiance which originates in the breaking through of forbidden tendencies, so post-exilic Judaism fluctuated between an enormously increased sense of guilt and a heightened feeling of self-righteousness. A heavy feeling of guilt would rest upon the community. It feared the Day of the Lord, the great Judgement which Jahve would hold. 'Our iniquities are increased over our head, and our trespass is grown up unto the heavens.'[1] But in the next moment it would feel itself justified before God and proudly raise its head. Then, as suddenly, it would come down from its exalted state, reminded by some external misfortune of the fact that it was encompassed by its own sins. It strove against the confession of its guilt—like Job, the man of Uz, who was both wicked and righteous—and yet only such a confession could give it relief. Psalm xxxii. 1-4 expresses it:

1. Blessed is he whose transgression is forgiven, whose sin is covered.[2]

3. When I kept silence, my bones waxed old through my roaring all the day long.

4. For day and night thy hand was heavy upon me: my moisture is turned into the drought of summer.

The congregation believe that if they do not see an immediate danger they are innocent, they even dare to challenge the strictest investigation by God. If, however, God's hand lies upon them their self-criticism becomes extremely severe. Their own sins now appear to them to be more numerous than the hairs on their heads.[3] The whole congregation humiliates itself: 'I acknowledged my sin unto thee, and mine iniquity have I not hid. I said, I will confess my transgressions unto the Lord; and thou forgavest the iniquity of my sin.'[4] We must not forget that the confessional nature of the Kol Nidre explained the vehement emotion and the subsequent relaxation of psychical tension felt by the believers. If, as

---

[1] Ezra ix. 6.   [2] =pardoned.   [3] Psalm xl. 12.   [4] Psalm xxxii. 5.

Smend suggests,[1] the community never passed out of this state of fluctuation between guilty consciousness and self-righteousness, and if every danger from without increased their sense of guilt, their psychical situation approximates to that of obsessional neurotic patients. The expectation of harm which we find disguised in the Kol Nidre formula is clearly discernible in the mental life of the time in which it probably took its origin. The community believed that they must needs live under the burden of God's wrath; according to Psalm xc. he drove generation after generation into death. A short life was looked upon as a particular sign of the fulfilment of God's ire. Thus the Kol Nidre, this Jewish *pater peccavi*, nowhere belies the traces of its origin.

We should be led too far astray if we attempted to quote parallel instances from the liturgy of other religions for the purposes of comparison. Certainly there are such phenomena, and no one who has studied the theories and practice of the remission of sins of the Middle Ages, the indulgences, confessions, exomologesis and absolutions, will deny the similarity of these religious practices to what is essential in the Kol Nidre. The anticipated removal of future sins in the remission of sins, and the constitutive elements of the confession (*contritio* and *confessio*) of the early Middle Ages, are plain enough to those who do not feel bound to adhere to the actual wording, but are seeking for the psychical kernel of the matter. The same objections against the remission of sins have been made from many quarters with the same justice or injustice as against the Kol Nidre.[2] The

---

[1] Rudolf Smend, *Lehrbuch der alttestamentlichen Religionsgeschichte*, Freiburg und Leipzig, 1893, S. 433.

[2] The differentiation between remission of punishment for sins and remission of the guilt of sins (*a culpa et poena*) is certainly secondary, and psychically corresponds completely with the doubts and obsessive thoughts of neurotics. This differentiation does not exist on certain occasions, as, for instance, in the indulgences of the Jubilee year. The erroneous belief that the remission of sins refers to future sins is analogous to the supposed abrogation of oaths in the Kol Nidre. Preachers and writers of the Middle Ages affirm that the so-called letters of confession and dispensations (*confessionalia*) actually refer to future sins. (See Franz Beringer, *Die Ablässe, ihr Wesen und Gebrauch*, Paderborn, 1906, S: 14.) The similarity of certain formulas of remission to the Kol Nidre is quite evident—for instance, the indulgences of the Jubilee year and the papal dis-

comparative investigation of religion should succeed in demonstrating the psychical indentity between the Kol Nidre[1] and the Catholic 'public confession' in the liturgy of the Middle Ages. I have no doubt that psychological religious research will find in the *Confiteor*,[2] which precedes the Mass, and in the *Kyrie Eleison*,[3] a similar liturgical formula, the theological theories concerning

---

pensations on the occasion of church feasts: *omnibus vere poenitentibus et confessis in festivitate . . . unum annum et quadraginta de injunctis sibi poenitentiis relaxamus.* (According to Al. Bendel, *Der kirchliche Ablass*, Rottweil a. N., 1847, S. 88.)

[1] The custom of the 'public confession' can be traced back very far. The oldest trace is said to be in old Slavonic formulas of confession from the ninth century (printed by Kopitar, *Glagolita Clozianus*, Wien, 1836, S. xxxv.). Those mentioned by Müllenhof and Scherer (*Denkmäler deutscher Poesie und Prosa*, 3. Auflage, i. S. 297) belong to the eleventh and twelfth centuries. In Lutheranism the general prayer of confession, which, like the Kol Nidre, is very often said at the beginning of the service in the German order, takes the place of the 'public confession'. Here, as well as in the Kol Nidre, a formula of absolution follows. It is interesting to note that the Vienna manuscript of the twelfth century published by Hoffmann expressly restricts the confession of sins to the day on which the members of the community wish to take the Lord's Supper. The public confession stands here in direct relation to the celebration of the Lord's Supper, just as the Kol Nidre does to the sacrifice on the Day of Atonement. Both rites are derivatives of the old totem meal. When in the *Didaché* of the Twelve Apostles (from the first half of the second century) the instruction is given, 'Meet together on the Lord's Day in order to break bread and give thanks, but first confess your sins so that your sacrifice may be pure' (Franz Ser. Renz, *Die Geschichte des Messopferbegriffes*, Freising, 1901, Bd. i. S. 144), the connection is just as clear as the Old Testament remission of sins of the community on the Day of Atonement before the commencement of the celebration. We see in all these various rites a confession of anticipated sins and a prayer for mercy on account of that human guilt which appears again in the subsequent service (in the repetition of parricide typified by the sacrifice).

[2] The *Confiteor* is spoken by the priest and ministrants and finishes with a formula of absolution. Like the Kol Nidre it serves as a preparation for the religious service. The confession of sins includes sins *cogitatione, verbo et opere*, and contrition is expressed by the explanation, '*Mea culpa, mea maxima culpa*' (compare Luther's cry 'My sin, my sin'). After this the priest goes up to the altar with the exhortation *Oremus* and begins the service. (See S. Rietschel, *Lehrbuch der Liturgik*, Berlin, 1900, Bd. i. S. 356.) In Lutheranism the *Confiteor*, from being a preparation of the priest, became a preparation of the congregation.

[3] The *Kyrie Eleison* has also a long liturgical history in its development from what was originally a cry of the congregation until it attained independent significance as *vox deprecationis*. How very similar the psychical process in this development is to that of the Kol Nidre becomes clear from what Rietschel says (*ibid.* S. 518): 'It is, however, quite unintelligible in the disconnected way in which it follows the *Introitus*, and it cannot be psychologically justified in this isolated position. The congregation's cry of repentance must be conveyed by means of a congregational *Confiteor* previously commanded in the liturgy. This *Confiteor* of the whole congregation must be distinguished from that of the particular confession, in that it shows greater generality of form and content (not "I" but "we").' Compare the abbreviation in the Kol Nidre and our suggested reconstruction of the missing stages.

which again present most of these puzzles and contradictions which can only be solved with the help of
psycho-analytical methods. In these religious practices,
too, we find a separation from the original context. They
have become more and more unrecognisable through
isolation, reversal and abbreviation. The similarity of
the Kol Nidre melody with the old Catholic hymns of
repentance is a sign of mental congruence. Finally,
reference may be made to the fact that the *Confiteor* and
the Collects for the purification of thoughts, etc., in
various liturgies are acts of preparations before the Lord's
Supper, intended, like the Kol Nidre, as a security
against the emergence of blasphemous and subversive
tendencies during the celebration. A more profound consideration will show that there is no essential difference
between these religious practices and the Kol Nidre:
grattez le juif et vous trouverez l'homme. It is surprising
that scholars have failed so long to notice these analogies.
It would be very unlikely that such human and natural
impulses as we have found in the Kol Nidre should not
recur in more or less pronounced forms in the religions
and customs of other peoples. At any rate, this seems to
be indicated by the saying, 'The way to hell is paved
with good intentions'.

As this first attempt to apply psycho-analytic methods
to a complicated liturgical problem shows, there are still
numerous unsolved questions in this field of psycho-
analytical work. I think, however, we should take it as
a good omen that the present solution started from
factors which up to now were either little appreciated or
not considered at all. An inner voice tells us that to
psycho-analysis also may be applied those beautiful and
prophetic words from Psalm cxviii. 22: 'The stone which
the builders refused is become the head stone of the
corner'.

SUPPLEMENTS, 1928

I

My friend and teacher, Dr. Karl Abraham, has raised the sound criticism to the above views, that they deal with the psycho-analytical interpretation of the Kol Nidre alone, instead of considering it a part of the complete ritual. He himself has attempted this latter method briefly,[1] and thereby made the yearly Feast of Atonement fully comprehensible. The rite of the Day of Atonement shows a most striking connection between the primitive ceremonial of the totem meal and the Kol Nidre. 'On the day before the feast, that is to say, therefore, a few hours before the Kol Nidre prayer, a rite takes place which represents a strange survival of the old sacrificial cult. In this ceremony a male person takes a cock, a woman a hen, as an expiatory sacrifice. The bird, with its legs tied together, is swung three times round the head of the atoning person who meanwhile recites a formula. The words of this formula are almost like an incantation. Their purport is: "This is my expiatory sacrifice, this is my representative, this cock is to die instead of me". The sacrificial bird, after the ceremony of swinging it three times, is thrown aside with a gesture of abhorrence, but afterwards is killed and eaten by the family.' Abraham alludes to the fact that according to the wording of the formula the bird represents the bringer of the sacrifice himself, and that the identity of this person with the totem can be proved in other cults. He says that before the beginning of the Feast of Atonement the totem meal is held in every house according to ancient customs and thus is repeated yearly the 'primal crime'. After the abolition of the official sacrifice the ceremony could not be carried out by the whole community and took refuge in a domestic cult. In like

[1] 'Der Versöhnungstag.' Remarks on Reik's 'Probleme der Religionspsychologie', *Imago*, vi., 1920, S. 80.

manner many other customs and religious views from heathenish times, which have been officially abolished, still live in the customs of the people. Abraham next points out that from this meal until the sunset of the next day the enjoyment of food and drink is entirely prohibited, that is to say, that the sinful meal is immediately followed by a prolonged fast. Now it is comprehensible why the abstention from all food represents the most suitable type of atonement. Just as a neurotic act of self-torture is a reaction against a sadistic impulse, so the fast is an act of self-sacrifice which includes self-punishment for the killing and eating of the totem. In the present celebration of divine service, which follows the meal in the home, nothing occurs but a repetition of the primal crime. There is still a communal rite for which the responsibility is shared by all, though this consists no longer in actions but in thoughts and spoken formulas, after the pattern of an obsessional neurosis. If my explanation of the Kol Nidre is accepted, the intellectual loosening of the bond with the father-god is seen to take the place of the killing of the totem. Abraham alludes to the ceremony in which, according to an ancient rite, the two oldest men of the congregation stepped forward, and in a solemn and formal manner gave consent to the utterance of the Kol Nidre; a custom which is not met anywhere else in the liturgy. On the Day of Atonement, every cantor, before he commences that part of the liturgy allotted to him, has to say a long and special prayer of his own. It is noteworthy that this procedure is omitted from the service of the previous evening. Here the cantor does not ask for God's assistance for the execution of his office, but receives his authority from the elders. Thus does the congregation arrogantly take the responsibility upon itself. Thereafter the Kol Nidre is sung solemnly three times. The sequence of events in the domestic ceremony, which corresponds to the sacrifice and eating, is comparable to that in the congregation ritual of the annulling of vows in the divine service. This demonstrates the inner homogeneity of the two acts, and forms an important support for Reik's idea. The isolation of the Kol Nidre from the rest of the liturgy of the Day of Atonement has a satisfactory explanation. The Kol Nidre is the substitute for the violent excesses against the father-god, that is, for the totem meal, which is followed by the great act of re- pentance; hence the Kol Nidre can only precede this repentance. The carnival and the subsequent period of fasting, as well as other examples, show that a period of atonement and renunciation is preceded by the excesses. Abraham gives a few impressive examples from the symptomatology of obsessional neuroses which show the same mechanisms. One should refer to Abraham's essay itself, which gives many interesting supplements and confirmations of my work, and I will only call atten- tion to a most significant detail which he has explained: 'Reik's idea of the bond-destroying significance of the Kol Nidre is confirmed by the conclusion of the liturgy of the Day of Atonement which merits our special attention. The solemn concluding prayer (*N'ilah*) ends in a confession. The Cantor pronounces the "*Sch'ma*" (Hear Israel!) three times, and the congregation thrice repeat it. After a further thrice repeated sentence the confession, "Jahve is the only God", follows, and is re- peated emphatically seven times. With this the liturgy of the day finishes.' Thus the Day of Atonement begins with the blasphemous abrogation of vows—or more correctly, the *B'rith* with Jahve—and ends with the emphatic announcement of his uniqueness and power. The bond is therewith re-established in the most solemn manner, reconciliation of the congregation with Jahve has taken place. The deepest meaning of the Day of Atonement now becomes evident: 'the slain father-god is acknowledged by his sons anew and on his side takes over again his obligations towards his children' (S. 89). Abraham's amazingly clear-sighted investigation, which psychologically inserts the Kol Nidre formula into the liturgy of the Day of Atonement, concludes with a résumé which confirms and completes what I have already said. 'The bond with Jahve involves the restraint of many impulses, and is a burden to the congregation which is only bearable if it may be broken at certain intervals. These intervals, however, cannot be left to individual choice. By the responsibility of all in common the *B'rith* was dissolved once a year, but again renewed after a short-lived gratification of rebellious impulses. Without this renewed confirmation, which nevertheless could only be effected after an abreaction of the hostile tendencies, the bond was not proof against internal and external threats. In this way the Day of Atonement originated, the liturgy of which begins with the gloomy sounds of the Kol Nidre telling of oppressive guilt, in order to end in the loud announcement of the uniqueness of God.'

II

Dr. Géza Róheim in a valuable paper, 'Zur Psychologie der Bundesriten', *Imago*, vi., 1920, S. 397, has quoted and investigated analytically numerous analogous customs which confirm my interpretation of the rites at the execution of the oath and bond.

THE SHOFAR[1]

(THE RAM'S HORN)

Wer weiss! Der Baum glaubt auf zu Dir zu rauschen—
Und doch ist's nur Dein Sturm, der durch ihn weht—
So—sprichst—vielleicht aus mir—Du—zu Dir selber . . .
Zwiesprach von Dir—mit Dir—ist mein Gebet!
              BEER-HOFMANN, *Jaákobs Traum.*

I. THE FIRST PROBLEM

SOME little time ago I was present at a gathering of
people who were greatly interested in music, and
the conversation turned on the origin of musical
art. As the various theories put forward did not seem to
throw much light on the subject, one of those taking
part in the discussion suggested that perhaps the sagas
and myths of ancient peoples could give some account
of the beginnings of music. He observed that a certain
measure of truth is often concealed in these produc-
tions of human phantasies, and that the expert student
may be able to interpret their drift.

Volume I of Ambros'[2] *History of Music* was consulted,
and furnished a bewildering abundance of myths describing the discovery of music among the Indians,
Chinese, Egyptians and Greeks.[3] The common feature
in these myths is that in them all the invention of music
and of the first musical instruments is ascribed to gods
and demi-gods: Orpheus, Arion, Hermes, Osiris, Athene
and Marsyas—everywhere it is a god who communicated his sufferings to human beings by means of sounds.
But it was pointed out that there is one exception to this
rule, and that the people upon whose religion and ethics

---

[1] Read before the Vienna Psycho-Analytical Society, January 5, 1919.
[2] A. W. Ambros, *Geschichte der Musik,* 3. Auflage, Leipzig, 1887, Bd. i.
[3] Two books by Engel, *Musical Myths and Facts,* 2 vols., London, 1870, and
the *Music of the Most Ancient Nations,* London, 1864, give a detailed review of
this material. Some allusions to myths of present-day savage peoples concerning the origin of music are found in Richard Wallaschek's *Primitive Music*
London, 1893, p. 259.

rests the greatest part of our civilisation had no myth of the origin of music, and did not derive it from God. The invention of the oldest musical instruments is mentioned briefly and casually in the Bible, and ascribed to an ordinary mortal named Jubal.

'And how does our scriptural authority explain this striking exception?' said our hostess, turning to me with friendly irony. The prohibition of images in the Old Testament immediately occurred to my mind, but was rejected—unjustly, as we shall see—and I had to admit with some shame that I could not give any explanation of this peculiar fact.

This was the rather trivial cause of my interest in the origin of music. My investigations gradually took me far away from my starting-point, but eventually brought me back to it after a long though not circuitous journey. I feel sure that the wide and surprising prospect that will be opened up will compensate somewhat for the tediousness of the journey.

In Genesis iv. 21, it is said that Adah bare Jubal, and that 'he was the father of all such as handle the harp and organ'. This tradition is interesting for several reasons: its deviation from other myths has already been mentioned, but its brevity, which contrasts with the more elaborate stories of the origin of music, is also worth noting, and, further, the name of the first musician is significant. The name Jubal is from the same root as *jôbēl* יובל,[1] which signifies ram's horn or trumpet; so that the name of the inventor is identified with that of an instrument which is of importance in a religious cult. Attempts have been made to interpret this fact, but

---

[1] This etymology, as well as the fraternal relationship of Jabel and Jubal in Genesis iv., might yield far-reaching conclusions as regards both the original meaning of the Cain-Abel story and the genealogical tree of the primitive family, if the following elucidation were taken into account.

Tradition in the Orient still maintains that Jubal was a Canaanite. This tradition, according to Chadrim, *Voyage en Perse*, tome v. p. 69, exists at the present time in Persia and Arabia, where the musicians and sinners are called Kaynè, *i.e.* descendants of Cain. Has not the obscure memory of an old deed of violence connected with the invention of music persisted in this derivation? Perhaps a comparison of the myths of Marsyas, Orpheus and other heroes of the first musical art would yield a number of surprising results.

without success; it still remains obscure. It may be
pointed out that some investigators have tried to recognise Abel, Cain's unfortunate brother, in Jubal. The
brief statement in Genesis has, therefore, only added a
new problem to the previous one.

It would certainly be appropriate to see whether we
cannot reach an explanation by investigating the function of music in ancient Judaism. We know that its most
important and most frequent use was in connection with
the religious cult. The reports about the function of
music come, however, from a relatively late period, and
we have, therefore, to fall back on hypotheses as to the
pre-Jahvistic period of music, and these can only be
supported by indefinite and meagre allusions in the Bible.
If we may believe such an eminent authority as Hugo
Gressmann,[1] music among the Hebrews was used in sorcery earlier than in religion. The bells on the vestments
of the high priest tinkled when he went into the Holy
Place in order that he should not die. Gressmann doubts
whether the belief that the sound of bells as a protection
against the wrath of God is primitive. In ancient times
bells and similar musical instruments were probably used
to drive away demons which take up their abode in or
about the Holy Place. Wellhausen found such bells used
as an apotropaic amulet among the heathen Arabs.[2]
Similar beliefs are found in every corner of the world.
In the Bacchanalian feasts, the Saturnalia, and the
Lupercalia, it was thought that the sound of cymbals
and bells drove away malicious demons who might im-
pair the fertility which the ceremonies were intended
to promote. Demons appear to hate sounds made by
blowing and the sound of large and small bells. The
Chinese from time immemorial beat the tamtam and
rattled chains in order to drive into darkness the dragon
who wishes to devour the son and heir. Among the Abys-
sinian Christians the sistrum is used simply as a demon

[1] Hugo Gressmann, *Musik und Musikinstrumente im Alten Testament*,
Giessen, 1903, S. 5.
[2] *Reste arabischen Heidentums*, 2. Auflage, S. 165.

rattle. According to Gressmann the same idea is still expressed to-day by the Catholic priests when they recite the formula for the consecration of church bells. Gressmann's explanation of these phenomena is certainly suggestive though not complete. He abstracts from them a defensive mechanism which is common to other protective rites or customs. Thus the Arabs call the moaning of demons heard in the desert *ažif al ǧinn*—an expression used also of musical instruments—and according to its intensity compare it with thunder, the sound of cymbals, beating of kettle-drums, ringing of bells, and other sounds. 'The noise which the *ǧinns* make is driven away by the noise of human beings.' We shall return to these homœopathic methods.

The story of the conquest of Jericho seems to record a magical application of music. In the tradition which has come down to us, the noise of the trumpets is a factor which merely accompanies a marvel of Jahve's omnipotence. What is the purpose of the noise? Perhaps it was originally a magic representation of the falling of the walls of the fortress which imitated the event it was intended to produce. Robertson Smith believes that the blowing of trumpets in the temple can also be explained from the point of view of magic—perhaps the imitation of thunder.[1]

Gressmann thinks, however, that an older though indistinct idea is also involved, and that the blowing of trumpets originally had the same object as the crying aloud and calling out of the priests of Baal on Carmel.[2] The Deity, who has so much to do and is perchance occupied elsewhere, has to be called loudly in order to attract his attention. Such an indelicate method of calling attention to oneself seems to us very improper, but it is certain that a similar tendency originally existed in prayer. Silent prayer is quite a late phenomenon. When Hannah uttered a silent prayer in the temple, the priest considered her action so extraordinary that he thought

---

[1] Robertson Smith, *The Religion of the Semites.*
[2] I Kings xviii. 28. Gressmann, *ibid.* S. 9.

she was intoxicated. The principle to be observed in intercourse with the Deity was originally—the louder the better. One does not speak with God, one cries (קרא), or calls out to Him (צעק).[1] Hosea[2] is the first to reject the crying-out, with the rite of self-cutting and scratching, as heathenish, and to demand instead a cry of the heart to God. Incidentally it may be remarked that the phrase 'It sounds like a Jewish school', which originated in the Middle Ages and has obtained such peculiar popularity in our beloved city, and which referred to the loudness and confused medley of voices in the temple, thus finds its historical explanation. The original purpose of the praying, which was really a crying to God, has become lost to the popular consciousness, and only occasionally breaks through in wit, as, for instance, in the following anecdote. An old man during the service on the Day of Atonement rebukes one of those praying, who is beating his breast very violently and very loudly confessing his sinfulness and remorse, in these words: 'Young man, force will do nothing with Him up there'. We must admit that Gressmann's work affords us a good deal of light, but it has yielded nothing really definite as to the origin of music in ancient Judaism.

Perhaps the present Jewish religious cult will help us. Here, however, we meet with an unexpected obstacle; kettle-drums, trumpets, zithers, flutes, triangles, cymbals and many percussive, wind, and string instruments which sounded at the great feasts of the ancient Jews, and enhanced their solemn mood, these are all silent

[1] It may at once be premised that not only do the expressions of the prayer change their form in the course of cultural development, but parallel with them the utterances of the god for whom they are intended. Jahve spoke in one way to his votaries in the primitive time, and in another way to those who held a deeper belief. Jahve on Sinai appears to the people in the burning thorn-bush with the sound of trumpets and earthquakes, but manifests himself to Elijah in another way; the Lord is not in the strong destroying wind, nor in the earthquake nor in the fire, but in the gentle breeze (1 Kings xix. 11-13). Michael says:

> Da flammt ein blitzendes Verheeren
> Dem Pfade vor des Donnerschlags;
> Doch deine Boten, Herr, verehren
> Das sanfte Wandeln deines Tags.
>
> (*Prolog im Himmel.*)

[2] Hosea vii. 14.

P

since that 9 Ab., August 17, A.D. 70, upon which date the fate of the Jews was decided for two thousand years. One instrument only has been retained by the unfortunate people in their dispersion and condemnation.[1] This instrument, however, is a remarkable one, and the puzzles it offers will now be our theme. At the outset it must be pointed out that we are stepping into the most obscure region of the Jewish liturgy, a *terra incognita* comparable to a primitive forest, reverently avoided by the science of religion, rich in confusing, mysterious, frequently even uncanny characteristics, but in which our curiosity is strained to the uttermost. It will demand our closest attention to remain sure of our bearings.

II. THE SHOFAR

The shofar is not only the sole primitive instrument which still plays a part in the ritual of Judaism, but it is also one of the oldest wind instruments known. Professor Steintal has expressed the opinion[2] that the shofar shows 'that quite in our neighbourhood, I might say among us, things are found which are prehistoric. . . .'

The horn of the antelope and primitive bull, and hollowed-out tusks of the mammoth are found as wind instruments in prehistoric burial-places.[3] While all other instruments had undergone technical improvements the shofar has retained its prehistoric simplicity and crudeness. But our interest in the shofar, which is already awakened by its antiquity, will be increased when we learn that it is not a musical instrument. It is said[4] that, 'no melody can be played on it and that it cannot produce different sounds'. Hipkins[5] states, however, that

---

[1] No importance need be attached to the modern and assimilative use of the organ, etc., in the Reform Service.

[2] Apropos of a report concerning the discovery of a shofar (*Verhandlungen der Gesellschaft für Anthropologie, Ethnologie und Urgeschichte*, 1880).

[3] Carl Stumpf, *Die Anfänge der Musik*, Leipzig, 1911, S. 35.

[4] *Realenzyklopädie für protestantische Theologie.*

[5] A. J. Hipkins, *Musical Instruments*, etc., Edinburgh, 1888, p. 12. The very few sounds which can be produced from the shofar also testify to its extreme age. Compare Wallaschek's remarks (*Primitive Music*, p. 151) on the sounds of other primitive instruments. 'An ancient pipe from the stone age (illustrated by

three sounds can be obtained by blowing the shofar. Busch's theory of the relationship of music to noise suggests itself here. We shall see that the remarkable characteristics of this primitive instrument afford only a suggestion of the many and important problems which arise from its function in the rite.

However, we must not anticipate, but first of all learn what a shofar is and what it looks like. The accompanying illustration portrays three examples of the shofar, and gives some idea of this peculiar instrument. Its chief features are its shape and the material of which it consists. In shape it is always curved, the horn of all animals except the bull may be used for it. The Talmud[1] and the *Shulḥan 'Aruk*[2] give the reason for this exception, namely, to avoid awakening the memory of the fatal episode of the golden calf. The shofar may be engraved but not painted. The *Mishnah Rosh ha-Shanah* (iii. 3) distinguishes two kinds of shofar; that used at the New Year's Feast was made from the horn of the wild goat, the *jaâl*, with the mouthpiece covered with gold, and that used on Fast Days was a ram's horn with the mouthpiece covered with silver. The shofar used in the synagogues at the present time has no ornamentation; and Adler is quite right in assuming[3] that 'it probably represents a more ancient form than the instrument described in the *Mishnah*'. A shofar that has been broken and stuck together must not be used; but if it has merely had a hole in it it may be used provided that the hole has been effectually closed so that the sound is not impaired.[4] Originally women and children were forbidden to hear the sound of the shofar; this prohibition, however, has been forgotten, and now they usually wait to hear it blown. Besides this curved horn, the straight

---

Fétis) shows the first four tones (*i.e.* one of the equal halves) of the diatonic scale. An instrument from ancient Mexico called by Baker, *Shalmei*, has the first five tones of the diatonic scale in major . . .', etc.

[1] *Mishnah Rosh ha-Shanah*, iii. 2.
[2] *Oraḥ Ḥayyim*, 586.
[3] Cyrus Adler, 'The Shofar. Its Use and Origin', *Annual Report of the Smithsonian Institution*, 1892, p. 442.
[4] *Mishnah Rosh ha-Shanah*, iii. 6.

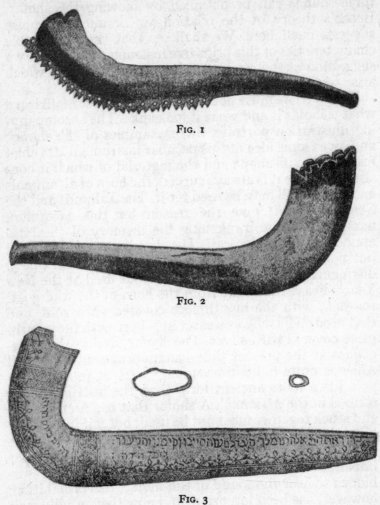

FIG. 1

FIG. 2

FIG. 3

The illustrations are taken from the *Annual Report of the Smithsonian Institution*, 1892, p. 440. Further illustrations of shofars are to be found in the *Jewish Encyclopædia*.

FIG. 1.—Shofar of the great Synagogue, Aldgate, London.

FIG. 2.—Shofar which was exhibited at the Anglo-Jewish Exhibition. Probably from the time before the banishment of the English Jews (1290).

FIG. 3.—Shofar with inscriptions.

variety and the trumpet are also used as wind instruments in the ancient Jewish cult. The difference lies only in the shape and material. The horn as an old and consecrated instrument is found as κερατίνη and σάλπιγξ among the Greeks, and as *lituus* and *buccina* among the Romans. The hypothesis is supported by numerous facts that these instruments have all evolved from a simple horn of an animal, and have been perfected by technical improvements and the use of bronze, silver and gold.[1] The primitive blow-horn, the progenitor of all these improved types, was gradually superseded by them, and remains only in the form of the shofar and the signal horn of primitive peoples. In Hebrew there are two words for the horn of the same animal, *keren* and *jôbel*, which originally denoted the animal itself. Adler has referred[2] to a similar ambiguity of the Hebrew *keren*, the English *horn*, and the Latin *cornu*—words which denote both a wind instrument and the horn of an animal; the German *horn* and the French *cornet* have the same double meanings.

Now that we have a general idea of the shofar we may pass on to its use in ancient Judaism. The law-giving on Sinai[3] was consummated amidst lightning and thunder and the terrifying sounds of the shofar. Abraham ibn Ezra believes that the Jews did not know of the shofar until the revelation on Sinai, and were far more terrified by the unusual sounds than by the storm that accompanied the revelation. In ancient Palestine the shofar was used for a summons or alarm. The people were assembled together by means of its raucous sounds when laws, orders and institutions had to be proclaimed. It proclaimed the year of *Jôbel*, which takes its name from the horn. The sound of the shofar was heard at every

---

[1] The Egyptians also had a similar bent horn called *chnue* which was blown at sacrifices. The Greek κέρας was made out of the horn of a bison or similar animal. The above supposed development of the horn instrument is confirmed by Varro, *De lingua lat.* v. 117: 'Ea (cornua), quae nunc sunt ex aere, tunc fiebant e bubulo cornu'. The matter is discussed further by Johann Weiss, *Die musikalischen Instrumente in den Heiligen Schriften des Testaments*, Graz, 1895, S. 92. For similar instruments among uncivilised people see Cyrus Adler, *ibid.* p. 448.

[2] *Ibid.* p. 450.

[3] Exodus xix. 16-19 and xx. 18.

solemn procession. When the *Arōn Elohim*, the Ark of the Covenant, was transferred to the new city of Zion,[1] David and the whole House of Israel conveyed the ark of Jahve amid jubilations and the sound of the shofar. The prophet Ezekiel[2] knew it as a signal horn:

'2. Son of man, speak to the children of thy people, and say unto them, When I bring the sword upon a land, if the people of the land take a man of their coasts, and set him for their watchman:

'3. If when he seeth the sword come upon the land, he blows the trumpet, and warn the people;

'4. Then whosoever heareth the sound of the trumpet, and taketh not warning; if the sword come, and take him away, his blood shall be upon his own head.

'5. He heard the sound of the trumpet, and took not warning; his blood shall be upon him. But he that taketh warning shall deliver his soul.

'6. But if the watchman see the sword come, and blow not the trumpet, and the people be not warned; if the sword come, and take any person from among them, he is taken away in his iniquity; but his blood will I require at the watchman's hand.'

In Jeremiah,[3] too, the shofar proclaims danger, and this fact is expressed in the same simple and deeply impressive manner as in the last quotation:

'19. My bowels, my bowels! I am pained at my very heart; my heart maketh a noise in me; I cannot hold my peace, because thou hast heard, O my soul, the sound of the trumpet, the alarm of war.'

In the Bible we read that the sound of the shofar, the blare of the horn, the *teru'ah* was heard in the mêlée. Job speaks of the *Kôl Shofar* in describing a battle.[4] The shofar serves, therefore, to terrify the enemy, as did the *barditus* of the ancient Germans.[5] Indeed its terrifying purpose is the most prominent feature of its

---

[1] 2 Samuel vi. 15, and 1 Chron. xiii. 7-9.   [2] Ezekiel xxxiii. 2-6.
[3] Jeremiah iv. 19.   [4] Job xxxix. 24.   [5] Judges vii. 18-22.

employment. This is evident not only from ibn Ezra's belief that the shofar was first heard on Mount Sinai, but also from the words of Amos: 'Shall a trumpet be blown in the city, and the people be not afraid?'[1]

To Isaiah the Lord says:[2] 'Cry aloud, spare not, lift up thy voice like a trumpet, and show thy people their transgression'. We recognise here an association, though a slight one, of the ram's horn with sin, an association which stands out most clearly in its use on New Year's Day and the Day of Atonement. Isaiah's exhortation, to which the above quotation forms the prelude, was given, as appears from its contents, on the occasion of a fast and feast of expiation. It becomes clear from this connection why on the Day of the Lord, the *Yom Jahve*, the divine judgement, which the prophets describe so impressively, is always accompanied by the sound of the shofar. Zephaniah, who foresaw Judas's downfall, proclaims,[3] 'A day of the trumpet and alarm against the fenced cities, and against the high towers'. Joel also proclaims the awful day,[4] 'Blow ye the trumpet in Zion, and sound an alarm in my holy mountain: let all the inhabitants of the land tremble: for the day of the Lord cometh, for it is nigh at hand'. The horn, however, will be heard not only on the Day of Judgement, but also on the Day of Resurrection, of National Resurrection, its solemn tones will sound forth:[5] 'And it shall come to pass in that day, that the great trumpet shall be blown, and they shall come which were ready to perish in the land of Assyria, and the outcasts in the land of Egypt, and shall worship the Lord in the holy mount at Jerusalem'.

The shofar was also blown at the coronation of a king. Absalom sends out spies and says:[6] 'As soon as ye hear the sound of the trumpet, then ye shall say, Absalom reigneth in Hebron'. The shofar is expressly mentioned at Solomon's anointment and at Jehu's proclamation.[7] Although the ram's horn had a multiplicity of uses it was never employed for trivial purposes; it is always at

[1] Amos iii. 6.   [2] Isaiah lviii. 1.   [3] Zephaniah i. 16.   [4] Joel ii. 1.
[5] Isaiah xxvii. 13.   [6] 2 Samuel xv. 10.   [7] 1 Kings i. 34, 39, and 2 Kings ix. 13.

solemn moments in the life of the people that it is heard, and even in secular events it is only on serious occasions, as in the din of battle, at the proclamation of a law, or on the approach of danger. It seems strange that the use of the instrument has been more and more restricted until finally it is blown only at two feasts in the religious life. The dissolution of the national state can only in part explain this fact. During the Middle Ages and to-day it is used on a number of occasions, though certainly in a very limited degree, among great Jewish communities in the East where its sound was heard in Old Testament times. It resounds in time of danger when an enemy or a flood threatens. According to the Talmud the shofar sounds when a boat is sinking,[1] and when a famine or drought is impending.[2] Here again the shofar is used as a signal.[3] But the blowing of the shofar has become more and more confined to the religious sphere.

Besides the use of the ram's horn on festival days it previously played a part on some occasions of which only obscure traces and remnants are to be found among the Galician and Polish Jews, for example, at excommunication. The great excommunication, the *Herem* of the Bible, is the same kind of institution as the taboo among the savages. The Talmud mentions the use of the

---

[1] [The blowing of the shofar at a time of serious danger and distress occurred as recently as 1913, when the steamship *Volturno* was burned at sea on October 10, 1913. The following account is taken from *The Burning of the 'Volturno'*, by Arthur Spurgeon, Cassell & Company, Limited, London, 1913, p. 35.

'The strangest part of the company on board was undoubtedly a group of Jews, mostly Russians, who were emigrating to New York. When the *Volturno* left Rotterdam the Feast of the Atonement was near, and therefore the Uranian Steamship Company obtained for the use of the Jewish passengers a sacred scrool and sacred horn, so that they could hold their celebrations during the voyage. I may add that the scrool, which is written on parchment in Hebrew characters, was loaned to the Company for the voyage by the Rotterdam synagogue at a cost of £50.

'There was a Rabbi at the head of this band of Jews, who, coming from the interior, had most of them never seen the sea, or ships that go down to the sea. One can imagine their horror when in the midst of a lonely ocean they found that the ship which kept them afloat upon the water was furiously burning. They brought out their scrool, they sounded their horn, they knelt down together on the deck and read the scrool, and recited their prayers many times during the day.'—TRANS.]

[2] *Ta'anit*, 16B.

[3] *Shulḥan 'Aruk, Oraḥ Ḥayyim*, 376, 1.

shofar on this occasion.[1] A black ram's horn was usually
blown. The Jewish museum in Budapest contains such a
Ḥerem-Shofar.[2] The solemn ceremony of the great excommunication consisted of a number of frightful curses
aided by the shofar. An impressive situation of this kind
is described in Gutzkow's drama *Uriel Acosta.* There is
also a good description of the ceremony in E. P. Oresko's
Meier Ezofowicz.

It must not be forgotten that this great excommunication also played a large part in ancient Judaism; and
that the shofar was sounded at a solemn ceremony on
July 27, 1656, when one of the greatest minds Judaism
has given to the world was cursed by the synagogue and
declared an outlaw. A second striking use of the shofar
in the Middle Ages occurred here and there in the East
on the occasion of the death of celebrated Rabbis.
Eisenmenger states that there are no funeral obsequies
among the Jews of high standing without the blowing of
the shofar. This custom is also mentioned in the Talmud.
A similar custom existed among the Romans; the *tuba*,
which was originally the same as the shofar, was blown at
funeral obsequies. Finally the shofar was found on the
tombstones in the Jewish catacombs with the inscription, 'To eternal life'. At the resurrection, therefore, the
ram's horn is also to be blown. The same belief must
certainly be firmly rooted in the Christian mind, as
suggested by the passage:[3] 'Cum tubae terribilis sonitu
concusserit orbem exitaeque animae sursum in sua vasa
redibunt'. F. Nork[4] who mentions these customs has also
given an explanation of them: The Rabbis teach that a
human being comes three times before the Divine Judgement; annually on New Year's Day or Day of the
Trumpet, after internment, and on the Day of Judgement; hence the shofar is blown on these occasions. The

---

[1] *Mo'ed Katan,* 16 and 17.
[2] I borrow this statement and some of the facts mentioned earlier from the
instructive paper 'Das Widderborn', by Berthold Kohlbach in the *Zeitschrift
des Vereines für Volkskunde,* 2. Heft, 1916, S. 115.
[3] 1 Thessalonians iv. 16, and 1 Corinthians xv. 52.
[4] *Etymologisch-symbolisch-mythologisches Realwörterbuch,* Stuttgart, 1845,
3. Bd. iii. S. 114.

ram's horn is also blown on the day when judgement is passed on the sins of an individual, as well as on the Day of the Great Judgement on the Jewish people. The sound of this peculiar instrument will be heard on the day of the national restoration, as on that of the resurrection of the individual.

We can now at last pass on to the most important, and to-day, the only use of the shofar, namely, its use in the great Jewish religious feasts. At the time the Sanctuary was at Jerusalem the ram's horn was blown at the consecration of water.[1] At the time of the *Mishnah, i.e.* up to the second century A.D., the shofar was blown at the daily service.[2] In the festal ritual, observed by modern Jews, the shofar is blown on the seventh day of the Feast of Tabernacles or *Sukkot* (*Hosha'na Rabbah*), and during the whole month *Elul*; this, nevertheless, depends on the degree of conservatism of the congregation. In some districts the blowing is omitted on these occasions, but it is one of the features of New Year's Day on which the shofar is blown several times, and it is an essential feature in the ritual of the *Yom Kippur* at the end of which the shofar is sounded. The *Rosh ha-Shanah* festival is simply impossible without such a ceremony, for its meaning would be lost without it. The statement in the Scriptures concerning the rôle of the shofar-blowing on this day is remarkably laconic yet very significant:[3] 'In the seventh month, in the first day of the month, shall ye have a sabbath, a memorial of blowing of trumpets, an holy convocation'. The festival of the New Year had not nearly the significance in ancient Judaism which it gained in the Middle Ages, and particularly in modern times. It is certain, however, that blowing the shofar is not the central feature of the service. According to Kohlbach's[4] view, the blowing on

---

[1] I cannot here go into the use of the shofar in the consecration of water as this ceremony needs special elucidation, which I shall give in another place.

[2] Lipmanns-Heller, *Kommentar zur Mischnah Támid*, iii. 8.

[3] Leviticus xxiii. 24, and Numbers xxix. 1.

[4] *Das Widderhorn*, S. 118.

this day is perhaps only for the purpose of drawing attention to the Day of Atonement which falls in this month: 'The *Zikron Teru'ah*, the anniversary of the sound of the horns, was merely to announce the people's day of repentance'. On the other hand, it is very certain that the Feast of Atonement was only instituted after Ezra's restoration of the Jewish law-giving, and that there is no other proof of such a use of the ram's horn. The expression, 'Day of the Sound of the Horns', must refer to something else. It would probably be more correct to associate the increasing significance of the shofar in the festival with the abolition of the sacrifice. The ram's horn was blown at the conclusion of morning prayer during the whole month *Elul*, and this custom has often been explained as a preparation of the people for the proximity of the great feast days in the month *Tishri*, namely, the New Year's Feast and the Feast of Atonement. This special preparation would perhaps form an adjunct to the Sanhedrin rule mentioned in the Talmud;[1] the Sanhedrin sent out messengers in the month *Elul* to warn Israel in time of the proximity of the New Year Festival. We shall certainly not be able to suppress a slight doubt as to whether such an extreme weakness of the Jewish memory for a date really forms the actual basis of such a warning. If it is correct that there are communities in Germany where the shofar is blown at both morning and evening prayer[2] in the month *Elul*, thus reminding believers of the approaching festival twice a day, our astonishment at such an extravagantly useless procedure can only increase.

Blowing the shofar forms the central point of the service of the *Rosh ha-Shanah* festival. Portions of the liturgy directly refer to this ceremonial, as, for instance, the hymn *Adonai Bekol Shofar*, in which the deliverance of Israel from its wretched bondage is celebrated with the sound of the shofar. It is difficult to give to the uninitiated an idea of the connection which caused the

---

[1] *Rosh ha-Shanah*, Mishnah, 3.
[2] According to Moses Isserles, *Shulḥan 'Aruk, Oraḥ Ḥayyim*, 581, note.

shofar-blowing to be inserted in the festal ritual. And it is still more difficult to describe the effect of this primitive instrument on the believers. The blowing of the ram's horn during the morning service is intimately connected with an insertion in the prayers of the forenoon (*Mussaf*), namely, the blowing of three groups of four sounds each separated by prayers and reflections; the first group is the so-called *malkiyot* (acknowledgement of God as Lord and King of the world); the second, the *zikronot* (memory of the covenant of God and Abraham's willingness to sacrifice, as well as the sacrifice of Isaac); and the third, the *shofarot* (rôle and use of the shofar). The shofar was sounded as a sort of conclusion to each of these three reflections. After the end of the forenoon service specially pious believers remain in the synagogue and listen once more to thirty sounds of the shofar without the prayers. According to a statement in the Talmud the festal rite of the shofar-blowing is really limited to morning prayer. At one time, however, the Romans held the blowing to be a sign of revolt, and on account of this the shofar-blowing was put off to a late hour in the forenoon when there could be no doubt as to its meaning.[1] It cannot be said, however, that this explanation sounds very plausible; it is only evident that the blowing of the ram's horn has now become separated from its context. It is difficult to overestimate the intensity of the effect of this ceremony on believers among the general mass of the people. The tones of this primitive, national and religious instrument are usually awaited with great tension, its reverberations are listened to with very deep and sincere emotion and contrition; yet these strong affects are quite out of proportion to the sounds which produce them. The importance of the rite in the mental life of the people is shown by their fasting right up to the conclusion of the shofar-blowing. It is necessary to have witnessed the praying multitude in order to estimate the effect as the people listen breath-

[1] See Ismar Eltbogen, *Der jüdische Gottesdienst in seiner geschichtlichen Entwicklung*, Leipzig, 1913, S. 140.

lessly to the Rabbi who pronounces the benediction before the blowing: 'Praised be the Lord our God, the King of the Universe, who sanctified us with His precepts and commanded us to hear the sound of the shofar'. The Rabbi, standing on the *Almenor* and clothed in the prayer-mantle, blows the shofar in three sets of sounds (12 + 9 + 9) in order to 'humiliate Satan' as it is put in a cabalistic work.[1] The congregation, which as a rule does not spare its voice during the prayers, listens to these sounds in silence, breathes again when, without any interruption, the blowing of the shofar has been purely and clearly accomplished. If the blower hesitates the tones do not sound pure and clear, and, as the people think, Satan is to blame; it is a bad omen and pestilence, famine or pogroms will overtake the community in the coming year. It is a long time since I heard the sounds of the shofar, and when recently, in the interest of this work, I heard the shofar blown on New Year's Day, I could not completely avoid the emotion which these four crude, fearsome, moaning, loud-sounding, and long-drawn-out sounds produced—I do not attempt to decide whether the reason for my emotion was the fact that I was accustomed to this sound from youth, or whether it was an effect which everyone might feel. The latter suggestion seems to be supported by the fact that Christians who have heard it for the first time, and to whom the rites of the feast as well as the significance of the ram's horn blowing are quite unintelligible, have testified to similar emotions. In any case we are again faced with a problem which seems to complicate the enigmatical characteristics already mentioned. Can the unusually strong emotion be due to the three sounds which are produced from the shofar? The three sets of sounds, which are only distinguished by change of rhythm, have different names in the ritual: *Teki'ah* (long sustained), *Shebarim* (interrupted), *Teru'ah* (blare or tremolo). A fourth set, *Teki'ah Gedolah*, is only a longer

---

[1] *Shene Luḥot ha-Berit,* 17B.

Teki'ah, distinguished from the primary form by a long sustained fifth. I here illustrate the basic forms for the use of musicians:

Teki'ah   Shebarim   Teru'ah   Teki'ah Gedolah

These highly primitive, long-drawn-out, abrupt and vibrating associations of sound cannot possibly contain in themselves the secret of their effect. The very worst works of our most modern musical composers put these sounds to shame so far as the art of composition and musical value are concerned. The sound of the shofar is more like the bellowing of a bull than music. The only remaining explanation is, that the listeners who are emotionally affected on hearing these sounds unconsciously form an affective association between the sounds of the shofar and something unknown to us, perhaps old events and experiences. This is by no means a rare thing; cow-bells, for instance, awaken painful homesickness in the Swiss, and every one of us perhaps knows a piece of music which, although valueless, still charms him, because it is associated with parts of his emotional life. According to the Talmud and official tradition there is a connection between blowing the shofar and Isaac's sacrifice; its origin, even, is traced to the horn of the ram then sacrificed instead of the youth. Is it possible that the blowing of the horn originally signified the bleating of that ram? But what could be the point of this, and why the powerful emotional effect? One might think that there must be strong reasons for the experience of this emotion by so many people, reasons which may be clear to some of them. But when we question believers they give us only obscure or evasive answers; it is obvious that they themselves are not clear about the causes of their psychical emotion on hearing the shofar.

Perhaps we shall obtain more information if we investigate the ideas which are specially connected with the shofar in this ritual. The Talmud,[1] as we know, associates the instrument with the tale of the sacrifice of Isaac, the so-called '*Akedah*:[2] 'And Abraham lifted up his eyes, and looked, and behold, behind him a ram caught in a thicket by his horns: and Abraham went and took the ram, and offered him up for a burnt offering in the stead of his son'. Rabbi Abbahu, according to the Talmud,[3] gives the tradition thus: 'Why is the ram's horn blown? The Eternal One spoke: "Blow into the ram's horn, so that I may be reminded in your favour how Isaac, Abraham's son, was bound as a victim".' This is, of course, a supplementary explanation of the custom. This view, however, recurs in the *Mussaf* prayer at the New Year's Feast and is a widespread one. Another Rabbi named Jôshia raises the following question in the Talmud:[4] 'It is written: "Hail to the people who understand the sound of the horn."[5] Do not the rest of the peoples know how to sound the alarm? What numerous wind instruments they have! How many buccinae, how many salpinxes! And thou proclaimest: "Hail to the people who understand the sound of the horn". But the fact remains that Israel understands how to procure the mercy of its Creator by means of the sound of the shofar. God rises from His seat of judgement and goes to the throne of mercy, and compassion moves His heart; He changes from the stern Judge into the merciful one.' The horn, which warns God of the willing sacrifice of the patriarch by reminding Him of the '*Akedah*, actually effects the mercy of the Lord. We certainly have to admit that behind this artificial and indeed ingenious exposition, the hidden meaning of which will occupy us later, traits of another, cruder and more primitive idea appear. 'They understand how to make themselves subservient

---

[1] *Rosh ha-Shanah*, 16A.
[2] Genesis xx. 1-12.
[3] *Rosh ha-Shanah*, 16A; *Genesis Rabbah*, 56, and *Leviticus Rabbah*, p. 29.
[4] *Leviticus Rabbah*, 29; *Talmud Rosh ha-Shanah*, 16B.
[5] Psalm lxxxix. 16.

to their Creator through blowing the shofar.'[1] It is said
in the morning prayer of New Year's Day, 'With the
shofar will I persuade Him, falling on my knees before
Him'; and the same idea recurs in the forenoon service
(*Mussaf*): 'We sound the shofar with the prayer in order
to persuade you, Almighty One'. Here the tones of the
shofar appear as a means of assuaging God without
reference to that sacrifice.

The *Zohar*[2] explains that God changes his judgement
of condemnation over Israel into one of pardon at the
sounding of the shofar. What is of first importance at the
shofar feast is that the blower should understand the
sounds, and not that he be merely skilled in blowing.
The shofar's task is therefore to soften the wrath of God
over the sinful but repentant people, and to move Him
to mercy. Another explanation, alleged[3] to be later, is
based on the use of the ram's horn on New Year's Day.
This is the Day of Judgement on which God determines
who is to die in the coming year.[4] In the Babylonian
Talmud Rabbi Yizḥak[5] teaches that the shofar is
blown at the *Rosh ha-Shanah* in order to confuse Satan.
Theologians have observed that this is a very late idea
because the figure of Satan first occurs in the religious
thought of the Jews at the time when the Book of Job
was written.[6] But it is necessary to be cautious in accept-
ing this chronology since a similar figure is often fore-
shadowed in the many varieties of demons which originated in the pre-monotheistic period and continued to
play a part in the beliefs of the people. The statement in
the Talmud that the first sound of the ram's horn con-
fuses Satan, and the second robs him of his senses so
that he cannot appear with his accusation, represents
Satan as the accuser, as he is in the Book of Job. According to the *Zohar* God grants the accuser the right to
summon all the dwellers upon earth before the seat of
judgement on New Year's Day, and this day is fixed so

---

[1] *Leviticus Rabbah*, 29.
[2] *Der Zohar*, ed. Smyrna, 1862, Bd. vi., Num. S. 298B.
[3] See Kohlbach, *ibid.* S. 122.   [4] *Rosh ha-Shanah*, i. 1.
[5] *Rosh ha-Shanah*, 16B.   [6] Job i. 6-12, and ii. 1-5.

that Satan may submit to God all the judicial matters in the world.[1]

'Besides the accuser there are two notaries (recording angels) with God. . . . Yet there is still time to turn back. If the sinner repents God tears up the sentence and asks, "Who can cite any reason for mercy in favour of the sinner?" Then the shofar sounds and echoes in heaven. When the two sounds of the shofar ring out, immediately all accusations brought by the accuser are thrown into confusion. The wrath of God ceases, His heart rejoices and is full of compassion.' 'Rosh ha-Shanah is the Day of Judgement and the slanderers appear against Israel'; when the echo of the shofar on earth,[2] i.e. the shofar in heaven, sounds forth 'a sound is heard which is uniformly harmonious (sic) and awakens mercy; when his compassion is stirred all the lamps in heaven are lit on every side'. These far-fetched and fancifully elaborated ideas find wide acceptance in circles which adhere to the Cabala. Jewish mysticism has adopted them and the Zohar as well as the Shelah (abbreviation for the title of an important cabalistic work, Shene Luḥot ha-Berit = the two law-tablets of Isaiah, Hurwitz) regard the three shofar sounds as having far-reaching and mysterious relationships to God. In a cabalistic work of the Middle Ages the devout utterance of the words קרעשׁ, 'O destroy utterly the devil', is recommended before the shofar-blowing. The name of God, יהוה, however, should be interpolated between the two words, whereby the effect of the prayer is supposed to be increased. This function of the shofar, namely, to confuse the devil, may be again illustrated from another source.

We know already that the ram's horn was blown during the whole of the month Elul, which precedes the Rosh ha-Shanah, to prepare Israel for the coming of this great day, and we may now add the confusing of Satan as a second motive of this custom. According to Jacob ben Asher (known also as Ba'al ha-Turim),[3] 'The shofar

---

[1] Zohar. Ra'ajah mehêmna for Leviticus xxiii. 4 Book, p. 196B.
[2] Zohar, 6, Bag Rag, 297B.   [3] Ed. Frankfurt a. Od., 1717, S. 216.

Q

is blown annually in the month *Elul* in order to warn
Israel to repent and return; also to mislead the devil'. In
Paul Christian Kirchner's notorious book,[1] which appeared in 1724, we find a clear reference to the idea of
the deception of Satàn, as it appeared at that time in
popular belief: 'Because the Jews pretend/that the LORD
GOD holds a great judgement on this day/and according
to the circumstances of the case writes down human
beings among either the righteous or the unrighteous/
and are also afraid/lest the devil should appear/and on
account of their sins/accuse them before GOD/as once he
accused Job/they desire to make a fool of him/and by
this thirty days' blowing/commencing in the month
Elul/to prevent him from knowing/which actually is
New Year's Day. O stupid Satan/who even in matters/
that everybody can know/must let yourself be so miserably deceived. Others, however, can suggest a sensible
reason/when they say/that this ceremony is provided so
that/they may remember the approaching time of re-
pentance/and prepare themselves accordingly.' When
we consider the people's conscious idea of the function
of blowing the ram's horn, we find no uniformity.

We have seen how Jewish mysticism, starting from
small beginnings, constantly developed more and more
complicated speculations about the shofar-blowing. Nor
did official Judaism, as represented by its Rabbis and
scholars, stop at the view that the shofar-blowing was
intended solely as a reminder. It saw in the old custom
higher and higher aims, ascribed to it a more and more
sublime meaning, and thought they perceived in it the
fulfilment of the most diverse intentions. We are be-
wildered at the confused mass of moral and theological
speculations which surround the blowing of the shofar.
The view of orthodox Judaism on the meaning of this
liturgical act may be quoted as a sample of this imposing
art of symbolical interpretation. I take the following
quotations from Dr. Michael Sachs:[2] 'The instrument

[1] *Jüdisches Zeremoniell*, etc., S. 111.
[2] *Festgebete der Israeliten*, Berlin, 1864, *Rosch-Haschanah*, 1. Teil, 5. Auflage,
S. 174.

itself, the ram's horn, is associated with the sacrifice of
Isaac. It is related to that great act of devotion to God
when Abraham was ready to sacrifice what was dearest
to him, and to the kindly promise of God, through the
ram which took the place of the patriarch prepared for
death.' The shofar-blowing ordained by God at the
beginning of the year is also a significant token sign. As
the sound of the horn is not wanting where the deliverance and revival of the Jews are proclaimed by the
prophets,[1] so 'the sound of the shofar carries us back
into the wonderful past of Israel, and anticipates its
ideal future, and at the same time becomes a call of
remembrance and hope'. As the shofar was heard at the
investiture and homage of the kings of Israel, so it
occurs at the beginning of the year as a homage to the
Lord and King of the world. The strangely fearful and
groaning sound of the instrument has also found its
symbolism. It is an awakening and warning summons to
the conscience that has fallen asleep in its sinful earthly
existence, to show repentance and courage. Maimonides,
who was one of the most important Jewish philosophers
of religion, writes: 'Although the blowing of the shofar
at the beginning of the year is a biblical command, it
means: Awake, ye sleepers! and ye stupefied ones, bestir
yourselves. Examine your deeds and return repentant.
. . . Look to your souls and improve your ways and your
doings. Let every one of you quit his sinful path and his
impious thoughts.' The sound of the shofar is, therefore,
a warning to prepare for the Day of Atonement, and is a
sort of application of the prophet's words which were
first spoken in a restricted sense: 'Shall a trumpet be
blown in the city, and the people not be afraid?'[2] The
shofar as a signal is a warning to return, a sign of impending punishment as on the Day of the Lord. Stern
argues that the wars and battles in which, according to
the Bible, the shofar was heard may be compared with
'the idea of conflict and struggle with sin'. How much

---

[1] Sachs, *ibid.* S. 175.   [2] Amos iii. 6.

these three sounds signify! 'History and life, past and future, national and religious matters, elevation and depression, allusion to the sublimity of God as well as to the sinfulness of human beings, all these various aspects and contrasts were felt in the tones of the shofar by the learned of the *Midrash*, the expositors and interpreters of the divine law'. This sound is also a serious warning to begin a new chapter of life. Stern concludes his exposition with these significant words: 'Now also the ancient voice may serve for a remembering, *i.e.* for introspection, for the rejuvenation and renewal of spiritual life and religious sincerity, a warning of eternal obligations towards a sacred covenant, to serve a noble past and a sublime future'. The first impression given by a declaration of this kind might surely be summed up in the words, 'Less would be more'. The association of the most diverse and heterogeneous component parts cannot possibly have its roots in the original institution of the custom. Thousands of years have contributed to it. One recognises further that if, for example, we get introspection from the memory of the horn of the ram at the sacrifice of Isaac, a struggle with sins from the real struggle with actual foes, and a renewal of religious sincerity from the national resurrection of Judaism, we have a perfect example of the 'anagogic' art of interpretation (Silberer). The original meaning of the ritual has been completely repressed, and the ritual has been made to carry the expression of feelings and thoughts proper to a high state of religion and moral development. Three crude and primitive shofar sounds have become a polyphonic symphony comprising all the essential elements of religion.

Apart from the New Year's Feast special importance in present-day ritual is assigned to the use of the shofar only on the Day of Atonement. At the conclusion of the ceremony a single long-sustained note (*Teḳi'ah*) is sounded once in the sense of *'ite missa est'*.[1] This horn signal is also to signify that now the glory of God, the *Shekinah*, which

---

[1] *Shulḥan 'Aruk, Oraḥ Ḥayyim*, § 623B. Note.

has taken part in the assembly, is returning to heaven.[1]
The *Cabala*, indeed, has a different interpretation for the
Teḳi'ah after the concluding prayer (*Ne'ilah*). 'The sound
is a warning of Isaiah's[2] promise that God in his love and
mercy will redeem Israel.'[3] This popular belief, that the
sound of the ram's horn is connected with the coming of
the Messiah as well as with the resurrection, has been
preserved with extraordinary persistency up to the
present day, and the favourite reference is to Isaiah
xxvii. 13: 'And it shall come to pass in that day, that
the great trumpet shall be blown, and they shall come
which were ready to perish in the land of Assyria, and
the outcasts in the land of Egypt, and shall worship the
Lord in the holy court at Jerusalem'.

I do not know how far I have succeeded in representing the nature and purpose of the shofar, but I can only
say that it is no easy matter to obtain a clear idea of this
subject, concerning which the most contradictory and
confusing ideas are found in Jewish and non-Jewish
literature.

III. A Way to the Interpretation

In turning to the numerous questions to which the
origin and use of this remarkable instrument give rise,
we find ourselves in a peculiar position. Although the
Cabalistic and Rabbinical expositions offer us an abundance of explanations of the most various kinds, science,
and particularly the science of religion, shows such
great caution that it leaves us almost completely in the
lurch. This, however, does not mean that studies of the
shofar are wanting. There are instructive articles on it[4]
which contain everything essential about the forms and
uses of the instrument. Adler compares the shofar with
signalling instruments of primitive peoples of a similar
nature. He states, incidentally, that the holy character

---

[1] Remark of David Halêvi.   [2] Isaiah lxiii. 9.
[3] *Zohar*, 6. Bd. p. 510A.
[4] *Jewish Encyclopædia*, vol. ix., Cyrus Adler, *ibid.*

of the shofar 'may be connected with the sacrificial use made of the goat', but does not go into details or indicate the path which leads to this assumption. The Talmud, after all, says the same thing, though in somewhat different words. This, however, should not be claimed as a scientific explanation. Berthold Kohlbach[1] supplies no explanation; and the same may be said of Scheftelowitz's detailed paper[2] to which we shall return. Articles and remarks on the ram's horn in journals, lexicons, encyclopædias and works on the history of religion may be added to these inadequate attempts.[3] A study of the literature of the science of religion is not exhilarating; an over-abundance of material is accompanied by an appalling vagueness respecting the origin and motive of the use of the shofar. If the present work should not be able to meet the criticisms launched against it, it may perhaps claim the modest service of having directed attention to the fact that there is a problem here, and, moreover, a problem whose significance is as great for the history of civilisation in general as for the science of religion, ethnology and the history of art in particular, not to mention folk psychology.

We shall make use of psycho-analysis for the elucidation of this problem, but at the same time a special attempt will be made to limit the application of psycho-analytic conclusions as much as possible, and only to employ its methods where they have proved serviceable with similar material.

To be candid, I must confess that I did not obtain my first clear enlightenment respecting the shofar from the rich material available, but from the peculiar Biblical passages occurring in Exodus xix. This chapter forms the introduction to a very important part of the Pentateuch, namely, the great covenant on Mount Sinai between God, Moses as mediator and the Jewish people,

---

[1] *Das Widderhorn.*
[2] 'Das Hörnermotiv in den Religionen', *Archiv für Religionswissenschaft*, Bd. xv.
[3] No conclusions should be drawn from the number of works quoted as to the amount of the material used by the author, as only such works are mentioned here as actually supply new and essential points concerning the shofar.

and is rich in all kinds of doubtful points. When the Jews were encamped before Mount Sinai for three months after the exodus, the Lord commanded Moses to ascend the mount and announced to him:[1] 'Now, therefore, if ye will obey my voice indeed, and keep my covenant, then ye shall be a peculiar treasure unto me above all people: for all the earth is mine'. The leader proclaims this to the people, and informs the Lord of their willingness. Then the Lord spoke: 'Lo, I come unto thee in a thick cloud, that the people may hear when I speak with thee, and believe thee for ever'. Now follows the prohibition to the people to approach the mountain; barriers are put round it. The ancient idea of the taboo of the Deity emerges here. He who touches the mountain is to die. 'When the trumpet soundeth long, they shall come up to the mount.' This last sentence is remarkable in many respects. It is disconnected and cannot be fitted into any of the three original writings from which the Sinai pericope originated, for nowhere is there even any mention of blowing the ram's horn, and nowhere have the people participated so far in what has taken place as to ascend the mountain. Baentsch asserts in his critical commentary,[2] 'The most likely assumption is that it belongs to an older form of the Horeb tradition'. Baentsch, therefore, ascribes this disconnected sentence to a source E1, and those between which it stands to a source E2. Even if we are correct in stating that this sentence has been inserted here from an older tradition and now acts independently and confusingly in the midst of a more recent tradition, we are still a long way from explaining everything. Baentsch is quite right when he says: 'It is not clear who is to give the signal, God or Moses, or somebody else'. To our limited lay mind it seems most likely that it is God who is to give the signal. He forbids and permits the ascent of the mountain. The blowing would therefore be equivalent to an expression of God's

---

[1] Exodus xix. 5.

[2] Baentsch, *Handkommentar zum Alten Testament*, Göttingen, 1903, Exodus, S. 174.

will. Objection will certainly be raised to the view that the wording, which says nothing of a blowing by God, must be adhered to. Who, therefore, will blow the ram's horn? A truly remarkable passage. Scepticism warns us to keep to the original text, 'impels me to turn up the original text', in the words of Faust. We are surprised to find here a word whose translation is only correct according to its meaning. The text has *jôbel* (יובל), *i.e.* ram, not קרן היובל, *keren ha'jobel*, *i.e.* ram's horn. The distinction is clear; in the first case, the translation must be 'when the ram sounds long', in the second, 'when one blows the ram's horn long'. In order to justify the translation 'ram's horn', it must be assumed that (יבול) *jôbel* signifies both ram and ram's horn. Gesenius[1] actually mentions both meanings, and refers to the passage we have quoted. Klostermann and, following him, Gressmann[2] have with some justice found that the development of the meaning from ram to ram's horn is peculiar. We feel that the holy text ought not to be amended merely to facilitate our comprehension of obscure passages. The ambition to understand everything immediately should not be encouraged. We will therefore translate the text according to the wording, and it will then read, 'when the ram sounds for a long time', *i.e.* gives forth sustained sounds. 'What ram?' we ask; but we must curb our impatience.

The theophany begins on the morning of the third day: 'And it came to pass on the third day in the morning, that there were thunders and lightnings, and a thick cloud upon the mount, and the voice of the trumpet exceeding loud; so that all the people that was in the camp trembled'. Here, again, we find the sound of the shofar or trumpet (we know that the trumpet was derived from the shofar). Everything earlier is intelligible; it is God who thunders and sends lightning, it is He who comes in a thick cloud. But who blows the trumpet or

---

[1] Wilhelm Gesenius, *Hebräisches und aramäisches Handwörterbuch über das Alte Testament*, Leipzig, 1915, 16 Auflage, S. 292.
[2] Gressmann, *ibid.* S. 29.

shofar? Now, however, occurs a most remarkable thing;
the whole mountain smoked because God came down in
fire on it, and it shook violently. 'And when the voice
of the trumpet sounded long, and waxed louder and
louder, Moses spake, and God answered him by a voice.'
Baentsch gravely comments on this passage as follows:[1]
'In the midst of this noise Elohim converses with Moses'.
A more grotesque idea is difficult to imagine than that
God conversed with Moses while the sounds of the
trumpet increased in volume. Scarcely less operatic is
Gressmann's conception of the theophany on Sinai when
he writes:[2] 'In this sea of fire, encircled by a thousand
flames, and amid the roar of noisy trumpets, dwells
Jahve, the majestic God'. The idea seems almost blasphemous when one considers that in a 'noise', to use
Baentsch's expression, of this kind, one cannot hear
one's own words, not to mention those of another
person, and that in these circumstances Jahve hands
over to Moses the fundamental teachings of morality
and religion. We are therefore content to state that here,
as in the question who is to blow the instrument which
was the signal for the ascent of the people, and in the
puzzle of the presence of a ram, there is an obscurity
which is difficult to penetrate, and evidently this was
why the matter has not been cleared up by exegesis. In
Exodus xx. 18 and 19, we have, further: 'And all the
people saw the thunderings, and the lightnings, and the
noise of the trumpet, and the mountain smoking: and
when the people saw it, they removed, and stood afar
off. And they said unto Moses, Speak thou with us, and
we will hear: but let not God speak with us, lest we die.'
Again an ambiguity: did the people hear or not hear
God's voice? We are only told of the sound of the horn,
and nowhere is it said that the people heard the Lord's
voice. Yet the people say they heard this voice, and God
Himself said that the people would hear His voice.

Any doubt as to whether the people actually heard

[1] Baentsch, *ibid*. S. 175.
[2] Hugo Gressmann, *Moses*, Göttingen, 1913, S. 196.

God's voice is eliminated by reference to Deuteronomy,[1] where Moses reminds the people of this great episode.[2]

'23. And it came to pass, when ye heard the voice out of the midst of the darkness (for the mountain did burn with fire), that ye came near unto me, even all the heads of your tribes, and your elders;

'24. And ye said, Behold, the Lord our God hath shewed us his glory and his greatness, and we have heard his voice out of the midst of the fire: we have seen this day that God doth talk with man, and he liveth.

'25. Now therefore why should we die? for this great fire will consume us: if we hear the voice of the Lord our God any more, then we shall die.

'26. For who is there of all flesh, that hath heard the voice of the living God speaking out of the midst of the fire, as we have, and lived?'

We will now consider some questions, contradictions and disparities in this description. A horn is to sound, but who is to blow it? The sound of the horn becomes louder and louder, Moses speaks and God answers loudly. Why the accompanying noise? The people see the smoking mountain, hear the sound of the horn and are terrified and afraid. This very same people assert that they have heard God's voice; but they have only heard the sound of the trumpet. I think that the conclusion cannot be rejected that all these contradictions can be solved at once if we assume that the sound of the horn is God's voice. If this is correct then we understand who is to give the signal for the ascent of the mountain, namely, He who alone has the right to do this, God Himself. We learn that God proclaims that the people will hear His voice; they have heard it, *i.e.* the sound of the horn. We can now understand the peculiar sentence, the sound of the horn waxed louder and louder, Moses spake, and God answered him by a voice: the sound of the horn is God speaking. Becoming louder

---

[1] Moses declares in Deut. iv. 12: 'And the Lord spake unto you out of the midst of the fire: ye heard the voice of the words, but saw no similitude; only ye heard a voice'.   [2] Deuteronomy v. 23-26.

means that the whole of the people are to hear what the
Lord has to proclaim. Baentsch's grotesque view of a
dialogue accompanied by a crescendo of sound, which
would be unimaginable even in a super-modern opera,
breaks down. The people see the smoking mountain,
hear the sound of the horn—these are the signs of God's
presence—and are afraid. Let us believe them when they
say they have heard God's voice out of the fire, *i.e.* the
sound of the shofar.

It is surprising that no Biblical commentator has come
to this obvious conclusion. No particular sagacity is
necessary for this, only a little courage and no prejudices; all that is required is to trust to the text and not
to make it coincide *à tout prix* with our modern views.
The fact that the sound of the horn is God's voice, which
reveals the inadequacy of all previous explanations of
this passage, receives a still more surprising confirmation in that the Old and New Testament actually speak
of the sound of the horn or trumpet as being God's
voice. This is to be taken seriously and literally, not
symbolically. For what else could be the meaning of the
prophet Zechariah's[1] proclamation: 'And the Lord God
shall blow the trumpet, and shall go with whirlwinds of
the south'? Who else but the Lord is to blow into the
horn in the passage in Isaiah[2] when the people of Israel
are to be gathered together again from all parts of the
earth? Blowing into the horn does not only correspond
to the call of God, it is His call. The people cannot compare His voice, both powerful and gentle, with anything
but the sound of the trumpet. John, in the Apocalypse,[3]
says, 'I was in the Spirit on the Lord's Day, and heard
behind me a great voice, as of a trumpet, saying, I am
Alpha and Omega, the first and the last'. When John
calls God's voice here μεγάλη ὡς σάλπιγγος (great as of a
trumpet) we need only drop the comparative particle:
the sound of the trumpet is God's voice. It is well
known that in other religions the gods are equipped with

[1] Zechariah ix. 14.   [2] Isaiah xxvii. 13.
[3] Revelation i. 10.

horns as wind instruments analogous to the shofar;
Triton among the Greeks, Heimdall among the Germans and Brahma among the Indians.

Our provisional conclusion is, therefore, that the
sound of the shofar is God's voice. It only needed the
application of the psycho-analytic method to arrive at
this. We paid attention to details, we took contradictions quite seriously, and we had the courage to take
what the text says in an unprejudiced and earnest
manner without being afraid of a threatening absurdity.
However, we must not conceal from ourselves that we
are still far from the solution of the questions with which
we are occupied. Why should the sound of the shofar be
God's voice? Why should this horn in particular have
such significance? If we remain loyal to the psycho-
analytic method we have to assume that the choice of
the ram's horn as the medium of the divine voice must
have a special and definite meaning. Does it signify perchance that God was once identified with a horned
animal, and in particular with a ram? Let us compare
Numbers xxiii. 22 on this point: 'God brought them out
of Egypt: he hath, as it were, the strength of an unicorn';
and Amos i. 2: 'The Lord will roar from Zion, and utter
his voice from Jerusalem'. We have certainly great
difficulty in understanding this vocal performance on the
part of Jahve now that we have so long been accustomed
to hear God's voice speaking to us softly, but impressively, in the growth and decay of nature; perhaps, however, the ancient Jews who were more closely in touch
with totemism were able to appreciate this quality.

According to Robertson Smith's[1] investigations it
seems there can no longer be any doubt of the existence
of a primitive form of religion out of which the cult of
Jahve developed. Scheftelowitz in his excellent article[2]
presents a selection of what is known about the primal
Semitic idea of a horned god and his totemistic proto-

---

[1] *Lectures on the Religion of the Semites.*
[2] *Das Hörnermotiv in den Religionen*, Bd. xv. S. 450. Compare also Marie
Bonaparte, 'Über die Symbolik der Kopftrophäen', *Imago*, 1928, Heft 1.

types. In all religions of the ancient Orient there was a
time when God was actually worshipped as a bull or a
ram. The bull Apis, the incarnation of Ptah; Chum, who
was represented with a goat's head; and Anubis, who had
the head of an animal with two upright horns, are
examples from the ancient Egyptians. The ancient
Babylonian gods have the surname bull (*buru*); Marduk
was represented as a bull, and the weather god Adad
and the god Elul were called 'great bull'. The moon god
Sinu is described in a hymn as 'strong young bull'. The
picture of an animal in the temple at Kyzikos represents
Dionysus; in Elis this god is evoked as bull, and in Argos
is called βουγένης; Poseidon is called 'bull-statured' (ταῦρος,
ταυρεῖος), and his feast, the feast of the bull (Ταύρια).
Zeus approaches Europa and Io in the form of a bull. In
the primary archaic period Zeus was presumably worshipped in the form of an animal, seeing that a silver-
horned head of a bull with a double axe between the
horns, the symbol of domination, was found at Mycenae.
The late Roman god, Ammon, who comes from the
Orient, has horns on his head like Pan, Bacchus, etc. The
Canaanites worshipped Baal under the image of a bull.
In the Bible itself are found numerous references to the
ancient Semitic cult of the bull. In the kingdom of Israel
images of a bull were worshipped at Dan and Bethel.[1] In
Exodus we hear of the sinful worship of the calf.[2] A
bronze image of a bull was found during excavations to
the east of the land of Jordan.[3]

If the god who was originally worshipped by the Jews
was a bull or a ram,[4] then we can understand why his
voice sounded from the horn of a ram. The position of
the ram as a totem animal follows from its especial
holiness as an expiatory sacrifice for guilt. The statement

[1] I Kings xii. 28. [2] Exodus xxxii.
[3] Benzinger, *Hebräische Archäologie*, 2. Auflage, S. 221, Abb. 229.
[4] There is no doubt that in the Jewish folk religion which was repressed by
the later prophetic one, Jahve had been worshipped under the image of a bull.
The supposition of Canaanite influence in this idea, which is shown also in the
designation of Jahve as a bull, אביר, is mentioned among other theories by L. B.
Paton in Hastings' *Encyclopædia of Ethics and Religion*, iii. (1910), p. 181. The
hypothesis of a common Semitic view is more probable.

of the prophet Amos, 'Jahve roars', betrays the original
and more direct nature of Jahve's demonstration. Let us
recall the literal translation of Exodus xix., 'When the
ram soundeth long, they shall come up to the mount.'
If this passage is inserted into the more recent report
from an older tradition, as textual criticism indicates, it
is very probable that the older view of the totemistic
god here stands side by side with the more highly
developed one. We have recognised that the voice of the
ram's horn is the voice of God. Modern exegesis, having
neglected this connection, has found it necessary to
assume a different voice. We thus see three historical
stages of development in the conception of the divine
voice, namely, the voice of the ram, the sounds which
God made by blowing a ram's horn, and the incom-
parable voice which is removed from all that is human
and animal, the voice of God, purified of all earthly
dross. It is evident that human beings recognise their
God by his voice, as the children do their mother in the
fairy tale of the wolf and the seven kids.

But how are we to explain the fact that the task of
sounding the voice of God was assigned to the horn?
Here again we obtain further help from the comparative
history of religion. It shows us that the horns, as symbols
of power and strength, are the sole remaining features of
an animal which originally must have embodied the
physical power of the gods.[1] In an ancient song of
exorcism against the female demon *Arayi*, the god
Brahmanaspati is entreated to come and impale *Arayi*
with his sharp horn. The war-god Indra is compared
with a sharp-horned wild bull who alone pushes away all
people. All Babylonian gods in the form of human
beings, and also the Phoenician Baal, wear a cap covered
with horns as a sign of godliness. Pan, who was originally
worshipped as a ram, wore horns, and likewise Bacchus
and the Satyrs. In Jewish belief such original god-forms
degenerated into demons. The Bible forbids the worship
of ram-shaped demons (שעירים). (The old Semitic bull-gods

---

[1] Scheftelowitz, *ibid.* S. 456.

appears later as demons, *shedim*.) In the *Midrash*,[1] we are told that the head of the demon (*shed*) resembles a calf from whose forehead a horn projects.[2] The ancient Christian belief that the devil has horns may be mentioned here as a relic of an earlier demon cult.

The development of the concept of God cannot be separated from the development of his cult. When Voltaire was told that God had created man in his own image, he remarked, 'L'homme le lui rend bien'. We know that those who acknowledge a god identify themselves with him. In the great sacrificial feasts of the ancients the believers wrapped themselves in the skin of the animal corresponding to their god, just as in the dancing festivals of savages of the present time. The aegis or goat's skin which is placed on statues of Athenae was worn by the Libyan women; the worshippers of Dagon, who brought a fish sacrifice, were wrapped in a fish-skin; and the Cyprians, when bringing the sheep-goddess a victim, wore sheep-skins. Similar customs in the cult of Dionysus are well known. A later form of this identification is the wearing of masks of animals, which is still found among savages of to-day. Because the gods of the Orient wore horns therefore their followers also assumed these emblems. Sumerian and Babylonian priests wore two horns on their cap, and the Salii, priests of Mars, wore a horn head-piece.[3] The Shamans of Kanaschinzen in Siberia and the Musquakie Indians of North America wear horned caps. The dress which Jahve arranged with so much detail for the high priests was originally the garment of God Himself.[4] Among the Jews of the Middle Ages there was a custom in the ceremonial of the New Year's Feast which can only be regarded as a primitive

[1] *Bamidbar Rabbah*, Par. xii.
[2] 3 M. 17, 7; 2 Chron. xi. 10; Isaiah xiii. 2.
[3] Scheftelowitz, *ibid*. S. 472.
[4] Further examples are given by Robertson Smith, *ibid*. p. 334. The view that with the putting on of a cloak the nature of its previous wearer passes over to the present one is general among the ancients and among primitive peoples. It may be mentioned in this connection that the passage in Gen. iii. 21, in which God gives the first human beings clothing of skins, receives a new illumination from this point. The customary metaphors in the Old and New Testament of the cloak of justice can also be traced back to this origin.

identification of this kind. Kirchner reports it in his above-mentioned book.[1] The Jews, after the prayers of the day before the New Year's Feast, go home, light candles and consecrate the Feast by eating sweet foods. 'They were also accustomed/to put on a ram's head/in remembrance of/the fact that/according to their belief/ Isaac was to have been sacrificed on this day/but in his place a ram was taken'. We consider that here there is a secondary and late motivation of that old ritual of identification with the god.

This identification by means of form, as we recognise it in the custom of the Middle Ages, was accompanied by identification by means of sounds. The savages who imitate their totem animals in their mask dances, also make the noise of the animal. In the totemistic secret societies and in the totem tribes the novice can only be accepted if he is ostensibly born again as a totem animal. Among the Carrier Indians, for instance, 'whenever anybody resolved upon getting received as *Lulem* or Bear, he would, regardless of the season, divest himself of all his wearing apparel and don a bear-skin, whereupon he would dash into the woods there to remain for the space of three or four days and nights in deference to the wonts of his intended totem animal. Every night a party of his fellow-villagers would sally out in search of the missing 'bear'. To their loud calls, *Yi!Kelulem* (Come on, Bear!) he would answer by angry growls in imitation of the bear.'[2] The raving and shrieking of the worshippers of Dionysus is explicable on similar lines. As civilisation advanced the skin of an animal was replaced by a mask, and the roaring which was originally to imitate the noise of the totem animal was replaced by the use of an instrument. Among the Jews identification with the Deity by putting on the head of a ram would likewise correspond to the wearing of masks by savages, and the shofar-blowing their wild

[1] *Jüdisches Zeremoniell*, etc., S. 112.
[2] Frazer, *The Golden Bough: Balder the Beautiful*, vol. ii. p. 274, Third Edition, 1911, London.

songs when they imitate the noise of the animal who is their totem god.

If we review the results of our study up to the present point we arrive at a preliminary explanation, and, as it seems, a not unimportant one, which indicates how the shofar-blowing came into the cult. The totemistic god of the early stage of the Jewish religion, who was represented as a bull or ram, was worshipped by imitating the bellowing of a bull or the bleating of a ram, just as the noise of the totem animal is imitated by the savages. The same identification with the deity was obtained by wearing the skin of a bull or ram. The wearing of horns, as specially representing the power of the god, was regarded later as a sign of the same metamorphosis. A technical advance, besides other factors unknown to us, must have led to the horn, which was originally worn on the head, being used as an instrument for blowing by the believers; but in this way also it helps the imitation of the totemistic god, namely, by imitating his voice. Its original purpose is still shown by its rôle in the ritual, as well as in its descent from a totemistic animal. The concept of God goes hand in hand with this evolution in those who believe in him: Jahve no longer roars, he blows the ram's horn, as at a similar stage Triton, Heimdall and Brahma received a wind instrument.

We have arrived at this point by the analytic method, and we have not found it necessary to adduce the results of the psycho-analytic investigation of religion. The questions which now obtrude can only be answered if we make use of Freud's totem theory for their explanation. There are many of these questions, of which the following may be mentioned. What was the original significance of the appropriation of the divine form and of the imitation of the divine voice by the believers? What is the meaning of the shofar-blowing in the present-day ritual of the Jewish religion? What is the explanation of the many official and mystical views which are united with this custom? What is the explanation of the strong affects which we have found in connection with it, and

R

what connection has the ritual with the New Year's Feast and the Feast of Atonement?

One of the results of the Freudian theory of *Totem und Tabu*, which is most essential and most valuable to the history of civilisation, is that it traces the totem sacrificial animal back to the father. This derivation permits the postulation of a historical origin of the concept of God, which is built on a hypothesis of events in the primitive horde. In the primitive horde the sons overcame, killed and devoured the potent father; this literal incorporation was the most primitive kind of identification with the beloved and hated man, and it became of the greatest significance for the subsequent period. The animal which presented itself as the nearest substitute for the father to the feelings of the conscience-stricken sons, who were tortured by remorse and desire, now became the object of an act of deferred obedience which ought to have been applied to the father himself. Tendencies to hatred and triumph persisted and secured their gratification by instituting the periodic festival of the totem meal. Freud investigated the development which led from the substitution of the totem animal for the father to the apotheosis of the father in an anthropomorphic form; and he was also able to re-establish again and again the critical share taken by the guilty conscience and defiance of the son in the further development of religion.

We now understand why the priest blows the shofar. It implies his identification with God, which he proclaims by imitating the divine voice, just as these sons of the primitive horde who murdered the father gradually indicated the father's nature and forms of expression. Just as the son's defiance and desire were re-expressed again and again in the totem meal in which hate and love towards the totem were fused in one act, so also is the same ambivalence expressed in the compulsive imitation of the paternal voice, which has become the voice of God. The identification with the father, which originated in the wish to possess his power and in the love for him strengthened by reaction, is continued when the father has found his surrogate in the totem animal, and still persisted in essence when the totem animal gave way to a higher concept of God. Besides this identification, which is so clear in the shofar-blowing, the second original purpose—the really primary one—of the ritual is not to be forgotten. We have perceived what this is from many remarks of the prophets, from the use of the shofar in battle, and especially from the theological explanations—it is to affect deeply and to terrify. We now also understand this feature: the sudden resounding tone of the shofar which calls to mind the bellowing of a bull at the slaughter, and which is the voice of the totemistic father-substitute, unconsciously recalls to every hearer that old outrage and awakens his hidden guilty conscience, which, in consequence of the child's repressed hostile wishes towards the father, slumbers in each individual and admonishes him to repent and improve. The shofar-blowing thus becomes a reminder of the resolution never again to carry out that old outrage, and to renounce the gratification of the unconscious wishes which supply the incitement. The marked impression which the sound of the shofar, this active acoustic reminder of the first serious and, indeed, unatonable and unforgettable crime of humanity, produces on the mass of believers, thus receives an explanation based on the unconscious motives of these strong and apparently disproportionate affects. The peculiarly fearsome, groaning, blaring and long-sustained tone of the shofar becomes intelligible in that it revives the memory of the bellowing of a bull; it derives its serious significance from the fact that, in the unconscious mental life of the listeners, it represents the anxiety and last death-struggle of the father-god—if the metaphor be not too forced, one may say, his swan-song. Thus it seems quite natural that this ancient instrument with its three crude sounds, the long-sustained tone, the interrupted notes and the tremolo, should make a greater impression on the listeners than the sound of an organ or bells. The explanation of the

origin of totemistic phenomena was obtained from the
analysis of children's phobias. An animal unconsciously
signifies to the little child a father-substitute, similar to
that of ancient and savage peoples. Identification with
the father-god, the totem, as a symptom of which we
have recognised the imitation of speech in the shofar-
blowing, may be compared with the behaviour of little
Hans—whom Freud analysed—in his imitation of a
horse, and also with the cackling and crowing of Árpád,
three and a half years old, reported by Ferenczi.[1] The
believer's unconscious terror at the sound of the shofar
finds its analogy in the mental life of children. A boy,
three years old, who suffered from a phobia of dogs would
tremble violently on hearing a dog bark, and show his
anxiety in words and facial expression. Among ancient
peoples as well as children the anxiety affect appears as
a reaction to unconscious hostile desires against the
father and his animal representative.

We may now attempt to construct a kind of history
of the shofar on the basis of our acquired knowledge.

When the form of the father was recognised in the
totem animal and was worshipped as a god, the believers
imitated his voice by means of onomatopoetic sounds.
The imitated roar of an animal signified both the presence of the god in the midst of his worshippers and
their equality with him. In the course of centuries an
instrument was evolved from the horn—the most striking emblem of that totemistic god—and was now used
as a means to imitate his voice.[2]

There is another point, relevant here, to which investigators of religion have paid no attention, although
it is a striking one, namely, that a shofar which is

---

[1] Already quoted in the preceding studies.

[2] It must be admitted that here a gap in the hypothesis occurs which I am
unable to fill. The above derivation can only furnish a part of the explanation
concerning the primordial course of events and leaves many points in obscurity.
How—to mention one example—did the primitive human being discover that
the horn can be used for blowing? In spite of these uncertainties and defects I
thought it as well not to omit the attempt at a hypothesis which leads from
established facts into the primordial time. Possibly the archæology of music
may reach new results with its help.

cracked or has a hole in it may be used if its sound is unimpaired, but must not be used if its tone is damaged by the defect. We know from analysis that such a prohibition would not exist without a serious reason. One reason is clear: the sound of the instrument must not be impaired for it is holy; the voice of God which it reproduces must not be caricatured. The second motive, however, seems to me to indicate in a more striking manner than the first one the connection of the instrument with the totemistic cult. The victim who originally was the totem itself must be completely free from defects; this regulation is strictly adhered to in all primitive religions. Leviticus[1] decrees that a sacrificial animal which has a defect or is mutilated is not to be offered. We cannot assume that this analogy is only a chance one. We know that the horn as an attribute of gods was a relic of the originally divine totem animal; the requirement is therefore quite reasonable, that the horn, withdrawn from its original function and used as a wind instrument, should possess the same faultlessness that is demanded in the totem animal when it is used as a victim.

Before we continue the history and use of the ram's horn, we must meet two objections which might endanger the validity of our hypothesis. We have said previously that it must have been a technical invention and an advance of civilisation which led to the horn being used for God's voice, *i.e.* as a wind instrument. We also know what circumstances favoured the horn being chosen for such a use; the horn as a sign of physical power became a representation of divine power. But what is the path which leads from the symbol of divine power to that of God's voice? Analytic experience suggests a more special significance for the horn in the godfigure, *i.e.* it is a sexual symbol representing the male penis. This symbol, like so many others, originates in a period in which everything was sexualised; and the form of the male organ must have played a definite part in the developmental history of the equation of horn and

[1] Leviticus xxii. 18-25.

penis.[1] Traces of this primitive identification still persist in language; *e.g.* the Ethiopian ΦGЗ = horn and signifies *phallus* in Egyptian;[2] in Italian slang, *corno* also signifies the male genital organ.[3] Storfer was able to prove the sexual significance of the horn in legends of the Middle Ages relating to the unicorn.[4] In the phrase 'to put horns on somebody', whose origin Marie Bonaparte has briefly explained, the idea is used in a sexual sense. The fear of a bull or goat in the phobias of children, where the anxiety is based on the thought of the horn by which the child fears to be tossed, may be compared with little Hans's fear of being bitten by a horse. The essential root of these infantile ideas is unconscious castration anxiety. It is fully in accordance with unconscious mental life that the instrument by which castration is carried out should be the father's penis.[5]

The son's sexual envy, increased by an incestuous mother fixation, was the most effective motive that led to parricide in the primitive horde. The fact that believers, who, on account of their unconscious feeling of guilt, identify themselves with the murderers, take possession of the horn of the totem animal, corresponds to the breaking through of the unconscious wish to get possession of the great penis of the father, *i.e.* to appropriate his sexual powers. Thus, one of the most important motives which led to the foundation of religion may be traced in its late manifestations.

Our conclusion, however, also enables us to understand the use of the horn as a transmitter of God's voice. This use is not only conditioned by a technical achievement, but also mentally determined and over-

---

[1] In cynical wit and obscene jokes we occasionally find the same identification, which is easily understood by the listener. Compare *Hamlet* iii. 2:

    OPHELIA: You are keen, my lord, you are keen!
    HAMLET: It would cost you a groaning to take off my edge.

[2] Müller, *Asien und Europa nach altägyptischen Denkmälern*, 1893, S. 358.
[3] Dr. S. Seligmann, *Der böse Blick und Verwandtes*, Berlin, 1910, Bd. ii. S. 136.
[4] A. J. Storfer, *Marias jungfräuliche Mutterschaft*, Berlin, 1914, S. 106.
[5] In the unconscious phantasies of children an operation on their own penis is also carried out by the paternal genital. Analysis shows that this phantasy emanates from spying on parental coitus, resulting in the child placing himself unconsciously in the mother's place.

determined. Strength is the common element in the representation of sexual power and of God's voice. It is clear from the analyses of obsessional patients in whom loud speaking seems to cause physical pain, and who themselves can only speak softly or in a whisper, that loud, uninhibited speaking is unconsciously equivalent in them to unbridled sexual activity.

Darwin has alluded to the significance of singing in the courting of animals, and his theory of the origin of music is built up on this foundation.[1] In the life of primitive peoples' song is ever a match-maker, and also among civilised peoples there always exists some relationship between music and erotism. The troubadours of the Middle Ages as well as modern love-lyrics testify to the libidinal rôle of singing. The sexual significance of speaking and singing has become almost entirely lost to consciousness, though relics like the *ansprechen einer Dame* ('to address a lady') or *besingen einer Schönen* ('serenading a beauty') at times indicate the old connection. There is no doubt, however, that the voice is sometimes interpreted by the unconscious as a kind of substitute for sexual power.[2] (Compare the usual female enthusiasm for tenors, etc.) It is therefore not surprising that the horn does not completely lose this old significance.

The second objection is a more serious one. It reproaches us with lack of logic. Although we have arrived at the conviction that the shofar-blowing is a part of an ancient ritual which is traceable to the totemistic cult, there is still a contradiction. The sounds issuing from the ram's horn have not the slightest resemblance to the bleating of a ram; rather they resemble, as we have stated, the roaring of a bull in pain. In our elucidation we have more than once drawn attention to the Semitic cult of the bull. The choice of a ram's horn would also be

---

[1] Charles Darwin, *Descent of Man*, London, 1888.
[2] Concerning the sexual significance of the voice, see Storfer, *ibid.* S. 84. Special explanations of the erotogenic nature of the mouth zone may be expected from further contribution to Abraham's *Selected Papers on Psycho-Analysis: The First Pregenital Stage of the Libido*, 1916, p. 248.

against its being traced back to this, like the express prohibition in the Talmud quoted above of using the horn of a bull or cow as a shofar. How can we reconcile this 'discordance' (*Unstimmigkeit*)—in a real as well as a transferred sense—with our assumptions? The objection is easy to refute, however serious it may seem at first sight, by a glance at the historical development of totemism among the Jews. The Kabiri, as the Jews are called in the Tel-el-Amarna papyri, were shepherds and not cattle-breeders on their immigration into Canaan (1400–1200 B.C.).[1] The poorly watered steppes of Palestine are not suited for cattle-breeding, and the nomadic Arabs keep only camels, finding cattle-breeding beneath their dignity. In the Biblical tales of the patriarchal period sheep-breeding stands everywhere in the foreground. Rachel signifies the mother sheep in Hebrew. About 700 B.C. rams' horns appeared on the sacrificial altar as they are found on the sacrificial altar excavated by Sellin[2] (from Ta'anak). It is therefore quite probable (especially if one considers the particular holiness of the sacrifice of the ram in Leviticus) that the ram was the totemistic deity of the Jews in the epoch preceding the domestication of sheep, etc. Nevertheless, the testimonies of the Jewish cult of the bull are so numerous and convincing that the assumption (which is also made by most modern students of the Bible) is justified that the Jews had worshipped the bull before their immigration. Whether the influence of a settled people, like the Babylonians, is apparent in this cult of the bull, or whether independent derivation of a primary Semitic idea has taken place, must be left undecided, though the latter hypothesis seems to me more probable. The ram's horn which is taken from the later totem animal has apparently been unable to obliterate the memory of the original totem. As in so many archaic relics which have come down to us, there also persists here, besides the

---

[1] Cf. Stade, Benzinger and others.
[2] *Denkschriften der Wiener kaiserl. Akademie der Wissenschaften., Phil.-hist. Klasse*, 1904, iv. Tafeln xii. und xiii.

testimony of an old stage of civilisation, the traces of a still older one whose institutions were superseded by the people. Humanity has dragged along, and will continue to do so unwittingly to the end, the chains of its bondage to earth.

The prohibition against using the horn of a bull as shofar was made at a time when the worship of the bull was already considered offensive, and, moreover, with the express provision that it was to avoid the memory of the calf, *i.e.* the earlier totem animal of the Jews. At this time, however, which was that of the composition of the Talmud, the connection of shofar-blowing with totemism was already lost to consciousness, for the horn of the ram was not regarded as a reminder of this. Its original significance was so far removed from consciousness that the horn was supposed to recall the sacrifice of the ram. The theological scholars, in their attractive, old-fashioned style, would say that here the devil is expelled by Beelzebub. From comparison with similar phenomena in the symptomatology of the obsessional neuroses the idea is suggested that a return of the repressed from repression is demonstrable in their process.[1]

Having met these two objections, we may continue to pursue the long path of the use of the ram's horn, and we shall now pass over thousands of years. The first accounts of the use of the shofar which we find in the Bible are naturally very late. We meet a surprising multiplicity of the uses of the instrument, for instance, its rôle in the proclamation of a king—who is a representative of God on earth—in times of danger, in battle, in assemblies, and as an alarm signal: everywhere it symbolises, no, it *is* the voice of God which admonishes, warns and exhorts.

These more profane functions of the shofar, which we find in the Biblical period by the side of its use in the cult, belong to a late epoch of development, and we shall not go far wrong if we assume that they already correspond to a displacement and generalisation which has

---

[1] Thus it comes about that Jahve 'roars' from the horn of the ram's horn in order to converse with Amos, and this suggests his original bovine character.

the purpose of repressing the original and totemistic significance of the instrument, and withdrawing this knowledge from consciousness. In a similar manner the incipient symptoms of the obsessional neurosis become more and more loosened from their causal connection and undergo far-reaching displacements and generalisations in the long course of the malady. Therefore the present rôle of the shofar in the religious ritual, in which it is associated with feelings of sin and expiation, reflect, in this limited use, a far earlier stage, and are consonant with the originally sanctified and consecrated function of the ram's horn. Here again the symptomatology of the obsessional neurosis presents a striking analogy. In the course of psycho-analytic treatment the highly complicated and very generalised symptoms of the compulsive action approximate more and more to those relatively simple initial actions of the compulsion, in which their mental origin may be recognised by analytic methods. This phenomenon of the re-approachment to an original situation becomes intelligible as an example of the mechanism of the return of repressed material.

We shall not hesitate, therefore, to admit that there is a certain psychical justification in the interpretations of the shofar-blowing given in the sublimated views of Jewish orthodoxy, since we may see in these interpretations refinements, corresponding to the contemporary level of civilisation, of factors which are connected with the memory of the origin of the ritual. The threatening danger and the pressing need which the shofar announces really exist: these are actually the urging of unconscious tendencies of hostility and rebellion against the father-god. There is likewise a real foundation for the warning of punishment, and the expression of terror: just as the primitive man must have been terrified when he heard the father's powerful voice, and just as the child, struggling with temptation, is frightened when it hears the father's voice, so the shofar reminds the congregation of the punishment awaiting it if again it commits the ancient crime. We also know from the idea

which Judaism associates with the judgement at the
Rosh ha-Shanah what punishment is awaiting the
sinners, namely, death. This threat of death appears in
a faded form when God decrees at the *Rosh ha-Shanah*
who is to die in the coming year. The memory of the sin
effected by the shofar-blowing, to which orthodoxy
refers, really exists in the action: God's voice recalls the
crime once committed against him. The ceremonial, like
the symptoms of the obsessional neurosis, is a protection
against a temptation perceived endopsychically.

This origin of the shofar also explains why it became
the promise of expiation of the old deed. If the congregation is reminded by the shofar of the transgression
against the old god, it becomes, at the same time, master
of the temptation to commit the crime again: God can
now forgive. Just as the sound of the shofar recalls the
downfall of Judaism as a punishment for the old deed, so
at the same time the sound of the shofar is the announcement of its restoration and renewal. It is God resurrected,
as it were, after His murder, promising help if His sons
will renounce all hostility towards Him. Pardon has now
come to them because they have atoned for their crime
in the thousands of years of suffering, in the dispersion
which the prophets regard as their divine punishment.
Reconciliation with the father, in which identification
seems to be the most essential feature, thus gives rise to
the happy prospect of the future. We must not forget,
however, that the shofar ritual, which signifies, like the
totem meal, the expiation of the old crime, at the same
time affords opportunity for its repetition. In the imitation of God's voice, in the usurpation of the divine horn
which is the most outstanding sign of the totem god, the
murder is committed once more *in nuce*. The reason why
the shofar-blowing has to be repeated—on New Year's
Day thirty times—is on account of the strength of the
unconscious impulses to parricide and the intensity of
the aversion to them. The constant attempt of these
forbidden impulses to break through necessitates their
continually renewed rejection and the constant remem-

brance of the fateful issue of that deed. The conscious faculty is for ever mobilising the shofar-blowing as a defence against them. Stern's observation is therefore really true—though in a sense surely not dreamed of by him—that the sound of the shofar goes back into the past and extends into the future of Judaism, and that it admonishes repentance, remorse and conversion.

Having thus brought the late interpretations of believing Judaism into agreement with our hypothesis, we are now under an obligation to explain the views of the Talmud, of the *Cabala*, and of the broad masses of the people from our standpoint. We are well aware that these views contain distortions, displacements and generalisations of the original meaning of the ceremonial; but our belief in a universal mental determinism is great enough to stimulate the expectation that traces of once rational associations can be found in those which are apparently absurd and far-fetched. Their later interpretations are all concerned with the secondary function of the shofar-blowing. We have to keep in mind the remarkable phenomenon that the sound of the shofar, which conjures up the memory of that old outrage, betrays the rebellion against God in the process of identification with Him. Similarly, in compulsive actions the tendencies to suppress and to give vent to forbidden feelings unite in a single symptom. According to the interpretation of Rabbi Joshia the shofar-blowing referred to in the verse of the psalm, 'Hail to the people who understand the sound of the horn . . .', signifies that the Jews, by means of the shofar-blowing, understand how to change the quality of the severe judge into the quality of mercy. The original and unconscious meaning of the verse is clear: 'Hail to the people who understand the sound of the horn', as a warning against that old outrage (and as the popular belief continues it, through their repentance to move the Lord to mercy). Thus, owing to a misunderstanding, the shofar-blowing became a means to persuade the Lord, to assuage Him, and to move Him to mercy. It is as though a prayer for indulgence were included in that open confession of sins which is implicit in the shofar-blowing, in the usurpation of God's voice.[1] It is clear that there is a compromise formation between two mental forces in conflict with each other in the *Mussaf* prayer of New Year's Day:

> Together with our prayer we raise the shofar,
> In order to persuade Thee, Almighty One, by it.

As a matter of fact the prayer for mercy really renews the old crime, in that the believers put themselves in the place of God. We understand why it is a good omen if the tones of the shofar are pure, and, on the other hand, a bad omen if they are indistinct and faltering. Resistance against blowing the shofar manifested in the faulty tones means for the unconscious an inner inhibition against the promise of repentance; the faltering of the blower corresponds to the endopsychic perception of a tendency consciously rejected, to desire the continuance of the sinful way of life. The wishing to remain in sin, *i.e.* the repetition of the old deed, results in misfortune for the whole community.

The belief which Jewish mysticism has taken up and further developed, that the sound of the horn is intended to confuse Satan in his accusations, becomes intelligible if we remember the psychogenesis of the idea of demons and the devil. Satan is the representation of the individual's hostile impulses projected into the external world. The reason for the projection was in great measure to ease the unconscious guilty conscience of the race. When later Satan becomes the accuser this development strictly corresponds to the mental mechanism of paranoiac hallucinations: the accusations which paranoiacs hear, and which are hurled upon them by spirits or the devil, are really self-reproaches projected into the external world. The accusation which Satan makes against the Jews is that of the murder of the old god: the voice of the accuser is really one's own conscience, one's own guilty consciousness. The shofar, which, as a token of

[1] A similar mental situation underlies the Kol Nidre prayer.

remembrance of the old guilt, was originally to serve the accuser as a *corpus delicti, i.e.* as a most effective weapon, becomes actually the means of his confusion. We see repeated here the same contrast between the conscious rôle which the shofar has to play in relationship to God. The sound of the shofar is to overcome Satan in the same way as the imitation of God's voice consciously helps the mastery of one's own hostile impulses. The wish contained in the phrase, 'Oh, destroy Satan', the saying of which, before the shofar-blowing, is recommended in a cabalistic work, is quite justified. Consciousness and love are turned against the unconscious temptation to hate which wishes to employ the shofar-blowing as a sign of the usurpation of the divine power, *i.e.* a repetition of the primal crime. This prayer is analogous to the continuance of neurotic protective measures, *i.e.* a new symptom of defence is formed to avoid the temptation which is contained in the defence symptom.[1] The recommendation to interpolate God's name in this sentence has quite consciously received the supplementary meaning, namely, to bring in God as a helper in the struggle. As a matter of fact, however, it is equivalent to a replacement of Satan by God, and thereby the person praying says, 'Oh, destroy God', actually expressing the wish which led to the erection of all the defence measures, and which was condemned by consciousness. We have already met this mechanism of the return of the repressed from repression. The interpolation is paralleled by the behaviour of Freud's obsessional patient who interspersed his prayers with blasphemous curses and insults against his conscious wish. The commonest form of such a disturbance of a religious practice by opposite trends of thought appears in the well-known occurrence of sacrilegious ideas in the midst of the prayers of pious people.

Our conception of the original significance of the shofar ceremonial facilitates our understanding of its rôle in excommunication, in cases of death, and in the

---

[1] Compare the Talmudic 'making fences around the law' with this extension of the precautionary measures.

idea of the Day of Judgement. It everywhere represents the presence of God; it is He who terrifies the excommunicated with His voice and intensifies the effect of the curses in the synagogue by the threat of death; its call, as it were, shows the uttered curses fulfilled in advance. It is clearly shown in the episode in 1 Samuel xv. 8 that the purpose of the excommunication was the killing of animal and man in honour of Jahve.[1] The sound of the shofar at death proclaims that the deceased has now expiated his guilt, that is, his participation in the great transgression of which he had made himself guilty through unconscious rebellious tendencies against God; and the last trump on the Day of Judgement is the terrible warning against the old sin renewed in each individual. The same sound has become, however, a good omen on the Jewish tombstones in the catacombs, an omen, namely, of resurrection, just as in the liturgy. In both cases the promise is dependent on the condition of impulse-renunciation. It is always worthy of note that these rites, like the rest of the religious rites of the shofar-blowing, bring back something of the pleasure which they are meant to prevent, because the command to fulfil them is executed. The compromise formations, which, in the obsessional neurosis, are the outcome of mental forces striving with one another, originate along the same psychic lines.

Some striking features of the shofar-blowing in the festal ritual demand explanation. We know that it was displaced from its original position in the service of New Year's Day—ostensibly on account of the persecution by the Romans. One of the unconscious motives of this displacement from the morning to the forenoon service becomes evident if we think of analogous mechanisms in neurotic symptom formation. Formerly the shofar-blowing was associated with reflections and prayers which explained its function, though this was certainly very much concealed; now it appears disconnected and com-

[1] F. Schwally, *Semitische Kriegsaltertümer*, Heft 1, Leipzig, 1901, S. 29, treats the excommunication as an old rite.

pletely isolated. This particular position, this detachment from the original context, is intended to impede
the destructive work of consciousness and of causal
investigation, just as in the isolation of an obsessional
symptom.

The real feature of the New Year's Feast, *i.e.* the beginning of a new life, is intimately associated with the
concept of expiation. It unites grief at the death of a god
with joy at his resurrection, as in the Dionysian and
Eleusinian feasts which were celebrated about the same
period.[1] These two factors were associated with the
fears and hopes of the congregation. The severe silence
which lies over the congregation during the blowing of
the shofar, and the glad sigh of relief after it is over,
would correspond to the confession of guilt and the expiation of the old crime: the believers, laden with their
guilty conscience, have now saved themselves for another
year from that death with which the Day of Judgement
threatened them. 'When at last it ceases to sound,' writes
Kirchner of the celebration of the New Year's Feast
among the Jews, 'the congregation calls out: "Hail to
the people/who can rejoice/they shall walk in the light
of thy countenance. At the ending of the service they
go home/to eat and drink/indeed, they are also exhorted
by the Rabbis/to be of good courage/because their sins
have been forgiven them by GOD."' The similarity of
this ritual to that of the Adonis celebration at Antioch,
where the priests consoled and anointed those previously
bewailing the death of the god—

> Be comforted, ye pious ones! for as the Lord is saved,
> So shall we be saved from our distress—

is striking, and illustrates the universality of the chief
psychical factors in religion, namely, guilty conscience,
desire for the father and defiance of the son.[2]

---

[1] As to the original date of the festival, see the *Jewish Encyclopædia*, vol.
viii. p. 254.

[2] As in the shofar-blowing, so in the meal which came to be the prototype of
the sacrificial ritual, the two opposite traits of subjection and rebellion were
united. There are a few remnants in the folk-custom of the New Year's Feast

The Feast of Atonement, although of a relatively more recent date, is rich in ceremonial which is of ancient origin. One may suppose that it is a derivation of that great piacular celebration which expiates the original sin and which the growing consciousness of guilt has created for its own mitigation. The meaning of the use of the shofar in the ritual of this feast is clear from the foregoing interpretation. The blowing at the end of the feast is characteristic. We have already recognised that the unconscious significance of blowing the horn is not only a sign of the most energetic repudiation of the old outrage, of making it invalid, and of reconciliation with the injured Deity, but is also a repetition of the outrage. We find again, therefore, the breaking through, one might almost say, the triumph of the consciously condemned rebellious impulses when the shofar is blown at the end of the great day of expiation, which actually serves for the expiation of that old sin. Guilty conscience, repentance and defiance are blended in a unity in the ceremonial of the shofar-blowing, just as in the great expiatory sacrifice which took place on this day when the old bull and ram totems were sacrificial animals.[1]

---

which prove that a totem meal originally took place at it; for example, the customary eating of sweetmeats, 'goat's horns', roots and dates. Ezra reports that the people on this day ate flesh and drank sweet beverages (Nehemiah viii. 10). In the twelfth century it was the custom in France for the Jews to put red apples on the table on this day: in Provence grapes, figs and a calf's head (compare the prohibition against making a shofar out of a calf's horn). Rabbi Jacob Mölin (fourteenth century) mentions the custom of eating apples with honey and a deer's head in memory of Abraham's sacrifice, the 'Aḳedah (compare the connection of the shofar-blowing with the horn of the ram sacrificed in Isaac's place). Another reason for eating an animal's head is to presage that the consumer will be 'ahead' and not backward in his undertakings during the ensuing year. Nuts, however, ought not to be eaten at the feast of the Rosh ha-Shanah, because the numerical value in the Hebrew word for nuts אבזין is equivalent to that of the letters of חטא = sin (chet with the exception of the vowel א = 17), and also for the reason that nuts stimulate the salivary glands, as a result of which the thoughts of the believers are turned away from their prayers and from the festival. (These references are taken from the Jewish Encyclopædia, vol. viii. p. 256, under 'New Year'.) The connection of eating nuts with sin expresses in a disguised form the guilty conscience felt as to the devouring of the father, appearing through a return of the repressed. The fear of having one's attention diverted corresponds to the defence against an access of pleasure in the never abandoned phantasy.

[1] In corroboration, reference may be made here to the temporal succession of the totem animals in Judaism, which we have assumed, and which, in connection with the psycho-analytic derivation of the sacrificial ritual, is suited at

S

We have still a word to say about the shofar-blowing in the month *Elul*. We know that it is officially a reminder of the approaching great feast of the month *Tishri*. The extension of the ceremonial to the preceding month is explained through the effect of that unconscious work of displacement which plays such a great part in the symptomatology of the obsessional neurosis. The seemingly abnormal forgetfulness of the Jews is offered as the motive of this extension, but the unconscious motives of this forgetfulness contribute most to its explanation, just as in similar phenomena in Freud's *Psychopathology of Everyday Life*. The most important motive is the refusal to remember the deed of parricide and god-murder, and the rejection of the unconscious feelings which at the same time awaken the temptation to repeat it. The unconscious work of displacement justifies the assumption that, simultaneously with increased fear of God, tenderness and subjection to Him, and even, under the cloak of these feelings, tendencies opposed to them, find their gratification in the extension of the shofar-blowing. Pleasure in the memory and in the temptation re-emerge each time behind the remorse for personal sin which the shofar-blowing awakens. It might be mentioned as a kind of proof of the correctness of this view that in the Middle Ages the Jews blew

the same time to throw light on the still puzzling ceremonial of this day. As is well known, the high priest sacrifices for himself a young bull, and for the people a goat, as expiatory victim. First the blood is smeared on the horns of the sacrificial altar and then sprinkled on it seven times. According to tradition (*M. Joma* v. 4, *Maimon* iii. 5) the blood of the bull was to be poured into the dish with the goat's blood; at any rate Leviticus xvi. 18 suggests that blood was applied mixed and not successively as in the Holy of Holies. The young bull appears here as the totem for the high priest as representative of the tradition, and the goat as the totem for the people. The intermixture of the blood of the two animals corresponds to the killing of the god, represented by the high priest, and the retaliative killing of the race, his murderers, in expiation of the deed. The 'reconciliatory character' of this deed becomes clearer if we consider similar rites in the puberty celebrations of the Australian blacks. In the Kuntamara ceremonies in central Australia, after thè subincision, the older men and the youths who have just been subincised collect together in the bed of the river, and all of them cut themselves with sharp knives and the father and son-generations are thus united; a tender bond is created between them for the overcoming of the existing opposition. The smearing of the horns of the altar, *i.e.* of God, has a remarkable analogy among the Australian blacks when the circumcised youth touches the head of an old man, who stands to him in the relationship of grandfather, with a little blood and a green branch.

the shofar during *Elul* because they wished to mislead Satan as to the time when the New Year's Feast, *i.e.* the Day of Judgement, would take place.[1]

We have recognised that memories of those most significant events which really led to the institution of religion are reflected in the ritual of the shofar-blowing. We can now ask how this trifling detail in the ritual obtained such an outstanding position. The ceremonial of the obsessional neurosis here also supplies an explanation. This ceremonial is generally concerned with the unimportant acts of life and expresses itself in foolish precepts and limitations. To the non-believer the shofar-blowing must seem trifling and foolish, so long as he fails to recognise that the mechanism of displacement is effective in the religious development of the custom. Just as in the compulsive actions of neurotics, so here a ceremonial has taken a marked position through displacement from real and most significant things to a very small and insignificant one. In the analysis of this apparently unimportant rite we have found that it leads to events of great consequence in the prehistoric period of human existence. Religious ritual has unconsciously held fast in a small trait to the essential thing which it does not venture to express in forms which appear to be more important. The believers, however, who endow the shofar-blowing with such strong effects behave unconsciously. They are like a person who devotes his whole care to a little worthless box. He is popularly regarded as eccentric, and no one guesses that this box represents his most valuable possession.

Another feature of the shofar ritual has also more than once shown how important, from a heuristic point of view, may be the comparison with the symptoms of the obsessional neurosis. I allude to the compromising nature of its psychogenesis. An act forbidden by God—the appropriation of the insignia of the father-god—is actually carried out in the name and by the command of

---

[1] According to our derivation this deception would, of course, represent a self-deception, a self-illusion by means of false facts.

God. Here the command of God, the primitive father, is obeyed and transgressed in the same action, just as in the 'defiant obedience' of obsessional patients. One can see how difficult it is for human nature to renounce a pleasure which has once been enjoyed.

The conservatism of the Jewish religious ritual in this and in other ceremonials is astonishing. The immortality and independence of time of unconscious impulses appear also in the ritual of Judaism. Strong impulses from the primal period of the people have found expression in the shofar-blowing in spite of all religious advance. The surprising tenacity and loyalty with which Judaism adheres to the old customs certainly claims a special explanation, which cannot, however, be given here. Perhaps the archaic structure of the mental life of the Jews, and their great ambivalency in comparison with that of other peoples, is of special weight here. Israel's love for Jahve could never conceal the strong impulses of hate and opposition with which it had to struggle.

We will now turn back to a question which was the starting-point of this study of the shofar. Why is the Biblical myth of the invention of music, which differs from other myths, not connected with a god or a hero? The answer is: because this myth would have come into conflict with the highly developed concept of God which obtained at the period of the composition of the Bible; it would have had to show all too clearly that Jahve has developed from a totem animal; and the fear of the discovery of an origin which was thought at this period to be a low one for a god may have been one of the strongest hindrances to such a tale. Jahve, it seems to me, has created a fateful precedent. We can see daily in the life of the Jews how similar concessions and concealments of a presumably humble origin are made in deference to the opinion of the world at large.

In the Bible the invention of music is ascribed to an ordinary mortal whose name only is known to us. Nevertheless, it is really this great distinction from the other (divine) singers and musicians, emphasised, no doubt, with a view to obliterating the trail, that has helped us to ascertain the real 'father' of those who play the flute and zither. Of course, this result could only be reached by disregarding the warning, 'La recherche de la paternité est interdite', which the scanty information of the Bible appears to give us. We have found it striking that the name Jubal coincides with the word *jôbel*, which means ram's horn. We learn, however, from the dictionary[1] that the word יובל in itself really signifies ram, and only ram's horn in a transferred sense. If we have the courage to take the statement in the Bible literally we can then translate it: the ram which is the father of all those who play the flute and zither. But is this the result of our laborious investigation? Yes, this is indeed the case. The Oriental method of expression, 'the father', may even be taken literally, for it was the sons who imitated the roaring of the father in the primitive society. We must not forget that in spite of this the text of the Biblical passage has come down to us censored and mutilated—the common noun, ram, has been changed into a proper noun in order to conceal the derivation from totemism. Two kinds of instruments, one of which, the flute, undeniably originated from the bones of an animal, have appeared instead of the horn of the shofar in a way that recalls obsessional neurotic displacement. We may even suppose that the name of the original totem animal, the bull, was replaced by that of the later one, the ram. This process would correspond to the prohibition against using a bull's horn as shofar, and to the introduction of a ram's horn into the ritual.

A survey of these last conclusions suggests that we have still to overcome a few difficulties. The alteration of the common noun, 'ram', into the name of a human being attracts our attention. How are we to make this development intelligible? Do we know of analogies from Semitic antiquity which make such displacements prob-

---

[1] The Talmud states that יובל is the Arabic expression for ram (*Rosh ha-Shanah*, c. 3, f. 26). Rabbi Akiba says he heard when he came to Arabia that the ram was there called *jôbel*.

able? It is easy to obtain relevant examples if we consider the proper names of the Old Testament.[1] Joshua's companion, for example, is called כלב dog; the name ראובן, Reuben, signifies lion; Rachel, Leah, Deborah, Simeon, Jonah, Terach, Hamor, Tola, Elon are all names of animals. In the Old Testament alone we find fifty-three names of animals which are used partly as names of persons and partly as names of tribes. These facts, which are in agreement with similar ones among all Semitic peoples, gave W. R. Smith[2] the idea that a trace of the old totemistic cult survives in such names. Further investigation of comparative religion and ethnology gave more and more plausibility to the view that the animal names originally denoted membership of a definite totem clan. Only in the historical period, when this origin was lost to the popular consciousness, were animal names

[1] Cf. George Kerber, *Die religionsgeschichtliche Bedeuting der hebräischen Eigennamen des Alten Testamentes*, Freiburg, 1897, S. 71. Biblical comparisons such as those occurring in Jacob's and Moses' blessings (Genesis xlix., Deuteronomy xxxiii.) can only thus be understood. The derivation, assumed above as certain, of proper and tribal names from totemism in pre-Jahvistic Judaism is questioned by the present science of the Old Testament. The existence of a totem cult in primitive Judaism has recently been vigorously denied. Present Biblical research is in full retreat from the positions which W. B. Smith has conquered. Lévy in the *Revue des études juives* (tome quarante-cinquième, Paris, 1902, p. 113) investigates the question of the origin of Hebraic names of animals, and comes to the conclusion, ' Au degré du développement qu'avaient atteint même les plus grossiers des peuples sémitiques, il serait absurde d'espérer trouver des exemples de totémisme pur'. Emil Kautzsch (*Biblische Theologie des Alten Testaments*, Tübingen, 1911) decides that totemism in Israel is not proved, and 'above all that any memory of it, even of its last remnant, has disappeared from the religion of Israel in the Old Testament'. We believe we have shown that residual phenomena are clearly perceptible, and we have even ventured the statement that without their assumption the understanding of the Old Testament is almost impossible. Other energetic opponents of a totemistic hypothesis in regard to prehistoric Judaism are Th. Nöldeke (*Zeitschrift der Deutschen Morgenländischen Gesellschaft*, 1886, S. 156) and P. de Lagarde (*Études sur les réligions sémitiques*, 2. Auflage, Paris, 1905, p. 112) and others. Eduard König, for instance (*Geschichte der alttestamentlichen Religion*, Gütersloh, 1912), holds the view that the names given to animals among the Jews had first been names of individuals. It may already be said that the attitude to the totemistic problem in religious development has become a shibboleth of students of religion.

[2] 'Animal Worship and Animal Tribes among the Arabs and in the Old Testament', *Journal of Philology*, vol. ix. p. 75, and *Kinship and Marriage in Early Arabia*, Cambridge, 1885. Besides R. Smith's disciple, A. Jevons (*Introduction to the History of Religion*, London, 1903), who regards the totemistic phase as the original one in all religions, J. Jacobs, T. K. Cheyne, A. H. Sayce, J. F. MacLennan, B. G. Gray, A. Lang have expressed agreement with the assumption of a totemistic cult. Only a few German investigators, like J. Benzinger and B. Stade, have followed them.

given to children in the hope that the characteristics of the animal concerned should be theirs (strength, courage, swiftness). This same development is demonstrable among the uncivilised peoples of the present time: the tribe calls itself after its totem animal.[1] This fact is so universal and so essential for the primitive organisation of the tribe that a whole series of ethnologists (A. K. Keans, Max Müller, Herbert Spencer, Lord Avebury, A. Lang, etc.) have been misled so far as to seek to explain the origin of totemism from it.[2] The totem-god is everywhere the name giver: the Australian black from a clan in which the kangaroo was worshipped merely called himself a kangaroo man or a kangaroo.

If we use this explanation for our Biblical passage, we shall find that we can perhaps correct and deepen our hypothesis. The name *jôbel*, ram, is not only the designation of the totem animal and the tribe who worship it, but at the same time the name of a member of the clan. Similarly, among the Arabs, an inferior tribe of *Hamdâh* is called *taur*, 'bull', a designation which each member of the tribe bore.[3]

We have stated that according to the Bible the totem animal, the ram, is the real inventor of music. We have recognised that the hidden meaning of this tale lies in the fact that the tribe had imitated the sounds of its totem animal in the holy songs which made up an essential part of its religious ritual. In virtue of the double function of the name ram—as designation of the totem and its worshippers—we are faced with the question, Whom have we really to regard as the 'father' of all those who play the flute and zither?

Comparison with the myths of other peoples comes to our aid here. We have already noted the remarkable deviation of Judaism from other myths, in that in Juda-

---

[1] Further remarks concerning the totemistic names of animals are to be found in J. G. Frazer's *Totemism and Exogamy*, London, 1910, vol. i. pp. 6, 7, 69, 338, 343.
[2] Freud, *Totem und Tabu*, S. 101, gives a review of these theories, which he associates as 'nominalistic'.
[3] R. Smith, *ibid.* p. 70.

ism the origin of music is traced back to a human descendant of Cain. It seems probable from our hypothesis that the sons imitated the voice of their slain father after the conflict in the primal horde. We find this father, or rather a later father-figure, the totem animal, in the Biblical saga—the ram is the father of those making music. We know, however, from ancient and savage peoples that the clan adopted the name of the paternal totem animal, and thus we may interpret the Biblical report in the sense that a man from the ram clan has been the inventor of music. Various factors suggest this. The sons who had taken possession of the father's dead body and believed they had gained possession of the paternal characteristics had great-grandsons who identified themselves with the paternal totem animal by clothing themselves in its skin, by imitation of its voice, and by eating its flesh. We must regard the adoption of the name of the totem animal as an act of such identification. In the myths of all peoples, however, it is precisely the rebellious son who is celebrated as the saviour, and as the inventor of all arts and sciences. All the institutions which mark the progress of primitive humanity are ascribed to him. For example, the invention of the flute and shepherd's pipe is ascribed to Marsyas and Midas, who rebelled against Apollo and fought with him. Again, in Australian tribes, different instruments and institutions can be traced back to certain mythical hawk-men.[1] Midas was originally an ass, Dionysus, who had the surname Dithyrambos, a he-goat, even as Jubal was a ram. We seem, therefore, to have found the trace of an old myth in the laconic statement in Genesis, which must have been similar to those of other peoples concerning the invention of music. We may suppose that memories of that primal episode, which we have denoted as so important for the beginnings of music, have been preserved in it in spite of all elaborations.

We know now the meaning of the Biblical statement

[1] For example, the circumcision among the Aranda and Loritja tribes, Strehlow, *ibid.* S. 11.

that the ram is the father of those who make music. The passage not only derives music from God like the rest of the myths, but it supplies a kind of abbreviated history of the art for those who can interpret it. Music originated in the imitation of the paternal voice, through imitation of the sounds of the animals which are worshipped by the clan as totem animal. We now also see that there is no deviation of the Jewish saga in principle from those of other peoples. Jubal, the inventor of music in the Bible, is a hero like Orpheus, Osiris and Attis, and has his story of suffering like these first artists. It is no ordinary mortal who, in the original pre-Biblical tradition, can boast of having discovered the secret of sounds. Here, too, it was only conflict with the gods that could bring a blessing.

The evolution of the meaning of the word 'ram', which advanced from the name of a totem animal to that of its adherents, and finally became a proper name, has shown itself to have great significance for the original sense of the Biblical passage. None of the distortions and concealments of a later period have been able to prevent psycho-analysis from reaching back to the primary content of the saga.

We have now become acquainted with a second motive which impeded the formation of a musical myth like those of other peoples. The myth exists already. Its main lines are found in this very saga of Jubal which surprised us by its deviation from the traditions of the rest of civilised peoples.

I feel that we have no reason to be proud of our discovery that music is traceable back to the imitation of the paternal voice.[1] The discovery has long been extant in the popular saying: 'As the cock crows the chicks twitter'.

---

[1] The derivation given above claims to have put forward only one factor in the evolution of music, and we have by no means forgotten that there are other very important factors brought out by Darwin, Spencer, Büchner and other students, which are of special significance for the origin of this art.

IV. The Shofar and the 'Bull-Roarer'

It will not have escaped the critical reader that we
have omitted to take into consideration in our explanations the connection maintained by official Judaism between the shofar and the horn of the ram which was
sacrificed instead of Isaac. It seems, however, that from
this association paths may be opened up leading to a far-
distant sphere, and meriting separate treatment.

We have found that a memory of the episode of the
sacrifice of Isaac, of Abraham's devotion to God and
willingness to sacrifice, of the 'Akedah, can be recognised
in the shofar-blowing. This particular narrative in Genesis xxii. 1-18 can be traced back to various sources, and
is preserved in a strongly modified form to which different periods of time have contributed. The original
meaning of the narrative shines through all the elaborations and super-impositions of the ages. It corresponds
exactly to the puberty rites which students have described among the Australians. In the initiation ceremonies of the Australian blacks, the young men are
made to feel afraid that they will be sacrificed to *balum*,
a mysterious monster. The preparations for the sacrifice
of the youths are the same as those reported in Genesis
for the sacrifice of Isaac. In the end pigs are sacrificed
in their place. Here, as there, the part played by the unconscious hostility of the fathers is unmistakable; for,
although they pretend that they are sorrowfully execut-
ing a higher command, in reality they wish to offer their
sons as victims. The command to kill the sons and Isaac
emanates ostensibly from the *balum* monster, *i.e.* from
the totem-god or the tribal father. Freud,[1] however, has
shown that here, just as in the divine sanction of the
sacrifice, there is a secondary idea which, by this displacement upon God, expresses the most complete denial
of the outrage originally committed against God Himself.

[1] *Totem und Tabu.*

The origin of the situation has to be sought in the scene of parricide which led to the institution of religion. Having recognised the unconscious meaning of the later displacement, we understand how it is that the command to kill Isaac emanates ostensibly from Jahve, and that of the Australian youths from *balum, daramulun* and similar totemistic beings. The association is determined by the unconscious memory of the men's own death-wishes against their fathers, and by the fear of retaliation on the part of their sons. Just as in Abraham the unconscious wish once existed to kill the father (Jahve), so also will it be stirred in the son who has become a man. And thus the command to sacrifice may be attributed to Jahve. The fear of retaliation affecting the father-generation, strengthened by memory of the father's own youth, and of the hostile wishes towards his own father which were then active, now leads to his own son being threatened with the fate of being devoured by the *balum* monster. The anticipated revenge for the unconscious hostile wishes of the sons is now transferred, as it were, to this monster, which, as a father-substitute, was once the object of similar impulses. Thus the sacrifice of a pig among the savages, and of a ram in the patriarchal saga, in place of the youth signifies not only a renunciation of the father's wish to gratify his impulse of hatred against his son, who appears to his unconscious as a *revenant* of his grandfather, but also its satisfaction. The animal is a father-substitute, and its sacrifice is a renewal of the old parricide. We are thus led, by this path also, towards an assimilation of the ram to the father-god.

Later tradition is quite correct in connecting the shofar-blowing with this report of Isaac's sacrifice; but it also comprises, though well enough concealed, the memory of the old blood-guilt. Like Isaac, all the members of the congregation would deserve to be killed on account of their hostile and unconscious intention against the father, whom they themselves have killed in virtue of the omnipotence of thought. Here also the impelling motive of the criminal wishes may be seen in the introduction of the horn, namely, sexual envy and jealousy.

A comparison of the puberty rites of savages with the ceremonies in which the shofar is blown promises, on the one hand, to furnish a further confirmation of our views concerning the origin and primary function of this still puzzling instrument, and, on the other hand, to deepen our understanding of the puberty rites of the savages.

In the men-feasts of primitive peoples the novices hear the sound of a remarkable instrument which plays a great part in the ceremonial, namely, the bull-roarer.[1] If we wish to know what this peculiar instrument is we must inquire of ethnologists, anthropologists, travelling students and missionaries. The bull-roarer is a holy instrument among all primitive peoples; it is kept carefully packed in the male club-house, and is only used on particular occasions, as at the rites of the initiation of youths, and in magical procedures to increase totem animals and plants. The instrument consists of a flat, narrow piece of wood in which there is a hole. It is whirled very quickly in the air by a long string threaded through the hole in the instrument, and a loud humming noise is produced. Women and children must not see it.

The bull-roarer is found all over the world, in Australia, South and West Africa, America, India, Sumatra, Solomon Islands, New Guinea, etc. Its existence in almost all European countries has been established. Its original association with religious ideas is shown in the country, where it is still used in connection with superstitious customs (for example, it is supposed to have a special effect on cattle). In towns it is found degraded to a top as a child's toy. The instrument has a venerable history. There is no doubt that the *rhombus* which was swung in the Dionysian mysteries was a bull-roarer.[2] Bull-roarers of the palæolithic period have even been discovered, and this fact led A. Lang to assume that the popular religion of that period must have been similar

---

[1] Cf. *Globus*, Bde lxviii. and lxix., and Schmeltz, *Das Schwirrholz*, Hamburg, 1896.   [2] *Encyclopædia of Ethics and Religion*, vol. ii. p. 890.

to that of the Australians. Professor A. C. Haddon[1] has expressed the opinion that the bull-roarer 'is perhaps the most ancient, widely-spread, and sacred religious symbol in the world'.

Students of religion differ concerning the position which the bull-roarer occupies in the religious life of primitive peoples. That it is a most important one is clear from the view adopted by a serious scholar, R. R. Marett.[2] He says, 'I have to confess to the opinion . . . that their (the divinities) prototype is nothing more or less than that well-known material and inanimate object the bull-roarer. Its thundering booming must have been eminently awe-inspiring to the first inventors, or rather discoverers, of the instrument, and would not unnaturally provoke the "animatistic" attribution of life and power to it. . . . Nevertheless, despite its want of animistic colouring, a genuine religion has sprung up out of the awe inspired by the bull-roarer.' The genesis of such an idea, of which the incorrectness is obvious, becomes intelligible from a number of facts which indicate the high importance of the bull-roarer among savages. Bull-roarers appear in many tribes actually as a tribal father, in others merely as the Supreme Being. Among most of the tribes of south-east Australia there are two bull-roarers, one of which, as shown by myths, represents the original totem-god, and the other his son.[3] The sound of the bull-roarer is often supposed to represent thunder, but always represents the voice of a spirit, of *daramulun*, of *tundun*, *mungan-ngaua*, *baiame*, etc. Among the Tami the bull-roarer is called *kani*, a name which also signifies the spirits of the dead. Among the

---

[1] A. C. Haddon, *The Study of Man*, p. 327.

[2] *Folk-lore*, vol. xi. (1900) p. 173. Marett, in his essay published in 1910, 'Savage Supreme Beings and the Bull-Roarer' (*Hibbert Journal*, vol. viii. pp. 394-410), acknowledges that his thesis went too far and develops new views regarding the bull-roarer.

[3] This view of the significance of the two bull-roarers is supported by the analogies revealed later. P. W. Schmidt puts forward the view that the two bull-roarers represent the tribal parents (*Der Ursprung der Gottesidee*, 1 Teil, Münster, 1912, S. 262). A. van Gennep, *Mythes et légendes d'Australie*, Paris, 1905, cap. vii. ('Les deux doctrines religieuses et le rhombe sacré', pp. lxiii-lxxxi), gives the myths as well as a good review of the bull-roarer in Australia.

Kai people it is called *ngosa*, which also means 'grand-father', and many tribes call it *balum*.

What has the bull-roarer to do with the puberty rites? It is the voice of that spirit which is supposed to devour or circumcise the youths and, according to the state-ments of travellers, has the purpose of terrifying the novices, perhaps also of warning them to observe strictly the precepts of the new society into which they are to be received. In the Arunta tribe the humming warns the women not to go near the place where the ceremony is taking place; they believe it is the voice of the spirit called *twanyirika*. The explanation given to account for the long absence of the youths while their wound heals is that *twanyirika* has carried them off into the bush. In the Wonghi tribe in New South Wales the noise of the bull-roarer is heard after the puberty opera-tion, which in this tribe consists in knocking out a tooth, and it is said that each youth meets a spirit named *thuremlin*, who kills him, makes him alive again and knocks out a tooth. We see, therefore, that the most essential function of the bull-roarer is to terrify the uninitiated, to whom its noise is the voice of a spirit.

We will now indicate what features the bull-roarer and the shofar have in common. Both are primitive instruments of noise, of great antiquity, and both evoke peculiar and marked affects in their hearers. Their names signify both an instrument and a totem god or a spirit (ram and ram's horn, *balum* and the totemistic gods of the Australian blacks, *twanyirika*, *daramulun*, *tundun*, etc., denoted as *balum*). The sound from both instru-ments produces the same impression. We have compared the sound of the shofar to the bellowing of a bull, which, according to our derivation, it really signifies. The bull-roarer, as its name suggests, makes a similar sound. The *balums* or *churingas* are carefully preserved in the male club-house, as the shofar is in the temple. Women and children must not see the bull-roarer, and originally the same was true of the shofar. Both instruments have a special rôle in the religious cult; the bull-roarer, as the

voice of a spirit, is to terrify the youths, just as the
sound of the shofar, which once was Jahve's voice, is to
make the faithful tremble. The sublimated psychological
motivation also is the same in the two rites. The Australian novices are warned to renounce their hostile and
incestuous wishes by the bull-roarer, whose sounds, like
those of the shofar, which reminds the worshippers of
Jahve of their burden of sin, represent a menace from
the spirit.

It will be appropriate here to glance at the development of the Jewish religion. Is the voice of Jahve, which,
according to the Bible, sounds from Sinai and terrifies
the Jews, essentially something more than that of *balum*
which terrifies the young candidates for the secret religion of totemism? The imposing apparatus which is
offered us in the Sinai pericope should not distract us,
for in both cases the members of the primitive clan, who
are now to become acquainted with the rigid fundamental laws of the religion of the tribe, are terrified by
mysterious and uncanny sounds in which they recognise
the voice of their terrible god. The distance between the
Decalogue and the crude laws which the Australian
elders communicate to the novices in the bush is by
no means as great as it seems at first sight. We obtain
an indication here that the story of Exodus was originally nothing but the tale of the great initiation of men,
and of the introduction of a clan into the cult of its
ancestors, which only after thousands of years became
the account of a revelation whose significance is valid
for all time.

We need not decide whether the failure to recognise
the similarity between the shofar and the bull-roarer of
initiation ceremonies is due to vested interest or to the
inattention of ethnologists and students of religion. The
jump from Jewish religious ceremonials to the religion
of the savages in central Australia is certainly a big one,
but there is no fundamental reason why there should not
be analogies between the rites of the highly developed
religion, which has unconsciously preserved memories of

its beginnings with strict conservatism, and the beliefs
of low primitive peoples.

We have already noted that the qualities common
to both instruments correspond with the unconscious
motives and the hidden meaning of their use in ritual.
We know that the shofar reminds the faithful of the
primal guilt which each individual unconsciously renews in harbouring death wishes against his father, and
that it warns them of the approaching punishment.
Analysis of the puberty rites[1] shows that the bull-roarer
has the same purpose, namely, to terrify the youths to
be initiated by its spirit sounds, and to compel them by
this and other threats to reject the anti-social wishes of
their childhood. The Day of Judgement and the beginning of a new life find a counterpart in the initiation of
youths. The threatened punishment by death in the
Rosh ha-Shanah and the liberation from this exigency
may be remembered and compared with the now unconscious meaning of the puberty rites which Frazer
called 'The Drama of Death and Resurrection'. The
death and rebirth of the youths is represented actually
among the savages and symbolically in the Jewish New
Year's Feast, in which the threat of death and the redemption are typified. A trace of this is recognisable in
the late comment of Maimonides that the shofar is to
awaken sinners out of their sleep. We may remember
that, according to the custom of the Middle Ages and of
the Eastern Jews, the shofar is blown at death just as it
is to sound at the resurrection. An analogy to the protective character of the sounds of the shofar, which is
emphasised by the *Cabala*, can even be recognised *in
embryo* in the following custom among the Australian
Unmatjera tribe.[2] After the subincision the youth 'must
be sure to make the bull-roarer swing, or else another
arakurta (a youth who has passed through the ceremony
of circumcision, but not through that of subincision),

---

[1] Compare the section on the puberty rites in the present work.
[2] Spencer and Gillen, *The Northern Tribes of Central Australia*, London, 1904,
p. 343.

who lives up in the sky, will come down and carry him away. If this *arakurta* hears the *luringa*—that is, the noise of the bull-roarer—he says, "That is all right", and will not harm him.'

We have still an objection to meet. Two factors differentiate the shofar essentially from the bull-roarer, namely, material and shape. A similarity of this kind between the two instruments is certainly difficult to establish, and we can only suggest an explanation for the difference. The Jews, in spite of their old culture—or on account of it—have probably retained the ancient instrument in their ritual in its primitive state; the savages have exchanged it for another one. That such an exchange has taken place is suggested by the fact that among the Minangkabauers of Sumatra, and frequently among other tribes, the bull-roarer is made from the frontal bone of a man who was noted for his bravery. It is no greater distance from a man's frontal bone to a ram's horn than from an anthropomorphic god to the old totem-god. Further, it is worth noting that in the puberty ritual it is not in all savage tribes that the bull-roarer, in particular, has to play the rôle corresponding to the shofar. While the novices remain in the stomach of the *balum* and their fathers make preparation for the circumcision, the men make a frightful noise, striking their shields, shrieking, blowing through their fists, which is done, as Schellong reports from Kaiser Wilhelms Land, 'for the unmistakable purpose of greatly intimidating the trembling youths within'. The shrieking and blowing into the fists is a primitive method of making a noise which is later replaced by the use of an instrument. Among the Karesau Islanders, according to a report of P. S. Schmidt, the youths are terrified by the mysterious sounds of flutes which are interpreted as the voice of the spirit. An increase in the volume of the sound represents a more urgent desire of the spirits to devour the youths.

A description of the ceremonies of initiation into the Kakian Society in the West of Ceram removes the last

T

doubt of the psychical identity between the shofar and the instruments used in such rites. The boys are thrown into an opening formed like a crocodile's jaw or cassowary's beak and the women are told that the demon has devoured them. The circumcised youths remain in the gloomy hut for several days, and during that time the chief takes a trumpet, lays its mouthpiece on the hand of each youth, and speaks through it in strange tones which imitate the voice of a spirit. He warns the youths, under threat of punishment by death, to keep strictly the rules of the society.

Although, to our surprise, science has not recognised the striking similarities between the ram's horn and the bull-roarer, it has, nevertheless, performed a great service in establishing the identity of the bull-roarer with an ancient ritual instrument. 'There is no doubt that the *rhombus* (ῥόμβος) which was whirled at the Greek mysteries was one.'[1] I borrow the following description of a ceremonial of this kind, in which the humming-top plays a rôle, from Jane Harrison's book,[2] which describes the origin of art, especially drama and sculpture, in ancient ritual. 'The celebrants in the very primitive ritual of the Mountain-Mother in Thrace were, we know, called *mimes*. In the fragment of his lost play, Aeschylus, after describing the din made by the "mountain gear" of the Mother, the maddening hum of the *bombykes*, a sort of spinning-top, the clash of the brazen cymbals and the twang of the strings, thus goes on: "And bull-voices roar thereto from somewhere out of the unseen, fearful *mimes*, and from a drum, an image, as it were, of thunder underground is borne on the air heavy with dread".' Here again we have the older form, the imitation of the bellowing of a bull, side by side with the newer one, the beating of drums and the top. Dionysus even is called the 'god of the loud cry', he is characterised as 'a sacred bull' and 'son of a bull'; at his feast in Ellis, the women sang of his coming 'with the feet of a bull'.[3] The festival

---

[1] *Encyclopædia Britannica*, vol. iv. p. 791.
[2] *Ancient Art and Ritual*, London, p. 47.
[3] Plutarch, *Quaest. Gr.* 36.

of this god, like the feats of Attis, Osiris, Orpheus and Tammuz, corresponds, in psychical motive, to the initiation ceremonies of savages.

Thus psychology recognises a similarity between such various instruments as the shofar of the Jews, the *rhombus* of the Greeks, the bull-roarer of the savages and the tops of our children. The same repressive forces that were at work in ancient Judea and Greece are active in Australia and Africa to-day.[1]

Ethnology has proposed the hypothesis of 'elementary thought' (Bastian), but it was reserved for psychoanalysis to find the fundamental affective basis of this concept and to endow it with living content. Only psycho-analysis could show that everywhere in primitive society similar institutions result from the play of mental forces which are eternally the same. Only psychoanalysis has been able to hear amidst the manifold and confusing richness of sounds the hidden dynamic melody which solemnly and eternally rises from the deep and dominates the chaos.

V. The Myth and Music

When we return home after a long and troublesome journey a great feeling of satisfaction comes over us as we view from a hill the long-left town. It seems to us as though a new and hitherto unknown attraction floats around it and illuminates it with a new light.

We may feel similarly as we now approach the starting-point of our investigation. We were led to this study by a strange anomaly in Jewish criticism, namely, that it did not appear to ascribe the invention of music to a god. It will be remembered that at the gathering mentioned at the commencement of this section on the shofar, the question was raised whether the ancient myth of the

---

[1] Ernest Jones, *Essays in Applied Psycho-Analysis*, 'The Madonna's Conception through the Ear: A Contribution to the Relation between Aesthetics and Religion', London, 1923, p. 261, has dealt with the bull-roarer and the significance of sound with special reference to their sexual symbolic meaning.

earliest peoples might not throw some light upon the origin of music.

We have discovered traces of an old myth in the revised Jewish saga which recalled an old act of violence associated with the invention of music. We found that the ram was denoted by the name Jubal, who was the father of musicians, and by following this indication to its totemistic meaning we arrived at the idea that the saga had originally told of a son-god's rebellion against the father-totem, the ram. It was actually the uncalled-for imitation of the sounds of the totem animal that showed us the path.

The myths of the ancients concerning the origin of music now require explanation. We will follow the suggestions contained in two articles by S. Reinach.[1] He shows that the original form of Marsyas, as well as of Apollo, was a divine ass or mule. The divine singer Orpheus, however, was worshipped as a fox in an earlier period, as Dionysus was worshipped as a bull or goat.

The fate of these young gods is similar to that of Osiris, Attis, Tammuz and Zagreus; Orpheus was torn to pieces by Maenads, Marsyas was flayed alive after a duel with Apollo, and Dionysus was torn asunder by the Titans. All these gods, who represent saviours, are lamented after their death by their worshippers, and come to life in a new form.

If the original content of the myths is investigated, we arrive at the idea that these gods had committed a serious offence against other gods, and die a horrible death by way of expiation. The death of Orpheus and the fact of his being devoured point, according to the law of retaliation, to the nature of the crime of which he had made himself guilty, namely, the killing and devouring of the divine primal father. In the myth of Marsyas the nature of the youthful hero's guilt stands out more clearly; he has brought on his fate by injuring Apollo in a duel. We may associate these young gods with the youths at the

---

[1] *Cultes, Mythes et Religions*, tome deuxième, Paris, 1906, pp. 85-122, and tome quatrième, Paris, 1912, pp. 29-44.

initiation of men among primitive peoples, when the
novices are ostensibly eaten by a spirit and then born
again. They are types of sons who are overtaken by the
revenge of the divine father.

In all these myths we find two gods, the offended
father-god and the son who has committed a crime
against the father and must severely atone for it. In many
myths, like that of Marsyas, the invention of a musical
instrument is actually mentioned as the cause of the
dispute with the divine father. If we call to mind the
sexual symbolism of music it is clear that the more
original motive is evident even in the late and distorted
form of the saga. The sons have taken possession of the
attributes of the father, just as in the lost myth of Jubal.
If, however, we follow Reinach's[1] view, that the elements of the myth can be traced back to parts of an old
ritual, we find that the worshippers of the god imitate
him in voice and form, by wearing an animal's skin and
roaring as in the Dionysian mysteries.

A surprising parallel is supplied by yet another
feature. Jubal, the inventor of music in Genesis, was
originally a ram, just as Marsyas was an ass and Orpheus a fox. The son-gods were garbed in a totemistic
costume, and thus indicate that they are of the same
origin as the gods whom they had overthrown. Perhaps
a later insurrection of the son is imaginatively thrown
back in this way into a past epoch and related in totemistic language. The Australian myths, described by A.
v. Gennep, also associate the invention of music with the
memory of an old act of violence: in many tribes the invention of the bull-roarer can be traced back to the
tribal father, a powerful spirit. This tribal father has
proved himself to be an ungrateful son towards the all-
father who is called *atnatu* among the Kai tribe, and he
dies an unnatural death as a punishment. In this case
the son has stepped into his father's place; and everywhere the bull-roarer imitates the voice of the father-
god, which is also described as thunder. The myths of

[1] *Ibid.* p. 87.

the ancients find a counterpart here. Among the Wirad-juri the spirit *baiame* kills *daramulun* who has deceived him and puts his voice into the trees of the forest. He makes bull-roarers from the trees which have received *daramulun's* voice. Among the Warramunga the son-god *murtu-murtu* is killed by wild dogs. *Murtu-murtu* is also identified with the bull-roarer.[1] Naturally all these gods are totemistic though they now appear as lizards, hawks, crows or emus.[2]

We have recognised the suffering of Dionysus and the death of Orpheus as expiations of the primitive crime with which they were burdened. According to Reinach, the oldest form of the myth is that in which the Maenads flayed Orpheus alive and devoured his bleeding body. According to another tradition, Orpheus caused the people to give up anthropophagy, and this story is particularly associated with the belief that the singer had appeased savage animals.

> Silvestres homines sacer interpresque Deorum
> Caedibus et victu foedo deterruit Orpheus,
> Dictus, ob hoc lenire tigres rabidosque leones,

sings Horace. Orpheus, the musician, like Dionysus, appears as a saviour and civiliser. We can understand from the psychogenesis of this saga how such an association came about: the guilty conscience of the son who killed and devoured the father-god instituted the law for the preservation of the totem, *i.e.* the prohibition against eating the fathers, which first assured the existence of the community. Music is here the representative of morality. The Abyssinians also have a saga which supports our idea of the origin of music. They ascribe the invention of music to the holy Vared in the time of Negus (king) Caleb. This pious man once noticed a worm vainly endeavouring to crawl up to the top of a tree, and saw it fall down seven times when nearing the top. The

---

[1] Spencer and Gillen, *The Northern Tribes of Central Australia*, London, 1904, p. 492.
[2] Cf. W. Schmidt's astral hypothesis concerning the Australian myths in *Der Ursprung der Gottesidee*, S. 258.

holy man supposed that it was revealed to him in this form how he himself, for seven years, had in vain sought to learn science and art in the schools. He swallowed the worm, whereupon enlightenment came to him, and he suddenly received the arts of reading, writing and music by divine revelation. We find here the devouring of the totem animal, the prototype of each later identification, and the beginnings of music as a result of it, united into one myth.

We have seen that music is everywhere connected with the primitive religion, and that everywhere it can be traced back to the first and most important stage of religious development, *i.e.* to totemism; and that imitation of the voice of the father or of the totem animal is found at the root of the invention.

* *
*

The origin of music is veiled in obscurity. In accounts handed down from the ancients and in reports of primitive peoples of the present time it never appears alone, but is always connected with the dance. Dance music of to-day is a special form of music, and certainly not the highest form of the art; and we have long been accustomed to enjoy music apart from the dance. Only a few female dancers are skilled in the art of dancing to music of the more serious kinds (Chopin, Liszt, Schubert, etc.); to other mortals like ourselves it seems unbecoming to make dance movements while listening to a Beethoven symphony at a concert. Nevertheless, this association of music demands investigation.

The dance first appears in ritual. Miriam sings to the Lord a song and dances; Jephtha's daughter celebrates her father's victory by dancing; David dances before the Ark of the Covenant, and the Jews around the golden calf; according to Psalm cxiv. the mountains skipped like rams and the little hills like lambs in honour of the Lord. The priests of Cybele danced at the resurrection feast of Attis to the raucous sound of cymbals, kettledrums, pipes and horns; the priests of Baal danced round the altar on Carmel;[1] and the priests of Mars performed their dances on the first day of the Cretan Zeus—everywhere in this period the art of dancing appears in the service of the cult. The worshippers danced at the celebrations of Dionysus and Bacchus and at the mysteries of Demeter. The dance was such an important part of the ancient mysteries that, according to Lucian,[2] to be excluded from the ceremonies was designated by the expression ἐξορχεῖσθαι, i.e. to leave the circle of the dance. The female Bacchantes danced at their service as the Dervishes do to-day. Pindar gave Apollo the title of 'the dancer'. Orpheus is said to have introduced the dance among the Dionysians. Aeschylus, the oldest of the Greek tragedians, prescribed the movements for the dancing choruses. Dancing was held in such esteem that it served to occupy the army besieging Troy; and Lycurgus prescribed dancing for the Spartans. Plato declared that all dancing was a religious performance. In Egypt religious processions moved along dancing and singing through the temple, and in Greece the chorus took measured steps and sang hymns to the glory of Apollo.

The dance, then, is a religious act of high importance. It represents the life and sufferings of a god. Lucian reports that the Indians imitated the dance of their deity. We know also that the gods danced. According to Jewish legends God danced with Eve,[3] the Muses danced, Hercules and Dionysus performed on Parnassus the choric dance with the Maenads.

The Jews who danced around the golden calf, David who danced before the Ark of the Covenant, the priests who skipped before the altar of Baal, not only danced before God; they imitated God, they identified themselves with Him. This becomes particularly clear if we compare their dances with those of primitive peoples,

---

[1] 1 Kings xviii. 26.
[2] The following remarks on the dance I borrow from *Die Religion in Geschichte und Gegenwart*, published by Schiele, from the *Encyclopædia Britannica*, and from monographs like F. de Ménil's *Histoire de la danse*, Paris, 1904.
[3] Eisenmenger, *Entdecktes Judentum*, i. S. 46.

which likewise belong to religious ritual.[1] 'Among the Mandan Indians, when the hunters failed to find the buffaloes on which the tribes depended for food, every man brought out of his lodge the mask made of a buffalo's head and horns, with the tail hanging down behind, which he kept for such an emergency, and they all set to dance buffalo. Ten or fifteen masked dancers at a time formed the ring, drumming and rattling, chanting and yelling; when one was tired out, he went through the pantomime of being shot with bow and arrow, skinned and cut up; while another, who stood ready with his buffalo-head on, took his place in the dance.' The North American dog and bear dances are pantomimic representations of these animals. The Kru dance of the Congo coast represents the movements of a gorilla. The Damara dance is an imitation of the movements of oxen and sheep. The Australian blacks and Tasmanians in their dances called corroborees imitate frogs and kangaroos. The mask dances of savages are representations of animals or spirits, just as the dances in the Dionysian celebrations are imitations of the divine goat.

If we carefully consider these examples, which could be easily augmented, and make use of Freud's theory of the animal dances of savages, we arrive at the following conclusion. The dances in the cult are first of all imitations of the movements of the god, who is represented at a certain stage of religious development as a totem animal. We know that the wearing of masks by the savages, and the corresponding covering in skins and disguises in the ancient religions, as in that of Dionysus, are likewise imitations of the totemistic god.

We now seem to have found in the traces of the first appearance of music in human civilisation a most essential factor, a factor of the highest importance in the history of musical art. Whatever may have been the origin of music we have now no doubt that the factor of imitation played a great part in its original development.

[1] Tylor, *Anthropology: An Introduction to the Study of Man and Civilization*, Second Edition, 1889, pp. 296-97.

We have seen that music, dance and mimicry always developed from imitation of the god whose first prototype was the father of the primitive horde, and who was changed later into the totem animal.

Dance, mimicry and song are united in a ritual which gave rise to tragedy and comedy. The content of the oldest Greek tragedy is the suffering of the divine goat Dionysus, and the lamentation of the goats over its fate. Aristotle explains in his *Poetics* that tragedy and comedy were originated by the leaders of Dithyrambos. Dithyrambos (the god of the two gates?) was originally an epithet of Dionysus, like Bromios (the god of the loud cry). He also mentions the hymn that was sung at the feast of Dionysus during the dance round the altar, and in which the deeds and sufferings of Dionysus were glorified. We know that the leaders of the Dithyrambos were the worshippers of Dionysus clothed in goat-skins, and that later they formed the chorus of the Greek tragedy. The hymn itself, however, originated in the imitation of the crying of Dionysus, *i.e.* the noise of the goat, and the choric dance in imitation of its springs and movements. Let us adopt Freud's suggestion that Dionysus, the son-god, has appeared in the place of the primitive father, the 'tragic' hero of the first tragedy who was killed by the rebellious sons.

I believe that the posthumous working of the great crime which occurred in the prehistoric period in the primal horde may still be found in the history of music. A compulsion of particular strength must again and again have caused later generations to retain firmly the memory of that primeval occurrence. It seems likely that the high psychic tension which the deed left behind, and the impossibility of its being mentally overcome, must in themselves have contributed in a high degree to the setting up of such a compulsion. The longing for the father and the triumph over the powerful adversary, lived over and over again in phantasy, must have made it possible for the sons to call up again and again the memory of the father's form, his movements and the tone of his voice. It forced the clan with compulsive strength to identify itself again and again by imitation of his voice and movements with the primal father whose return is represented for individuals by their own father.[1]

When the animal, in the form of the totem, became the substitute of the father, its voice and movements were imitated. In the feasts of the savages and in the ritual of the ancient mysteries we see humanity at a stage which was the direct continuation of that prehistoric development. When, however, the deity regained its human character and a son-god repressed the father-god, this ritual was retained in altered form, as shown by the compulsive lamentation over the death of the Semitic gods (Attis, Adonis).

The first crude and primitive music, which is of unknown origin, has somewhere in this development—probably in the totemistic period—encroached upon the evolution of the prehistoric cult; it originally helped to imitate the voice of the paternal god, and only much later acquired other functions. The same may be said of the dance which was intended to represent the movements of the totem animals.

The memory of the killing and devouring of the father of the primal horde and the triumph over him, has led to the periodic celebration of the totem meal[2] in which the crime of parricide is repeated. Robertson Smith has discovered the ceremonial of such a totem meal in the description by the patriarch Nilus of the sacrificial customs of the Bedouins about the end of the fourth century A.D. The victim, a camel, was laid on a rough altar of stones, and those participating in the celebra-

---

[1] Perhaps imagination may supplement the above account by reverting to the primal situation and seeking there the prototype of all that happened later. After the murder of the father in the primitive horde, a great silence overcame the sons caused by the presence of the dead person who lay in their midst, and gave the most eloquent expression to their identification with the slain person. (Compare my short essay 'Die Bedeutung des Schweigens', *Imago*, 5. Jahrgang, 1919, Heft 5). In the howling which broke this silence their triumph broke through. The growing guilty conscience must later have changed the howling in the annual slaughter of the totem into a compulsive outburst of grief.

[2] Freud, *Totem und Tabu*, S. 134.

tion went three times round the altar singing. Here again we find music in a religious cult; it has developed into a religious song out of an imitation of the cry of the animal, just as the dance, the earlier imitation of the movements of the animal, has developed into a kind of procession.

In the original periodic totem meals of the tribe, the imitation of the voice of the totem animal has the same unconscious purpose as the devouring of the totem animal itself, namely, to retain and enjoy the victory over the father. At the same time, however, the grief and guilty conscience of the believers is recognisable in this identification, just as the desire to be reunited with the father is apparent in the totem meal.

This hypothesis leads us to examine other results of Robertson Smith's researches from a new side, namely, the grief at the sacrifice and the dancing and rejoicing in connection with it.[1] Robertson Smith draws attention to the fact that 'in the annual piacula of the Baal religion there was also a formal act of mourning, which, however, was not an expression of penitence for sin, but a lament over the dead god', like the corresponding lamentation in the Adonis cult. 'The origin and primary significance of the obligatory lamentation is sufficiently transparent; for the death of the god is originally nothing else than the death of the theanthropic victim, which is bewailed by those who assist at the ceremony, exactly as the Todas bewail the slaughter of the sacred buffalo. On the same principle the Egyptians in Thebes bewailed the death of the ram which was annually sacrificed to the god Amen . . . and then clothed the idol in its skin and buried the carcass in a sacred coffin. Here the mourning is for the death of the sacrosanct victim, which, as the use of the skin indicates, represents the god himself.' Smith is convinced that 'a form of lamentation over the victim was part of the oldest sacrificial ritual, and that this is the explanation of such rites as the howling (ὀλολυγή) which accompanied Greek sacrifices. . . .

---

[1] *Lectures on the Religion of the Semites*, London, 1901, p. 430.

Among the Semites the shouting (*hallel, tahlīl*) that
accompanied the sacrifice, may probably, in its oldest
form, have been a wail over the death of the victim,
though it ultimately became a chant of praise (Hallelujah).' He refers to the fact that the roots הלל and ילל
(Arabic ولول), to chant praises and 'to howl' are closely
connected.

Robertson Smith refers, in his explanation, to yet
another custom, that of the cult dance. The dance was
usually an expression of religious joy as several passages
in the Old Testament prove. The 'leaping' dance of the
priests of Baal[1] is associated, however, with a sorrowful
appeal. In Syrian the same verb in different conjuga-
tions signifies 'to dance' and 'to grieve'. In the usual
sacrificial cult the attitude of reverential respect which
in the ancient period was observed at the death of the
victim, had changed to savage rejoicing, and the shrieking underwent a corresponding change of meaning. The
expiatory rites, however, were permanently accompanied by expressions of grief.

This highly gifted scholar recognises with keen insight that the forms of grief observed in these rites were
not originally the expression of regret for sins, but solely
an obligatory lamentation over the death of the totem
victim. These prescribed forms of grief are not an expression of great sorrow, but have a compulsive character and a particular significance.

Our findings up to the present enable us to corroborate Smith's views in all essential points and to correct
them in some minor ones. The comparison of the compulsive nature of the grief with the symptoms of pathological grief in neurotics provides the explanation. The
ambivalence of the father complex was transferred to
the totem animal, the later substitute of the father, and
was the chief factor in determining the conduct of its
worshippers. The compulsive form of the grief at the
death of the victim is explained by the mental ambivalence towards the totem animal. The rising feeling of

[1] 1 Kings xviii. 26.

triumph over the death of the father-image had to be
suppressed by an increase of grief; the bewailing over
the death was necessarily compulsive because leakages
from the unconscious threatened to question the seriousness and sincerity of the grief—these are processes of
mental life which may easily be observed in neurotics at
the present time.

Robertson Smith is quite right in understanding the
howling at the sacrifice as compulsive lamentation,
which later passed into rejoicing. Analytic experience
here again refers us to the ambivalence which enables us
to explain similar mental phenomena. The compulsive
howling was to drown the feelings of satisfaction over
the death of the divine animal, because these unconscious feelings strove for expression. Little children are
often compelled to cry and make other expressions of
grief on the death of their parents, because tendencies
of an opposite nature threaten to break through into
consciousness.

Robertson Smith's view of the alteration in the meaning
of the howling is certainly correct, but his explanation
needs supplementing. There probably was a period in
which the howling, taken as a compromise action, signified both a lamentation and a cry of triumph over the
death of the totem-god. The howling was at first, perhaps, only an expression of triumph, a cry of satisfaction and joy over the death of the paternal rival; but as
the unconscious feeling of guilt in the religions increased
in strength, it became more and more an expression of
grief and bewailing. The transition from cries of sorrow
to cries of joy corresponds completely with the two-
period actions of neurotics, in which, at first, the one
motive of the ambivalence is brought to expression and,
thereupon, isolated from it, its opposite. The more the
real significance of the sacrifice, *i.e.* originally the
slaughter of the father-god, was lost to consciousness,
the more energetically could vent be given to the cry
of triumph as an expression of satisfaction, because it
was detached from its original cause. The feelings of joy

and satisfaction finally make it possible to repress the expressions of grief and lamentation. This return of the primary impulse is a clear sign of the constant emergence in religion of the defiance of the son. We have in the shofar-blowing, which expresses at the same time both grief and joyous hope by imitating the voice of the totemistic god, a further proof that the impulses striving with one another were once united.

The dance also was originally an expression of the wildest triumph, and then changed into a rite full of grief in order to become again a sign of the most joyous vital feeling. The dance as a ritual has disappeared from the life of civilised people—except in the view of certain æsthetic critics who designate manifestations of dancing as religious service—but it still exists as such in almost all savage peoples, among the half-civilised peoples of India and Thibet where the priests dance in the masks of animals, and also among the Mohammedan dervishes. Incidentally the dance of the East Jewish *Chassidim* as an act of religious service may be recalled. The dances at the solstice celebrations are also an ancient remnant of originally religious rites. However paradoxical it may sound, the dance in our latitudes has still been preserved, although in unrecognisable form, in prayer, that religious act which seems to us the most important. The positions and gestures in prayer are only residue phenomena of old dances. The kneeling and prostration, the squatting (among Indian sects), various customs in prayer like the swaying of the body (among the Eastern Jews), hand-clapping, hopping and jumping (in Buddhism) have developed from primitive dance movements and positions.

We have seen that music and the dance play an important part in religious cults, and that their real development begins from the point where they have become utilised to support the imitation of the primitive father-god. Traces of their early religious function appear very clearly in their further evolution. We know that the drama originated in the feasts of Dionysus in which the suffering of the young god was glorified. But another kind of art also has its origin here. Opera and operetta have developed from the dithyrambic hymn which was sung and danced. Already in Menander we find the beginnings of opera. Music, acting and poetry are united in the original prototype of the feast of Dionysus, *i.e.* the funeral rites of the son-deity, in the same way as they are associated in the mask dances of savages even to-day. Richard Wagner[1] wishes to see them reunited, so that the highest development of art in his view falls into line with its earliest beginnings. The religious sanctity which Wagner ascribes to his work of art becomes intelligible through this reversion to the condition of its pristine holy usage.

According to our view the original cultural significance of music has developed out of the religious cults. We have seen it appear at first in the celebration of festivals at the death of a god. Robertson Smith calls this celebration 'the commemoration of a mythical tragedy'. We know the nature of the tragedy which took place at the outset of human culture, and of which the later memory was shown in the celebrations of the death of the son-god, namely, the murder of the primal father by the sons of the horde. A religious festival in which the worshippers of the god imitated him in voice and movement and identified themselves with him has developed from the bewailing of the death of the youthful god who expiated the murder in later forms of religion. One might perhaps speak in this sense of the birth of music from the soul of tragedy. The advance of civilisation brought instruments to support the human voice. It is characteristic that the first instruments, like the shofar, and the material of which they were constructed, were both taken from totem animals, and still serve to imitate the noise of the animal. The song of the chorus, which developed from lamentation over the death of Adonis and Dionysus, betrayed its derivation. Neither has it lost its original significance, the imitation of the voice of the father who has become a

[1] *Kunstwerk der Zukunft.*

god, when it is sung in modern churches in praise of God. The hallelujah which the choir sounds forth originated in the howling which bewailed the dead.

It is not my intention to pursue the development of music in the whole richness and multiplicity of its rôles in religious service from ancient and mediæval up to modern times. It need only be pointed out that this art has never lost its intimate relationship with religion, for not only does it accompany the religious service in the notes of bells and organ, and in singing, but its greatest masters, Bach and Beethoven, have again and again enlisted the force of its sounds in the service of religion. The brightest genius of music, A. W. Mozart, who was born in the pious city of a hundred churches and a thousand bells, could not entirely free his creations from the influence of religious feeling.

Perhaps music, like the other arts, had magical tendencies in the beginning.[1] If so, the imitation of the voice of a god in ancient cults and the imitation of an animal in the totemistic rites of the savages could also be easily understood from this standpoint.

SUPPLEMENT

VI. THE MOSES OF MICHELANGELO AND THE EVENTS ON SINAI

The following somewhat condensed remarks are intended to show that the knowledge arrived at by following analytic paths may throw new and surprising light on some of the most important questions of the science of religion. Their fragmentary character will indicate that they are to be taken only as suggestions and hints for the exponents of this particular science. The importance of the questions raised, and the fact that the value of this contribution to their answer has yet to be tested, justifies this summary treatment; and their inclusion

[1] S. Reinach, 'L'art et magie', in *Cultes, Mythes et Religions*, tom. 8, pp. 125-36.

in a larger context makes it a necessity. If, therefore, the problems discussed are treated here in a manner which is more suggestive than explicit, the disadvantage is perhaps alleviated by the fact that, so far as I know, they are shown in an entirely new aspect.

In order to simplify the approach to these great questions we will start from one of the most significant works of sculptural art. The magnificent marble statue of Moses, which Michelangelo executed for the tomb of Pope Julius II.—it is supposed in the years 1512 to 1516 —and which is exhibited in the church of S. Pietro in Vincoli at Rome, has exercised a profound effect upon almost all those who have seen it. Hermann Grimm has called it the 'crown of modern sculpture'. It has repeatedly been designated the Olympian Zeus of our time. Many æstheticians and connoisseurs, of whom I need only mention H. Grimm, Jakob Burckhardt, Henry Thode, C. Justi, W. Lübke, have expressed themselves enthusiastically about the statue, while there are others who have been impressed quite differently. Some critics are candid enough to express feelings of marked repulsion on viewing it. They say that they are repulsed by the relatively small head, whose animal-like character strikes them, and by the brutal force which seems to radiate from the statue. Even Karl Justi remarks that the profile with the horns has about it 'something of the satyr, something of hard defiance'; and Jules Michelet calls the Moses 'sublimement bestial'. A modern writer on art, Karl Scheffler, has recently expressed in the following words[1] the feeling of repugnance he felt in the presence of the gigantic force of the figure: 'Besides the effective arrangement of the figure there is a really terrifying savagery in it. *A human being sits there like an infuriated bison, whose mere glance makes one tremble*[2]—in whose form there is, however, a certain carnal naturalness, an indiscretion quite foreign to the antique, and thoroughly

---

[1] I owe the reference to this passage from *Italien. Tagebuch einer Reise,* Leipzig, 1913, to a kind communication from Fräulein Renée Ranzenhofer of Vienna.

[2] The italics are mine.

in keeping with the Renaissance; this stormy and technically over-smooth statue has just the effect of a monumental portrait of the artist himself.' Something of the ambiguous effect of the work must have been conscious to Michelangelo's contemporaries. A gentle horror was always mingled with their admiration of the master, for they called him at one time 'the divine', and at another 'the terrible'.

Like the artist his greatest work forbids any intimacy: the animal-like profile is just as decisively aloof as the breath of divinity which floats around the head of this Moses. Nevertheless, those who feel this resting form to be uncanny and repulsive cannot escape the impression of its grandiose and superhuman effect. Most of the criticisms of the statue ascribe to it the overpowering influence which is proper to the great man of God, the kingly prophet and priest. In some it would seem as if this Moses is no longer looked upon as a representative of Jahve and a leader of the people, but as the Deity himself. Coyer already wrote of the statue:[1] 'Puisqu'il a plu aux hommes de révêtir la Divinité de la forme humaine, c'est ainsi qu'il faudrait figurer le Père éternel'. He therefore puts the Moses of the artist in the place of the fearful God of the Old Testament and speaks as if Jahve were incarnate in him. The Jews of the time of Michelangelo appear to have had similar views, for Basari states that the inhabitants of the Ghetto made a pilgrimage, 'like flocks of cranes', to the Basilica of Eudoxia on the Sabbath 'in order to worship Moses'. Michelangelo's biographer adheres to this statement, which sounds so improbable, in spite of other authors' objections.

The facial expression of the hero has been interpreted in the most different ways.[2] Thode found in it a 'mixture of anger, pain and disdain', while Dupaty says, 'Ce front auguste semble n'être qu'un voile transparent, qui couvre

---

[1] *Voyage en Italie et de Hollande*, Paris, 1775, i. p. 268.
[2] Cf. Freud, *Collected Papers*, 'The Moses of Michelangelo', vol. iv., London, 1925, p. 257.

à peine un esprit immense'. Lübke says one seeks in vain
the expression of higher intelligence in the head, 'there
is nothing in this compressed forehead but the quality of
terrific anger, and of an energy that will overcome everything'. Borinsky[1] sees in the statue the ideal of the 'con-
templative man of action'; the look is directed into the
far distance and he sees nothing in his proximity. Münz,
Guillaume, Steinmann, etc., express similar judgements.
Gabriel Thomas[2] condenses these views in the words,
'Mais surtout le regard haut et ferme, dirigé vers un but
lointain nous relève le chef social et religieux, le vrai
pasteur d'un peuple, qui lui obéit sans le comprendre,
le fondateur d'une nation, mais qui façonne encore
la race, la pétrit comme un limon; c'est en un mot le
prophète souverain, interprète de Jehovah qu'il a vu face
à face.'

There is still another doubtful point and one which is
of primary significance for the understanding of this
work, namely, the question whether Moses is represented here as an ideal figure of no particular period, or
whether the master wished to portray him at a definite
and important moment of his life. It is clear that this
question cannot be decided without a detailed investigation of the motives underlying the energy portrayed
in the figure. At the same time, however, the investigation will reflect the individual spectator's conception of
the character of the statue.

To speak briefly, the great artist's figure of Moses gives
us many riddles to solve. The effect which it exercises on
almost all critics is a strong one, but in many of them it
is not clear and uniform. In the eyes of some visitors the
monument assumes the shape of an enormous animal, in
those of others it passes imperceptibly into the figure of
the Deity himself. Is it not possible to find the deeper
reasons for this divergence of opinion respecting the
æsthetic effect and conception of this work of art? As a
model for our investigation we will take a work which has

---

[1] Karl Borinsky, *Das Rätsel Michelangelos*, München, 1908, S. 123.
[2] *Michel-Ange poète*, Paris, 1892, p. 151.

treated the Moses of Michelangelo in a manner similar to psycho-analysis, and which has disclosed new and convincing meaning in the statue. The findings of this work will appear in an altered light from our investigation.

Connoisseurs assure us that the horned head and compressed forehead of the law-giver, as well as his facial expression, contribute essentially to the fact that the impression produced by the masterpiece oscillates between attraction and repulsion. An understanding of this detail will perhaps give an explanation of the 'ambivalent' effect of the Moses.

It is well known that the horns on the head of this statue as well as on many other representations of Moses can be traced back to an incorrect translation of a passage in the Bible. Exodus xxxiv. 29-30 says: 'And it came to pass, when Moses came down from mount Sinai with the two tables of testimony in Moses' hand, when he came down from the mount, that Moses wist not that the skin of his face shone while he talked with him. And when Aaron and all the children of Israel saw Moses, behold, the skin of his face shone; and they were afraid to come nigh him.' The Vulgate and *Aquila* incorrectly, it is said, translate the Hebrew word קרן 'was horned' instead of 'shone', so that according to these texts Moses appears before the Jews with horns. In this way Moses made his entry into plastic art *cornuta facie*; for textual criticism was no business of the Renaissance.

Many factors indicate, however, that the 'misunderstanding' to which Michelangelo, as well as other artists, fell a victim in no way deserves to be put on one side with a casual excuse and allusion to the lack of textual criticism. The Hebrew word has actually both meanings. It means 'to shine' as well as 'to be horned'. It may even be supposed that the meaning to shine is the later and more developed one. Thus the halo round Moses' head was originally a pair of horns which were only later changed into a light. Why then did the leader come down from Sinai with horns on his head?

The text expressly says that the shining of Moses' face was caused by his association with Jahve; it is, therefore, the reflection of the Deity which hovers over the great man's head. The change of sense in the Hebrew word meaning 'to shine', as well as our earlier elucidations, force us to assume that Moses has identified himself with God by assuming the attribute of horns; he has become God. The horns were the sign of the vanquished totem-god.

We see here a part of the old totemistic idea of God surviving unaltered in a higher and more developed stage of Judaism—a part which was then adapted to changed views. The horns and the halo are historically only different attributes of the Deity; the one repressed the other, and in the repressing element we again find the repressed in an altered form. Modern science, which boasts of its impartiality, has unconsciously followed the same path as the peoples who have forced their own ideas of God into the background as inconsistent with their consciousness. All too quickly has science relegated the representation of the hero of the Middle Ages to the lumber room, and, impelled by unconscious tendencies, has replaced the idea of the hero with horns by that of the hero shining with the divine halo.

The Vulgate and Michelangelo are right: Moses is horned; he bears the symbol of the animal-god feared and admired of old in the primitive period, a symbol which only gave way to the more sublime attribute of light in the course of centuries. We are accustomed to represent the Deity in a sublime form, but we must not forget that Jahve, who on Sion proclaimed the Law for all time amidst thunder and earthquake, was not always the majestic Lord of Creation. In recognising that the overwhelming greatness of Jahve is of humble origin, we must take care not to underestimate the significance and powerful impression produced by the superseded animal-deity. A comparison of forgotten and repudiated ancestors, in regard to quality and value, with representatives of a newly created line should not necessarily be to the advantage of the latter. But it is in any case easier to do homage to the new god officially than to eliminate the submerged though continuous influence of the one who is said to have been superseded.

Many points now become clear. The double effect of the great artist's statue of Moses, *i.e.* the alternation of attraction and repulsion, no longer puzzles us. This double effect is produced, on the one hand, by our admiration and reverence for the divine character of the figure, and on the other hand by our unconscious resistance against the traits which tend to remind us, without our knowing it, of an idea of God which we believed we had overcome. The bestial profile of Moses, the contrast between tranquillity and mobility, between the elementary and impulsive savageness and the superhuman self-domination, as well as the strangely disdainful and threatening expression of the eyes, all obtain a new significance. The strong and almost uncanny effect of Moses rests for a great part on the fact that he is really half animal, half god. This fact explains many of the criticisms, that of Coyer, for instance, who sees an image of the Deity in the figure, and also the impression of other connoisseurs who hold directly opposite views. When Scheffler says, 'A human being sits there like an infuriated bison, whose mere glance makes one tremble', he is unconsciously using a quite correct comparison. Moses of the saga has really become a bull because he identifies himself with Jahve. The horns on the head of Michelangelo's marble statue are a remnant of this old, suppressed, but unconquered idea. The animal-like savageness, the suppression of which appears in the figure, constitutes a second indication of the original nature of the hero.

It may be remarked here that the development which has become clear in our interpretation might perhaps have importance for the history of the nimbus, aureole and halo. As is well known, these attributes, like their transformed derivatives, the radiated and the ordinary crown, have been traced back to the lustre of the light deities.[1] Yet, perhaps this association, the justice of which cannot be questioned, is only secondary and was first established when the gods were projected into heaven. The ray of light, like the horn, becomes the symbol of divine power particularly in its sexual form.[2] The sun, which ancient peoples, savages and neurotics have correlated with the father[3] in myths, confers its life-giving force upon its worshippers, like the totem animal, which is also a father-image. We meet here also the replacement of one idea by another, and the transformations and displacements which are determined by the historical development of the people and by the influence of repression. The horns of the totemistic god and the rays of the light god are appropriated by the believers. A Babylonian during the religious service wears two horns like those of the bull-god he worships. In the art of the early Middle Ages God the Father is represented with two rays on his head, like his representatives on earth, the saints, popes and kings. 'Inspiration' through God becomes later the more spiritualised form of identification, in which there is unmistakably a trace of the more original and more material form of identification. The deeply rooted view that with the divine insignia the divine spirit is also conferred, was long to persist in human history. The institution of hereditary imperialism testifies to the existence of this primitive view even at this day, as does also the saying, 'To whom God gives dignity, He also gives understanding'. Everyone knows how rare it is for experience to confirm such a belief, and yet how tenaciously the belief is popularly retained.

Let us now turn back to the Biblical text to which it

---

[1] Cf. Ludolf Stephani, 'Nimbus und Strahlenkranz in der alten Kunst', *Mémoires de l'Académie des Sciences de St-Pétersbourg*, vi. série t. ix., St. Petersburg, 1859, as well as the article 'Heiligenschein' in the *Realenzyclopädie für protestantische Theologie*.

[2] Cf. W. Schwartz, 'Der Sonnenphallos der Urzeit', *Zeitschrift für Ethnologie*, vi. S. 167.

[3] Cf. Freud, *Collected Papers*, 'Psycho-Analytic Notes upon an Auto-Biographical Account of a Case of Paranoia (Dementia Paranoides)', London, 1925, vol. iii. p. 390.

was necessary to refer in our interpretation of the Moses
of Michelangelo. We have learned that Moses went down
from Sinai with a shining countenance after his conversation with Jahve. The subsequent text[1] describes how
the hero, whenever he appeared before Jahve, removed
a veil which he wore over his face, and how, on leaving
the holy place, he again put on the veil. There is a close
connection between this report and the earlier one, although its precise nature is not yet apparent.

Gressmann distinguishes two phases in the whole tradition.[2] The first takes place on Sinai and concerns a
single mythical event; the second relates to an act
which is repeated and which occurs at Jahve's tabernacle. The essential thing in both phases is the priestly
function which Moses fulfils in putting on the veil. The
custom is here the primary thing; the saga is ætiological
and is to explain the origin of the custom. According to
Gressmann the saga answers the question, 'Why did
Moses put a veil over his face when he conversed with
the people as representative of Jahve?'; for it describes
how his skin shone so much by intercourse with God that
the Israelites were afraid to approach him. Gressmann
points out that according to the traditional text, Moses
wore the veil in the interval as a private individual when
he had nothing to do with either Jahve or with the
people as the representative of Jahve, and only removes
it when officiating as priest.

This remarkable account reverses the order of things,
and can only be explained by an intentional alteration of
the text. The original meaning of the passage is that
Moses wears the veil during his priestly functions. Now
it is difficult to explain why exception should be taken
to the traditional custom and an alteration made in it.
Gressmann believes he can find the basis for this subsequent alteration in the fact that the 'veil' is to be interpreted as a mask, and even goes a step further by sug-

[1] Exodus xxxiv. 33.
[2] *Mose und seine Zeit, ein Kommentar zu den Mosesagen,* Göttingen, 1913,
S. 247.

gesting that the mask was really the countenance of the Deity. He refers to the rites of ancient and primitive peoples in which human beings represented gods, took their names and put on the masks or clothing of the deity. The mask made them not only representatives of the god but the deity himself.[1] 'According to present tradition, Moses, through intercourse with God, became His equal in splendour. Originally it would have been said that Moses became a light-radiating deity by means of the mask; and if it is now said that Moses put on the mask in order to diminish the fear of the Israelites at his radiance, an obscuring of the original idea must be supposed to have taken place. It is natural for primitive people, as we can observe in children, to be afraid of a mask even if they know who is concealed by it.'

We can supplement this illuminating explanation by tracing back the old ritual to the totemistic period, where we find a custom in which Moses puts on the mask of an animal, i.e. the skin of the totem, in order to fill the Jews with anxiety; and in which ritual he imitates the voice of the bull or ram in order to terrify them. The radiance of the god has here replaced the cruder religious view. We have recognised the horns on Moses' head as a remnant of the skin of the totem animal which the priests used to put on in order to identify themselves with the deity. The veil which Moses puts on shows quite clearly the origin of the old saga.

We have, therefore, to distinguish three phases in the tradition, which only becomes intelligible through psycho-analytic acquaintance with unconscious processes. In the first phase the young hero, Moses, has taken possession of the skin of the father-god, and has thus become God himself according to the ancient idea. A trace of this phase can be recognised in the representation of the horned Moses. The second phase has replaced the skin of the animal, which is incompatible with the higher concept of God, by radiance; but the light on Moses' face still comes from Jahve. We can see that in this phase

[1] Gressmann, *ibid.* S. 151.

also Moses makes himself almost equal to the Deity by taking over the divine attribute. The Jews were afraid before him as though he were Jahve himself. The third phase portrays the distorted return of the repressed totemistic origin of the divine attribute. The veil recurs now in the form of a mask and serves for a protection against the dangerous radiance of Moses' countenance. The original identity of the radiance and the mask had become unconscious and now it was not known what to do with the tradition of a veil or mask. Secondary elaboration associated the more original form of the godhead with the later form in a manner which was at once tolerable to consciousness and compatible with the demands of causality. The mask is a protection against the sight of the god-like man, and in reality of the Deity himself.

The Biblical report, however, again shows that this phase, which owes its origin to the advance of repression and which arose from the erroneous conception of the function of the veil, could not withstand the return of repressed tendencies. Moses now appears before Jahve without a veil and only wears a mask when he is not officiating as priest. This phase which psychologically demonstrates the victory of the repressed really represents a reconstruction of the original meaning of the tale. This becomes clear if we consider that the whole saga was only associated with the more developed Jewish cult quite late; it was woven into the religious view of that time, though it originally arose in an epoch when Jahve was not yet the law-giving God of Sinai. At this period Moses did not use a mask, or skin of an animal, in intercourse with God; for he tore the skin from the God, and thereby became God himself. Every priest was also God. Moses, who speaks to Jahve in the tabernacle, is a later figure; because Moses himself was Jahve, the presence of Jahve seems to be duplicated. When, however, Moses wears the veil or mask in order to terrify the Jews, he wishes unconsciously to deter them from a repetition of the deed which he had carried out, and which would this time be directed against his own person. Psycho-analytically the situation can be explained as follows. The identification with the father-god, by putting on the skin of the totem, was the result of the son's elementary wish to take the place of the father. The wearing of the paternal skin of the animal is a symptom both of triumph over the father and of the father's triumph—both of the father's defeat and of his victory—since the son who overcame the father is compelled to take over the paternal rôle. The son, who has thus advanced to the state of father, finds himself compelled by his unconscious fear of retaliation to use towards the younger generation the same means of intimidation and paternal authority which he had himself overcome.

A good parallel to this event is furnished by the puberty rites of savages, in which the representatives of the father-generation terrify the youths by disguising themselves as totem animals, and force the youths' obedience by means of this disguise.

It is impossible to understand these sagas of Moses if we do not recognise that acts and customs, originally rejected by religion, became sanctioned when carried out in the name of religion. In other words, forbidden things which religion endeavours to prevent from breaking out return in changed form in the later and higher stages of the evolution of religion. Realisation of the compromising character of religious compulsion, which is so similar to that of neurotic compulsion, supplies the decisive explanation also in this case. Religion demands later the introduction of the forbidden thing in altered form, while it bitterly combats it in undisguised form. Gressmann is wrong in assuming that there is no analogy to the tale of Moses' veil in the history of the Israelitish priesthood. The turban which Aaron wears and which has a plate of pure gold on the front of it with the inscription 'Holiness to the Lord'[1] points to the same divine origin. Here the same process is repeated; an attri-

---

[1] Exodus xxviii. 36-38.

bute, torn from the resisting god, is worn at God's express command, and even becomes a token of protection against Jahve. This priestly token, however, is not essentially different from the amulet which Jahve ordains shall be worn on the forehead, and which, even to-day, survives in the Jewish ritual as *tephillim*. In all these religious totems, from the horns taken from the totem animal to the frontlets of the present Jewish religion, as well as in the love and admiration for the divine father, there persists unconsciously a part of that revolutionary defiance which led to the appropriation of Jahve's attributes, and which testifies to the immortality and indestructibility of unconscious impulses.

If our reconstruction is correct, most important conclusions regarding the hidden meaning of the Sinai pericope must result from it. The course of events at the institution of the Jahvistic religion, as well as the position of the law-giver Moses in religious history, gained a new life. We know already what actually happened on the mountain. Moses became God in that he killed Jahve and appropriated the horns of this originally totemistic god, his power and the sign of his privileged position. Perhaps an old suppressed myth told of a struggle there between the animal-god Jahve and the hero Moses, similar in nature and effect to that between the dragon and Siegfried who possessed himself of the animal's skin, or that between Achelous and Heracles who secured the horn of his adversary. Tradition, contrary to its wish, has preserved the memory of such a murderous struggle when it reports that Moses is horned through conversation with Jahve, *i.e.* has become the successor of the totem-god.

But the period in which this insurrection against the father-god took place cannot be that of totemism; totemism is entirely a father-religion. The son-religions only developed later, long after an anthropomorphic god had been instituted; only traces of the early totemism exist in this period of the development of civilisation. If we wish to understand the history of Sinai we must assume

that a later *coup d'état* by the son is, as it were, projected
into an earlier period and told in totemistic language.
This retrogression to primal ideas and the use of unconscious totemism for a new phenomenon reproduces,
however, involuntarily and unwittingly, a long-forgotten
and real event; the overpowering of the father of the
primitive horde was the prototype of all later revolu-
tions of the sons.

Here also an eternally recurring process emerges from
the deep, where consciousness has kept it imprisoned for
thousands of years: no new god may assume his domination who does not succeed in killing the old one, or at least
in overcoming him inwardly and stepping into his place.
We have arrived at so bold a conclusion that confirmatory tests are no less necessary than desirable. If it is
found to be correct it must lead to a revision of our idea
of the nature and essence of the Jewish religion.

We ought to examine our view from several aspects.
We will, however, postpone this for the present and turn
to the narrative, Exodus xxxii. 1-35, which describes
the return of Moses from Sinai, the moment at which
Michelangelo has represented him. We feel that we ought
to find indications here of what took place on Sinai.
Events of great and persistent emotional significance,
such as we have reconstructed, cannot, in spite of all
efforts of the conscious censorship and of later generations, be suppressed without leaving recognisable traces.
Even wounds healed long ago leave cicatrices behind.

When Moses comes down with the Laws and sees the
golden calf, around which the Jews are dancing, he
dashes the holy tablets to pieces in ungovernable rage
at the foot of the mountain, seizes the calf, burns it in the
fire, crushes it to powder, strews the ashes on the water
and gives it to the children of Israel to drink. The tale
is remarkable for its precision and logical sequence of
events. On closer examination, however, we find the
precision is only apparent and the sequence of events
shows a few treacherous gaps. We will not enter into the
hypotheses of the learned concerning the apportionment

of single verses, later editions and insertions, nor discuss
the distinction of the different sources and redactions,
but we will content ourselves with calling attention to
some of the most striking features of the report. According to the tradition, Moses reduced the calf to powder
after he had burned it; but burnt gold cannot be ground
to powder. Further, it is not quite clear what is meant by
the sentence, 'and gave it to the sons of Israel to drink'.
It is usually considered that the pronoun refers to the
ashes, but this is contradicted by the text since the
article does not agree. It is also peculiar that Deuteronomy ix. 21, where the event is also related, does not
mention such a drink, but speaks of a brook from Sinai
which is not spoken of in Exodus xxxii. Critics of the
Bible have also noted numerous contradictions and
peculiarities in the preceding and following verses. After
Moses (verse 8) has learned from the Lord himself the
fall of the people he behaves (verse 18) as though he
knew nothing about it. Verse 35 speaks of a punishment
of the sins of the people by God, while verses 20-30
mention the punishment carried out by Moses. Other
features demand explanation, the fact, for instance, that
the object of the idolatrous service is expressly denoted
as a calf; this is a deviation from the widely spread cult
of the bull among the Jews and neighbouring peoples.
Gressmann considers it very probable that the image
was a young bull, and that it was called a calf out of
contempt by Hosea.[1] We are also surprised that the high
priest Aaron, who knew better than others the nature of
God, himself prepared the calf, and that Moses did not
reproach him for it. The people demanded of Aaron, 'Up,
make us a god which shall go before us'. The people,
therefore, demand a guiding god, a divine leader for their
future pilgrimage. But, according to verse 4, the people
had said of the image: 'These be thy gods, O Israel,
which brought thee up out of the land of Egypt'; thus
the god takes his significance from his past deeds. And
further, where does the plural in the passage just quoted

[1] *Mose und seine Zeit*, S. 204.

come from? We are only acquainted with the representation of a single calf. Most of the critical Biblical editions substitute the singular, 'This is your god', etc., though, as we think, without sufficient justification for the emendation.

We shall revert to this and a few other details, but for the present keep to the tale as a whole. According to the unanimous pronouncements of Biblical scholars, the cast image represents a god, and the god, moreover, of early Judaism, which must have been similar to that of neighbouring peoples. How strongly the cult of the bull was spread among the Jews and what a lasting effect it exercised is best seen from the fact that images of a bull in Bethel and Dan enjoyed divine honours under Jeroboam I., and that the prophets, especially Hosea, directed their bitterest attacks against the worshippers of the bull.

There is a great gulf between the totem-god, the bull, and Jahve the celestial God who announces his commands amidst thunder and lightning, but it is diminished if we remember that each more advanced stage of religion has striven to deny and degrade the gods of the earlier periods, and to exalt the god worshipped at present.

This process can be compared with a widespread phantasy, namely, the so-called family romance of neurotics.[1] This phantasy, which appears particularly in day-dreams, has for its object the replacement of the dreamer's parents by socially higher ones. The real father is represented by a more noble person of the rank of prince or king, from whom the dreamer derives his descent. The denial of the father, which can regularly be shown to be a constituent of such a phantasy, and which is an expression of the son's unconscious hostility, is, however, not radical and complete. The new father who replaces the ostensibly lower one retains many of his characteristics—a proof of the son's original and re-

---

[1] Otto Rank, *Der Mythus von der Geburt des Helden. Schriften zur angewandten Seelenkunde*, Wien und Leipzig, Heft 5, S. 64.

tained tenderness. The removal of the father thus becomes equivalent to his elevation. The imagined self-elevation which results from the ostensibly higher descent is one of the most essential factors in the family romance.

The process of the replacement of one god by another seems more intelligible now that we understand the genesis and motives of the family romance. The bull around which the Jews dance, and which they worship as a deity, is not only the precursor of Jahve, it is Jahve himself in his old form. The new god so highly exalted is really a variant of the old god now denied and despised, just as the noble father of the family romance is in reality the 'low' father of earlier childhood. *The recognition of the psychological identity of Jahve and the golden image of the bull furnishes the key to an understanding of the whole tale.*

In order to grasp the hidden meaning of the saga we must also remember the close connection which exists between object and image in the ideas of primitive peoples. To ancient and primitive peoples an image is not the representation of an object as we see it, it is the object itself. Primitive people assume an identity where we find only a similarity. What Moses does to the image of the calf he does to the calf itself, *i.e.* to the living animal.

The Exodus story takes on a new significance in the light of this double identity of Jahve and the bull and of the bull and the image. In grinding the golden bull to powder, Moses destroys not an idol but Jahve himself. The conception of the image as an idol, an inferior thing, to be rejected as heathenish, serves the interests of a tendentious distortion. It belongs to a later period which had lost the real meaning of the saga, and which now unconsciously brings the old totem-god into sharp contrast with the more developed idea of a god. In the meantime the old relation of identity of image and original must have been loosened, and a distinction, though not a clearly defined one, must have arisen between them.

x

In this way we arrive at a reconstruction of a primary kernel of the story, in which Moses killed the old and feared bull-god. We find, therefore, in the story handed down to us the product of the retouching and elaboration of innumerable generations. We have found a duplicated form of the deity in the saga and can distinguish in this deity an anthropomorphic god, the one who appeared to Moses in a tempest on Sinai, and the totem-god of a past epoch. The mechanism of division, well known to us from dream life, has thus come into play: a personality appears in several forms often mutually incompatible. Psycho-analytic acquaintance with unconscious processes enables us to assume that ambivalent attitudes of the individual towards the personality concerned correspond with different parts of such a divided whole, so that, for example, hostile impulses towards the father are gratified in a figure which appears contemptible, while feelings of tenderness and piety flow on to a distinct and elevated form of the father. The distribution of affects in the Moses saga now becomes clear. The hero's conscious love and attachment to God is turned upon Jahve, while the unconscious tendencies to rebellion and hatred find their gratification in the destruction of the bull. The intensity of the latter kind of impulses has even led to a great reaction, since in the saga the bull is actually destroyed out of loyalty and love for Jahve. Moses' behaviour may be described as parallel to the two-period acts of neurotics. On Sinai he subjects himself submissively and full of devotion to the Deity whom he destroys in a rage at the foot of the mountain.[1] The ambivalent feelings are thus gratified one after another without meeting strong internal resistance. The duplicated presence of the Deity in this scene on Sinai, just as in the ritual of sacrifice, has an essential meaning, though one which, perhaps, can only

[1] It seems to me probable that the original story did not tell of an image but of the killing of a real bull. The insertion of an image served, perhaps unconsciously, to disguise the real meaning of the saga. Here again is to be observed the totemistic clothing, which ought to warn us that we have to distinguish between reality and phantasy in the tale.

be understood genetically. In the destruction of the golden calf, as in the sacrifice, satisfaction is offered to the father-god in return for the injury perpetrated on him, in an action which really signifies a repetition of the injury. Just as a compulsive act, which unconsciously signifies a mockery of the father, becomes, in virtue of a reaction of increased love, a conscious act to sanctify his memory, so the killing of Jahve in the form of a bull, which is incompatible with the religious ideas of a later period, becomes a deed performed *ad maiorem gloriam dei*. It is worth noting that the act as such was preserved in the late setting, little altered, and that affects of rage and hate equally persist in the tale.

The primary character of the saga, which we have thus reconstructed, is the same as that yielded by our analysis of the shofar ritual and by our interpretation of Michelangelo's representation of Moses. A number of difficult questions find an unexpected solution by means of it. The tale of the destruction of the golden bull is a replica, transferred to the foot of Mount Sinai, of the description of the events on the summit. If we view the tale in this way the passage relating to the drinking of the water containing the gold becomes quite reasonable. We may regard the reduction of the slain animal to powder, and the throwing of this powder into water, as secondary characteristics, and the eating of the calf by the people as primary; for this event cannot be concealed by the apparent precision in the description of Moses' separate acts in his treatment of the calf. The eating of the calf in common is a sacramental meal which carries us back to totemism. Baentsch's explanation will show how far our conception diverges from the common view of commentators.[1] This author assumes that the people received from Moses their own sins to drink, and that the drinking had a bad effect upon them, *i.e.* that many became ill and died. This view is certainly secondary and has nothing to do with the 'original meaning of the tale' as Baentsch imagines.

[1] *Handkommentar*, S. 272.

I would prefer to assume that we are here dealing with a variant of the report of that covenant meal of which, according to Exodus xxiv. 11, Moses and the elders partook on Sinai. The connection is quite clear; for we are told that Moses and the representatives of the people ate and drank before God, while previously the offering of young bulls to Jahve as well as the conclusion of the covenant between God and the people is mentioned. Through devouring the bulls—the totem animals—the Jews had concluded a covenant with the totem-god, in that they incorporated the totem in themselves. The meal of the covenant is a totem meal celebrated by the tribe, and the holy bond between those eating together is renewed. This primal type of the communion, in which the body of the Lord is devoured, thereby establishing the bond between Him and His worshippers, seems to me to recur in the legend in which Moses gives the calf to the children of Israel to eat. Later additions and distortions became necessary because the identity of the totem animal with Jahve was repressed.[1] The sacramental meal of Moses and the elders not only preserves their identification with the Deity, but also repeats the first incorporation, *i.e.* the devouring of the god. It is easy to understand how these events fit into the foundation of the new religion which took place on Sinai. At the emergence of a new belief, the primal crime which really led to the formation of the religion has to be recommitted and the old god must be killed again.

> Victims fall here,
> Neither lamb nor steer,
> But human sacrifice unheard of.

As we have seen, a bull victim actually falls; but certainly it is only a substitute for that first great 'unheard of' human sacrifice, the murder of the primeval representative of God.

---

[1] Also in the report of the covenant meal on Sinai it is not expressly mentioned that bulls formed the object of the meal, but this is clear from the analysis of the sacrificial and covenant ritual, as Robertson Smith and Freud have shown.

Some other contradictions can now be solved quite easily. The judgement which Moses holds over the people is certainly a late variant, because he himself has forsaken God, *i.e.* has brought about God's fall. The punishment meted out to the Jews proceeds originally from the offended Deity and falls very heavily on Moses. Moses' entreaty to Jahve for mercy for the sinning people belongs to a later period; originally, as is clear from another reference, it is the guilty conscience of the hero that speaks. Moses offers himself to the Lord as an object of punishment. The fiction that he was the representative of the people was later worked into this tradition in order to conceal the trace of Moses' deed and to establish a logical relationship between this offer, which was justified by retributive law, and the people's crime—a process which is quite analogous to the secondary elaboration of dream life.

The attitude of the high priest Aaron also becomes intelligible through the psychological analysis; it is he who, according to one version, makes the calf, and later finds only insufficient excuses for doing so. According to other versions the people make the golden animal. In the earlier time, when no exception was taken to the identity of the bull with Jahve, the making of the totem animal belonged to the priestly function of Aaron, and this function was only rejected when the old idea of a god was repressed. The tradition now shows two successive phases on the same temporal plane, and attempts to unify the contradictory views, to motivate Aaron's procedure, and to represent it as logical. One can see in this attempt the strict counterpart to a neurotic symptom-formation which often endeavours against all logic to establish a consistent connection.

We have learned that the science of the Bible finds in the expression 'calf' for the image worshipped by the Jews a contemptuous distortion of the designation 'bull'. This explanation, which can only be true in a limited application to a later period, does not seem to me to be sufficient. We are inclined to take the statement in the Bible quite

seriously and to believe that a calf was indeed worshipped by the Jews at the foot of Sinai. Perhaps the
context may contribute something to the understanding
of this feature. Chap. xxxii. 1 says: 'And when the people
saw that Moses delayed to come down out of the mount,
the people gathered themselves together unto Aaron,
and said unto him, Up, make us gods,[1] which shall go
before us; for as for this Moses, the man that brought us
up out of the land of Egypt, we wot not what is become
of him'. Gressmann rightly finds this wish to be a peculiar
one,[2] 'for in such a situation one would expect that
Israel would above all require a successor for Moses.
The meaning of the words cannot possibly be that the
'God' should be Moses' successor; one would assume that
the question of a successor as a matter of course had
already been decided in favour of Aaron. Gressmann
thinks, therefore, that the people's wish means 'since
Moses our Leader can no longer fulfil the request for a
god who should go before us, we ask you'. This interpretation presupposes that Moses ascended the mountain in
order to fetch someone for the people who should go
before them. When, however, Moses does not return, the
people demand this guiding god of Aaron. This explanation is undoubtedly correct, but it can only refer to a
period in which the attempt was already being made to
change the meaning of the original connection of ideas,
and in which the secondary elaboration is taken to represent the essential and complete state of affairs. The
people's demand for a god is based expressly on the supposed death of Moses. Further, the character of this god
is denoted as that of a conducting and guiding god.
Gressmann himself has to admit that the demand for a
substitute for the leader Moses was more to be expected
than the peculiar wish for a god. He refuses, however, to
assume that God is to be Moses' successor. But supposing no distinction exists between this God and Moses? or

---

[1] [Gods is the translation in the Authorised Version. The German text
quoted a translation in which the singular form, 'a god', is preferred.—TRANS.]
[2] *Mose und seine Zeit*, S. 200.

conversely, if Moses is to be the successor of a god? What prevents us from assuming that the people, in demanding the image of a god to go before them and guide them, are expressing nothing but the wish for Moses, and uttering their longing for the one who has disappeared?

The people base their desire on Moses' absence: the wished-for god was, like him, to be the leader of the people; a substitute for the hero is necessary; according to primitive ideas the representation of a person is identical with that person himself; the admired and beloved man whose absence the Jews endured with difficulty enjoyed an almost divine veneration—all these reasons, when combined with a consideration of the actual wording of the text, indicate that the golden calf was an image of Moses. Curiously enough, the people, in expressing their wish to Aaron, speak of Moses as having led them out of Egypt, and signify at the same time the image as the god who had led them out of Egypt. This detail in their way of expressing themselves points to the original identity of the graven calf and Moses.

It may be objected that the people knew Moses as a human being and would not worship him under the image of a calf. But we may answer this objection by pointing out that in primitive totemism the difference between a human being and an animal is not very pronounced, since anthropomorphic gods were originally worshipped in the form of animals. And further, we have the report in Exodus that Moses descended from Sinai horned, *i.e.* with the qualities of an animal. Finally, welcome support is obtained from our earlier findings. If Jahve was worshipped as a bull, Moses, whose son-like character we have recognised from the latent meaning of the Sinai saga, is quite rightly depicted as a calf. The name Moses, which is derived from the Egyptian *mesu* = child (compare the theophoric names Tuthmosis, Rameses), points to the fact that the liberator of the Jews represents a son-type. Our interpretation is the more probable when we remember that the whole saga has been projected back into the totemistic period.

If the golden animal which the Jews worship is really an image of Moses, as we suppose, its designation as a calf becomes clearer: the 'calf' would be the totemistic name of Jahve's son. The cult of this young animal, which has taken the place of the paternal bull, would correspond somewhat with the 'adoration' of Michelangelo's statue of Moses by the Jews in Rome during the Middle Ages, mentioned by Vasari.

It cannot be denied that the above ideas have increased the difficulties of explanation, and matters appear to have become still more obscure and complicated. We now understand that the image of the golden calf represents the substitute for the leader who was thought to be lost—the belief that individual traits are universally determined has been proved in this instance also—and when we look more closely at the circumstances of Moses' return and of the adoration of the calf, the people's extreme joy seems intelligible, but new contradictions arise. It is also safe to assume that the image of the animal was a representation of Jahve, of the totemistic bull-god. Which is the correct idea?

Perhaps we shall get over this difficulty by referring again to a trifling detail and inquiring after its hidden meaning. We know that Biblical criticism has emended the text in two passages where it is related that the Jews worshipped the golden calf in these words, 'These are your gods, O Israel, which have led you out of Egypt'. Although we have found this emendation to be intelligible, since the plural in the text could not possibly refer to one image, we consider it goes too far to meet the complacent intelligence of Bible readers. Though we may fail to arrive immediately at a clear understanding of small but peculiar points like this, we shall still adhere to the belief that they have a definite meaning. Psycho-analysis, which has given us so strong a belief in the universal validity of mental determinism, has also taught us to curb our impatience and to wait until the understanding of such anomalies reaches us—as it does often from an unexpected quarter.

Commentators have observed that in another passage in the Bible[1] mention is made of the worship of two golden calves. It is related there that King Jeroboam had two golden calves made, and spoke to the people as follows: 'It is too much for you to go up to Jerusalem: behold thy gods, O Israel, which brought thee up out of the land of Egypt'. In this instance we find two calves, their cult, which is charged to the king as a sin, and strangely enough, the same reference as in the Exodus narrative to these having been the gods who led Israel out of Egypt. If we apply this passage to the explanation of the first one, we must assume that in the Sinai account also there were originally two images of animals. Our interpretation suggests what the two images represented: the one Jahve, the bull, and the other Moses, the calf. Certain tendencies must have led to the distortion of this circumstance, and the result was the appearance of only one animal-image, namely, the calf, in the narrative in Exodus, and of two animal-images, *i.e.* again two calves, in the report in Kings. In one of the passages, therefore—apart from the misleading plural in the people's exclamation—one image is eliminated, and in the second, the number is retained but the image of a bull has been changed into that of a calf. In both cases there is an alteration which affects the image of Jahve, originally the totemistic bull, and from this fact, as well as from the result of the correction, we can infer the nature of the tendency which compelled interference with the text. Both narratives reject the cult of the images of animals as heathenish, and as having been borrowed from the inferior neighbouring peoples; looked at in this way the golden calf could give no offence. The image of a bull as representative of Jahve would have shown too clearly that the same totemistic cult had been prominent in the previous religious history of the Jews. The narrative would have been a direct contradiction to the prohibition of images in the Decalogue—and the more so, since there is no question of an image of an idol, but of

[1] I Kings xii. 28.

Jahve himself. The suppression of the image of the bull
in the text is equivalent to an unconscious execution of
this command; it extends the precautions against the
temptation until the bare mention of the sinful and rejected idol is avoided. A deeper psychological insight
into the motives of the elimination of Jahve can only be
obtained after a study of the religious evolution of the
Jews. We can, however, see that not only does the
omission of the bull in the tradition signify a very great
respect, dictated by the awe which extends the prohibition of images to the avoidance of even the thought of the
image of the bull and of Jahve, but that this measure
shows also all the characteristics of a defiant obedience. Like the compromise of a neurotic symptom, it not
only eliminates Jahve's image but Jahve himself from
the cult. This neglect, however, is more than compen-
sated for by promoting him to the position of the world's
law-giver. We must not forget that the elevation of Jahve
to the position of an eternal God, dictated by a relatively increased love, coincided with the annihilation of
the same god, in virtue of an unconscious hate. Similarly, in the family romance of puberty a social promotion
of the father is combined with the imagined destruction
of his own personality.[1]

The assumption of the original presence of two animal-
images in the scene on Sinai, one representing Jahve as
bull and one Moses as calf, suggests a period of Jewish
religious development in which a son-deity was worshipped as well as the father-god. We have reason to
suppose that the details of the text have partly betrayed
this development in the replacement of the plural by the
singular. There must have existed a period in which the
son-god Moses had repressed the father-god Jahve, and

[1] It is not to be denied that similar motives to those we found in the history
of the editing of the story may unconsciously have prevented students of the
Bible from recognising the connection pointed out above, and, for example,
have contributed to the emendation of the text (one calf instead of two). The
fact that commentators have admitted the identity of the primitive cult of
Jahve with the worship of animals does not constitute an objection to this
assertion, since the psychical attitude of the reader in the Exodus scene, in
which the distance between the two cults is made obvious, is a special one.

when his own cult was in the foreground. This process coincides with what we found in the analysis of the horned Moses. A son overpowers the father and now takes his place. We may recall the suggestion that a late insurrection of the son was related in the language of the totemistic past. It is, therefore, no accident that in the saga the Jews actually worship a calf. The young of a bull can only be represented thus. It also becomes clear that it was precisely the son who overthrew the father: *On n'est jamais trahi que par les siens*.

In this stage of development, of which we still find relics, the Jewish religion must have been similar to that of the neighbouring peoples in which young son-deities like Attis, Adonis and Dionysus were worshipped. In the Exodus narrative we find traces of a subsequent period in which father and son deities stood side by side and were equivalent objects of religious worship. When the Jews say, 'These are the gods which have brought you up out of the land of Egypt', they mean Jahve and Moses. Progressive development led to the son-god being assigned a subordinate position while the father-god was elevated to still higher supramundane heights. When Hosea says, 'Jahve has led Israel out of Egypt through a prophet', he has already accomplished this change; he has already reduced Moses unconsciously to the rank of a mediator, and put him back into the place of a servant —even though consciously he wished to distinguish him by this pronouncement. The motive of this development is clear; it was chiefly guilty conscience and the longing for the father that led to this reversion. The replacement of the father-god by the son was a revolution of the most savage and cruel character; his victory signified the overthrow of the hated but also beloved and admired father. This turning-point was suited better than any other to stimulate the tender side of the ambivalence towards the father. We believe we can recognise here, though as it were in a mist, the outlines of a hitherto unknown or not appreciated development of the Jewish religion, which will enable us to understand the simi-

larities and differences between the evolution of the Jews
and their religion, and that of other contemporary or
later peoples. The replacement of the religion of the
father by that of the son, as well as the juxtaposition of
the two types of god, can also be followed in the religious
development of other peoples. The particular feature of
Judaism is that the father finally attains the victory and
undisputedly holds the domination in firm hands. The
revolution of the son has broken down and Jahve is the
only God—there is none other but He. If we compare this
final result with the content of the Christian religion we
see that Christ has taken over the revolutionary inheritance of Moses, and that he has striven with more success
to overthrow the father and put himself in his place.

Special psychical factors within Judaism must have
been at work to produce such a powerful reaction against
the subjugation of the father—a reaction which was
mainly caused by guilty conscience and which resulted
in the absolute monarchy of Jahve. It is clear that the
psychology of religion cannot in future afford to neglect
this point if it is to explain the religion and natural
peculiarities of the Jews, their belief in their being the
chosen people, their thousands of years of suffering.

The significance for the history of religion of our reconstruction of these processes, if it were quite certain,
would not be trivial. Through it the Jews approximate
to their ancient neighbours, in religious nature and development, to a far higher degree than was hitherto
thought: Judaism also had experienced an advance of
the revolutionary son-deity, but the advance miscarried
in consequence of psychological peculiarities which had
developed in the mental life of the race. The son-god
could not maintain himself beside the father, still less
over him. He became, on the contrary, a servant of the
father-deity, a mediator between him and his believers.[1]

The parallel between Moses and Christ, to which we

[1] The similarities to the figure of Christ are just as striking as the differences
between the religious conceptions of the two mediators. The similarity in the
early period preponderated so very much that Islam bracketed Moses and
Christ together.

can only make a passing reference, holds also for that delineation of the prophet which we have derived from the projection of a later development of religion into the totemistic period. In the language of the earlier animal worship, Moses is represented as a calf, and Christ as the divine lamb. In both cases a totemistic father-deity, which is indicated unconsciously and suppressed in editions of the Bible, corresponds to the young animal. The alteration of bull to ram as the totemistic precursor of Jahve may have originated through the condensation of myths of two tribes with a different totem.[1]

It is relatively easy to resolve further doubts of our view of the development of the Exodus saga, so far as they are based on the Biblical text. Most of them can be dispelled by a reference to the way in which the Biblical text originated, *i.e.* through allusion to the resettings and additions, distortions and other secondary processes which were continued through generations, and which were demanded by the constant advance of repression. We therefore need not fear the apparent contradiction that Moses, in destroying the golden calf, annihilated himself. We know that Moses originally destroyed the bull, and that the calf was only later put in its place. In virtue of this transformation the destruction of the bull became a praiseworthy deed in the service of the Deity, instead of a severe crime against Him. The replacement of the bull by the calf points to two feelings which we consider led essentially to the alteration of the text. If in the tradition Moses had really killed a bull, the original connection would have become recognisable much better and more quickly to the Semitic listeners of the early period. The ancient Semites, who

[1] It would suit well with this derivation if it should prove to be correct that the God of Sinai was approximated to Jahve through the teaching of the Kenites, and his supremacy based on the fusion of the tribes of Israel among themselves and with the tribes of Kadesh, as some students assume. (Cf. Rudolf Kittel, *Geschichte des Volkes Israel*, 2. Auflage, Gotha, 1912, S. 552.) Perhaps it was the god of the tribe of Moses who repressed on Sinai the other gods of the tribe. The hypothesis assumed above of a fusion of the tribes in which the totemistic god of the tribe which is politically or culturally superior puts that of the others into the background seems to come nearer to the truth than the idea of an exchange of totem within the people.

stood so much nearer to totemistic ideas than we do, could not have failed to understand from the story that the saga of the destruction of the bull originally described the destruction of a god and, moreover, of Jahve. The substitution, therefore, on the one hand, serves the purpose of making unrecognisable the real meaning of the saga, and, on the other, in the choice of the substituted object satisfies the ever-increasing guilty conscience. When Moses destroys the calf he also kills himself and expiates the guilt which he had incurred through the destruction of the father- and bull-deity, Jahve. Therefore, according to the inexorable law of retaliation, he takes upon himself the punishment of death ordained for the murder of a member of the tribe.

From the points of view both of psychology and of the history of religion, the destruction of the calf corresponds to the sacrificial death of Christ, the *Agnus Dei*. We now also understand why Moses offered himself to Jahve on Sinai as victim for the sins of the people; behind his striking magnanimity we recognise an unconscious guilty conscience which is as fully justified as it is in neurotics. When Moses entreats the Lord to strike him out of the Book of Life if He does not forgive the people, he acts as Christ does when He takes the Cross on Himself for suffering humanity—both are Saviours and sinners conscious of their guilt.[1]

---

[1] Psychological reasons thus justify the ancient assertion of similarities between Moses, Christ and Orpheus. S. Reinach might just as well have chosen Moses as Orpheus for the hero of his *Histoire générale des Religions*. Moses would even have been better. This scholar has, moreover, cleverly brought out the similarity between Moses and Orpheus in the preface to his book, *Orpheus*, Paris, 1909, Deuxième édition, p. 7. 'L'image d'Orphée, charmant les animaux aux sons de sa lyre, est le seul motif mythologique, qui paraisse plusieurs fois, dans les peintures des catacombes chrétiennes. Les Pères de l'Église se sont persuadés qu'Orphée avait été l'élève de Moïse; ils ont vu en lui une "figure", ou plutôt une "préfiguration" de Jésus, parce que lui aussi, venu pour enseigner les hommes, avait été à la fois leur bienfaiteur et leur victime.' He expressly adds: 'La critique moderne cherche l'explication de ces ressemblances ailleurs que dans l'hypotèse aventureuse d'une intimité entre Moïse et Orphée. Elle reconnaît d'ailleurs, que l'Orphisme n'a pas seulement des traits communs avec le judaïsme et le christianisme, mais avec d'autres religions plus lointaines, comme le buddhisme, et même avec les croyances tout à fait primitives de sauvages actuels.' He is quite right in tracing these common qualities to factors which exist in all religions, 'puisés au tréfonds de la nature humaine et nourris de ses plus chères illusions' (p. viii).

The act of destroying the calf is a condensation, since the image of the animal signifies both Jahve and Moses. This condensation, as in dreams, is made possible by a special strength of the identification. The making use of the totemistic representation of the son's revolution in the myth corresponds to the utilisation of early infantile 'prehistoric' ideas in later dreams which elaborate actual conflicts. In destroying the image, which was originally Jahve, Moses destroys himself; the retaliation appears particularly clearly in this one act which unites the crime and its expiation. At the same time, however, both the opposite strong feelings break through in the compromise action; hate and rage against Jahve in his destruction, love and devotion in the self-destruction expiating this deed.

The double personality of Moses as man and prophet and as calf does not weaken our hypothesis. We find here again one of those duplications which we have already discovered—the human figure is the later one, the animal form the earlier.

The ambivalence also comes out clearly in the splitting of the personality, and it is significant that Moses' destruction of his own animal-image represents a reaction to his crime which is actually repeated simultaneously in this act. In order to understand the saga one has to conceive the human figure of Moses, who appears as a loyal servant of his master Jahve, as a figure inserted into the original content at a later period, which is to some degree comparable to the god in the sacrificial ritual who himself commands the sacrifice, i.e. the killing and devouring of his own ego.

This conception also enables us to justify from a new point of view our explanation of the covenant meal which Moses gives the Jews. With the replacement of the father-religion by the son-religion the old totem meal is renewed as a sign of the community of the covenant. The father has yielded to the son here as elsewhere: the tribe no longer eats the body and blood of the father, with which the tribe sanctifies and identifies itself, but of the son.[1] The identity of the eating of the calf by the people, as described in Exodus, and the Christian communion in which the believers eat the body of the Saviour, is quite clear.

It would be desirable, at this point, to compare the saga of Moses destroyed as a calf with the myth of the totemistic son-deities of antiquity who are overtaken by a similar fate, namely, Dionysus-Zagreus, Orpheus and Attis, and to bring Mithras, who kills the bull alone, into line with Moses and thus to deepen our knowledge. We will, however, merely record our opinion that the nature of Moses' tragic guilt, through which he dies before reaching the Holy Land,[2] and which is so insufficiently explained elsewhere in the Old Testament, is now clear. Originally it was another, a higher Person, who destroyed the golden calf (i.e. Moses), and Moses only stepped into his place when this circumstance became lost to consciousness. The representation of the tradition, like that of dreams, renders possible the condensation into one act of two opposed acts. Only by a repeated reversal of the situation, as in dream interpretation, can a complete understanding be obtained. In the tradition of the deed we distinguish, firstly, an original phase in which Moses killed the bull (Jahve); secondly, a phase in which Jahve killed the calf (Moses) as a punishment for his crime; and only the third and last gives the form that has been handed down and made possible through an identification of the two figures in which Moses kills the golden calf. This complicated series of transformations of the original saga reveals the activity of almost all the mechanisms of dream work, especially condensation, displacement and reversal of the situation. We can further observe to what an extent secondary elaboration has concealed from commentators and everyone else the real meaning of the saga.

We may also observe the similarity of the mental

---

[1] Freud, *Totem und Tabu*, p. 142.

[2] In this trait of Moses becomes recognisable the sexual element in the revolution, since the stepping into the Holy Land represents a symbol of the consummated incest.

forces and mechanisms in the development of the Exodus
tale to those in the saga of Jubal. In both cases we recognise a composite figure in the figure of the animal
(ram, calf) in which we see united a totemistic father-
god and his revolutionary son. But the similarity between the two legends goes far beyond the dynamics
of the psychical processes, and extends to the primal
material of the sagas. Jubal, like Moses, has killed the
totemistic father-god and taken possession of his power.
Jubal identifies himself with the slain animal by imitating
its voice; Moses, by wearing the horned mask.[1]

The interpretation of a single dream element often
unexpectedly illuminates other parts of the dream; and
the discovery of a connection between such elements,
which is latent and far removed from the manifest and
apparently rational association, regularly discloses their
over-determination. Similarly, the new light we have obtained from our analysis of the Sinai legend falls also on
other parts of Moses' history in which no one thought
there were any puzzles, and illumines even certain more
obscure problems of the science of religion which suddenly seem to demand another formulation. From the
complex of new questions which here assail us, we will
only select those which most noticeably require an
altered consideration. The remainder must stand over
until they can take their place in another context.

The sin which the people commit in worshipping the
golden calf is really twofold; it breaks two commandments of the Decalogue simultaneously, namely, the
command, 'Thou shalt have no other gods before me',
and that which forbids the making an image of things,
either in heaven, on earth, or in the water under the
earth. Ought there not to be an inner connection between the two commands? Commentators have pointed
out that the passage which follows the prohibition
against making images includes at the same time the
preceding prohibition from worshipping them. This pass-

---

[1] It must here be added that in the Jubal myth also the totemistic clothing
signified a projection to far earlier stages of development.

age is, 'Thou shalt not bow down thyself to them, nor
serve them: for I the Lord thy God am a jealous God',
etc. Frazer is quite right in supposing that the Biblical
prohibition of images did not originate in any aversion
from art on principle, but that it had the object of withdrawing a tool from the magic condemned by religion.[1]

Now it seems to me possible that one of the most
essential motives of the prohibition was the fear lest individuals should make images of the god in order to sup-
plant him by magic. The fact that ancient kings demanded that their images should be objects of divine
worship seems to indicate that such cases really occurred.
The instance, however, which we have found in the
analysis of the legend of the golden calf is even more
significant. By means of the image which represents
Moses, Jahve is deposed and another god, Moses, set up
in his place. The prohibition has, therefore, the purpose
of protecting the Deity against the unconscious ambi-
tions and hostile wishes of His worshippers to remove
Him from His proper position. The primary attitude to
the worship of idols is thus revealed. Perhaps it was precisely the son-deity against whose rivalry Jahve wished
to secure himself. The consequence of the prohibition in
the Jewish religion seems at least to indicate this, as does
also the fact that with the victory of Christianity the
prohibition is removed and the Son of God appears in
plastic representations.

On the other hand, there must of course have been
other motives for the prohibition, one of which appears
in the episode of the golden calf. We have recognised
that Moses actually annihilates Jahve in destroying the
bull image. The tale is incomprehensible so long as the
very strong belief of the ancients in the power of magical procedures is not taken into account. If one makes
an image of a person and carries out a hostile act against
it, the same thing will happen to the person himself; this
is a positive belief among ancient human beings and
among the savages of to-day. 'Every night when the

---

[1] Frazer, *The Golden Bough: The Magic Art*, vol. i. p. 87.

sun-god Ra sank down to his home in the glowing west he was assailed by hosts of demons under the leadership of the arch-fiend Apepi. All night long he fought them, and sometimes by day the powers of darkness sent up clouds even into the blue Egyptian sky to obscure his light and weaken his power. To aid the sun-god in this daily struggle a ceremony was daily performed in his temple at Thebes. A figure of his foe Apepi, represented as a crocodile with a hideous face or a serpent with many coils, was made of wax, and on it the demon's name was written in green ink. Wrapt in a papyrus case, on which another likeness of Apepi had been drawn in green ink, the figure was then tied up with black hair, spat upon, hacked with a stone knife, and cast on the ground. There the priest trod on it with his left foot again and again, and then burned it in a fire made of a certain plant or grass.'[1] We have here a magical rite in the service of piety, just as in the legend of the golden calf. Apepi, like the bull, is a god who has to cede his domination to a higher one and now is reduced to a demon. The service which the Egyptian priests offer to their god, Ra, by the process of destruction was not always genuine, and in this it is similar to Moses' zeal in the destruction of the worship of the bull; the affect was once directed against that god who is now to be protected. The unconscious hostility was only later transferred to the god who is now reduced to an idol. It thus becomes clear that the prohibition of images, which is so closely connected with the old belief that the image was identical with the original, served at first to combat hostile magic at a time when God had not yet retired to heaven, and when those who were unfavourable to Him might injure Him by magical rites directed against His image. The crude and simple god of primeval mankind had to protect himself from the consequences of the hostile acts like the savages of our time, who have a superstitious fear of being painted or sketched because thereby they hand over a part of their ego to strangers.

[1] Frazer, *ibid.* p. 67.

We see that the motive of protecting the Deity appears in both reasons for the prohibition, and that the unconscious hostility of Jahve's first worshippers against their God could not have been trifling since such severe prohibitions were required to restrain it.

It is scarcely permissible to conclude from the absence of the images of God that a specially high stage of religious development has been reached. But it may be affirmed that such a feature is only to be met with in religions which can boast a fairly long history. The result of the psycho-analytic review of the prohibition of images suggests that it was mainly instituted to protect the Deity from the magic of His worshippers. According to Freud, the principle of magic is based on the belief in the 'omnipotence of thought', and especially in that of wishes that are condemned as wicked. The prohibition of images suggests the repression of these rejected impulses and the victory of tender and reverential ones. Psycho-analysis agrees with the findings of exegesis and textual criticisms which show that the prohibition of images was only introduced into the Decalogue at a very late period.[1]

Perhaps we may assume that the feast celebrated by the Jews, in which the golden image of the bull was worshipped, was similar in character to the mysteries of the south-east Australians, *i.e.* it was an initiation of men, or totem feast. The worship and later destruction of the image by a priest or man of God would be quite comparable to the Australian cult. The high priest's willing-

---

[1] It is surprising to find that the idea of the formlessness of God is not quite unknown even among primitive peoples. Andrew Lang calls attention to the fact that even among peoples who have idols the cult of the Highest Being is without image, and refers to the Ahane of the Virginians, the chief god of the Bantu, and of the Sudan blacks, etc. Lang even makes use of this fact for his hypothesis of an original monotheism. The formlessness is specially striking in the religion of the tribes of south-east Australia who are at a very low level, and neither carry on agriculture or cattle-breeding, nor use metals or pottery. In almost all South Australian peoples there is no image of their Highest Being; only among a few one is manufactured for the mysteries, but must be immediately destroyed afterwards under penalty of death. Hartland's objection to Lang's argument ('The High Gods of Australia', *Folk-lore*, 1898, ix. p. 314), that the fact that the aborigines have no 'idols' is not a question of religion, but of the development of art, in no way goes to the root of the matter, as W. Schmidt has correctly shown (*Ursprung der Gottesidee*, S. 239).

ness to set up an image of the bull, and other traits, suggest that in the original saga the festival was counted among those sanctified and demanded by the Deity, and that it was only regarded as idolatrous as the result of repression.

The magical procedure of the priests of Ra in Egypt, who cause the image of Apepi to die so many deaths, is reminiscent of the Bible text which reports a destruction of the image of an animal in several ways (grinding to dust, making into powder, casting into water). The really immortal father must be killed again and again; the hostile and aggressive impulses directed against him revive ever anew, and their opposites must as constantly be mobilised to overpower them. The father cannot be murdered; he has a thousand heads like the Hydra, which is, perhaps, itself a mythical representation of the father.

The destruction of the holy tablets by Moses seems to corroborate our view of the original meaning of the Horeb tradition from another standpoint. We cannot here attempt to solve the almost inextricable skein of the text; but our attention is attracted to a detail which has hitherto not been considered worthy of Biblical research. Exodus xxxii. 19 describes the descent of Moses and those accompanying him from the holy mountain in the following words: 'And it came to pass, as soon as he came nigh unto the camp, that he saw the calf, and the dancing: and Moses' anger waxed hot, and he cast the tables out of his hands, and brake them beneath the mount'. The next verse describes the destruction of the golden calf carried out in the most violent rage.

What is Moses' reason for thus treating undoubtedly holy objects like the tablets? It seems peculiar that this remarkable feature has been so little considered in the abundant literature of the events on Sinai; and yet it stands in marked contrast to everything we know concerning the careful and reverential treatment of holy objects. These objects are regarded with great awe; they must not be touched if one does not wish to perish. It is as though these objects were charged with an unknown power, which is dangerous to anyone approaching them.[1] The objects of the cult of Jahve are taboo: Uzzah is suddenly killed by Jahve because, with the best intention, he stretched out his hand towards the ark which was about to fall.[2] Moses was allowed to carry the tablets without being killed by Jahve because God had chosen him as mediator. But was he allowed to destroy that which bore God's writing? Did he not thereby make himself guilty of a terrible crime against the Deity? Any thought about this feature must lead to a mistrust of the usual explanation of the episode.

This feeling is further increased when we note the striking parallel between the destruction of the tablets and that of the golden calf. Both acts are carried out in the most extreme anger; the object in the one case is an object of the cult of the Jahvistic religion, in the other a heathenish idol. The difference, however, is, in virtue of our earlier findings, not nearly so profound as it might seem at first sight.

We are also struck by the fact that the number two again emerges, and this time in relation with the tablets; we have already found it in the original version of the legend of the golden calf.

But the impression we obtain from the tablet episode is different. On reading it again now it seems as though the holy tablets and their destruction receive a new meaning, or, on the other hand, as though their original meaning becomes clear. Up to now we have had the idea that Moses destroyed the tablets in an outburst of violent rage, because he no longer thought the faithless Jews worthy of their possession.

If we again employ the old analogy of saga and dream, we have to bear in mind that the affect of the act is the thing that really matters ; hate or rage must really have been the strongest motive which impelled the divine

---

[1] Concerning taboo and its psychic motivation, see Freud, *Totem und Tabu*, S. 17.
[2] 2 Samuel vi. 6-9.

man to do this act. But the traditional association is peculiar and stimulates our interest. A high priest who destroys a holy relic in anger over the unbelief of a community is certainly not a usual figure. We were surprised that the objects which experienced the effect of Moses' anger were the holy tablets, the treasure of the Jewish religion which he had received from God's hands. We can quite understand that his zeal towards God might make him destroy the idol of the golden calf, but why he should commit sacrilege against the holy tablets needs explanation. It is not easy to understand how Moses could so far forget himself and his priestly office as to commit the offence against the sacrosanct gifts of Jahve. The destruction of the tablets, according to the ancient view, is a *crimen laesae maiestatis*, against which rage at the sin of the people is at most an extenuating circumstance.

Psycho-analytic experience teaches us daily of what little importance conscious and logical reasoning is compared with the impelling and unconscious motives of human mental life. Conscious reasoning readily takes the place of these other motives when they wish to retain their incognito, just like the willing servant of a strict master. But closer observation dispels the apparent logic even in our Biblical narrative. The conscious motive of the breaking of the tablets soon appears as a cover for the secret tendencies we believe we see. We must admit only the fact (Moses destroys the holy tablets) and the affects (anger and rage) as established; the causal relation between these affects and the sin of the Jews will prove to have been a subsequent construction.

We have already alluded to the peculiar repetition which is contained in the Horeb tradition. Moses, coming down from Sinai, destroys the tablets and the golden calf in a terrible rage—both are objects of religious worship. We are almost tempted to conclude from the identity of acts and affects that the two objects must have been originally identical, or at least related images of God. If we neglect the traditional and artificial connection, and remember that the essential motive of an act may be reconstructed *a posteriori* from its effect, we might infer that Moses destroys the holy tablets because he is over-come by rage against them. But is not this absurd? Had the divine leader, who bore Jahve's eternal laws engraved on stone to deliver to his people, originally the intention of breaking up the tablets? And what would be the mean-ing of such excessive anger against inanimate objects? If the tablets were the image of a heathen god, like the golden calf, one could understand this anger. They are, however, no image, but the material upon which God's finger wrote His laws; and they originate not from El or Baal, or a pre-Mosaic god of another Semitic tribe, but from Jahve Himself, the God of Israel. There remain, however, Moses' peculiar treatment of the tablets and the striking similarity between their destruction and that of the golden calf; and these, as well as other factors of which we shall speak directly, compel us to believe, in spite of all difficulties, that the scene has a meaning which has been hitherto unrecognised, and that it must have some connection with that other episode of the golden calf.

We mentioned earlier that we are convinced of the superior force of unconscious impulses and unimpressed by the apparent logical precision of the narrative. But is the logic of the Horeb tradition in general and of the legend of the tablets really so unimpeachable? Modern Biblical exegesis has established here such numerous errors and contradictions and so many mutually incom-patible reports that even the most fervent believer in the Bible can scarcely accept the text unless he is prepared to make great intellectual sacrifices.

We will only mention a few of these features. The tale in Exodus states that the tablets bore the law by which Israel undertook to enter into a bond with Jahve, *i.e.* they were stone archives of a kind familiar to excavators. Who wrote the tablets? According to Exodus xxxiv. 27, Moses wrote them, and according to Deuteronomy iv. 13

and ix. 10, God Himself wrote them. Their contents are just as uncertain as the writer of the tablets. The Elohist version states that the Decalogue was on the tablets, while the Jahvist assumes that they contained the law of the covenant,[1] which was quite different. But here we meet new difficulties arising from the distribution of the commandments on the two stones. Augustinus, Calvin and a great number of Jewish and Catholic theologians have occupied themselves with the question as to which or how many commandments might have appeared on the one or other tablet.[2] In what writing were the tablets executed? One may ask whether Egyptian hieroglyphics or a specific Semitic writing (otherwise old Canaanitish) was used in Israel at the time of Moses. Underlying this question, however, there is the far more important one, namely, whether written characters were known at all at the time of the foundation of the Jahvistic religion.[3]

There are other serious difficulties which concern the text. Exodus xxiv. 12 says, 'And the Lord said unto Moses, Come up to me into the mount and be there: and I will give thee tables of stone, and a law, and commandments which I have written; that thou mayest teach them'. According to the present text it looks as though Moses was to receive stone tablets on which the law was written. But the link suggested by the copula (') between the words tablet and *Torah* does not agree with this; at most the translation should run, 'the stone tablets, that is to say, a law and commandments'. If the Decalogue was on the tablets as appears from Deuteronomy v. 22, the designation 'law and commandment' is

[1] Exodus xxxiv. 14-26.
[2] It is usually assumed that on one of the tablets there were the commandments of *pietas*, and on the other of *probitas*.
[3] The above doubts as to the character of the writing on the stone tablets have often been discussed. A short time ago Berger, *Mélanges*, Hartwig Derenbourg, 1909, 15 ff. ('*Comment était écrit le Décalogue?*'), affirmed that the 'writing of God' (Exodus xxxii. 16), according to analogy with the Phœnician כלב אלם which signified a consecrated dog, is the holy script of the Egyptian hieroglyphics. The circumstance also that the Petrie expedition (*Researches in Sinai*, fig. 139) found on the Sinai peninsula inscriptions in a Semitic writing not yet deciphered, and belonging to the eighteenth dynasty, cannot remove the above doubts, since we have no facts by which to date the life of a historical (?) figure like that of Moses.

inaccurate, since it seems to indicate something more ample. Moreover, these things are communicated to Moses so that he may lead and guide the people in accordance with them. Here a contradiction arises from the fact that private indoctrination of that kind, by which, as Wellhausen[1] says, the divine law is to be imparted to Moses 'as a sort of spiritual potency', does not agree with the public character of the law tablets. Further, we do not understand why Moses is to remain on the mountain for forty days and nights if he has only to fetch the divine tablets which were already prepared. In view of these contradictions, Gressmann considers that neither the Jahvist nor the Elohist versions knew anything of the law tablets in their oldest form, but only of the personal instruction of Moses by Jahve.[2] The introduction of the law tablets can only be understood by assuming a projection of later institutions into a previous period of lower culture. Presumably it was the custom in later periods to write laws on stone tablets, as shown by the examples of the Hammurabi law, of the Solonic pyramids of the law in the Stoa Basileios at Athens, and of the Punic sacrificial tariff of Marseilles.

If, however, the saga originally contained nothing about the law tablets—and in the text there is only the transference of a later institution into an epoch devoid of writing, as one supposes—wherein existed the necessity of introducing such tablets at all? The assumption of the anachronistic use of stones throws no further light on the numerous contradictions and variations of the text of which we have quoted a part. If we accept Gressmann's view we can only admit it as one of the factors which determined the present form of the text. The particular holiness of the tablets, their destruction and the remaking of new stones, clearly point to the fact that the narrative still conceals a latent content besides its manifest one, and that the stones are not out of their proper place.

---

[1] Wellhausen, *Komposition des Hexateuchs*, 2. Auflage, S. 90.
[2] Gressmann, *ibid.* S. 186.

In our search for this unrecognised meaning of the tablet story we again meet a few puzzling features. The old saga suggests no reason why the tablets were deposited in the Holy Ark; only later narrators state they were deposited there.[1] Gressmann sagaciously draws attention to the fact that this feature is absurd if the tablets bore the laws. Laws exist for publication; and for this reason they were later engraved on stone tablets and exhibited in holy places. The Elohist version even asserts[2] that both sides of the stone, the back and the front, were written upon, so that one can only imagine the stone as standing by itself. The information as to the storing of the stones, therefore, disagrees strongly with the purpose of the tablets if they have the law engraved upon them. Suppose, however, the tablets were not originally stone archives, but had another function? The tradition which brings them into connection with the Ark may be a justifiable one. But if the stones were not law tablets, what were they?

We shall, perhaps, get more insight into their nature if we make use of our earlier discussions. We know that according to the original text Moses descended Sinai in order to bring the Jews a God who should lead them, but later editing replaced this real and portable God by the teaching of Jahve, *i.e.* the law. Gressmann is quite right when he says that those who contrast the bull, as a false symbol of God, with the Ark as the correct one, must suppose that Moses descends from the mountain either with the Ark or with the god of the Ark, which is the same thing.[3] The law tablets do not fit into this scheme. Gressmann regards them as foreign bodies here : 'For Moses has ascended the mountain in order to procure a God to guide Israel, and it does not appear why he returns with the law tablets which would be giving stones for bread'.

We think that Gressmann has allowed himself to depart all too easily from the correct path. Moses was to

[1] Gressmann, *ibid.* S. 189. [2] Exodus xxxii. 15.
[3] Gressmann, *ibid.* S. 211.

bring down from Sinai a guiding god, and in reality he brings down a stone, but *the stone was originally the god*. The mechanism of condensation comes into action here, in that the primitive stone-god and a sacred object of the later, more advanced period, the law tablets, are simultaneously represented in one thing.

Our interpretation, therefore, suggests that in an earlier version Moses had actually brought down God, *i.e.* a stone-god, from Sinai; the holy stone was the portable god who was to accompany the Jews on their journey. Therefore, in contrast to Gressmann and most of the other commentators, we consider that the introduction of the tablets into the text represents the remodelling of an already existing tradition which was to serve the interests of certain definite tendencies. We believe we can reconstruct the nature and effect of these tendencies. In a period long before the writing of any history the stone became a god, just as the animal and, later, the tree. We believe that the tradition which we have found in the Sinai saga must be regarded as a dim memory of that period. This saga later conflicted with the more developed concept of God and succumbed to the repression of many generations. In the strife between the creator of the world, *i.e.* Jahve in his superhuman form, and the cruder picture of the deity as stone, the more primitive idea, which was incompatible with the higher cultural views of the period, was considered disturbing in an ever-increasing degree. There is nothing to prevent us from assuming that both ideas of God existed for a long period beside each other in the saga, just as the *Massēba* was retained quite late beside the altar as a requisite for the cult. But the more the people realised that the stone-god represented a painful memory of a period which conflicted severely with the high culture and the purified religion of their own time, the more the stone, in its original significance, had to give way. A complete elimination of this feature was impossible because of the all too virile and conservative tradition; perhaps the particular holiness of the stone was still too near the people's consciousness to permit a usurpation of the report. This holiness had been preserved in the version that has come down to us; for although the stone is no longer God Himself, it is the special work of His hands. This process of reinterpretation as a result of unconscious tendencies is a phenomenon of folk-psychology which has an individual parallel in the screen-memories against the early impressions of childhood. In both cases clear memories of apparently trifling facts conceal those of experiences which, although more important and of greater effect upon life, seek to avoid consciousness in a later period.

The memory of the holiness of the stones, when the stone cult began to be lost to consciousness, suggested the possibility of a new and valid connection. The tale could be assimilated to the new forms of religious and moral life by making the stones into law tablets which Moses bore from Sinai, and which were already known at that time and whose divine origin was believed in. The holy nature of the stones was preserved in this compromise, but their primary identification with God was at the same time so completely obliterated that it could not be recognised. The crude stone which in far-off primeval times had been worshipped as God was transferred in ennobled form into a later and higher period of culture. Modern tendencies that seek to replace the personal God of the positive religions by a special Moral Principle, better suited to our more sceptical time, furnish, I believe, a rough analogy to what may have occurred in that earlier age in the minds of the elaborators.

This remodelling process is comparable to the secondary work of consciousness in dream formation. By operating for centuries upon tradition it has changed the form of a part of the mental life of the people until that which had become consciously unintelligible and unconsciously painful, but which had survived as a foreign element in the more advanced epoch, has become a rational and unobjectionable part of the saga. The same process shows also the psychical conflict in the minds of the people. Incapable of denying the past, but not prepared to recognise it since it had become incompatible with the character of the time, the Judaism of this transitional period arrived at a compromise; single symptoms reflect clearly enough the ambivalent attitude to the past. Feelings of loyalty and contempt, of love and hostility towards the fathers, are thus comprised in one expression.

The analogy of this change of meaning with the alteration of the bull saga of Sinai is instructive. While the bull, the totem of the oldest time, appears in the later tradition of the golden calf as an abhorrent idol, the younger god, the stone, is so changed that he can assume his place and his divine derivation in the saga. This unequal treatment of obliterated representations of God is not unimportant for their future history. The image of the bull as god must have been more remote from the Jews at the time of Moses than the cult of the stone, the survival of which is proved by numerous testimonies. In the analysis of the legend of the golden calf we have emphasised that a projection of actual occurrences into an ancient circle of totemistic ideas is to be observed; here we meet rather the fusion of old and outworn views with more recent concepts.

We were struck with the fact that Moses first of all broke up the stone tablets and then pulverised the golden calf. We have affirmed that this parallelism is quite sensible; we have further assumed that the affect of anger which the saga records reflects the real feeling of the hero, and that a secondary relationship was created in the association of the affect with the sin of the people. We now recognise that this supposition, which is based on experience from the analytical psychology of dreams and neuroses, really meets the actual conditions. When Moses breaks up the holy tablets he actually destroys God, the primeval stone-god, just as he destroys God when he pulverises the animal totem, *i.e.* the golden calf. The saga of the breaking up of the tablets represents a duplicate of the other saga—a duplicate in which, in spite of the most intensive remodelling and frequent rearrangement of the material, Moses' destruction of such a holy object is more clearly recognisable as a religious crime.

In spite of all disguises, this sacrilegious motive occurs three times in the one Sinai episode—in the horns of Moses, in the breaking up of the tablets, and in the destruction of the calf—and thus shows how difficult the psychical overpowering of the occurrence must have been to the Jews. The elementary power of the rage and hate which breaks through in the deed, and the reaction of love which attributes it to zeal for the Deity, betrays how mighty was that mental struggle of the people which preceded and followed this deed.

In the Biblical account Moses' rage was directed to the people rather than to the image. And we must now ask whether the selection of the people as the object of this displacement had not its particular reasons. Psychoanalysis teaches us that such displacements have their full mental justification in spite of their secondary nature. We have to recognise that the chief purpose of the legend of Moses' anger at the people's infidelity to God was to conceal the fact that his own deed was a crime against this God. The object was to make the leader appear the most pious and zealous defender of Jahve by means of the misleading report of a deed which, in its original character, would naturally have been followed by his condemnation. We entertain no doubt of the filial love of Hamlet who wishes ferociously to revenge the murder of his father, and yet we know that in his unconscious phantasies he himself had been his father's murderer. But, beyond the religious and deeply moral purpose of the association of Moses' deed with the infidelity of the people, we must recognise a further and more active motive. Moses is only a representative of the Jewish people; in him they recognised themselves with all their virtues and weaknesses. It is, therefore, reasonable that the people should be prepared to take over the guilt of the leader, since they have actually co-operated in the crime; they have burdened themselves with guilt through unconscious impulses of hostility and rebellion against God. If we recall the latent meaning of the first Greek drama and that of the Sinai myth we find that besides definite differences they have much in common. In both cases a hero, or God, burdens himself with heavy guilt; but whereas the Greek Chorus appears only in the rôle of the spectator bewailing the suffering hero, the Jewish people take his tragic guilt upon themselves so that he may be freed from it. The guilt, however, is the same—a monstrous offence against the Deity. If the development of the Greek drama had lasted longer, it would perhaps have resembled the Jewish tradition, in which the return of a repressed situation is secured by the guilty conscience of the people. Perhaps, however, constitutional and historically determined peculiarities account for the difference between the mental attitude of the two peoples toward their mythical heroes. When we pass from the study of the psychic mechanisms which elaborated the saga to that of the impulse-components expressed in it, we must not overlook another factor which greatly facilitated the association of Moses' deed with the people, namely, the masochism which is concealed in the assumption of the guilt. This important factor in the psychology of the Jewish people, whose misunderstanding has led to far-reaching error, early began its activity and has persisted into present times. Perhaps none of the modern civilised people have so great a sense of guilt as the Jews, who in the course of thousands of years have sought and attained again and again the gratification of masochistic and self-punitive tendencies. An element of archaic mental life, which in other peoples has long since given place to a more stable mental condition, has persisted in Judaism and contributed essentially to its isolation.

The reversal in the Biblical setting[1] of the original

---

[1] The mechanism appearing here corresponds to the reversal of situation in the dream. The circumstance elucidated above gains its deeper meaning from the fact that Moses, as the representative of the revolutionary people, has repressed Jahve and put himself in his place. Thus he becomes the symbol of

state of things cannot deceive us. The offence of the Jews against God does not lie in the worship of the bull, but in the destruction of the image which is Jahve himself, in the revolution against the totem animal. The unconscious feeling of guilt sought, and eventually found, a cause in the worship of idols; but even in the secondary rationalisation there lies some truth, since the cult of the bull appeared later as an infidelity to Jahve equivalent to an insurrection against God.

Finally, we have also to admit the justification of the subsequent association of Moses' affect of rage with the sins of the people. We have learned that Moses has stepped into Jahve's place; he has the horns of the bull totem which made the Jews afraid before him as they were before God; he becomes the mediator. On account of this, Jahve's destruction is at the same time his own destruction. The people who revolt against Jahve will likewise be disloyal to his human successor and representative. The account in Exodus of the people's grumbling and the numerous insurrections against Moses confirm this interpretation. The leader revenges the murder of his beloved and hated prototype, because he feared to experience from the mob the same fate as his prototype. A Brutus who succeeds to power well knows that anyone who trusts to the love and loyalty of the masses builds upon sand. This part of our interpretation approaches the conception of the commentators who argue that the destruction of the golden calf and the tablets was a warning and an example.[1]

---

impulses which live in the people and which had for their content the rebellion against the domination of the father-god. The tale of the building of the Tower of Babel shows the existence of these tendencies in primitive Judaism more clearly.

[1] Here again, of course, reservations demanded by the formal differences between the original tale and its later modifications have to be made. For, if our interpretation is justified, Moses, according to the traditional version, has sufficient reason to hate the people. The people worship him since the calf is an image of Moses. And his attitude towards this worship of himself can consciously only be one of refusal and rejection, since it represents the aim of those unconscious wishes which he had repressed as malicious. We already understand the attitude of the prophet as an example of the mechanism of the reversal of affect, and it is now further explained by the above-mentioned unconscious identification with Jahve. The believers repeat in the cult of the

We may now briefly refer to the fact that the number (two) of the tablets is identical with that of the animals worshipped by the Jews. Moses, who has identified himself with the animal-god, is worshipped as a calf, the young of the bull, and has perhaps become in the form of a stone also the image of the original god. The breaking of the stones, like the destruction of the calf, would signify self-destruction in the service of unconscious self-punitive tendencies.

Our investigation has shown us that the numerous contradictions and uncertainties of the text are expressions of unconscious knowledge of and reaction to the real content of the saga. The appearance at one time of Jahve and at another of Moses as the writer of the tablets illustrates the oscillation between father-god and son-god. The uncertainty about what was on the tablets, as to how the inscriptions were distributed, in what writing it was transcribed, etc., point to the fact that the doubt aroused by the ambivalence extended to substitutive objects and activities; it is a sure sign that the original nature of the stones has unconsciously remained known. The construction of new tablets which Moses made at God's command to replace the broken ones is not only a continuation of the misleading tradition, but comprises the victory and the re-establishment of the domination of the destroyed father-god. The return to the *status quo ante* indicates that the love, increased by the reaction of remorse and feelings of guilt, has become overwhelming, just as the Biblical legend, in which the events as a whole are finally handed down, enables us to recognise the exclusiveness of Jahve as God.

It must be noted here that the gifted author of the study of the Moses of Michelangelo, which we have already quoted, had already recognised as essential the same traits in the statue as those which stand out in the

---

son-god the crime which they once committed against the father, and the same hostile and defiant impulses will be aroused against him. The eating of the calf only takes the place of that of the bull as the eating of the body of Christ in the Last Supper continues the old totem meal in which the tribe partook of the flesh of the divine father.

present analytic interpretation of the Biblical tradition. The gesture of Michelangelo's hero, whose finger is buried in his beard, he has described as the sign of a relinquished movement directed masochistically against himself, and suggests that the powerful store of feeling which rages in the leader's breast is hushed by the memory of his mission. In yet another detail the same author has perceived the psychological mechanism, namely, in the fact that Moses reverses the holy tablets and holds them upside down. We may recall that our surprise at the treatment of the holy stones was the starting-point of our interpretation of the episode. We have found the essence of the events of Sinai in the suppression and rejection of rebellious tendencies against God, and in the victory of the conscious impulses of love over the unconscious feelings of hate and rage. According to the testimony of this author, Michelangelo's statue represents the renunciation of the gratification of the individual's strong affects in the service of a higher idea.

We must now endeavour to reply to certain objections. It will be said that our interpretation, as far as it proceeds from the Sinai report, may be a probable one, but that it contradicts the religious *niveau* of Judaism reached at that time. Where, it will be asked, are found traces of Jewish homage to a stone fetish? Our reply is that the religious views of a people at any particular stage are never completely free from memories of earlier ideas; and, further, that the expression, fetish, does not seem appropriate here. Robertson Smith[1] has already rejected the designation fetishism from the worship of holy stones as 'a popular term, which conveys no precise idea, but is vaguely supposed to mean something very savage and contemptible. And no doubt the worship of unshapen blocks is, from the artistic point of view, a very poor thing, but from a purely religious point of view, its inferiority to image worship is not so evident. The host in the mass is artistically as much inferior to the Venus of Milo as a Semitic *Maṣṣēba* was, but no one

[1] *Lectures on the Religion of the Semites*, London, 1901, p. 209.

will say that mediæval Christianity is a lower form of religion than Aphrodite worship.' The holy pillar of stone is in general widely spread among the Semites. The *Maṣṣēba* may be justly denoted as the first and the most primitive prototype of the altar. The sacred stones mentioned by Herodotus are called *ansab* (sing. *noṣb*), *i.e.* stones set up, pillars. Such monolithic pillars or stone heaps are constantly mentioned in the oldest part of the Scriptures.[1] The Pentateuchal law condemns the use of these pillars as idolatrous. The religious significance of the *Maṣṣēba* can be inferred from the fact that it was originally considered as God by the Canaanites and Hebrews. The stone erected by Jacob was not thought of as a boundary stone but as an image of God, since it is anointed, and the place where it stood is called 'God's house'.[2] In the primitive religion of the Israelites the stone, like the altar in later Judaism, was smeared with blood. When in certain parts of the Bible one or several stones appear as testimony of a bond, we should not think of them in the modern sense as memorials, but take the statements quite seriously; the stone as God was made a witness. This meaning is not incompatible with the later appearance of Jahve and the stone side by side as isolated and quite independent concepts, as, for instance, when Joshua calls the stone to witness at the conclusion of the bond in Sichem, 'For it hath heard all the words of the Lord which he spake unto us'.[3] This duplication of the idea of God, like the double presence of God in the sacrificial cult, can only be explained historically. The former identity of the two later separate images of God is proved by the designation צוּר 'rock' for God, by numerous other references and by the prophets' rejection of the worship of the *Maṣṣēba*.[4] On the

---

[1] At Sichem: Joshua xxiv. 26; Bethel: Genesis xxviii. 18; Gibeath: Genesis xxxi. 45; Gilgal: Joshua iv. 5; Mizpah: 1 Samuel vii. 12; Gibeon: 2 Samuel xx. 8; En-rogel: 1 Kings i. 9.

[2] Genesis xxviii. 22.   [3] Joshua xxiv. 27.

[4] The twelve stone pillars erected by Moses at the conclusion of the covenant, Exodus xxiv. 4, for the twelve tribes of Israel, as witnesses, according to the old idea of the solemn deed, are probably identical with the earlier tribal gods.

other hand, many ritual prescriptions become explicable through the regressive discovery of the repressed significance of the stone, and many metaphors and turns of expression in the Old Testament lose their puzzling character.

It may be remarked here that a careful study of stone totemism, which may have been once universal, would lead to surprising results for the science of religion. E. Sidney Hartland believes that 'Many of the menhirs in Europe and Asia Minor have probably been actually figures of deities. Rocks, boulders and standing stones have been worshipped as gods or as inhabited by gods all over the world. Wherever men have been struck by the appearance or position of a rock or stone, they have regarded it with awe as uncanny, and in innumerable cases they have ultimately erected it into a divinity, brought offerings, and put up prayers before it. Instances need not be cited; they are found in every quarter of the globe.'[1]

The much-discussed metaphor,[2] 'Look unto the rock whence ye are hewn, and to the hole of the pit whence ye are digged. Look unto Abraham your father, and unto Sarah that bare you,' becomes intelligible in virtue of the original identity of stone, human being and anthropomorphic deity in the primitive mental life. The psychoanalytic theory of the genesis of sexual symbolism finds a brilliant confirmation in this prophetic metaphor, which shows irrefutably that what to-day appears as a symbol is only a remnant of former conceptual and linguistic identity.

The reconstruction of the original significance of the holy stones becomes important for the elucidation of obscure problems of the cult. This is best seen in the development of the altar. In the old law[3] it is prescribed that the altar shall be built out of earth or unhewn stones. Robertson Smith[4] has already recognised that

---

[1] James Hastings, *Encyclopædia of Religion and Ethics*, vol. ii., Edinburgh, 1920, p. 864.
[2] Isaiah li. 1-2.
[3] Exodus xx. 24-25, and 1 Samuel xiv. 32.
[4] *Ibid.* p. 201.

the table on which the victim was to be offered up to the
Deity cannot possibly be regarded as the origin of the
altar, since 'the table is not a very primitive article of
furniture'. This keen scholar has expressed the opinion
that 'the altar is only a modification of the *noṣb*, and
that the rude Arabian usage is the primitive type out of
which all the elaborate altar ceremonies of the more cul-
tivated Semites grew'. We cannot pursue here the very
complicated and not easily perceptible development of
the stone altar; we only wish to point out that our explanation might be made the starting-point for such an
investigation.

The prohibition[1] against making use of hewn stone for
the building of the altar ('For if thou lift up thy tool
upon it, thou has polluted it') shows an old taboo to prevent injury to the Deity still evident in a later prescrip-
tion of the cult. It is as though the hewing of a stone
were equivalent to an injury of the Deity who originally
was the stone itself and later was represented as living in
the stone.[2] The blood of the victim consecrated to the
god was smeared on the altar. In this primitive form of
giving nourishment, the Deity appears more convincing
and nearer to nature than later when the origin of the
altar in a primitive stone-god had been forgotten. If the
path which leads from the crude stone to the imposing
and richly decorated altar were pursued, a light would be
thrown on a significant element in the historical development of civilisation, provided the important rôle of the
stone-god were fully appreciated.

One detail which should bring us back to our starting-
point shows how necessary it is to supplement the
genetic method of research by that of folk-psychology.
Here again only the use of psycho-analytic methods and

---

[1] Exodus xx. 25.

[2] How far contemporary Biblical exegesis is from recognising the really
effective mechanisms of mental life is shown by Baentsch's explanation (*Handkommentar zu Exodus*, S. 188), according to which the prohibition to use stones
worked with iron for the altar shows a hostility to culture surviving from
nomadic times. Analytic investigation, on the contrary, shows that the prohibition is a reflection of the earlier one against killing the Deity, originally the
father, which marks the beginning of cultural evolution.

conclusions can lead to deeper knowledge and render intelligible the original significance of elements in the mental life of the people which have become unconscious.

The horns of the altar, on which the blood of the victim was smeared and which were looked upon as affording protection,[1] have been explained in the most diverse ways. Kautzsch[2] has stated that it is extremely probable that the horns go back to the custom of spreading the skin of the animal victim together with the horns over the altar. Baentsch[3] holds a similar view, and adds that it scarcely agrees with the representation of the Deity in the form of an animal. Wolf Baudissin[4] supposes that 'this decoration may perhaps be explained from the fact that horned animals were sacrificed on the altar; or possibly the horns have merely the practical purpose of forming a handle for those beseeching protection by which they may take hold of the altar'. We are certainly little inclined to accept so rationalistic an explanation. It contradicts above all the rôle of the horns in the sacrificial ritual, which is quite disregarded in Baudissin's second explanation, and in the first is not brought into any psychologically sufficient relationship to this constituent part of the altar. Neither the æsthetic hypothesis of the horns as a decoration, nor the purely practical one which interprets them as a sort of divine clothes-pegs, will fit the primitiveness of the views of that period.

Our interpretation enables us to make an attempt to explain this detail in the cult which, as I think, is as well suited to the psychological as to the historical development. When a little child puts on a soldier's helmet he does so by no means as a game, without seriousness or emotion; he means rather, 'I am a soldier'. The altar which bears the horns of the ram was, therefore, originally identified with the ram, the old totem-god. We have

---

[1] i Kings i. 50, ii. 28.
[2] Karl Kautzsch, *Biblische Theologie des Alten Testaments*, Tübingen, 1911, S. 26.
[3] *Ibid.* S. 234.
[4] In the *Realenzyklopädie für protestantische Theologie*, etc.

expressed the opinion that a totem stone was worshipped as god, together with—more probably after—
the totem animal. The altar which later developed from
the holy stone still bears the most important totem of
the animal-god, and bears it at a time which had long
since advanced to the cult of Jahve. A remnant of the
repressed totem still projects into a period which is
proud of the cultural height to which it has attained.
But the horns were still considered to be the vital elements of the altar, and such a significant displacement
on to a trifling thing, a displacement so similar to that
found in neurotic symptoms, is unintelligible without
the psycho-analytic investigation of the psychical processes. In spite of all later developments, we can state
on the basis of this feature that the stone once had
divine significance, that the stone was once really God.[1]

After a long journey we have again arrived at the
horns, the totem of the prehistoric totem-god which became the symbol of the power and awfulness of this
primitive god. We have again found them in the old Israelitish altar structure and in the shofar ritual, and we
believe that, although the people have long abandoned
totem worship, their significance is unconsciously determined by their original character, for the interpretation
of Michelangelo's masterpiece has shown the significance
and affective value which they retain for the spectators'
unconscious.

Our analysis of the Sinai legend has not brought us a
complete understanding of the events which, owing to

---

[1] The keeping of the tablets in the Ark is explicable in view of this earliest
meaning of the holy stone and from comparison with similar cults of the ancient
Orient. It goes without saying that the prehistoric worship of holy stones was
not confined to these Jews. The part played by holy stones among the Arabs,
and the custom of fondling and kissing such stones, is to be traced back, like the
worship of the Kaaba, to their primary divinity. Holy stones were known in the
Phœnician temples. The stone pillars of Melkart in the temple at Tyre represented Heracles. Similarly, the two pillars of the temple of Solomon were originally images of gods. The Hermes in Greece, the lingam stones in India, and the
holy stones appearing in the religion of the American and Australian uncivilised
peoples point to the conclusion that the cult of the stone has represented a
transitional stage in all religions. Perhaps the pillars in the Greek temples may
derive their elevation and magnificence from a far less conspicuous stone which
was once the object of divine worship.

the choice of the religion of Jahve, became of decisive importance in the history of the world. However, we have formed a dim conception of what is really essential in the process which culminated in Jahve's proclamation that he alone is the God of Israel and that Israel is His chosen people. The covenant between Jahve and the Jews, with which the peculiar fate of the Jews and their belief that they are the chosen people was to be bound up, was founded on the repression of the strongest unconscious affects. Without a knowledge of the deciding factors there can be no understanding of the problems of the Jewish religion.

Here ends our task, which was to indicate a new path for the science of religion leading to an unknown realm. We greet the truth which we see rising before us, as Moses, who dimly saw the Promised Land from Mount Nebo, and yearned for it from afar.

INDEX